In the series as a whole, indexes have been placed sometimes after single works, sometimes after groups of works. It may help readers in the use of these if they are told exactly where to look for them. Indexes will be found as follows:

In vols. IV, VI, VII, VIII at the end.

In vol. I after *Analytica Posteriora*; after *De Sophisticis Elenchis*.

In vol. II after *Physica*; after *De Caelo*; after *De Generatione et Corruptione*.

In vol. III after *Meteorologica*; after *De Anima*; after *Parva Naturalia*; after *De Mundo*; after *De Spiritu*.

In vol. V after *De Partibus Animalium*; after *De Incessu Animalium*; after *De Generatione Animalium*.

In vol. IX after *Ethica Nicomachea*; after *Magna Moralia*; after *De Virtutibus et Vitiis*.

In vol. X after *Politica*; after *Oeconomica*; after *Atheniensium Respublica*.

In vol. XI after *Rhetorica*; after *Rhetorica ad Alexandrum*; after *Poetica*.

THE WORKS OF ARISTOTLE

TRANSLATED INTO ENGLISH
UNDER THE EDITORSHIP

OF

W. D. ROSS, M.A.

FELLOW AND TUTOR OF ORIEL COLLEGE
DEPUTY PROFESSOR OF MORAL PHILOSOPHY IN THE UNIVERSITY OF OXFORD

VOLUME IX

ETHICA NICOMACHEA

By W. D. ROSS

MAGNA MORALIA

By St. GEORGE STOCK

ETHICA EUDEMIA
DE VIRTUTIBUS ET VITIIS

By J. SOLOMON

OXFORD UNIVERSITY PRESS

Oxford University Press, Ely House, London W. 1
GLASGOW NEW YORK TORONTO MELBOURNE WELLINGTON
CAPE TOWN SALISBURY IBADAN NAIROBI LUSAKA ADDIS ABABA
BOMBAY CALCUTTA MADRAS KARACHI LAHORE DACCA
KUALA LUMPUR HONG KONG

FIRST EDITION 1915
REPRINTED LITHOGRAPHICALLY IN GREAT BRITAIN
BY LOWE AND BRYDONE (PRINTERS) LTD., LONDON
FROM SHEETS OF THE FIRST EDITION
1944, 1949, 1954, 1963, 1966

ETHICA NICOMACHEA

BY

W. D. ROSS

FELLOW AND TUTOR OF ORIEL COLLEGE
DEPUTY PROFESSOR OF MORAL PHILOSOPHY IN THE
UNIVERSITY OF OXFORD

OXFORD UNIVERSITY PRESS

PREFACE

THIS translation is based on Bywater's text, and I have departed from it only occasionally, where there seemed to be a good deal to be gained by doing so.

There is considerable difficulty in translating terms which are just crystallizing from the fluidity of everyday speech into technical meanings; and in my treatment of such words as *λόγος* or *ἀρχή* I cannot hope to please everybody. Any attempt to render such a term always by a single English equivalent would produce the most uncouth result, and would be in principle wrong. I have tried, however, to limit my renderings of such terms to a reasonably small number of alternatives, so that the thread of identical significance may not be entirely lost.

I am much indebted to my wife, whose suggestions have in many places helped me to make the translation clearer or more like English.

W. D. ROSS,

July 1925.

CONTENTS

3. Pleasure in doing virtuous acts is a sign that the virtuous disposition has been acquired: a variety of considerations show the essential connexion of moral virtue with pleasure and pain.

4. The actions that produce moral virtue are not good in the same sense as those that flow from it: the latter must fulfil certain conditions not necessary in the case of the arts.

B. *Definition of moral virtue.*

5. Its genus: it is a state of character, not a passion nor a faculty.

6. Its differentia: it is a disposition to choose the mean.

7. This proposition illustrated by reference to the particular virtues.

C. *Characteristics of the extreme and mean states: practical corollaries.*

8. The extremes are opposed to each other and to the mean.

9. The mean is hard to attain, and is grasped by perception, not by reasoning.

D. *Inner side of moral virtue: conditions of responsibility for action.*

III. 1. Praise and blame attach to voluntary actions, i.e. actions done (1) not under compulsion, and (2) with knowledge of the circumstances.

2. Moral virtue implies that the action is done (3) by choice; the object of choice is the result of previous deliberation.

3. The nature of deliberation and its objects: choice is deliberate desire of things in our own power.

4. The object of rational wish is the end, i.e. the good or the apparent good.

5. We are responsible for bad as well as for good actions.

III. 6—V. 11. THE VIRTUES AND VICES

A. *Courage.*

6. Courage concerned with the feelings of fear and confidence—strictly speaking, with the fear of death in battle.

7. The motive of courage is the sense of honour: characteristics of the opposite vices, cowardice and rashness.

8. Five kinds of courage improperly so called.

9. Relation of courage to pain and pleasure.

B. *Temperance.*

10. Temperance is limited to certain pleasures of touch.

11. Characteristics of temperance and its opposites, self-indulgence and 'insensibility'.

12. Self-indulgence more voluntary than cowardice: comparison of the self-indulgent man to the spoilt child.

B. *The chief intellectual virtues.*

3. Science—demonstrative knowledge of the necessary and eternal.

4. Art—knowledge of how to make things.

5. Practical wisdom—knowledge of how to secure the ends of human life.

6. Intuitive reason—knowledge of the principles from which science proceeds.

7. Philosophic wisdom—the union of intuitive reason and science.

8. Relations between practical wisdom and political science.

C. *Minor intellectual virtues concerned with conduct.*

9. Goodness in deliberation, how related to practical wisdom.

10. Understanding—the critical quality answering to the imperative quality practical wisdom.

11. Judgement—right discrimination of the equitable: the place of intuition in morals.

D. *Relation of philosophic to practical wisdom.*

12. What is the use of philosophic and of practical wisdom? Philosophic wisdom is the formal cause of happiness; practical wisdom is what ensures the taking of proper means to the proper ends desired by moral virtue.

13. Relation of practical wisdom to natural virtue, moral virtue, and the right rule.

BOOK VII. CONTINENCE AND INCONTINENCE. PLEASURE

A. *Continence and incontinence.*

VII. 1. Six varieties of character: method of treatment: current opinions.

2. Contradictions involved in these opinions.

3. Solution of the problem, in what sense the incontinent man acts against knowledge.

4. Solution of the problem, what is the sphere of incontinence: its proper and its extended sense distinguished.

5. Incontinence in its extended sense includes a brutish and a morbid form.

6. Incontinence in respect of anger less disgraceful than incontinence proper.

7. Softness and endurance: two forms of incontinence—weakness and impetuosity.

8. Self-indulgence worse than incontinence.

9. Relation of continence to obstinacy, incontinence, 'insensibility', temperance.

BOOKS VIII, IX. FRIENDSHIP

6. Relation of friendship to unanimity.
7. The pleasure of beneficence.
8. The nature of true self-love.

F. *The need of friendship.*

9. Why does the happy man need friends?
10. The limit to the number of friends.
11. Are friends more needed in good or in bad fortune?
12. The essence of friendship is living together.

BOOK X. PLEASURE. HAPPINESS

A. *Pleasure.*

X. 1. Two opposed views about pleasure.
2. Discussion of the view that pleasure is the good.
3. Discussion of the view that pleasure is wholly bad.
4. Definition of pleasure.
5. Pleasures differ with the activities which they accompany and complete: criterion of the value of pleasures.

B. *Happiness.*

6. Happiness is good activity, not amusement.
7. Happiness in the highest sense is the contemplative life.
8. Superiority of the contemplative life further considered.
9. Legislation is needed if the end is to be attained: transition to *Politics*.

I. 1094^{a} 1, 2 = *M. M.* 1182^{a} 32–5 3–5 = *E. E.* 1219^{a} 13–17, *M. M.* 1184^{b} 9–11, 1197^{a} 3–10 22–4 = *E. E.* 1214^{b} 6–11 24–8 = *E. E.* 1218^{b} 10–14 ^{b} 22–1095^{a} 2 = *E. E.* 1216^{b} 35–1217^{a} 10 1095^{a} 14–19 = *E. E.* 1217^{a} 18–22 22, 23 = *E. E.* 1214^{b} 6–9 26–8 = *E. E.* 1217^{b} 2–16, *M. M.* 1182^{b} 9 28–30 = *E. E.* 1214^{b} 28–1215^{a} 7 ^{b} 17–19 = *E. E.* 1215^{a} 32–^{b} 1, 1216^{a} 27–9 19, 20 = *E. E.* 1215^{b} 30–5 22, cf. *E. E.* 1216^{a} 16 26–30 = *E. E.* 1216^{a} 19–22 1096^{a} 5–7 = *E. E.* 1215^{a} 25–32 17–19 = *E. E.* 1218^{a} 1–10 19–22, 23–9 = *E. E.* 1217^{b} 25–34, *M. M.* 1183^{a} 9–12, 1205^{a} 8–14 29–34 = *E. E.* 1217^{b} 34–1218^{a} 1 34–^{b} 5 = *E. E.* 1218^{a} 10–15 ^{b} 30, 31 = *E. E.* 1217^{b} 16–23 32–5 = *E. E.* 1217^{b} 23–5, 1218^{b} 1–4 1097^{a} 22–4 = *E. E.* 1218^{b} 10–12 ^{b} 16–20 = *M. M.* 1184^{a} 14–38 23–33 = *E. E.* 1219^{a} 2–8 1098^{a} 5–7 = *E. E.* 1219^{a} 9–18 7–12 = *E. E.* 1219^{a} 18–23 12–18 = *E. E.* 1219^{a} 23–35 18–20 = *E. E.* 1219^{a} 35–9 33–^{b} 3 = *E. E.* 1218^{b} 22–4 ^{b} 9–12 = *E. E.* 1216^{b} 26–35 12–16 = *E. E.* 1218^{b} 32–4, *M. M.* 1184^{b} 2–5 20–2 = *E. E.* 1219^{a} 39–^{b} 3 23–5 = *E. E.* 1214^{a} 30–^{b} 6 31–1099^{a} 3 = *E. E.* 1215^{a} 20–5, 1219^{a} 23–5, *M. M.* 1185^{a} 9–13 1099^{a} 3–7 = *E. E.* 1219^{b} 9, 10 24–31 = *E. E.* 1214^{a} 1–8 ^{b} 7, 8 = *E. E.* 1214^{a} 25, 26 9–11 = *E. E.* 1214^{a} 14–24 14–20 = *E. E.* 1215^{a} 12–19 32–1100^{a} 1 = *E. E.* 1217^{a} 24–9 1100^{a} 1–5 = *E. E.* 1219^{a} 35–9, ^{b} 4–6, *M. M.* 1185^{a} 3–9 10, 11 = *E. E.* 1219^{b} 6–8, *M. M.* 1185^{a} 6–9 1101^{a} 14–16 = *E. E.* 1219^{a} 38, 39 ^{b} 10–14, 21–7 = *E. E.* 1219^{b} 11–16, *M. M.* 1183^{b} 20–30 31–4 = *E. E.* 1219^{b} 8, 9 1102^{a} 28–32 = *E. E.* 1219^{b} 32–6 32–^{b} 3 = *E. E.* 1219^{b} 36–1220^{a} 2 ^{b} 3–11 = *E. E.* 1219^{b} 16–26 7 = *E. E.* 1219^{a} 25 13, 14 = *E. E.* 1219^{b} 27–32 1103^{a} 3–10 = *E. E.* 1220^{a} 4–13

II. 1103^{a} 17–23 = *E. E.* 1220^{a} 39–^{b} 5, *M. M.* 1185^{b} 38–1186^{a} 8 ^{b} 26–30 = *E. E.* 1216^{b} 21–5 1104^{a} 11–27 = *M. M.* 1185^{b} 13–32 27–^{b} 3 = *E. E.* 1220^{a} 22–34 ^{b} 16–18 = *E. E.* 1220^{a} 34–7 18–25 = *E. E.* 1221^{b} 39–1222^{a} 5 1105^{a} 7, 8 = *E. E.* 1223^{b} 22–4 ^{b} 19–28 = *E. E.* 1220^{b} 6–20, *M. M.* 1186^{a} 9–19 1106^{a} 26–^{b} 16 = *E. E.* 1220^{b} 21–35 ^{b} 36–1107^{a} 2 = *E. E.* 1227^{b} 5–9 1107^{a} 8–17 = *E. E.* 1221^{b} 18–26, *M. M.* 1186^{a} 36–^{b} 1 28–1108^{b} 6 = *E. E.* 1220^{b} 35–1221^{b} 3 1108^{a} 35–^{b} 6 = *E. E.* 1233^{b} 16–26, *M. M.* 1192^{b} 18–29 ^{b} 11–15 = *E. E.* 1222^{a} 17–22 15–19 = *M. M.* 1186^{b} 11–13 23–6 = *M. M.* 1186^{b} 13–17 35–1109^{a} 19 = *E. E.* 1222^{a} 22–^{b} 4, 1234^{b} 6–13, *M. M.* 1186^{b} 4–11, 17–32 1109^{a} 20–30 = *M. M.* 1186^{b} 32–1187^{a} 4

III. 1109^{b} 30–5 = *E. E.* 1223^{a} 9–23, *M. M.* 1187^{b} 31–4 35, 1110^{a} 1 = *E. E.* 1224^{a} 9–11 1110^{a} 4–^{b} 7 = *E. E.* 1225^{a} 2–27 ^{b} 9–17 = *M. M.* 1188^{b} 16–23 24–1111^{a} 15 = *E. E.* 1225^{a} 36–^{b} 16 30–1111^{a} 15 =

M. M. 1188^b 25–38 1111^a 24 = *E. E.* 1223^a 28–36, ^{b} 18–24, *M. M.* 1187^b 37–1188^a 5, 1188^a 23–5 ^{b} 4–34 = *E. E.* 1225^b 16–1226^a 17, *M. M.* 1189^a 1–22 ^{b} 5, 6 = *E. E.* 1228^a 11–14 1112^a 13–^{b} 8 = *E. E.* 1226^a 20–^{b} 9 13–17 = *M. M.* 1189^a 22–^{b} 3 14, 15 = *E. E.* 1226^b 30–6 21–3 = *E. E.* 1226^a 2–4 30, 31 = *M. M.* 1189^b 6–8 34–^{b} 9 = *M. M.* 1189^b 9–25 ^{b} 11–20, 1113^a 5–7 = *E. E.* 1226^b 9–13, 1227^a 5–18, ^{b} 25–33 1113^a 9–12 = *E. E.* 1226^b 13–17, 1227^a 3–5 15–31 = *E. E.* 1227^a 18–31 33–^{b} 2 = *E. E.* 1227^a 38–^{b} 1 ^{b} 11–14 = *E. E.* 1223^a 4–9 14–17 = *M. M.* 1187^a 5–13 17–21 = *E. E.* 1222^b 15–20, *M. M.* 1187^b 4–9 21–30 = *M. M.* 1187^a 13–19 1114^a 13–21 = *M. M.* 1187^b 20–30 21–31 = *M. M.* 1187^a 23–9 ^{b} 26, 27, 1115^a 4–6 = *E. E.* 1228^a 23–6 1115^a 6–9 = *E. E.* 1228^a 26–^{b} 4 10–^{b} 6 = *E. E.* 1229^a 32–^{b} 21, *M. M.* 1190^b 9–21 ^{b} 7–17 = *E. E.* 1228^b 18–1229^a 11, *M. M.* 1191^a 17–36 17–24 = *E. E.* 1230^a 26–33 26–28 = *E. E.* 1229^b 28, 29 1116^a 12–15 = *E. E.* 1229^b 32–1230^a 4 16–^{b} 3 = *E. E.* 1229^a 11–13, *M. M.* 1191^a 5–13 ^{b} 3–23 = *E. E.* 1229^a 14–16, 1230^a 4–21, *M. M.* 1190^b 22–32 23–1117^a 9 = *E. E.* 1129^a 20–29, *M. M.* 1190^b 35–1191^a 4 1117^a 9–22 = *E. E.* 1229^a 18–20, *M. M.* 1191^a 13–17 22–7 = *E. E.* 1229^a 16–18, *M. M.* 1190^b 32–5 ^{b} 20–3 = *E. E.* 1230^a 33–8, *M. M.* 1191^a 36–8 27–1118^b 8 = *E. E.* 1230^b 21–1231^a 26, *M. M.* 1191^b 5–10 1118^b 16–21 = *E. E.* 1221^b 15–17 1119^a 5–11 = *E. E.* 1230^b 13–18, 1231^a 26–34 33–^{b} 1 = *E. E.* 1230^b 3–7

IV. 1119^b 22–32 = *E. E.* 1231^b 27–38, *M. M.* 1191^b 39–1192^a 8 1121^b 21–34 = *E. E.* 1232^a 10–15, *M. M.* 1192^a 8–10 1122^a 18–1123^a 33 = *E. E.* 1233^a 31–^{b} 15, *M. M.* 1192^a 37–^{b} 17 1123^a 34–1125^a 35 = *M. M.* 1192^a 21–36 ^{b} 5–15 = *E. E.* 1232^b 31–1233^a 9 1124^a 4–12 = *E. E.* 1232^b 14–21 ^{b} 6–9 = *E. E.* 1232^b 10–12 1125^a 17–34 = *E. E.* 1233^a 9–30 ^{b} 26–1126^b 10 = *E. E.* 1231^b 5–26, *M. M.* 1191^b 23–38 1126^a 8–28 = *E. E.* 1221^b 9–15 ^{b} 11–1127^a 12 = *E. E.* 1233^b 29–38, *M. M.* 1193^a 20–7 1127^a 13–^{b} 32 = *E. E.* 1233^b 38–1234^a 3, *M. M.* 1193^a 28–38 ^{b} 33–1128^b 9 = *E. E.* 1234^a 4–23, *M. M.* 1193^a 11–19 1128^b 10–33 = *E. E.* 1233^b 26–9, *M. M.* 1193^a 1–10

V. 1129^a 3–1130^a 13 = *M. M.* 1193^a 39–^{b} 19 1131^a 10–^{b} 24, 1132^b 21–1133^b 28 = *M. M.* 1193^b 19–1194^b 3 1134^a 24–1135^a 5 = *M. M.* 1194^b 3–1195^a 8 1135^a 8–1136^a 9 = *M. M.* 1195^a 8–^{b} 4 1136^a 10–^{b} 14 = *M. M.* 1195^b 4–34 ^{b} 15–1137^a 4 = *M. M.* 1196^a 33–^{b} 3 1137^a 31–1138^a 3 = *M. M.* 1198^b 24–33 1138^a 4–^{b} 13 = *M. M.* 1195^b 35–1196^a 33

VI. 1138^b 18–34 = *E. E.* 1249^a 21–^{b} 6, *M. M.* 1196^b 4–11 35–1139^b 13 = *M. M.* 1196^b 11–34 1139^b 14–18 = *M. M.* 1196^b 34–7 18–36 = *M. M.* 1196^b 37–1197^a 1 1140^a 1–23 = *M. M.* 1197^a 3–13 24–^{b} 30 = *M. M.* 1197^a 13–20 ^{b} 31–1141^a 8 = *M. M.* 1197^a 20–3 1141^a 9–20 = *M. M.* 1197^a 23–30 20–^{b} 3 = *M. M.* 1197^a 32–^{b} 11 21, 33–^{b} 2 = *E. E.* 1217^a 33 1142^a 31–^{b} 33 = *M. M.* 1199^a 4–14 ^{b} 34–1143^a 18 = *M. M.* 1197^b 11–17 1143^a 19–24 = *M. M.* 1198^b 34–1199^a 3 1144^a 6–22 = *E. E.* 1227^b 19–1228^a 2 23–^{b} 1 = *M. M.* 1197^b 17–27 ^{b} 1–1145^a

6 = *M. M.* 1197b 36–1198b 8   b 18–20 = *E. E.* 1216b 6   1145a 6–11 = *M. M.* 1198b 8–20

VII. 1145a 15–b 2 = *M. M.* 1200b 4–19   b 21–1146a 4 = *M. M.* 1200b 20–1201a 6   1146a 9–b 5 = *M. M.* 1201a 9–39   b 6–1147b 19 = *M. M.* 1201a 39–1202a 8   1147b 20–1148b 14 = *M. M.* 1202a 29–b 9   1148b 15–1149a 20 = *M. M.* 1202a 19–29   1149a 24–b 26 = *M. M.* 1202b 9–29   b 8–13 = *M. M.* 1202a 23–6   26–1150a 8 = *M. M.* 1203a 18–25   1150a 9–b 19 = *M. M.* 1202b 29–38   b 19–28 = *M. M.* 1203a 29–b 11   29–36 = *M. M.* 1203a 11–18, 25–9   1151a 1–28 = *M. M.* 1203a 29–b 11   15–19 = *E. E.* 1227a 7–9, b 22–30   29–b 22 = *M. M.* 1202a 8–19   b 32–1152a 33 = *M. M.* 1203b 11–1204a 18   1152b 1–8 = *M. M.* 1204a 19–31   10, 11 = *M. M.* 1205a 7, 8   11, 12 = *M. M.* 1206a 31   12–20 = *M. M.* 1204a 31–b 4   33–1153a 7 = *M. M.* 1204b 4–20   1153a 7–15 = *M. M.* 1204b 20–1205a 7   20–3 = *M. M.* 1205b 37–1206a 25   23–7 = *M. M.* 1206a 25–30   b 7–9 = *M. M.* 1205a 25–b 2   25–8 = *M. M.* 1205b 33–7   29–31 = *M. M.* 1205a 16–25, b 2–13

VIII. 1155a 3–31 = *E. E.* 1234b 18–1235a 4, *M. M.* 1208b 3–7   32–b 8 = *E. E.* 1235a 4–28, *M. M.* 1208b 7–20   b 8–13 = *E. E.* 1235a 29–33, *M. M.* 1208b 22–6   17–27 = *E. E.* 1235b 13–1236a 7, *M. M.* 1208b 36–1209a 3   27–1156a 5 = *E. E.* 1236a 7–15, *M. M.* 1208b 27–36   1156a 6–b 6 = *E. E.* 1236a 15–b 26   b 7–17 = *E. E.* 1236b 26–32, *M. M.* 1209a 3–7   17–1157a 25 = *E. E.* 1237b 8–30, *M. M.* 1209b 11–17   1158b 1–3 = *E. E.* 1238b 15–17, *M. M.* 1211b 4–8   11–28 = *E. E.* 1238b 18–30, 1239a 6–12, *M. M.* 1211b 8–17   1159a 12–b 1 = *E. E.* 1239a 21–b 2, *M. M.* 1210b 2–20   b 1–24 = *E. E.* 1239b 6–1240a 4   25–1160a 8 = *E. E.* 1241b 12–17, *M. M.* 1211a 6–12   1160a 8–30 = *E. E.* 1241b 24–6   35 = *E. E.* 1241b 36   b 22–1161a 9 = *E. E.* 1241b 27–32, 38–40   1161a 30–b 10 = *E. E.* 1241b 17–24, 1242a 13–19   b 11–33 = *E. E.* 1242a 1–13   34, cf. *E. E.* 1238a 34   1162a 29–33 = *E. E.* 1242a 19–32   34–b 4 = *E. E.* 1242b 2–21   b 21–1163a 23 = *E. E.* 1242b 31–1243b 14   1163a 24–b 27 = *E. E.* 1242b 2–21

IX. 1163b 32–1164b 21 = *E. E.* 1243b 14–38, *M. M.* 1210a 24–b 2   1164b 22–1165a 35 = *E. E.* 1244a 1–36   1166a 1–b 29 = *E. E.* 1240a 8–b 39, *M. M.* 1210b 32–1211a 6, 1211a 15–36   b 30–1167a 21 = *E. E.* 1241a 1–15, *M. M.* 1211b 39–1212a 13   1167a 22–b 16 = *E. E.* 1241a 15–34, *M. M.* 1212a 14–27   b 17–1168a 27 = *E. E.* 1241a 35–b 9, *M. M.* 1211b 20–39   1168a 28–35 = *M. M.* 1212a 28–b 3   35–b 10 = *M. M.* 1211a 36–b 3   b 6–10 = *E. E.* 1240b 1–4   10–1169b 2 = *M. M.* 1212b 8–23   1169b 3–1170b 19 = *E. E.* 1244b 1–1245b 19, *M. M.* 1212b 24–1213b 2   1170b 20–1171a 20 = *E. E.* 1245b 19–26, *M. M.* 1213b 3–17   1171a 21–b 28 = *E. E.* 1244b 1–1245b 19, 1245b 26–1246a 25, *M. M.* 1213b 3–17

ETHICA NICOMACHEA

BOOK I

1 EVERY art and every inquiry, and similarly every action 1094a and pursuit, is thought to aim at some good; and for this reason the good has rightly been declared[1] to be that at which all things aim. But a certain difference is found among ends; some are activities, others are products apart from the activities that produce them. Where there are ends apart from the actions, it is the nature of the products to be better than the activities. Now, as there are many actions, arts, and sciences, their ends also are many; the end of the medical art is health, that of shipbuilding a vessel, that of strategy victory, that of economics wealth. But where such arts fall under a single capacity—as bridle-making and the other arts concerned with the equipment of horses fall under the art of riding, and this and every military action under strategy, in the same way other arts fall under yet others—in all of these the ends of the master arts are to be preferred to all the subordinate ends; for it is for the sake of the former that the latter are pursued. It makes no difference whether the activities themselves are the ends of the actions, or something else apart from the activities, as in the case of the sciences just mentioned.

2 If, then, there is some end of the things we do, which we desire for its own sake (everything else being desired for the sake of this), and if we do not choose everything for the sake of something else (for at that rate the process would go on to infinity, so that our desire would be empty and vain), clearly this must be the good and the chief good. Will not the knowledge of it, then, have a great influence on life? Shall we not, like archers who have a mark to aim at, be more likely to hit upon what is right? If so, we

[1] Perhaps by Eudoxus; cf. 1172b9.

must try, in outline at least, to determine what it is, and of which of the sciences or capacities it is the object. It would seem to belong to the most authoritative art and that which is most truly the master art. And politics appears to be of this nature; for it is this that ordains which of the sciences
1094b should be studied in a state, and which each class of citizens should learn and up to what point they should learn them; and we see even the most highly esteemed of capacities to fall under this, e.g. strategy, economics, rhetoric; now, since politics uses the rest of the sciences, and since, again, it legislates as to what we are to do and what we are to abstain from, the end of this science must include those of the others, so that this end must be the good for man. For even if the end is the same for a single man and for a state, that of the state seems at all events something greater and more complete whether to attain or to preserve; though it is worth while to attain the end merely for one man, it is finer and more godlike to attain it for a nation or for city-states. These, then, are the ends at which our inquiry aims, since it is political science, in one sense of that term.

Our discussion will be adequate if it has as much clear- 3
ness as the subject-matter admits of, for precision is not to be sought for alike in all discussions, any more than in all the products of the crafts. Now fine and just actions, which political science investigates, admit of much variety and fluctuation of opinion, so that they may be thought to exist only by convention, and not by nature. And goods also give rise to a similar fluctuation because they bring harm to many people; for before now men have been undone by reason of their wealth, and others by reason of their courage. We must be content, then, in speaking of such subjects and with such premisses to indicate the truth roughly and in outline, and in speaking about things which are only for the most part true and with premisses of the same kind to reach conclusions that are no better. In the same spirit, therefore, should each type of statement be *received*; for it is the mark of an educated man to look for precision in each class of things just so far as the nature of the subject admits;

it is evidently equally foolish to accept probable reasoning from a mathematician and to demand from a rhetorician scientific proofs.

Now each man judges well the things he knows, and of these he is a good judge. And so the man who has been educated in a subject is a good judge of that subject, and 1095[a]
the man who has received an all-round education is a good judge in general. Hence a young man is not a proper hearer of lectures on political science;[1] for he is inexperienced in the actions that occur in life, but its discussions start from these and are about these; and, further, since he tends to follow his passions, his study will be vain and unprofitable, because the end aimed at is not knowledge but action. And it makes no difference whether he is young in years or youthful in character; the defect does not depend on time, but on his living, and pursuing each successive object, as passion directs. For to such persons, as to the incontinent, knowledge brings no profit; but to those who desire and act in accordance with a rational principle[2] knowledge about such matters will be of great benefit.

These remarks about the student, the sort of treatment to be expected, and the purpose of the inquiry, may be taken as our preface.

[1] Cf. 'Young men, whom Aristotle thought
Unfit to hear moral philosophy.'
(*Troilus and Cressida*, II. ii. 166 f.)

[2] Of all the words of common occurrence in the *Ethics*, the hardest to translate is λόγος. Till recently the accepted translation was 'reason'. But it is, I think, quite clear that normally λόγος in Aristotle does not stand for the faculty of reason, but for something grasped by reason, or perhaps sometimes for an operation of reason. Its connexion with reason is so close as to make 'irrational' the most natural translation of ἄλογος. But for λόγος I have used, according to the shade of meaning uppermost in each context, such renderings as 'rational principle', 'rational ground', 'rule' (ὀρθὸς λόγος I always render 'right rule'), 'argument', 'reasoning', 'course of reasoning'. The connexion between reason and its object is for Aristotle so close that not infrequently λόγος occurs where strict logic would require him to be naming the faculty of reason, and it is possible that in some of the latest passages of his works in which λόγος occurs it has come to mean 'reason'—which it certainly had come to mean, not much later in the history of philosophy.

The meaning of λόγος in Aristotle is discussed by Professor J. L. Stocks in *Journal of Philology*, xxxiii (1914), 182–94, *Classical Quarterly*, viii (1914), 9–12, and by Professor J. Cook Wilson in *Classical Review*, xxvii (1913), 113–17.

Let us resume our inquiry and state, in view of the fact 4
that all knowledge and every pursuit aims at some good, what it is that we say political science aims at and what is the highest of all goods achievable by action. Verbally there is very general agreement; for both the general run of men and people of superior refinement say that it is happiness, and identify living well and doing well with being happy; but with regard to what happiness is they differ, and the many do not give the same account as the wise. For the former think it is some plain and obvious thing, like pleasure, wealth, or honour; they differ, however, from one another—and often even the same man identifies it with different things, with health when he is ill, with wealth when he is poor; but, conscious of their ignorance, they admire those who proclaim some great ideal that is above their comprehension. Now some[1] thought that apart from these many goods there is another which is self-subsistent and causes the goodness of all these as well. To examine all the opinions that have been held were perhaps somewhat fruitless; enough to examine those that are most prevalent or that seem to be arguable.

Let us not fail to notice, however, that there is a difference between arguments from and those to the first principles. For Plato, too, was right in raising this question and asking, as he used to do, 'are we on the way from or to the first principles?'[2] There is a difference, as there is in a race-course between the course from the judges to the turning-
1095b point and the way back. For, while we must begin with what is known, things are objects of knowledge in two senses—some to us, some without qualification. Presumably, then, *we* must begin with things known to *us*. Hence any one who is to listen intelligently to lectures about what is noble and just and, generally, about the subjects of political science must have been brought up in good habits. For the fact is the starting-point, and if this is sufficiently plain to him, he will not at the start need the reason as well; and the man who has been well brought up has or can

[1] The Platonic School; cf. ch. 6.
[2] Cf. *Rep.* 511 B.

easily get starting-points. And as for him who neither has nor can get them, let him hear the words of Hesiod:[1]

Far best is he who knows all things himself;
Good, he that hearkens when men counsel right;
But he who neither knows, nor lays to heart
Another's wisdom, is a useless wight.

5 Let us, however, resume our discussion from the point at which we digressed.[2] To judge from the lives that men lead, most men, and men of the most vulgar type, seem (not without some ground) to identify the good, or happiness, with pleasure; which is the reason why they love the life of enjoyment. For there are, we may say, three prominent types of life—that just mentioned, the political, and thirdly the contemplative life. Now the mass of mankind are evidently quite slavish in their tastes, preferring a life suitable to beasts, but they get some ground for their view from the fact that many of those in high places share the tastes of Sardanapallus. A consideration of the prominent types of life shows that people of superior refinement and of active disposition identify happiness with honour;[3] for this is, roughly speaking, the end of the political life. But it seems too superficial to be what we are looking for, since it is thought to depend on those who bestow honour rather than on him who receives it, but the good we divine to be something proper to a man and not easily taken from him. Further, men seem to pursue honour in order that they may be assured of their goodness; at least it is by men of practical wisdom that they seek to be honoured, and among those who know them, and on the ground of their virtue; clearly, then, according to them, at any rate, virtue is better. And perhaps one might even suppose this to be, rather than honour, the end of the political life. But even this appears somewhat incomplete; for possession of virtue seems actually compatible with being asleep, or with lifelong inactivity, and, further, with

[1] *Op.* 293, 295–7 Rzach. [2] a 30.

[3] Mr. C. M. Mulvany has pointed out (*C. Q.* xv (1921), 87) that there is a continuous sentence from l. 14 to l. 30, and that *τὸ ἀγαθὸν καὶ τὴν εὐδαιμονίαν οὐκ ἀλόγως ἐοίκασιν ἐκ τῶν βίων ὑπολαμβάνειν* (14–16) goes with *οἱ δὲ χαρίεντες . . . τιμήν* as with *οἱ μὲν πολλοὶ . . . ἡδονήν*.

1096a the greatest sufferings and misfortunes; but a man who was living so no one would call happy, unless he were maintaining a thesis at all costs. But enough of this; for the subject has been sufficiently treated even in the current discussions. Third comes the contemplative life, which we shall consider later.[1]

The life of money-making is one undertaken under compulsion, and wealth is evidently not the good we are seeking; for it is merely useful and for the sake of something else. And so one might rather take the aforenamed objects to be ends; for they are loved for themselves. But it is evident that not even these are ends; yet many arguments have been thrown away in support of them. Let us leave this subject, then.

We had perhaps better consider the universal good and 6
discuss thoroughly what is meant by it, although such an inquiry is made an uphill one by the fact that the Forms have been introduced by friends of our own. Yet it would perhaps be thought to be better, indeed to be our duty, for the sake of maintaining the truth even to destroy what touches us closely, especially as we are philosophers or lovers of wisdom; for, while both are dear, piety requires us to honour truth above our friends.

The men who introduced this doctrine did not posit Ideas of classes within which they recognized priority and posteriority (which is the reason why they did not maintain the existence of an Idea embracing all numbers); but the term 'good' is used both in the category of substance and in that of quality and in that of relation, and that which is *per se*, i. e. substance, is prior in nature to the relative (for the latter is like an offshoot and accident of being); so that there could not be a common Idea set over all these goods. Further, since 'good' has as many senses as 'being' (for it is predicated both in the category of substance, as of God and of reason, and in quality, i. e. of the virtues, and in quantity, i. e. of that which is moderate, and in relation, i. e. of the useful, and in time, i. e. of the right opportunity,

[1] 1177a 12–1178a 8, 1178a 22–1179a 32.

and in place, i. e. of the right locality and the like), clearly it cannot be something universally present in all cases and single; for then it could not have been predicated in all the categories but in one only. Further, since of the things answering to one Idea there is one science, there would have been one science of all the goods; but as it is there are many sciences even of the things that fall under one category, e.g. of opportunity, for opportunity in war is studied by strategics and in disease by medicine, and the moderate in food is studied by medicine and in exercise by the science of gymnastics. And one might ask the question, what in the world they *mean* by 'a thing itself', if (as is the case) in 'man himself' and in a particular man the account of man is one and the same. For in so far as 1096^b they are man, they will in no respect differ; and if this is so, neither will 'good itself' and particular goods, in so far as they are good. But again it will not be good any the more for being eternal, since that which lasts long is no whiter than that which perishes in a day. The Pythagoreans seem to give a more plausible account of the good, when they place the one in the column of goods; and it is they that Speusippus seems to have followed.

But let us discuss these matters elsewhere[1]; an objection to what we have said, however, may be discerned in the fact that the Platonists have not been speaking about *all* goods, and that the goods that are pursued and loved for themselves are called good by reference to a single Form, while those which tend to produce or to preserve these somehow or to prevent their contraries are called so by reference to these, and in a secondary sense. Clearly, then, goods must be spoken of in two ways, and some must be good in themselves, the others by reason of these. Let us separate, then, things good in themselves from things useful, and consider whether the former are called good by reference to a single Idea. What sort of goods would one call good in themselves? Is it those that are pursued even when isolated from others, such as intelligence, sight, and certain

[1] Cf. *Met.* 986^a 22–6, 1028^b 21–4, 1072^b 30–1073^a 3, 1091^a 29–^{b} 3, ^{b} 13–1092^a 17.

pleasures and honours? Certainly, if we pursue these also for the sake of something else, yet one would place them among things good in themselves. Or is nothing other than the Idea of good good in itself? In that case the Form will be empty. But if the things we have named are also things good in themselves, the account of the good will have to appear as something identical in them all, as that of whiteness is identical in snow and in white lead. But of honour, wisdom, and pleasure, just in respect of their goodness, the accounts are distinct and diverse. The good, therefore, is not some common element answering to one Idea.

But what then do we mean by the good? It is surely not like the things that only chance to have the same name. Are goods one, then, by being derived from one good or by all contributing to one good, or are they rather one by analogy? Certainly as sight is in the body, so is reason in the soul, and so on in other cases. But perhaps these subjects had better be dismissed for the present; for perfect precision about them would be more appropriate to another branch of philosophy.[1] And similarly with regard to the Idea; even if there is some one good which is universally predicable of goods or is capable of separate and independent existence, clearly it could not be achieved or attained by man; but we are now seeking something attainable. Perhaps, however, some one might think it worth while to recognize this with a view to the goods that *are* attainable
1097a and achievable; for having this as a sort of pattern we shall know better the goods that are good for us, and if we know them shall attain them. This argument has some plausibility, but seems to clash with the procedure of the sciences; for all of these, though they aim at some good and seek to supply the deficiency of it, leave on one side the knowledge of *the* good. Yet that all the exponents of the arts should be ignorant of, and should not even seek, so great an aid is not probable. It is hard, too, to see how a weaver or a carpenter will be benefited in regard to his own craft by knowing this 'good itself', or how the man who has viewed the Idea itself will be a better doctor or

[1] Cf. *Met.* Γ. 2.

general thereby. For a doctor seems not even to study health in this way, but the health of man, or perhaps rather the health of a particular man; it is individuals that he is healing. But enough of these topics.

7 Let us again return to the good we are seeking, and ask what it can be. It seems different in different actions and arts; it is different in medicine, in strategy, and in the other arts likewise. What then is the good of each? Surely that for whose sake everything else is done. In medicine this is health, in strategy victory, in architecture a house, in any other sphere something else, and in every action and pursuit the end; for it is for the sake of this that all men do whatever else they do. Therefore, if there is an end for all that we do, this will be the good achievable by action, and if there are more than one, these will be the goods achievable by action.

So the argument has by a different course reached the same point; but we must try to state this even more clearly. Since there are evidently more than one end, and we choose some of these (e.g. wealth, flutes,[1] and in general instruments) for the sake of something else, clearly not all ends are final ends; but the chief good is evidently something final. Therefore, if there is only one final end, this will be what we are seeking, and if there are more than one, the most final of these will be what we are seeking. Now we call that which is in itself worthy of pursuit more final than that which is worthy of pursuit for the sake of something else, and that which is never desirable for the sake of something else more final than the things that are desirable both in themselves and for the sake of that other thing, and therefore we call final without qualification that which is always desirable in itself and never for the sake of something else.

Now such a thing happiness, above all else, is held to be;
for this we choose always for itself and never for the sake 1097b
of something else, but honour, pleasure, reason, and every virtue we choose indeed for themselves (for if nothing

[1] Cf. Pl. *Euthyd.* 289 C.

resulted from them we should still choose each of them), but we choose them also for the sake of happiness, judging that by means of them we shall be happy. Happiness, on the other hand, no one chooses for the sake of these, nor, in general, for anything other than itself.

From the point of view of self-sufficiency the same result seems to follow; for the final good is thought to be self-sufficient. Now by self-sufficient we do not mean that which is sufficient for a man by himself, for one who lives a solitary life, but also for parents, children, wife, and in general for his friends and fellow citizens, since man is born for citizenship. But some limit must be set to this; for if we extend our requirement to ancestors and descendants and friends' friends we are in for an infinite series. Let us examine this question, however, on another occasion;[1] the self-sufficient we now define as that which when isolated makes life desirable and lacking in nothing; and such we think happiness to be; and further we think it most desirable of all things, without being counted as one good thing among others—if it were so counted it would clearly be made more desirable by the addition of even the least of goods; for that which is added becomes an excess of goods, and of goods the greater is always more desirable. Happiness, then, is something final and self-sufficient, and is the end of action.

Presumably, however, to say that happiness is the chief good seems a platitude, and a clearer account of what it is is still desired. This might perhaps be given, if we could first ascertain the function of man. For just as for a flute-player, a sculptor, or any artist, and, in general, for all things that have a function or activity, the good and the 'well' is thought to reside in the function, so would it seem to be for man, if he has a function. Have the carpenter, then, and the tanner certain functions or activities, and has man none? Is he born without a function? Or as eye, hand, foot, and in general each of the parts evidently has a function, may one lay it down that man similarly has a function apart from all these? What then can this be?

[1] i. 10, 11, ix. 10.

Life seems to be common even to plants, but we are seeking what is peculiar to man. Let us exclude, therefore, the life of nutrition and growth.[1] Next there would be a life of 1098a
perception, but *it* also seems to be common even to the horse, the ox, and every animal. There remains, then, an active life of the element that has a rational principle; of this, one part has such a principle in the sense of being obedient to one, the other in the sense of possessing one and exercising thought. And, as 'life of the rational element' also has two meanings, we must state that life in the sense of activity is what we mean; for this seems to be the more proper sense of the term. Now if the function of man is an activity of soul which follows or implies a rational principle, and if we say 'a so-and-so' and 'a good so-and-so' have a function which is the same in kind, e.g. a lyre-player and a good lyre-player, and so without qualification in all cases, eminence in respect of goodness being added to the name of the function (for the function of a lyre-player is to play the lyre, and that of a good lyre-player is to do so well): if this is the case, [and we state the function of man to be a certain kind of life, and this to be an activity or actions of the soul implying a rational principle, and the function of a good man to be the good and noble performance of these, and if any action is well performed when it is performed in accordance with the appropriate excellence: if this is the case,] human good turns out to be activity of soul in accordance with virtue, and if there are more than one virtue, in accordance with the best and most complete.

But we must add 'in a complete life'. For one swallow does not make a summer, nor does one day; and so too one day, or a short time, does not make a man blessed and happy.

Let this serve as an outline of the good; for we must presumably first sketch it roughly, and then later fill in the details. But it would seem that any one is capable of carrying on and articulating what has once been well outlined, and that time is a good discoverer or partner in such a work; to which facts the advances of the arts are due;

[1] Omitting τε and τὴν in l. 1, with most MSS.

for any one can add what is lacking. And we must also remember what has been said before,[1] and not look for precision in all things alike, but in each class of things such precision as accords with the subject-matter, and so much as is appropriate to the inquiry. For a carpenter and a geometer investigate the right angle in different ways; the former does so in so far as the right angle is useful for his work, while the latter inquires what it is or what sort of thing it is; for he is a spectator of the truth. We must act in the same way, then, in all other matters as well, that our main task may not be subordinated to minor questions. Nor must we demand the cause in all matters
1098b alike; it is enough in some cases that the *fact* be well established, as in the case of the first principles; the fact is the primary thing or first principle. Now of first principles we see some by induction, some by perception, some by a certain habituation, and others too in other ways. But each set of principles we must try to investigate in the natural way, and we must take pains to state them definitely, since they have a great influence on what follows. For the beginning is thought to be more than half of the whole, and many of the questions we ask are cleared up by it.

We must consider it, however, in the light not only of our 8
conclusion and our premisses, but also of what is commonly said about it; for with a true view all the data harmonize, but with a false one the facts soon clash. Now goods have been divided into three classes,[2] and some are described as external, others as relating to soul or to body; we call those that relate to soul most properly and truly goods, and psychical actions and activities we class as relating to soul. Therefore our account must be sound, at least according to this view, which is an old one and agreed on by philosophers. It is correct also in that we identify the end with certain actions and activities; for thus it falls among goods of the soul and not among external goods. Another belief which harmonizes with our account is that the happy man lives well and does well; for we have practi-

[1] 1094b 11–27.

[2] Pl. *Euthyd.* 279 AB, *Phil.* 48 E, *Laws,* 743 E.

cally defined happiness as a sort of good life and good action. The characteristics that are looked for in happiness seem also, all of them, to belong to what we have defined happiness as being. For some identify happiness with virtue, some with practical wisdom, others with a kind of philosophic wisdom, others with these, or one of these, accompanied by pleasure or not without pleasure; while others include also external prosperity. Now some of these views have been held by many men and men of old, others by a few eminent persons; and it is not probable that either of these should be entirely mistaken, but rather that they should be right in at least some one respect or even in most respects.

With those who identify happiness with virtue or some one virtue our account is in harmony; for to virtue belongs virtuous activity. But it makes, perhaps, no small difference whether we place the chief good in possession or in use, in state of mind or in activity. For the state of mind may exist without producing any good result, as in a man who 1099a
is asleep or in some other way quite inactive, but the activity cannot; for one who has the activity will of necessity be acting, and acting well. And as in the Olympic Games it is not the most beautiful and the strongest that are crowned but those who compete (for it is some of these that are victorious), so those who act win, and rightly win, the noble and good things in life.

Their life is also in itself pleasant. For pleasure is a state of *soul*, and to each man that which he is said to be a lover of is pleasant; e.g. not only is a horse pleasant to the lover of horses, and a spectacle to the lover of sights, but also in the same way just acts are pleasant to the lover of justice and in general virtuous acts to the lover of virtue. Now for most men their pleasures are in conflict with one another because these are not by nature pleasant, but the lovers of what is noble find pleasant the things that are by nature pleasant; and virtuous actions are such, so that these are pleasant for such men as well as in their own nature. Their life, therefore, has no further need of pleasure as a sort of adventitious charm, but has its pleasure in itself. For, besides what we have said, the man who does not rejoice in noble actions is not even good; since no one would call a man just who did not enjoy acting justly, nor any man liberal who did not enjoy liberal actions; and similarly in all other cases. If this is so, virtuous actions must be in themselves pleasant. But they are also *good* and *noble*, and have each of these attributes in the highest degree, since the good man judges well about these attributes; his judgement is such as we have described.[1] Happiness then is the best, noblest, and most pleasant thing in the world, and these attributes are not severed as in the inscription at Delos—

> Most noble is that which is justest, and best is health;
> But pleasantest is it to win what we love.

For all these properties belong to the best activities; and these, or one—the best—of these, we identify with happiness.

Yet evidently, as we said,[2] it needs the external goods as well; for it is impossible, or not easy, to do noble acts with-
1099b out the proper equipment. In many actions we use friends and riches and political power as instruments; and there are some things the lack of which takes the lustre from happiness, as good birth, goodly children, beauty; for the man who is very ugly in appearance or ill-born or solitary and childless is not very likely to be happy, and perhaps a man would be still less likely if he had thoroughly bad children or friends or had lost good children or friends by death. As we said,[2] then, happiness seems to need this sort of prosperity in addition; for which reason some identify happiness with good fortune, though others identify it with virtue.

For this reason also the question is asked, whether 9
happiness is to be acquired by learning or by habituation or some other sort of training, or comes in virtue of some divine providence or again by chance. Now if there is *any* gift of the gods to men, it is reasonable that happiness should be god-given, and most surely god-given of all human things inasmuch as it is the best. But this question would perhaps be more appropriate to another inquiry; happiness

[1] I.e., he judges that virtuous actions are good and noble in the highest degree. [2] 1098b 26-9.

seems, however, even if it is not god-sent but comes as a result of virtue and some process of learning or training, to be among the most godlike things; for that which is the prize and end of virtue seems to be the best thing in the world, and something godlike and blessed.

It will also on this view be very generally shared; for all who are not maimed as regards their potentiality for virtue may win it by a certain kind of study and care. But if it is better to be happy thus than by chance, it is reasonable that the facts should be so, since everything that depends on the action of nature is by nature as good as it can be, and similarly everything that depends on art or any rational cause, and especially if it depends on the best of all causes. To entrust to chance what is greatest and most noble would be a very defective arrangement.

The answer to the question we are asking is plain also from the definition of happiness; for it has been said [1] to be a virtuous activity of soul, of a certain kind. Of the remaining goods, some must necessarily pre-exist as conditions of happiness, and others are naturally co-operative and useful as instruments. And this will be found to agree with what we said at the outset; [2] for we stated the end of political science to be the best end, and political science spends most of its pains on making the citizens to be of a certain character, viz. good and capable of noble acts.

It is natural, then, that we call neither ox nor horse nor any other of the animals happy; for none of them is capable of sharing in such activity. For this reason also a boy is 1100a
not happy; for he is not yet capable of such acts, owing to his age; and boys who are called happy are being congratulated by reason of the hopes we have for them. For there is required, as we said,[3] not only complete virtue but also a complete life, since many changes occur in life, and all manner of chances, and the most prosperous may fall into great misfortunes in old age, as is told of Priam in the Trojan Cycle; and one who has experienced such chances and has ended wretchedly no one calls happy.

[1] 1098a 16.
[2] 1094a 27.
[3] 1098a 16–18.

Must no one at all, then, be called happy while he lives; **10**
must we, as Solon says,[1] see the end? Even if we are to lay down this doctrine, is it also the case that a man *is* happy when he is *dead*? Or is not this quite absurd, especially for us who say that happiness is an activity? But if we do not call the dead man happy, and if Solon does not mean this, but that one can then safely *call* a man blessed as being at last beyond evils and misfortunes, this also affords matter for discussion; for both evil and good are thought to exist for a dead man, as much as for one who is alive but not aware of them; e.g. honours and dishonours and the good or bad fortunes of children and in general of descendants. And this also presents a problem; for though a man has lived happily up to old age and has had a death worthy of his life, many reverses may befall his descendants—some of them may be good and attain the life they deserve, while with others the opposite may be the case; and clearly too the degrees of relationship between them and their ancestors may vary indefinitely. It would be odd, then, if the dead man were to share in these changes and become at one time happy, at another wretched; while it would also be odd if the fortunes of the descendants did not for *some* time have *some* effect on the happiness of their ancestors.

But we must return to our first difficulty;[2] for perhaps by a consideration of it our present problem might be solved. Now if we must see the end and only then call a man happy, not as being happy but as having been so before, surely this is a paradox, that when he is happy the attribute that belongs to him is not to be truly predicated
1100b of him because we do not wish to call living men happy, on account of the changes that may befall them, and because we have assumed happiness to be something permanent and by no means easily changed, while a single man may suffer many turns of fortune's wheel. For clearly if we were to keep pace with his fortunes, we should often call the same man happy and again wretched, making the happy man out to be a 'chameleon and insecurely based'.[3] Or is this keeping pace with his fortunes quite wrong? Success

[1] Hdt. i. 32. [2] Cf. l. 10. [3] Source unknown.

or failure in life does not depend on these, but human life, as we said,[1] needs these as mere additions, while virtuous activities or their opposites are what constitute happiness or the reverse.

The question we have now discussed confirms our definition. For no function of man has so much permanence as virtuous activities (these are thought to be more durable even than knowledge of the sciences), and of these themselves the most valuable are more durable because those who are happy spend their life most readily and most continuously in these; for this seems to be the reason why we do not forget them. The attribute in question,[2] then, will belong to the happy man, and he will be happy throughout his life; for always, or by preference to everything else, he will be engaged in virtuous action and contemplation, and he will bear the chances of life most nobly and altogether decorously, if he is 'truly good' and 'foursquare beyond reproach'.[3]

Now many events happen by chance, and events differing in importance; small pieces of good fortune or of its opposite clearly do not weigh down the scales of life one way or the other, but a multitude of great events if they turn out well will make life happier (for not only are they themselves such as to add beauty to life, but the way a man deals with them may be noble and good), while if they turn out ill they crush and maim happiness; for they both bring pain with them and hinder many activities. Yet even in these nobility shines through, when a man bears with resignation many great misfortunes, not through insensibility to pain but through nobility and greatness of soul.

If activities are, as we said,[4] what gives life its character, no happy man can become miserable; for he will never do the acts that are hateful and mean. For the man who is truly good and wise, we think, bears all the chances of life **1101a**
becomingly and always makes the best of circumstances, as a good general makes the best military use of the army at his command and a good shoemaker makes the best shoes out of the hides that are given him; and so with all other

[1] 1099a 31–b 7.
[2] Durability.
[3] Simonides, fr. 4 Diehl.
[4] l. 9.

craftsmen. And if this is the case, the happy man can never become miserable—though he will not reach *blessedness*, if he meet with fortunes like those of Priam.

Nor, again, is he many-coloured and changeable; for neither will he be moved from his happy state easily or by any ordinary misadventures, but only by many great ones, nor, if he has had many great misadventures, will he recover his happiness in a short time, but if at all, only in a long and complete one in which he has attained many splendid successes.

Why then should we not say that he is happy who is active in accordance with complete virtue and is sufficiently equipped with external goods, not for some chance period but throughout a complete life? Or must we add 'and who is destined to live thus and die as befits his life'? Certainly the future is obscure to us, while happiness, we claim, is an end and something in every way final. If so, we shall call happy those among living men in whom these conditions are, and are to be, fulfilled—but happy *men*. So much for these questions.

[1]That the fortunes of descendants and of all a man's II
friends should not affect his happiness at all seems a very unfriendly doctrine, and one opposed to the opinions men hold; but since the events that happen are numerous and admit of all sorts of difference, and some come more near to us and others less so, it seems a long—nay, an infinite—task to discuss each in detail; a general outline will perhaps suffice. If, then, as some of a man's own misadventures have a certain weight and influence on life while others are, as it were, lighter, so too there are differences among the misadventures of our friends taken as a whole, and it makes a difference whether the various sufferings befall the living or the dead (much more even than whether lawless and terrible deeds are presupposed in a tragedy or done on the stage), this difference also must be taken into account; or rather, perhaps, the fact that doubt is felt whether the dead share
1101b in any good or evil. For it seems, from these considerations,

[1] Aristotle now returns to the question stated in 1100a 18–30.

that even if anything whether good or evil penetrates to them, it must be something weak and negligible, either in itself or for them, or if not, at least it must be such in degree and kind as not to make happy those who are not happy nor to take away their blessedness from those who are. The good or bad fortunes of friends, then, seem to have some effects on the dead, but effects of such a kind and degree as neither to make the happy unhappy nor to produce any other change of the kind.

12 These questions having been definitely answered, let us consider whether happiness is among the things that are praised or rather among the things that are prized; for clearly it is not to be placed among *potentialities*.[1] Everything that is praised seems to be praised because it is of a certain kind and is related somehow to something else; for we praise the just or brave man and in general both the good man and virtue itself because of the actions and functions involved, and we praise the strong man, the good runner, and so on, because he is of a certain kind and is related in a certain way to something good and important. This is clear also from the praises of the gods; for it seems absurd that the gods should be referred to our standard, but this *is* done because praise involves a reference, as we said, to something else. But if praise is for things such as we have described, clearly what applies to the best things is not praise, but something greater and better, as is indeed obvious; for what we do to the gods and the most godlike of men is to call them blessed and happy. And so too with good *things*; no one praises happiness as he does justice, but rather calls it blessed, as being something more divine and better.

Eudoxus also seems to have been right in his method of advocating the supremacy of pleasure; he thought that the fact that, though a good, it is not praised indicated it to be better than the things that are praised, and that this is what God and the good are; for by reference to these all other things are judged. *Praise* is appropriate to virtue, for as a result of virtue men tend to do noble deeds; but *encomia* are

[1] Cf. *Top.* 126^b4; *M.M.* 1183^b20.

bestowed on acts, whether of the body or of the soul. But perhaps nicety in these matters is more proper to those who have made a study of encomia; to us it is clear from what
1102a has been said that happiness is among the things that are prized and perfect. It seems to be so also from the fact that it is a first principle; for it is for the sake of this that we all do all that we do, and the first principle and cause of goods is, we claim, something prized and divine.

Since happiness is an activity of soul in accordance with 13
perfect virtue, we must consider the nature of virtue; for perhaps we shall thus see better the nature of happiness. The true student of politics, too, is thought to have studied virtue above all things; for he wishes to make his fellow citizens good and obedient to the laws. As an example of this we have the lawgivers of the Cretans and the Spartans, and any others of the kind that there may have been. And if this inquiry belongs to political science, clearly the pursuit of it will be in accordance with our original plan. But clearly the virtue we must study is human virtue; for the good we were seeking was human good and the happiness human happiness. By human virtue we mean not that of the body but that of the soul; and happiness also we call an activity of soul. But if this is so, clearly the student of politics must know somehow the facts about soul, as the man who is to heal the eyes or the body as a whole must know about the eyes or the body; and all the more since politics is more prized and better than medicine; but even among doctors the best educated spend much labour on acquiring knowledge of the body. The student of politics, then, must study the soul, and must study it with these objects in view, and do so just to the extent which is sufficient for the questions we are discussing; for further precision is perhaps something more laborious than our purposes require.

Some things are said about it, adequately enough, even in the discussions outside our school, and we must use these; e. g. that one element in the soul is irrational and one has a rational principle. Whether these are separated as the parts of the body or of anything divisible are, or are distinct by definition but by nature inseparable, like convex and concave in the circumference of a circle, does not affect the present question.

Of the irrational element one division seems to be widely distributed, and vegetative in its nature, I mean that which causes nutrition and growth; for it is this kind of power of the soul that one must assign to all nurslings and to embryos, 1102b and this same power to full-grown creatures; this is more reasonable than to assign some different power to them. Now the excellence of this seems to be common to all species and not specifically human; for this part or faculty seems to function most in sleep, while goodness and badness are least manifest in sleep (whence comes the saying that the happy are no better off than the wretched for half their lives; and this happens naturally enough, since sleep is an inactivity of the soul in that respect in which it is called good or bad), unless perhaps to a small extent some of the movements actually penetrate to the soul, and in this respect the dreams of good men are better than those of ordinary people. Enough of this subject, however; let us leave the nutritive faculty alone, since it has by its nature no share in human excellence.

There seems to be also another irrational element in the soul—one which in a sense, however, shares in a rational principle. For we praise the rational principle of the continent man and of the incontinent, and the part of their soul that has such a principle, since it urges them aright and towards the best objects; but there is found in them also another element naturally opposed to the rational principle, which fights against and resists that principle. For exactly as paralysed limbs when we intend to move them to the right turn on the contrary to the left, so is it with the soul; the impulses of incontinent people move in contrary directions. But while in the body we see that which moves astray, in the soul we do not. No doubt, however, we must none the less suppose that in the soul too there is something contrary to the rational principle, resisting and opposing it. In what sense it is distinct from the other elements does not concern us. Now even this seems to have a share in a rational principle, as we said;[1] at any rate in the continent man it obeys the rational principle—and presumably in the temperate and brave man it is still more obedient; for in him it speaks, on all matters, with the same voice as the rational principle.

Therefore the irrational element also appears to be twofold. For the vegetative element in no way shares in a rational principle, but the appetitive and in general the desiring element in a sense shares in it, in so far as it listens to and obeys it; this is the sense in which we speak of 'taking account' of one's father or one's friends, not that in which we speak of 'accounting' for a mathematical property.[2] That the irrational element is in some sense persuaded by a rational principle is indicated also by the giving of advice
1103a and by all reproof and exhortation. And if this element also must be said to have a rational principle, that which has a rational principle (as well as that which has not) will be twofold, one subdivision having it in the strict sense and in itself, and the other having a tendency to obey as one does one's father.

Virtue too is distinguished into kinds in accordance with this difference; for we say that some of the virtues are intellectual and others moral, philosophic wisdom and understanding and practical wisdom being intellectual, liberality and temperance moral. For in speaking about a man's character we do not say that he is wise or has understanding but that he is good-tempered or temperate; yet we praise the wise man also with respect to his state of mind; and of states of mind we call those which merit praise virtues.

[1] I. 13.

[2] It is impossible in English to reproduce the play on the meanings of λόγον ἔχειν, translated above 'have a rational principle' and here 'take account of' and 'account for'. Aristotle's point is that the ἄλογον (the faculty of desire) can be said to have λόγος only in the sense that it can obey a λόγος presented to it by reason, not in the sense that it can originate a λόγος—just as many people can 'take account of' a father's advice who could not 'account for' a mathematical property.

BOOK II

1 VIRTUE, then, being of two kinds, intellectual and moral, intellectual virtue in the main owes both its birth and its growth to teaching (for which reason it requires experience and time), while moral virtue comes about as a result of habit, whence also its name (ἠθική) is one that is formed by a slight variation from the word ἔθος (habit). From this it is also plain that none of the moral virtues arises in us by nature; for nothing that exists by nature can form a habit contrary to its nature. For instance the stone which by nature moves downwards cannot be habituated to move upwards, not even if one tries to train it by throwing it up ten thousand times; nor can fire be habituated to move downwards, nor can anything else that by nature behaves in one way be trained to behave in another. Neither by nature, then, nor contrary to nature do the virtues arise in us; rather we are adapted by nature to receive them, and are made perfect by habit.

Again, of all the things that come to us by nature we first acquire the potentiality and later exhibit the activity (this is plain in the case of the senses; for it was not by often seeing or often hearing that we got these senses, but on the contrary we had them before we used them, and did not come to have them by using them); but the virtues we get by first exercising them, as also happens in the case of the arts as well. For the things we have to learn before we can do them, we learn by doing them, e.g. men become builders by building and lyre-players by playing the lyre; so too we become just by doing just acts, temperate by 1103b
doing temperate acts, brave by doing brave acts.

This is confirmed by what happens in states; for legislators make the citizens good by forming habits in them, and this is the wish of every legislator, and those who do not effect it miss their mark, and it is in this that a good constitution differs from a bad one.

Again, it is from the same causes and by the same means that every virtue is both produced and destroyed, and similarly every art; for it is from playing the lyre that both good and bad lyre-players are produced. And the corresponding statement is true of builders and of all the rest; men will be good or bad builders as a result of building well or badly. For if this were not so, there would have been no need of a teacher, but all men would have been born good or bad at their craft. This, then, is the case with the virtues also; by doing the acts that we do in our transactions with other men we become just or unjust, and by doing the acts that we do in the presence of danger, and being habituated to feel fear or confidence, we become brave or cowardly. The same is true of appetites and feelings of anger; some men become temperate and good-tempered, others self-indulgent and irascible, by behaving in one way or the other in the appropriate circumstances. Thus, in one word, states of character arise out of like activities. This is why the activities we exhibit must be of a certain kind; it is because the states of character correspond to the differences between these. It makes no small difference, then, whether we form habits of one kind or of another from our very youth; it makes a very great difference, or rather *all* the difference.

2 Since, then, the present inquiry does not aim at theoretical knowledge like the others (for we are inquiring not in order to know what virtue is, but in order to become good, since otherwise our inquiry would have been of no use), we must examine the nature of actions, namely how we ought to do them; for these determine also the nature of the states of character that are produced, as we have said.[1] Now, that we must act according to the right rule is a common principle and must be assumed—it will be discussed later,[2] i. e. both what the right rule is, and how it is related to the
1104a other virtues. But this must be agreed upon beforehand, that the whole account of matters of conduct must be given in outline and not precisely, as we said at the very beginning[3] that the accounts we demand must be in accordance with

[1] a31–b25. [2] vi. 13. [3] 1094b 11–27.

the subject-matter; matters concerned with conduct and questions of what is good for us have no fixity, any more than matters of health. The general account being of this nature, the account of particular cases is yet more lacking in exactness; for they do not fall under any art or precept but the agents themselves must in each case consider what is appropriate to the occasion, as happens also in the art of medicine or of navigation.

But though our present account is of this nature we must give what help we can. First, then, let us consider this, that it is the nature of such things to be destroyed by defect and excess, as we see in the case of strength and of health (for to gain light on things imperceptible we must use the evidence of sensible things); both excessive and defective exercise destroys the strength, and similarly drink or food which is above or below a certain amount destroys the health, while that which is proportionate both produces and increases and preserves it. So too is it, then, in the case of temperance and courage and the other virtues. For the man who flies from and fears everything and does not stand his ground against anything becomes a coward, and the man who fears nothing at all but goes to meet every danger becomes rash; and similarly the man who indulges in every pleasure and abstains from none becomes self-indulgent, while the man who shuns every pleasure, as boors do, becomes in a way insensible; temperance and courage, then, are destroyed by excess and defect, and preserved by the mean.

But not only are the sources and causes of their origination and growth the same as those of their destruction, but also the sphere of their actualization will be the same; for this is also true of the things which are more evident to sense, e.g. of strength; it is produced by taking much food and undergoing much exertion, and it is the strong man that will be most able to do these things. So too is it with the virtues; by abstaining from pleasures we become temperate, and it is when we have become so that we are most able to abstain from them; and similarly too in the
case of courage; for by being habituated to despise things 1104b
that are terrible and to stand our ground against them

we become brave, and it is when we have become so that we shall be most able to stand our ground against them.

We must take as a sign of states of character the pleasure 3
or pain that ensues on acts; for the man who abstains from bodily pleasures and delights in this very fact is temperate, while the man who is annoyed at it is self-indulgent, and he who stands his ground against things that are terrible and delights in this or at least is not pained is brave, while the man who is pained is a coward. For moral excellence is concerned with pleasures and pains; it is on account of the pleasure that we do bad things, and on account of the pain that we abstain from noble ones. Hence we ought to have been brought up in a particular way from our very youth, as Plato says,[1] so as both to delight in and to be pained by the things that we ought; for this is the right education.

Again, if the virtues are concerned with actions and passions, and every passion and every action is accompanied by pleasure and pain, for this reason also virtue will be concerned with pleasures and pains. This is indicated also by the fact that punishment is inflicted by these means; for it is a kind of cure, and it is the nature of cures to be effected by contraries.

Again, as we said but lately,[2] every state of soul has a nature relative to and concerned with the kind of things by which it tends to be made worse or better; but it is by reason of pleasures and pains that men become bad, by pursuing and avoiding these—either the pleasures and pains they ought not or when they ought not or as they ought not, or by going wrong in one of the other similar ways that may be distinguished. Hence men[3] even define the virtues as certain states of impassivity and rest; not well, however, because they speak absolutely, and do not say 'as one ought' and 'as one ought not' and 'when one ought or ought not', and the other things that may be added. We assume, then, that this kind of excellence tends to do what is best with regard to pleasures and pains, and vice does the contrary.

The following facts also may show us that virtue and vice are concerned with these same things. There being three

[1] *Laws*, 653 A ff., *Rep.* 401 E–402 A.

[2] a 27–b 3.

[3] Probably Speusippus is referred to.

objects of choice and three of avoidance, the noble, the advantageous, the pleasant, and their contraries, the base, the injurious, the painful, about all of these the good man tends to go right and the bad man to go wrong, and especially about pleasure; for this is common to the animals, and also it accompanies all objects of choice; for even the noble and the advantageous appear pleasant.

Again, it has grown up with us all from our infancy; this 1105^{a} is why it is difficult to rub off this passion, engrained as it is in our life. And we measure even our actions, some of us more and others less, by the rule of pleasure and pain. For this reason, then, our whole inquiry must be about these; for to feel delight and pain rightly or wrongly has no small effect on our actions.

Again, it is harder to fight with pleasure than with anger, to use Heraclitus' phrase[1], but both art and virtue are always concerned with what is harder; for even the good is better when it is harder. Therefore for this reason also the whole concern both of virtue and of political science is with pleasures and pains; for the man who uses these well will be good, he who uses them badly bad.

That virtue, then, is concerned with pleasures and pains, and that by the acts from which it arises it is both increased and, if they are done differently, destroyed, and that the acts from which it arose are those in which it actualizes itself—let this be taken as said.

4 The question might be asked, what we mean by saying[2] that we must become just by doing just acts, and temperate by doing temperate acts; for if men do just and temperate acts, they are already just and temperate, exactly as, if they do what is in accordance with the laws of grammar and of music, they are grammarians and musicians.

Or is this not true even of the arts? It is possible to do something that is in accordance with the laws of grammar, either by chance or at the suggestion of another. A man will be a grammarian, then, only when he has both done

[1] Fr. 85 Diels, θυμῶι μάχεσθαι χαλεπόν· ὅ τι γὰρ ἂν θέληι, ψυχῆς ὠνεῖται.

[2] 1103^{a} 31–^{b} 25, 1104^{a} 27–^{b} 3.

something grammatical and done it grammatically; and this means doing it in accordance with the grammatical knowledge in himself.

Again, the case of the arts and that of the virtues are not similar; for the products of the arts have their goodness in themselves, so that it is enough that they should have a certain character, but if the acts that are in accordance with the virtues have themselves a certain character it does not follow that they are done justly or temperately. The agent also must be in a certain condition when he does them; in the first place he must have knowledge, secondly he must choose the acts, and choose them for their own sakes, and thirdly his action must proceed from a firm and unchangeable character. These are not reckoned in as
1105b conditions of the possession of the arts, except the bare knowledge; but as a condition of the possession of the virtues knowledge has little or no weight, while the other conditions count not for a little but for everything, i. e. the very conditions which result from often doing just and temperate acts.

Actions, then, are called just and temperate when they are such as the just or the temperate man would do; but it is not the man who does these that is just and temperate, but the man who also does them *as* just and temperate men do them. It is well said, then, that it is by doing just acts that the just man is produced, and by doing temperate acts the temperate man; without doing these no one would have even a prospect of becoming good.

But most people do not do these, but take refuge in theory and think they are being philosophers and will become good in this way, behaving somewhat like patients who listen attentively to their doctors, but do none of the things they are ordered to do. As the latter will not be made well in body by such a course of treatment, the former will not be made well in soul by such a course of philosophy.

Next we must consider what virtue is. Since things that 5
are found in the soul are of three kinds—passions, faculties, states of character, virtue must be one of these. By passions

I mean appetite, anger, fear, confidence, envy, joy, friendly feeling, hatred, longing, emulation, pity, and in general the feelings that are accompanied by pleasure or pain; by faculties the things in virtue of which we are said to be capable of feeling these, e. g. of becoming angry or being pained or feeling pity; by states of character the things in virtue of which we stand well or badly with reference to the passions, e. g. with reference to anger we stand badly if we feel it violently or too weakly, and well if we feel it moderately; and similarly with reference to the other passions.

Now neither the virtues nor the vices are *passions*, because we are not called good or bad on the ground of our passions, but are so called on the ground of our virtues and our vices, and because we are neither praised nor blamed for our passions (for the man who feels fear or anger is not praised, nor is the man who simply feels anger blamed, but the man who feels it in a certain way), but for our virtues 1106a
and our vices we *are* praised or blamed.

Again, we feel anger and fear without choice, but the virtues are modes of choice or involve choice. Further, in respect of the passions we are said to be moved, but in respect of the virtues and the vices we are said not to be moved but to be disposed in a particular way.

For these reasons also they are not *faculties*; for we are neither called good nor bad, nor praised nor blamed, for the simple capacity of feeling the passions; again, we have the faculties by nature, but we are not made good or bad by nature; we have spoken of this before.[1]

If, then, the virtues are neither passions nor faculties, all that remains is that they should be *states of character*.

Thus we have stated what virtue is in respect of its genus.

6 We must, however, not only describe virtue as a state of character, but also say what sort of state it is. We may remark, then, that every virtue or excellence both brings into good condition the thing of which it is the excellence and makes the work of that thing be done well; e. g. the excellence of the eye makes both the eye and its work good;

[1] 1103a 18–b 2.

for it is by the excellence of the eye that we see well. Similarly the excellence of the horse makes a horse both good in itself and good at running and at carrying its rider and at awaiting the attack of the enemy. Therefore, if this is true in every case, the virtue of man also will be the state of character which makes a man good and which makes him do his own work well.

How this is to happen we have stated already,[1] but it will be made plain also by the following consideration of the specific nature of virtue. In everything that is continuous and divisible it is possible to take more, less, or an equal amount, and that either in terms of the thing itself or relatively to us; and the equal is an intermediate between excess and defect. By the intermediate in the object I mean that which is equidistant from each of the extremes, which is one and the same for all men; by the intermediate relatively to us that which is neither too much nor too little—and this is not one, nor the same for all. For instance, if ten is many and two is few, six is the intermediate, taken in terms of the object; for it exceeds and is exceeded by an equal amount; this is intermediate according to arithmetical proportion. But the intermediate relatively to us is not to be taken so; if ten pounds are too
1106b much for a particular person to eat and two too little, it does not follow that the trainer will order six pounds; for this also is perhaps too much for the person who is to take it, or too little—too little for Milo,[2] too much for the beginner in athletic exercises. The same is true of running and wrestling. Thus a master of any art avoids excess and defect, but seeks the intermediate and chooses this—the intermediate not in the object but relatively to us.

If it is thus, then, that every art does its work well—by looking to the intermediate and judging its works by this standard (so that we often say of good works of art that it is not possible either to take away or to add anything, implying that excess and defect destroy the goodness of works of art, while the mean preserves it; and good artists, as we say, look to this in their work), and if, further,

[1] 1104a 11–27.

[2] A famous wrestler.

virtue is more exact and better than any art, as nature also is, then virtue must have the quality of aiming at the intermediate. I mean moral virtue; for it is this that is concerned with passions and actions, and in these there is excess, defect, and the intermediate. For instance, both fear and confidence and appetite and anger and pity and in general pleasure and pain may be felt both too much and too little, and in both cases not well; but to feel them at the right times, with reference to the right objects, towards the right people, with the right motive, and in the right way, is what is both intermediate and best, and this is characteristic of virtue. Similarly with regard to actions also there is excess, defect, and the intermediate. Now virtue is concerned with passions and actions, in which excess is a form of failure, and so is defect, while the intermediate is praised and is a form of success; and being praised and being successful are both characteristics of virtue. Therefore virtue is a kind of mean, since, as we have seen, it aims at what is intermediate.

Again, it is possible to fail in many ways (for evil belongs to the class of the unlimited, as the Pythagoreans conjectured, and good to that of the limited), while to succeed is possible only in one way (for which reason also one is easy and the other difficult—to miss the mark easy, to hit it difficult); for these reasons also, then, excess and defect are characteristic of vice, and the mean of virtue;

For men are good in but one way, but bad in many.[1]

Virtue, then, is a state of character concerned with choice, lying in a mean, i.e. the mean relative to us, this being 1107a determined by a rational principle, and by that principle by which the man of practical wisdom would determine it. Now it is a mean between two vices, that which depends on excess and that which depends on defect; and again it is a mean because the vices respectively fall short of or exceed what is right in both passions and actions, while virtue both finds and chooses that which is intermediate. Hence in respect of its substance and the definition which states its

[1] Fr. eleg. adesp. 16, Diehl.

essence virtue is a mean, with regard to what is best and right an extreme.

But not every action nor every passion admits of a mean; for some have names that already imply badness, e.g. spite, shamelessness, envy, and in the case of actions adultery, theft, murder; for all of these and suchlike things imply by their names that they are themselves bad, and not the excesses or deficiencies of them. It is not possible, then, ever to be right with regard to them; one must always be wrong. Nor does goodness or badness with regard to such things depend on committing adultery with the right woman, at the right time, and in the right way, but simply to do any of them is to go wrong. It would be equally absurd, then, to expect that in unjust, cowardly, and voluptuous action there should be a mean, an excess, and a deficiency; for at that rate there would be a mean of excess and of deficiency, an excess of excess, and a deficiency of deficiency. But as there is no excess and deficiency of temperance and courage because what is intermediate is in a sense an extreme, so too of the actions we have mentioned there is no mean nor any excess and deficiency, but however they are done they are wrong; for in general there is neither a mean of excess and deficiency, nor excess and deficiency of a mean.

We must, however, not only make this general statement, 7
but also apply it to the individual facts. For among statements about conduct those which are general apply more widely, but those which are particular are more genuine, since conduct has to do with individual cases, and our statements must harmonize with the facts in these cases. We may take these cases from our table. With regard to feelings of
1107b fear and confidence courage is the mean; of the people who exceed, he who exceeds in fearlessness has no name (many of the states have no name), while the man who exceeds in confidence is rash, and he who exceeds in fear and falls short in confidence is a coward. With regard to pleasures and pains—not all of them, and not so much with regard to the pains—the mean is temperance, the excess self-indulgence. Persons deficient with regard to the pleasures are not often

found; hence such persons also have received no name. But let us call them 'insensible'.

With regard to giving and taking of money the mean is liberality, the excess and the defect prodigality and meanness. In these actions people exceed and fall short in contrary ways; the prodigal exceeds in spending and falls short in taking, while the mean man exceeds in taking and falls short in spending. (At present we are giving a mere outline or summary, and are satisfied with this; later these states will be more exactly determined.[1]) With regard to money there are also other dispositions—a mean, magnificence (for the magnificent man differs from the liberal man; the former deals with large sums, the latter with small ones), an excess, tastelessness and vulgarity, and a deficiency, niggardliness; these differ from the states opposed to liberality, and the mode of their difference will be stated later.[2]

With regard to honour and dishonour the mean is proper pride, the excess is known as a sort of 'empty vanity', and the deficiency is undue humility; and as we said[3] liberality was related to magnificence, differing from it by dealing with small sums, so there is a state similarly related to proper pride, being concerned with small honours while that is concerned with great. For it is possible to desire honour as one ought, and more than one ought, and less, and the man who exceeds in his desires is called ambitious, the man who falls short unambitious, while the intermediate person has no name. The dispositions also are nameless, except that that of the ambitious man is called ambition. Hence the people who are at the extremes lay claim to the middle place; and we ourselves sometimes call the intermediate person ambitious and sometimes unambitious, and sometimes praise the ambitious man and sometimes the unambitious. The reason of our doing this will be stated 1108a
in what follows;[4] but now let us speak of the remaining states according to the method which has been indicated.

With regard to anger also there is an excess, a deficiency, and a mean. Although they can scarcely be said to have

[1] iv. 1.

[2] 1122a 20-9, b 10-18.

[3] ll. 17-19.

[4] b 11-26, 1125b 14-18.

names, yet since we call the intermediate person good-tempered let us call the mean good temper; of the persons at the extremes let the one who exceeds be called irascible, and his vice irascibility, and the man who falls short an inirascible sort of person, and the deficiency inirascibility.

There are also three other means, which have a certain likeness to one another, but differ from one another: for they are all concerned with intercourse in words and actions, but differ in that one is concerned with truth in this sphere, the other two with pleasantness; and of this one kind is exhibited in giving amusement, the other in all the circumstances of life. We must therefore speak of these too, that we may the better see that in all things the mean is praiseworthy, and the extremes neither praiseworthy nor right, but worthy of blame. Now most of these states also have no names, but we must try, as in the other cases, to invent names ourselves so that we may be clear and easy to follow. With regard to truth, then, the intermediate is a truthful sort of person and the mean may be called truthfulness, while the pretence which exaggerates is boastfulness and the person characterized by it a boaster, and that which understates is mock modesty and the person characterized by it mock-modest. With regard to pleasantness in the giving of amusement the intermediate person is ready-witted and the disposition ready wit, the excess is buffoonery and the person characterized by it a buffoon, while the man who falls short is a sort of boor and his state is boorishness. With regard to the remaining kind of pleasantness, that which is exhibited in life in general, the man who is pleasant in the right way is friendly and the mean is friendliness, while the man who exceeds is an obsequious person if he has no end in view, a flatterer if he is aiming at his own advantage, and the man who falls short and is unpleasant in all circumstances is a quarrelsome and surly sort of person.

There are also means in the passions and concerned with the passions; since shame is not a virtue, and yet praise is extended to the modest man. For even in these matters one man is said to be intermediate, and another to exceed,

as for instance the bashful man who is ashamed of everything; while he who falls short or is not ashamed of anything at all is shameless, and the intermediate person is modest. Righteous indignation is a mean between envy and spite, and these states are concerned with the pain and 1108^{b}
pleasure that are felt at the fortunes of our neighbours; the man who is characterized by righteous indignation is pained at undeserved good fortune, the envious man, going beyond him, is pained at all good fortune, and the spiteful man falls so far short of being pained that he even rejoices.[1] But these states there will be an opportunity of describing elsewhere;[2] with regard to justice, since it has not one simple meaning, we shall, after describing the other states, distinguish its two kinds and say how each of them is a mean;[3] and similarly we shall treat also of the rational virtues.[4]

8 There are three kinds of disposition, then, two of them vices, involving excess and deficiency respectively, and one a virtue, viz. the mean, and all are in a sense opposed to all; for the extreme states are contrary both to the intermediate state and to each other, and the intermediate to the extremes; as the equal is greater relatively to the less, less relatively to the greater, so the middle states are excessive relatively to the deficiencies, deficient relatively to the excesses, both in passions and in actions. For the brave man appears rash relatively to the coward, and cowardly relatively to the rash man; and similarly the temperate man appears self-indulgent relatively to the insensible man, insensible relatively to the self-indulgent, and the liberal man prodigal relatively to the mean man, mean relatively to the prodigal. Hence also the people at the extremes push the intermediate man each over to the other, and the

[1] Aristotle must mean that while the envious man is pained at the good fortune of others, whether deserved or not, the spiteful man is pleased at the *bad* fortune of others, whether deserved or not. But if he had stated this in full, he would have seen that there is no real opposition.

[2] The reference may be to the whole treatment of the moral virtues in iii. 6–iv. 9, or to the discussion of shame in iv. 9 and an intended corresponding discussion of righteous indignation, or to the discussion of these two states in *Rhet.* ii. 6, 9, 10.

[3] 1129^{a}26–^{b}1, 1130^{a}14–^{b}5, 1131^{b}9–15, 1132^{a}24–30, 1133^{b}30–1134^{a}1.

[4] Bk. vi.

brave man is called rash by the coward, cowardly by the rash man, and correspondingly in the other cases.

These states being thus opposed to one another, the greatest contrariety is that of the extremes to each other, rather than to the intermediate; for these are further from each other than from the intermediate, as the great is further from the small and the small from the great than both are from the equal. Again, to the intermediate some extremes show a certain likeness, as that of rashness to courage and that of prodigality to liberality; but the extremes show the greatest unlikeness to each other; now contraries are defined as the things that are furthest from each other, so that things that are further apart are more contrary.

1109a To the mean in some cases the deficiency, in some the excess is more opposed; e. g. it is not rashness, which is an excess, but cowardice, which is a deficiency, that is more opposed to courage, and not insensibility, which is a deficiency, but self-indulgence, which is an excess, that is more opposed to temperance. This happens from two reasons, one being drawn from the thing itself; for because one extreme is nearer and liker to the intermediate, we oppose not this but rather its contrary to the intermediate. E. g., since rashness is thought liker and nearer to courage, and cowardice more unlike, we oppose rather the latter to courage; for things that are further from the intermediate are thought more contrary to it. This, then, is one cause, drawn from the thing itself; another is drawn from ourselves; for the things to which we ourselves more naturally tend seem more contrary to the intermediate. For instance, we ourselves tend more naturally to pleasures, and hence are more easily carried away towards self-indulgence than towards propriety. We describe as contrary to the mean, then, rather the directions in which we more often go to great lengths; and therefore self-indulgence, which is an excess, is the more contrary to temperance.

That moral virtue is a mean, then, and in what sense it is **9**
so, and that it is a mean between two vices, the one involving

excess, the other deficiency, and that it is such because its character is to aim at what is intermediate in passions and in actions, has been sufficiently stated. Hence also it is no easy task to be good. For in everything it is no easy task to find the middle, e.g. to find the middle of a circle is not for every one but for him who knows; so, too, any one can get angry—that is easy—or give or spend money; but to do this to the right person, to the right extent, at the right time, with the right motive, and in the right way, *that* is not for every one, nor is it easy; wherefore goodness is both rare and laudable and noble.

Hence he who aims at the intermediate must first depart from what is the more contrary to it, as Calypso advises—

> Hold the ship out beyond that surf and spray.[1]

For of the extremes one is more erroneous, one less so; therefore, since to hit the mean is hard in the extreme, we must as a second best, as people say, take the least of the evils; and this will be done best in the way we describe.

1109b But we must consider the things towards which we ourselves also are easily carried away; for some of us tend to one thing, some to another; and this will be recognizable from the pleasure and the pain we feel. We must drag ourselves away to the contrary extreme; for we shall get into the intermediate state by drawing well away from error, as people do in straightening sticks that are bent.

Now in everything the pleasant or pleasure is most to be guarded against; for we do not judge it impartially We ought, then, to feel towards pleasure as the elders of the people felt towards Helen, and in all circumstances repeat their saying;[2] for if we dismiss pleasure thus we are less likely to go astray. It is by doing this, then, (to sum the matter up) that we shall best be able to hit the mean.

But this is no doubt difficult, and especially in individual cases; for it is not easy to determine both how and with

[1] *Od.* xii. 219 f. (Mackail's trans.). But it was Circe who gave the advice (xii. 108), and the actual quotation is from Odysseus' orders to his steersman.

[2] *Il.* iii. 156–60.

whom and on what provocation and how long one should be angry; for we too sometimes praise those who fall short and call them good-tempered, but sometimes we praise those who get angry and call them manly. The man, however, who deviates little from goodness is not blamed, whether he do so in the direction of the more or of the less, but only the man who deviates more widely; for *he* does not fail to be noticed. But up to what point and to what extent a man must deviate before he becomes blameworthy it is not easy to determine by reasoning, any more than anything else that is perceived by the senses; such things depend on particular facts, and the decision rests with perception. So much, then, is plain, that the intermediate state is in all things to be praised, but that we must incline sometimes towards the excess, sometimes towards the deficiency; for so shall we most easily hit the mean and what is right.

BOOK III

1 SINCE virtue is concerned with passions and actions, and on voluntary passions and actions praise and blame are bestowed, on those that are involuntary pardon, and sometimes also pity, to distinguish the voluntary and the involuntary is presumably necessary for those who are studying the nature of virtue, and useful also for legislators with a view to the assigning both of honours and of punishments.

Those things, then, are thought involuntary, which take place under compulsion or owing to ignorance; and that is 1110a
compulsory of which the moving principle is outside, being a principle in which nothing is contributed by the person who is acting or is feeling the passion, e.g. if he were to be carried somewhere by a wind, or by men who had him in their power.

But with regard to the things that are done from fear of greater evils or for some noble object (e.g. if a tyrant were to order one to do something base, having one's parents and children in his power, and if one did the action they were to be saved, but otherwise would be put to death), it may be debated whether such actions are involuntary or voluntary. Something of the sort happens also with regard to the throwing of goods overboard in a storm; for in the abstract no one throws goods away voluntarily, but on condition of its securing the safety of himself and his crew any sensible man does so. Such actions, then, are mixed, but are more like voluntary actions; for they are worthy of choice at the time when they are done, and the end of an action is relative to the occasion. Both the terms, then, 'voluntary' and 'involuntary', must be used with reference to the moment of action. Now the man acts voluntarily; for the principle that moves the instrumental parts of the body in such actions is in him, and the things of which the moving principle is in a man himself are in his power to do or not to do. Such actions, therefore, are voluntary, but in the abstract perhaps involuntary; for no one would choose any such act in itself. For such actions men are sometimes even praised, when they endure something base or painful in return for great and noble objects gained; in the opposite case they are blamed, since to endure the greatest indignities for no noble end or for a trifling end is the mark of an inferior person. On some actions praise indeed is not bestowed, but pardon is, when one does what he ought not under pressure which overstrains human nature and which no one could withstand. But some acts, perhaps, we cannot be forced to do, but ought rather to face death after the most fearful sufferings; for the things that 'forced' Euripides' Alcmaeon to slay his mother[1] seem absurd. It is difficult sometimes to determine what should be chosen at what cost, and what should be endured in return for what gain, and yet more difficult to abide by our decisions; for as a rule what is expected is painful, and what we are forced to do is base, whence praise and blame are bestowed on those who have been compelled or have not.

1110b What sort of acts, then, should be called compulsory? We answer that without qualification actions are so when the cause is in the external circumstances and the agent contributes nothing. But the things that in themselves are involuntary, but now and in return for these gains are worthy of choice, and whose moving principle is in the agent, are in themselves involuntary, but now and in return for these gains voluntary. They are more like voluntary acts; for actions are in the class of particulars, and the particular acts here are voluntary. What sort of things are to be chosen, and in return for what, it is not easy to state; for there are many differences in the particular cases.

But if some one were to say that pleasant and noble objects have a compelling power, forcing us from without, all acts would be for him compulsory; for it is for these

[1] Μάλιστα μέν μ' ἐπῆρ' ἐπισκήψας πατήρ,
ὅθ' ἅρματ' εἰσέβαινεν εἰς Θήβας ἰών.

Alcmeon, fr. 69, Nauck.

objects that all men do everything they do. And those who act under compulsion and unwillingly act with pain, but those who do acts for their pleasantness and nobility do them with pleasure; it is absurd to make external circumstances responsible, and not oneself, as being easily caught by such attractions, and to make oneself responsible for noble acts but the pleasant objects responsible for base acts. The compulsory, then, seems to be that whose moving principle is outside, the person compelled contributing nothing.

Everything that is done by reason of ignorance is *not* voluntary; it is only what produces pain and repentance that is *in*voluntary. For the man who has done something owing to ignorance, and feels not the least vexation at his action, has not acted voluntarily, since he did not know what he was doing, nor yet involuntarily, since he is not pained. Of people, then, who act by reason of ignorance he who repents is thought an involuntary agent, and the man who does not repent may, since he is different, be called a not voluntary agent; for, since he differs from the other, it is better that he should have a name of his own.

Acting by reason of ignorance seems also to be different from acting *in* ignorance; for the man who is drunk or in a rage is thought to act as a result not of ignorance but of one of the causes mentioned, yet not knowingly but in ignorance.

Now every wicked man is ignorant of what he ought to do and what he ought to abstain from, and it is by reason of error of this kind that men become unjust and in general bad; but the term 'involuntary' tends to be used not if a man is ignorant of what is to his advantage—for it is not mistaken purpose that causes involuntary action (it leads rather to wickedness), nor ignorance of the universal (for *that* men are *blamed*), but ignorance of particulars, i. e. of the circumstances of the action and the objects with which it is concerned. For it is on these that both pity and 1111a
pardon depend, since the person who is ignorant of any of these acts involuntarily.

Perhaps it is just as well, therefore, to determine their nature and number. A man may be ignorant, then, of who he is, what he is doing, what or whom he is acting on, and sometimes also what (e.g. what instrument) he is doing it with, and to what end (e.g. he may think his act will conduce to some one's safety), and how he is doing it (e.g. whether gently or violently). Now of all of these no one could be ignorant unless he were mad, and evidently also he could not be ignorant of the agent; for how could he not know himself? But of what he is doing a man might be ignorant, as for instance people say 'it slipped out of their mouths as they were speaking',[1] or 'they did not know it was a secret', as Aeschylus said of the mysteries,[2] or a man might say he 'let it go off when he merely wanted to show its working', as the man did with the catapult. Again, one might think one's son was an enemy, as Merope did,[3] or that a pointed spear had a button on it, or that a stone was pumice-stone; or one might give a man a draught to save him, and really kill him; or one might want to touch a man, as people do in sparring, and really wound him. The ignorance may relate, then, to any of these things, i.e. of the circumstances of the action, and the man who was ignorant of any of these is thought to have acted involuntarily, and especially if he was ignorant on the most important points; and these are thought to be the circumstances of the action and its end. Further,[4] the doing of an act that is called involuntary in virtue of ignorance of this sort must be painful and involve repentance.

Since that which is done under compulsion or by reason of ignorance is involuntary, the voluntary would seem to be that of which the moving principle is in the agent himself,

[1] Reading in l. 9 *λέγοντάς* with (apparently) Aspasius and *αὐτούς* with the Aldine edition.

[2] Aeschylus was acquitted by the Areopagus on a charge of revealing the Eleusinian mysteries. In Pl. *Rep.* 563 C we have *οὐκοῦν κατ' Αἰσχύλον, ἔφη, ἐροῦμεν ὅτι νῦν ἦλθ' ἐπὶ στόμα.* Professor H. Jackson (in *J. of P.* xxvii. 159 f.) connects the two references and suggests that Aeschylus, charged with betraying the mysteries, replied, 'I said the first thing which occurred to me', and perhaps added, 'not knowing that there was anything in it which had to do with the mysteries'. He conjectures, further, that the true reading of the present passage is *οἷον λέγοντές φασιν ἐκπεσεῖν αὐτοὺς ἃ οὐκ εἰδέναι ὅτι ἀπόρρητα ἦν.* This emendation is, however, not very probable.

[3] In the *Cresphontes* of Euripides; v. Nauck[2], 497 f.

[4] Reading *τοῦ δέ* in l. 19, with Thurot.

he being aware of the particular circumstances of the action. Presumably acts done by reason of anger or appetite are not rightly called involuntary.[1] For in the first place, on that showing none of the other animals will act voluntarily, nor will children; and secondly, is it meant that we do not do voluntarily *any* of the acts that are due to appetite or anger, or that we do the noble acts voluntarily and the base acts involuntarily? Is not this absurd, when one and the same thing is the cause? But it would surely be odd to describe as involuntary the things one ought to desire; and we ought both to be angry at certain things and to have an appetite for certain things, e. g. for health and for learning. Also what is involuntary is thought to be painful, but what is in accordance with appetite is thought to be pleasant. Again, what is the difference in respect of involuntariness between errors committed upon calculation and those committed in anger? Both are to be avoided, but the irrational 1111[b]
passions are thought not less human than reason is, and therefore also the actions which proceed from anger or appetite are the man's actions. It would be odd, then, to treat them as involuntary.

2 Both the voluntary and the involuntary having been delimited, we must next discuss choice;[2] for it is thought to be most closely bound up with virtue and to discriminate characters better than actions do.

Choice, then, seems to be voluntary, but not the same thing as the voluntary; the latter extends more widely. For both children and the lower animals share in voluntary action, but not in choice, and acts done on the spur of the moment we describe as voluntary, but not as chosen.

Those who say it is appetite or anger or wish or a kind of opinion do not seem to be right. For choice is not common to irrational creatures as well, but appetite and anger are. Again, the incontinent man acts with appetite,

[1] A reference to Pl. *Laws* 863 B, ff., where anger and appetite are coupled with ignorance as sources of wrong action.

[2] Προαίρεσις is a very difficult word to translate. Sometimes 'intention', 'will', or 'purpose' would bring out the meaning better; but I have for the most part used 'choice'. The etymological meaning is 'preferential choice'.

but not with choice; while the continent man on the contrary acts with choice, but not with appetite. Again, appetite is contrary to choice, but not appetite to appetite. Again, appetite relates to the pleasant and the painful, choice neither to the painful nor to the pleasant.

Still less is it anger; for acts due to anger are thought to be less than any others objects of choice.

But neither is it wish, though it seems near to it; for choice cannot relate to impossibles, and if any one said he chose them he would be thought silly; but there may be a wish even for impossibles, e.g. for immortality. And wish may relate to things that could in no way be brought about by one's own efforts, e.g. that a particular actor or athlete should win in a competition; but no one chooses such things, but only the things that he thinks could be brought about by his own efforts. Again, wish relates rather to the end, choice to the means; for instance, we wish to be healthy, but we choose the acts which will make us healthy, and we wish to be happy and say we do, but we cannot well say we choose to be so; for, in general, choice seems to relate to the things that are in our own power.

For this reason, too, it cannot be opinion; for opinion is thought to relate to all kinds of things, no less to eternal things and impossible things than to things in our own power; and it is distinguished by its falsity or truth, not by its badness or goodness, while choice is distinguished rather by these.

Now with opinion in general perhaps no one even says it
1112a is identical. But it is not identical even with any kind of opinion; for by choosing what is good or bad we are men of a certain character, which we are not by holding certain opinions. And we choose to get or avoid something good or bad, but we have opinions about what a thing is or whom it is good for or how it is good for him; we can hardly be said to opine to get or avoid anything. And choice is praised for being related to the right object rather than for being rightly related to it, opinion for being truly related to its object. And we choose what we best know to be good, but we opine what we do not quite know; and it is not the same

people that are thought to make the best choices and to have the best opinions, but some are thought to have fairly good opinions, but by reason of vice to choose what they should not. If opinion precedes choice or accompanies it, that makes no difference; for it is not this that we are considering, but whether it is *identical* with some kind of opinion.

What, then, or what kind of thing is it, since it is none of the things we have mentioned? It seems to be voluntary, but not all that is voluntary to be an object of choice. Is it, then, what has been decided on by previous deliberation? At any rate choice involves a rational principle and thought. Even the name seems to suggest that it is what is chosen before other things.

3 Do we deliberate about everything, and is everything a possible subject of deliberation, or is deliberation impossible about some things? We ought presumably to call not what a fool or a madman would deliberate about, but what a sensible man would deliberate about, a subject of deliberation. Now about eternal things no one deliberates, e.g. about the material universe or the incommensurability of the diagonal and the side of a square. But no more do we deliberate about the things that involve movement but always happen in the same way, whether of necessity or by nature or from any other cause, e.g. the solstices and the risings of the stars; nor about things that happen now in one way, now in another, e.g. droughts and rains; nor about chance events, like the finding of treasure. But we do not deliberate even about all human affairs; for instance, no Spartan deliberates about the best constitution for the Scythians. For none of these things can be brought about by our own efforts.

We deliberate about things that are in our power and can be done; and these are in fact what is left. For nature, necessity, and chance are thought to be causes, and also reason and everything that depends on man. Now every class of men deliberates about the things that can be done by their own efforts. And in the case of exact and self-contained sciences there is no deliberation, e.g. about the letters of the 1112b alphabet (for we have no doubt how they should be written); but the things that are brought about by our own efforts, but not always in the same way, are the things about which we deliberate, e.g. questions of medical treatment or of money-making. And we do so more in the case of the art of navigation than in that of gymnastics, inasmuch as it has been less exactly worked out, and again about other things in the same ratio, and more also in the case of the arts than in that of the sciences; for we have more doubt about the former. Deliberation is concerned with things that happen in a certain way for the most part, but in which the event is obscure, and with things in which it is indeterminate. We call in others to aid us in deliberation on important questions, distrusting ourselves as not being equal to deciding.

We deliberate not about ends but about means. For a doctor does not deliberate whether he shall heal, nor an orator whether he shall persuade, nor a statesman whether he shall produce law and order, nor does any one else deliberate about his end. They assume the end and consider how and by what means it is to be attained; and if it seems to be produced by several means they consider by which it is most easily and best produced, while if it is achieved by one only they consider how it will be achieved by this and by what means *this* will be achieved, till they come to the first cause, which in the order of discovery is last. For the person who deliberates seems to investigate and analyse in the way described as though he were analysing a geometrical construction[1] (not all investigation appears to be deliberation—for instance mathematical investigations—but all deliberation is investigation), and what is last in the order of analysis seems to be first in the order of becoming. And if we come on an impossibility, we give up the search, e.g. if we need money and this cannot be got; but if a thing appears possible we

[1] Aristotle has in mind the method of discovering the solution of a geometrical problem. The problem being to construct a figure of a certain kind, we suppose it constructed and then analyse it to see if there is some figure by constructing which we can construct the required figure, and so on till we come to a figure which our existing knowledge enables us to construct.

try to do it. By 'possible' things I mean things that might be brought about by our own efforts; and these in a sense include things that can be brought about by the efforts of our friends, since the moving principle is in ourselves. The subject of investigation is sometimes the instruments, sometimes the use of them; and similarly in the other cases—sometimes the means, sometimes the mode of using it or the means of bringing it about. It seems, then, as has been said, that man is a moving principle of actions; now deliberation is about the things to be done by the agent himself, and actions are for the sake of things other than themselves. For the end cannot be a subject of deliberation, but only the means; nor indeed can the particular facts be a subject of it, as whether this is bread or has been baked as it should; 1113a
for these are matters of perception. If we are to be always deliberating, we shall have to go on to infinity.

The same thing is deliberated upon and is chosen, except that the object of choice is already determinate, since it is that which has been decided upon as a result of deliberation that is the object of choice. For every one ceases to inquire how he is to act when he has brought the moving principle back to himself and to the ruling part of himself; for this is what chooses. This is plain also from the ancient constitutions, which Homer represented; for the kings announced their choices to the people. The object of choice being one of the things in our own power which is desired after deliberation, choice will be deliberate desire of things in our own power; for when we have decided as a result of deliberation, we desire in accordance with our deliberation.

We may take it, then, that we have described choice in outline, and stated the nature of its objects and the fact that it is concerned with means.

4 That *wish* is for the end has already been stated;[1] some think it is for the good, others for the apparent good. Now those who say that the good is the object of wish must admit in consequence that that which the man who does not choose aright wishes for is not an object of wish (for if it is to be

[1] 1111b 26.

so, it must also be good; but it was, if it so happened, bad); while those who say the apparent good is the object of wish must admit that there is no natural object of wish, but only what seems good to each man. Now different things appear good to different people, and, if it so happens, even contrary things.

If these consequences are unpleasing, are we to say that absolutely and in truth the good is the object of wish, but for each person the apparent good; that that which is in truth an object of wish is an object of wish to the good man, while any chance thing may be so to the bad man, as in the case of bodies also the things that are in truth wholesome are wholesome for bodies which are in good condition, while for those that are diseased other things are wholesome—or bitter or sweet or hot or heavy, and so on; since the good man judges each class of things rightly, and in each the truth appears to him? For each state of character has its own ideas of the noble and the pleasant, and perhaps the good man differs from others most by seeing the truth in each class of things, being as it were the norm and measure of them. In most things the error seems to be due to pleasure; for it appears a good
1113b when it is not. We therefore choose the pleasant as a good, and avoid pain as an evil.

The end, then, being what we wish for, the means what 5
we deliberate about and choose, actions concerning means must be according to choice and voluntary. Now the exercise of the virtues is concerned with means. Therefore virtue also is in our own power, and so too vice. For where it is in our power to act it is also in our power not to act, and *vice versa*; so that, if to act, where this is noble, is in our power, not to act, which will be base, will also be in our power, and if not to act, where this is noble, is in our power, to act, which will be base, will also be in our power. Now if it is in our power to do noble or base acts, and likewise in our power not to do them, and this was what being good or bad meant,[1] then it is in our power to be virtuous or vicious.

The saying[2] that 'no one is voluntarily wicked nor involun-

[1] 1112a 1 f.

[2] Fr. adesp. (? Solon), Bergk^3, p. 1356 f.

tarily happy ' seems to be partly false and partly true; for no one is involuntarily happy, but wickedness *is* voluntary. Or else we shall have to dispute what has just been said, at any rate, and deny that man is a moving principle or begetter of his actions as of children. But if these facts are evident and we cannot refer actions to moving principles other than those in ourselves, the acts whose moving principles are in us must themselves also be in our power and voluntary.

Witness seems to be borne to this both by individuals in their private capacity and by legislators themselves; for these punish and take vengeance on those who do wicked acts (unless they have acted under compulsion or as a result of ignorance for which they are not themselves responsible), while they honour those who do noble acts, as though they meant to encourage the latter and deter the former. But no one is encouraged to do the things that are neither in our power nor voluntary; it is assumed that there is no gain in being persuaded not to be hot or in pain or hungry or the like, since we shall experience these feelings none the less. Indeed,[1] we punish a man for his very ignorance, if he is thought responsible for the ignorance, as when penalties are doubled in the case of drunkenness;[2] for the moving principle is in the man himself, since he had the power of not getting drunk and his getting drunk was the cause of his ignorance. And we punish those who are ignorant of anything in the laws that they ought to know and that is not difficult, and so too in the 1114a
case of anything else that they are thought to be ignorant of through carelessness; we assume that it is in their power not to be ignorant, since they have the power of taking care.

But perhaps a man is the kind of man not to take care. Still they are themselves by their slack lives responsible for becoming men of that kind, and men make themselves responsible for being unjust or self-indulgent, in the one case by cheating and in the other by spending their time in drinking bouts and the like; for it is activities exercised on particular objects that make the corresponding character.

[1] This connects with the words of l. 24 f. 'unless they have acted . . . as a result of ignorance for which they are not themselves responsible.'

[2] As by the law of Pittacus; cf. *Pol.* 1274b 19, *Rhet.* 1402b 9.

This is plain from the case of people training for any contest or action; they practise the activity the whole time. Now not to know that it is from the exercise of activities on particular objects that states of character are produced is the mark of a thoroughly senseless person. Again, it is irrational to suppose that a man who acts unjustly does not wish to be unjust or a man who acts self-indulgently to be self-indulgent. But if *without* being ignorant a man does the things which will make him unjust, he will be unjust voluntarily. Yet it does not follow that if he wishes he will cease to be unjust and will be just. For neither does the man who is ill become well on those terms. We may suppose a case in which he is ill voluntarily, through living incontinently and disobeying his doctors. In that case it was *then* open to him not to be ill, but not now, when he has thrown away his chance, just as when you have let a stone go it is too late to recover it; but yet it was in your power to throw it, since the moving principle was in you. So, too, to the unjust and to the self-indulgent man it was open at the beginning not to become men of this kind, and so they are unjust and self-indulgent voluntarily; but now that they have become so it is not possible for them not to be so.

But not only are the vices of the soul voluntary, but those of the body also for some men, whom we accordingly blame; while no one blames those who are ugly by nature, we blame those who are so owing to want of exercise and care. So it is, too, with respect to weakness and infirmity; no one would reproach a man blind from birth or by disease or from a blow, but rather pity him, while every one would blame a man who was blind from drunkenness or some other form of self-indulgence. Of vices of the body, then, those in our own power are blamed, those not in our power are not. And if this be so, in the other cases also the vices that are blamed must be in our own power.

Now some one may say that all men desire the apparent good, but have no control over the appearance, but the end appears to each man in a form answering to his character.
1114b We reply that if each man is somehow responsible for his state of mind, he will also be himself somehow responsible

for the appearance; but if not, no one is responsible for his own evildoing, but every one does evil acts through ignorance of the end, thinking that by these he will get what is best, and the aiming at the end is not self-chosen but one must be born with an eye, as it were, by which to judge rightly and choose what is truly good, and he is well endowed by nature who is well endowed with this. For it is what is greatest and most noble, and what we cannot get or learn from another, but must have just such as it was when given us at birth, and to be well and nobly endowed with this will be perfect and true excellence of natural endowment. If this is true, then, how will virtue be more voluntary than vice? To both men alike, the good and the bad, the end appears and is fixed by nature or however it may be, and it is by referring everything else to this that men do whatever they do.

Whether, then, it is not by nature that the end appears to each man such as it does appear, but something also depends on him, or the end is natural but because the good man adopts the means voluntarily virtue is voluntary, vice also will be none the less voluntary; for in the case of the bad man there is equally present that which depends on himself in his actions even if not in his end. If, then, as is asserted, the virtues are voluntary (for we are ourselves somehow partly responsible for our states of character, and it is by being persons of a certain kind that we assume the end to be so and so), the vices also will be voluntary; for the same is true of them.

With regard to the virtues in *general* we have stated their genus in outline, viz. that they are means and that they are states of character, and that they tend, and by their own nature, to the doing of the acts by which they are produced, and that they are in our power and voluntary, and act as the right rule prescribes. But actions and states of character are not voluntary in the same way; for we are masters of our actions from the beginning right to the end, if we know the particular facts, but though we control the beginning of
our states of character the gradual progress is not obvious, 1115a
any more than it is in illnesses; because it was in our power, however, to act in this way or not in this way, therefore the states are voluntary.

Let us take up the several virtues, however, and say which they are and what sort of things they are concerned with and how they are concerned with them; at the same time it will become plain how many they are. And first let us speak of courage.

That it is a mean with regard to feelings of fear and 6
confidence has already been made evident;[1] and plainly the things we fear are terrible things, and these are, to speak without qualification, evils; for which reason people even define fear as expectation of evil. Now we fear all evils, e.g. disgrace, poverty, disease, friendlessness, death, but the brave man is not thought to be concerned with all; for to fear some things is even right and noble, and it is base not to fear them—e.g. disgrace; he who fears this is good and modest, and he who does not is shameless. He is, however, by some people called brave, by a transference of the word to a new meaning; for he has in him something which is like the brave man, since the brave man also is a fearless person. Poverty and disease we perhaps ought not to fear, nor in general the things that do not proceed from vice and are not due to a man himself. But not even the man who is fearless of these is brave. Yet we apply the word to him also in virtue of a similarity; for some who in the dangers of war are cowards are liberal and are confident in face of the loss of money. Nor is a man a coward if he fears insult to his wife and children or envy or anything of the kind; nor brave if he is confident when he is about to be flogged. With what sort of terrible things, then, is the brave man concerned? Surely with the greatest; for no one is more likely than he to stand his ground against what is awe-inspiring. Now death is the most terrible of all things; for it is the end, and nothing is thought to be any longer either good or bad for the dead. But the brave man would not seem to be concerned even with death in *all* circumstances, e.g. at sea or in disease. In what circumstances, then? Surely in the noblest. Now such deaths are those in battle; for these take place in the greatest and noblest danger. And these are corre-

[1] 1107a 33–b 4.

spondingly honoured in city-states and at the courts of monarchs. Properly, then, he will be called brave who is fearless in face of a noble death, and of all emergencies that involve death; and the emergencies of war are in the highest degree of this kind. Yet at sea also, and in disease, the brave man is fearless, but not in the same way as the seamen; 1115b
for he has given up hope of safety, and is disliking the thought of death in this shape, while they are hopeful because of their experience. At the same time, we show courage in situations where there is the opportunity of showing prowess or where death is noble; but in these forms of death neither of these conditions is fulfilled.

7 What is terrible is not the same for all men; but we say there are things terrible even beyond human strength. These, then, are terrible to every one—at least to every sensible man; but the terrible things that are *not* beyond human strength differ in magnitude and degree, and so too do the things that inspire confidence. Now the brave man is as dauntless as man may be. Therefore, while he will fear even the things that are not beyond human strength, he will face them as he ought and as the rule directs, for honour's sake; for this is the end of virtue. But it is possible to fear these more, or less, and again to fear things that are not terrible as if they were. Of the faults that are committed one consists in fearing what one should not, another in fearing as we should not, another in fearing when we should not, and so on; and so too with respect to the things that inspire confidence. The man, then, who faces and who fears the right things and from the right motive, in the right way and at the right time, and who feels confidence under the corresponding conditions, is brave; for the brave man feels and acts according to the merits of the case and in whatever way the rule directs. Now the end of every activity is conformity to the corresponding state of character. This is true, therefore, of the brave man as well as of others. But courage is noble.[1] Therefore the end also is noble; for each thing is defined by its end.

[1] Reading, as Ramsauer suggests, καὶ τῷ ἀνδρείῳ δὴ ἡ ⟨δὲ⟩ ἀνδρεία καλόν.

Therefore it is for a noble end that the brave man endures and acts as courage directs.

Of those who go to excess he who exceeds in fearlessness has no name (we have said previously that many states of character have no names[1]), but he would be a sort of madman or insensible person if he feared nothing, neither earthquakes nor the waves, as they say the Celts do not; while the man who exceeds in confidence about what really is terrible is rash. The rash man, however, is also thought to be boastful and only a pretender to courage; at all events, as the brave man *is* with regard to what is terrible, so the rash man wishes to *appear*; and so he imitates him in situations where he can. Hence also most of them are a mixture of rashness and cowardice; for, while in these situations they display confidence, they do not hold their ground against what is really terrible. The man who exceeds in fear is a coward; for he fears both what he ought not and as he ought not, and all the similar
1116a characterizations attach to him. He is lacking also in confidence; but he is more conspicuous for his excess of fear in painful situations. The coward, then, is a despairing sort of person; for he fears everything. The brave man, on the other hand, has the opposite disposition; for confidence is the mark of a hopeful disposition. The coward, the rash man, and the brave man, then, are concerned with the same objects but are differently disposed towards them; for the first two exceed and fall short, while the third holds the middle, which is the right, position; and rash men are precipitate, and wish for dangers beforehand but draw back when they are in them, while brave men are keen in the moment of action, but quiet beforehand.

As we have said, then, courage is a mean with respect to things that inspire confidence or fear, in the circumstances that have been stated;[2] and it chooses or endures things because it is noble to do so, or because it is base not to do so.[3] But to die to escape from poverty or love or anything painful is not the mark of a brave man, but rather of a coward;

[1] 1107b 2, cf. 1107b 29, 1108a 5.
[2] Ch. 6.
[3] 1115b 11–24.

for it is softness to fly from what is troublesome, and such a man endures death not because it is noble but to fly from evil.

8 Courage, then, is something of this sort, but the name is also applied to five other kinds. (1) First comes the courage of the citizen-soldier; for this is most like true courage. Citizen-soldiers seem to face dangers because of the penalties imposed by the laws and the reproaches they would otherwise incur, and because of the honours they win by such action; and therefore those peoples seem to be bravest among whom cowards are held in dishonour and brave men in honour. This is the kind of courage that Homer depicts, e.g. in Diomede and in Hector:

First will Polydamas be to heap reproach on me then;[1]

and

For Hector one day 'mid the Trojans shall utter his vaulting harangue:
"Afraid was Tydeides, and fled from my face."[2]

This kind of courage is most like to that which we described earlier,[3] because it is due to virtue; for it is due to shame and to desire of a noble object (i. e. honour) and avoidance of disgrace, which is ignoble. One might rank in the same class even those who are compelled by their rulers; but they are inferior, inasmuch as they do what they do not from shame but from fear, and to avoid not what is disgraceful but what is painful; for their masters compel them, as Hector[4] does:

But if I shall spy any dastard that cowers far from the fight,
Vainly will such an one hope to escape from the dogs.

And those who give them their posts, and beat them if they retreat,[5] do the same, and so do those who draw 1116b
them up with trenches or something of the sort behind them; all of these apply compulsion. But one ought to be brave not under compulsion but because it is noble to be so.

[1] *Il.* xxii. 100. [2] *Il.* viii. 148, 149. [3] Chs. 6, 7.
[4] Aristotle's quotation is more like *Il.* ii. 391–3, where Agamemnon speaks, than xv. 348–51, where Hector speaks. [5] Cf. Hdt. vii. 223.

(2) Experience with regard to particular facts is also thought to be courage; this is indeed the reason why Socrates thought courage was knowledge.[1] Other people exhibit this quality in other dangers, and professional soldiers exhibit it in the dangers of war; for there seem to be many empty alarms in war, of which these have had the most comprehensive experience; therefore they seem brave, because the others do not know the nature of the facts. Again, their experience makes them most capable in attack and in defence, since they can use their arms and have the kind that are likely to be best both for attack and for defence; therefore they fight like armed men against unarmed or like trained athletes against amateurs; for in such contests too it is not the bravest men that fight best, but those who are strongest and have their bodies in the best condition. Professional soldiers turn cowards, however, when the danger puts too great a strain on them and they are inferior in numbers and equipment; for they are the first to fly, while citizen-forces die at their posts, as in fact happened at the temple of Hermes.[2] For to the latter flight is disgraceful and death is preferable to safety on those terms; while the former from the very beginning faced the danger on the assumption that they were stronger, and when they know the facts they fly, fearing death more than disgrace; but the brave man is not that sort of person.

(3) Passion also is sometimes reckoned as courage; those who act from passion, like wild beasts rushing at those who have wounded them, are thought to be brave, because brave men also are passionate; for passion above all things is eager to rush on danger, and hence Homer's 'put strength into his passion'[3] and 'aroused their spirit and passion'[4] and 'hard he breathed panting'[5] and 'his blood boiled'.[6] For all such expressions seem to indicate the stirring and onset of passion. Now brave men act for honour's sake,

[1] Xen. *Mem.* iii. 9. 1 f., iv. 6. 10 f., Pl. *Prot.* 350, 360.

[2] The reference is to a battle at Coronea in the Sacred War, *c.* 353 B.C., in which the Phocians defeated the citizens of Coronea and some Boeotian regulars.

[3] This is a conflation of *Il.* xi. 11 or xiv. 151 and xvi. 529.

[4] Cf. *Il.* v. 470, xv. 232, 594.

[5] Cf. *Od.* xxiv. 318 f.

[6] The phrase does not occur in Homer; it is found in Theocr. xx. 15.

but passion aids them; while wild beasts act under the influence of pain; for they attack because they have been wounded or because they are afraid, since if they are in a forest they do not come near one. Thus they are not brave because, driven by pain and passion, they rush on danger without foreseeing any of the perils, since at that rate even asses would be brave when they are hungry; for blows will not drive them from their food;[1] and lust also makes 1117a adulterers do many daring things. [Those creatures are not brave, then, which are driven on to danger by pain or passion.] The 'courage' that is due to passion seems to be the most natural, and to be courage if choice and motive be added.

Men, then, as well as beasts, suffer pain when they are angry, and are pleased when they exact their revenge; those who fight for these reasons, however, are pugnacious but not brave; for they do not act for honour's sake nor as the rule directs, but from strength of feeling; they have, however, something akin to courage.

(4) Nor are sanguine people brave; for they are confident in danger only because they have conquered often and against many foes. Yet they closely resemble brave men, because both are confident; but brave men are confident for the reasons stated earlier,[2] while these are so because they think they are the strongest and can suffer nothing. (Drunken men also behave in this way; they become sanguine). When their adventures do not succeed, however, they run away; but it was[2] the mark of a brave man to face things that are, and seem, terrible for a man, because it is noble to do so and disgraceful not to do so. Hence also it is thought the mark of a braver man to be fearless and undisturbed in sudden alarms than to be so in those that are foreseen; for it must have proceeded more from a state of character, because less from preparation; acts that are foreseen may be chosen by calculation and rule, but sudden actions must be in accordance with one's state of character.

(5) People who are ignorant of the danger also appear brave, and they are not far removed from those of a

[1] Cf. *Il.* xi. 558-62. [2] 1115b 11-24.

sanguine temper, but are inferior inasmuch as they have no self-reliance while these have. Hence also the sanguine hold their ground for a time; but those who have been deceived about the facts fly if they know or suspect that these are different from what they supposed, as happened to the Argives when they fell in with the Spartans and took them for Sicyonians.[1]

We have, then, described the character both of brave men 9
and of those who are thought to be brave.

Though courage is concerned with feelings of confidence and of fear, it is not concerned with both alike, but more with the things that inspire fear; for he who is undisturbed in face of these and bears himself as he should towards these is more truly brave than the man who does so towards the things that inspire confidence. It is for facing what is painful, then, as has been said,[2] that men are called brave. Hence also courage involves pain, and is justly praised; for it is harder to face what is painful than to abstain from what is pleasant. Yet the end which courage sets before it would
1117b seem to be pleasant, but to be concealed by the attending circumstances, as happens also in athletic contests; for the end at which boxers aim is pleasant—the crown and the honours—but the blows they take are distressing to flesh and blood, and painful, and so is their whole exertion; and because the blows and the exertions are many the end, which is but small, appears to have nothing pleasant in it. And so, if the case of courage is similar, death and wounds will be painful to the brave man and against his will, but he will face them because it is noble to do so or because it is base not to do so. And the more he is possessed of virtue in its entirety and the happier he is, the more he will be pained at the thought of death; for life is best worth living for such a man, and he is knowingly losing the greatest goods, and this is painful. But he is none the less brave, and perhaps all the more so, because he chooses noble deeds of war at that cost. It is not the case, then, with all the virtues that the exercise of them is pleasant, except in so far as it

[1] At the Long Walls of Corinth, 392 B.C. Cf. Xen. *Hell.* iv. 4. 10.
[2] 1115b7–13.

reaches its end. But it is quite possible that the best soldiers may be not men of this sort but those who are less brave but have no other good; for these are ready to face danger, and they sell their life for trifling gains.

So much, then, for courage; it is not difficult to grasp its nature in outline, at any rate, from what has been said.

After courage let us speak of temperance; for these seem
10 to be the virtues of the irrational parts. We have said[1] that temperance is a mean with regard to pleasures (for it is less, and not in the same way, concerned with pains); self-indulgence also is manifested in the same sphere. Now, therefore, let us determine with what sort of pleasures they are concerned. We may assume the distinction between bodily pleasures and those of the soul, such as love of honour and love of learning; for the lover of each of these delights in that of which he is a lover, the body being in no way affected, but rather the mind; but men who are concerned with such pleasures are called neither temperate nor self-indulgent. Nor, again, are those who are concerned with the other pleasures that are not bodily; for those who are fond of hearing and telling stories and who spend their days on anything that turns up are called gossips, but not self-indulgent, nor are those who are pained at the loss of money or of friends.

Temperance must be concerned with bodily pleasures, **1118a**
but not all even of these; for those who delight in objects of vision, such as colours and shapes and painting, are called neither temperate nor self-indulgent; yet it would seem possible to delight even in these either as one should or to excess or to a deficient degree.

And so too is it with objects of hearing; no one calls those who delight extravagantly in music or acting self-indulgent, nor those who do so as they ought temperate.

Nor do we apply these names to those who delight in odour, unless it be incidentally; we do not call those self-indulgent who delight in the odour of apples or roses or incense, but rather those who delight in the odour of

[1] 1107b 4–6.

unguents or of dainty dishes; for self-indulgent people delight in these because these remind them of the objects of their appetite. And one may see even other people, when they are hungry, delighting in the smell of food; but to delight in this kind of thing is the mark of the self-indulgent man; for these are objects of appetite to him.

Nor is there in animals other than man any pleasure connected with these senses, except incidentally. For dogs do not delight in the scent of hares, but in the eating of them, but the scent told them the hares were there; nor does the lion delight in the lowing of the ox, but in eating it; but he perceived by the lowing that it was near, and therefore appears to delight in the lowing; and similarly he does not delight because he sees 'a stag or a wild goat',[1] but because he is going to make a meal of it. Temperance and self-indulgence, however, are concerned with the kind of pleasures that the other animals share in, which therefore appear slavish and brutish; these are touch and taste. But even of taste they appear to make little or no use; for the business of taste is the discriminating of flavours, which is done by wine-tasters and people who season dishes; but they hardly take pleasure in making these discriminations, or at least self-indulgent people do not, but in the actual enjoyment, which in all cases comes through touch, both in the case of food and in that of drink and in that of sexual intercourse. This is why a certain gourmand[2] prayed that his throat might become longer than a crane's, implying that
1118b it was the contact that he took pleasure in. Thus the sense with which self-indulgence is connected is the most widely shared of the senses; and self-indulgence would seem to be justly a matter of reproach, because it attaches to us not as men but as animals. To delight in such things, then, and to love them above all others, is brutish. For even of the pleasures of touch the most liberal have been eliminated, e. g. those produced in the gymnasium by rubbing and by the consequent heat; for the contact characteristic of the self-indulgent man does not affect the whole body but only certain parts.

[1] *Il.* iii. 24.

[2] Philoxenus; cf. *E.E.* 1231a 17, *Probl.*, 950a 3.

11 Of the appetites some seem to be common, others to be peculiar to individuals and acquired; e. g. the appetite for food is natural, since every one who is without it craves for food or drink, and sometimes for both, and for love also (as Homer says)[1] if he is young and lusty; but not every one craves for this[2] or that kind of nourishment or love, nor for the same things. Hence such craving appears to be our very own. Yet it has of course something natural about it; for different things are pleasant to different kinds of people, and some things are more pleasant to every one than chance objects. Now in the natural appetites few go wrong, and only in one direction, that of excess; for to eat or drink whatever offers itself till one is surfeited is to exceed the natural amount, since natural appetite is the replenishment of one's deficiency. Hence these people are called belly-gods, this implying that they fill their belly beyond what is right. It is people of entirely slavish character that become like this. But with regard to the pleasures peculiar to individuals many people go wrong and in many ways. For while the people who are 'fond of so and so' are so called because they delight either in the wrong things, or more than most people do, or in the wrong way, the self-indulgent exceed in all three ways; they both delight in some things that they ought not to delight in (since they are hateful), and if one ought to delight in some of the things they delight in, they do so more than one ought and than most men do.

Plainly, then, excess with regard to pleasures is self-indulgence and is culpable; with regard to pains one is not, as in the case of courage, called temperate for facing them or self-indulgent for not doing so, but the self-indulgent man is so called because he is pained more than he ought at not getting pleasant things (even his pain being caused by pleasure), and the temperate man is so called because he is not pained at the absence of what is pleasant and at his abstinence from it.

[1] *Il.* xxiv. 130.
[2] Reading τῆς δὲ τοιᾶσδε as Bywater suggests, and omitting the comma before οὐκέτι.

1119a The self-indulgent man, then, craves for all pleasant things or those that are most pleasant, and is led by his appetite to choose these at the cost of everything else; hence he is pained both when he fails to get them and when he is merely craving for them (for appetite involves pain); but it seems absurd to be pained for the sake of pleasure. People who fall short with regard to pleasures and delight in them less than they should are hardly found; for such insensibility is not human. Even the other animals distinguish different kinds of food and enjoy some and not others; and if there is any one who finds nothing pleasant and nothing more attractive than anything else, he must be something quite different from a man; this sort of person has not received a name because he hardly occurs. The temperate man occupies a middle position with regard to these objects. For he neither enjoys the things that the self-indulgent man enjoys most—but rather dislikes them—nor in general the things that he should not, nor anything of this sort to excess, nor does he feel pain or craving when they are absent, or does so only to a moderate degree, and not more than he should, nor when he should not, and so on; but the things that, being pleasant, make for health or for good condition, he will desire moderately and as he should, and also other pleasant things if they are not hindrances to these ends, or contrary to what is noble, or beyond his means. For he who neglects these conditions loves such pleasures more than they are worth, but the temperate man is not that sort of person, but the sort of person that the right rule prescribes.

Self-indulgence is more like a voluntary state than 12
cowardice. For the former is actuated by pleasure, the latter by pain, of which the one is to be chosen and the other to be avoided; and pain upsets and destroys the nature of the person who feels it, while pleasure does nothing of the sort. Therefore self-indulgence is more voluntary. Hence also it is more a matter of reproach; for it is easier to become accustomed to its objects, since there are many things of this sort in life, and the process of habituation to them is free from danger, while with terrible objects the reverse is

the case. But cowardice would seem to be voluntary in a different degree from its particular manifestations; for it is itself painless, but in these we are upset by pain, so that we even throw down our arms and disgrace ourselves in other ways; hence our acts are even thought to be done under compulsion. For the self-indulgent man, on the other hand, the particular acts are voluntary (for he does them with craving and desire), but the whole state is less so; for no one craves to be self-indulgent.

The name self-indulgence is applied also to childish faults;[1] for they bear a certain resemblance to what we have been considering. Which is called after which, makes no differ- 1119b
ence to our present purpose; plainly, however, the later is called after the earlier. The transference of the name seems not a bad one; for that which desires what is base and which develops quickly ought to be kept in a chastened condition, and these characteristics belong above all to appetite and to the child, since children in fact live at the beck and call of appetite, and it is in them that the desire for what is pleasant is strongest. If, then, it is not going to be obedient and subject to the ruling principle, it will go to great lengths; for in an irrational being the desire for pleasure is insatiable even if it tries every source of gratification, and the exercise of appetite increases its innate force, and if appetites are strong and violent they even expel the power of calculation. Hence they should be moderate and few, and should in no way oppose the rational principle—and this is what we call an obedient and chastened state—and as the child should live according to the direction of his tutor, so the appetitive element should live according to rational principle. Hence the appetitive element in a temperate man should harmonize with the rational principle; for the noble is the mark at which both aim, and the temperate man craves for the things he ought, as he ought, and when he ought; and this is what rational principle directs.

Here we conclude our account of temperance.

[1] ἀκόλαστος, which we have translated 'self-indulgent', meant originally 'unchastened' and was applied to the ways of spoilt children.

1119b

BOOK IV

LET us speak next of liberality. It seems to be the mean with regard to wealth; for the liberal man is praised not in respect of military matters, nor of those in respect of which the temperate man is praised, nor of judicial decisions, but with regard to the giving and taking of wealth, and especially in respect of giving. Now by 'wealth' we mean all the things whose value is measured by money. Further, prodigality and meanness are excesses and defects with regard to wealth; and meanness we always impute to those who care more than they ought for wealth, but we sometimes apply the word 'prodigality' in a complex sense; for we call those men prodigals who are incontinent and spend money on self-indulgence. Hence also they are thought the poorest characters; for they combine more vices than one. Therefore the application of the word to them is not its proper use; for a 'prodigal' means a man who has a
1120a single evil quality, that of wasting his substance; since a prodigal is one who is being ruined by his own fault,[1] and the wasting of substance is thought to be a sort of ruining of oneself, life being held to depend on possession of substance.

This, then, is the sense in which we take the word 'prodigality'. Now the things that have a use may be used either well or badly; and riches is a useful thing; and everything is used best by the man who has the virtue concerned with it; riches, therefore, will be used best by the man who has the virtue concerned with wealth; and this is the liberal man. Now spending and giving seem to be the using of wealth; taking and keeping rather the possession of it. Hence it is more the mark of the liberal man to give to the right people than to take from the right sources and not to take from the wrong. For it is more characteristic

[1] ἄ-σωτος = one who is not saved, who is ruined.

of virtue to do good than to have good done to one, and more characteristic to do what is noble than not to do what is base; and it is not hard to see that giving implies doing good and doing what is noble, and taking implies having good done to one or not acting basely. And gratitude is felt towards him who gives, not towards him who does not take, and praise also is bestowed more on him. It is easier, also, not to take than to give; for men are apter to give away their own too little than to take what is another's. Givers, too, are called liberal; but those who do not take are not praised for liberality but rather for justice; while those who take are hardly praised at all. And the liberal are almost the most loved of all virtuous characters, since they are useful; and this depends on their giving.

Now virtuous actions are noble and done for the sake of the noble. Therefore the liberal man, like other virtuous men, will give for the sake of the noble, and rightly; for he will give to the right people, the right amounts, and at the right time, with all the other qualifications that accompany right giving; and that too with pleasure or without pain; for that which is virtuous is pleasant or free from pain—least of all will it be painful. But he who gives to the wrong people or not for the sake of the noble but for some other cause, will be called not liberal but by some other name. Nor is he liberal who gives with pain; for he would prefer the wealth to the noble act, and this is not characteristic of a liberal man. But no more will the liberal man take from wrong sources; for such taking is not characteristic of the man who sets no store by wealth. Nor will he be a ready asker; for it is not characteristic of a man who confers benefits to accept them lightly. But he will take from the right sources, e.g. from his own possessions, not as something [1120b] noble but as a necessity, that he may have something to give. Nor will he neglect his own property, since he wishes by means of this to help others. And he will refrain from giving to anybody and everybody, that he may have something to give to the right people, at the right time, and where it is noble to do so. It is highly characteristic of a liberal man also to go to excess in giving, so that he

leaves too little for himself; for it is the nature of a liberal man not to look to himself. The term 'liberality' is used relatively to a man's substance; for liberality resides not in the multitude of the gifts but in the state of character of the giver, and this is relative to the giver's substance.[1] There is therefore nothing to prevent the man who gives less from being the more liberal man, if he has less to give. Those are thought to be more liberal who have not made their wealth but inherited it; for in the first place they have no experience of want, and secondly all men are fonder of their own productions, as are parents and poets. It is not easy for the liberal man to be rich, since he is not apt either at taking or at keeping, but at giving away, and does not value wealth for its own sake but as a means to giving. Hence comes the charge that is brought against fortune, that those who deserve riches most get it least. But it is not unreasonable that it should turn out so; for he cannot have wealth, any more than anything else, if he does not take pains to have it. Yet he will not give to the wrong people nor at the wrong time, and so on; for he would no longer be acting in accordance with liberality, and if he spent on these objects he would have nothing to spend on the right objects. For, as has been said, he is liberal who spends according to his substance and on the right objects; and he who exceeds is prodigal. Hence we do not call despots prodigal; for it is thought not easy for them to give and spend beyond the amount of their possessions. Liberality, then, being a mean with regard to giving and taking of wealth, the liberal man will both give and spend the right amounts and on the right objects, alike in small things and in great, and that with pleasure; he will also take the right amounts and from the right sources. For, the virtue being a mean with regard to both, he will do both as he ought; since this sort of taking accompanies proper giving, and that which is not of this sort is contrary to it, and accordingly the giving and taking that accompany each other are present together in the same man, while the
1121a contrary kinds evidently are not. But if he happens to

[1] Omitting δίδωσιν, as Bywater suggests.

spend in a manner contrary to what is right and noble, he will be pained, but moderately and as he ought; for it is the mark of virtue both to be pleased and to be pained at the right objects and in the right way. Further, the liberal man is easy to deal with in money matters; for he can be got the better of, since he sets no store by money, and is more annoyed if he has not spent something that he ought than pained if he has spent something that he ought not, and does not agree with the saying of Simonides.[1]

The prodigal errs in these respects also; for he is neither pleased nor pained at the right things or in the right way; this will be more evident as we go on. We have said[2] that prodigality and meanness are excesses and deficiencies, and in two things, in giving and in taking; for we include spending under giving. Now prodigality exceeds in giving and not taking, and falls short in taking, while meanness falls short in giving, and exceeds in taking, except in small things.

The characteristics of prodigality are not often combined; for it is not easy to give to all if you take from none; private persons soon exhaust their substance with giving, and it is to these that the name of prodigals is applied—though a man of this sort would seem to be in no small degree better than a mean man. For he is easily cured both by age and by poverty, and thus he may move towards the middle state. For he has the characteristics of the liberal man, since he both gives and refrains from taking, though he does neither of these in the right manner or well. Therefore if he were brought to do so by habituation or in some other way, he would be liberal; for he will then give to the right people, and will not take from the wrong sources. This is why he is thought to have not a bad character; it is not the mark of a wicked or ignoble man to go to excess in giving and not taking, but only of a foolish one. The man who is prodigal in this way is thought much better than the mean man

[1] Reading Σιμωνίδου, as Bywater suggests. The reference may be to any one of three sayings of Simonides, which are recorded in *Rhet.* 1391^{a} 8; Athenaeus xiv. 656 C–E; Plutarch, *An seni resp. gerenda sit*, 1, p. 783 E.

[2] 1119^{b} 27.

both for the aforesaid reasons and because he benefits many while the other benefits no one, not even himself.

But most prodigal people, as has been said,[1] also take from the wrong sources, and are in this respect mean. They become apt to take because they wish to spend and cannot do this easily; for their possessions soon run short. Thus they are forced to provide means from some other source.
1121b At the same time, because they care nothing for honour, they take recklessly and from any source; for they have an appetite for giving, and they do not mind how or from what source. Hence also their giving is not liberal; for it is not noble, nor does it aim at nobility, nor is it done in the right way; sometimes they make rich those who should be poor, and will give nothing to people of respectable character, and much to flatterers or those who provide them with some other pleasure. Hence also most of them are self-indulgent; for they spend lightly and waste money on their indulgences, and incline towards pleasures because they do not live with a view to what is noble.

The prodigal man, then, turns into what we have described if he is left untutored, but if he is treated with care he will arrive at the intermediate and right state. But meanness is both incurable (for old age and every disability is thought to make men mean) and more innate in men than prodigality; for most men are fonder of getting money than of giving. It also extends widely, and is multiform, since there seem to be many kinds of meanness.

For it consists in two things, deficiency in giving and excess in taking, and is not found complete in all men but is sometimes divided; some men go to excess in taking, others fall short in giving. Those who are called by such names as 'miserly', 'close', 'stingy', all fall short in giving, but do not covet the possessions of others nor wish to get them. In some this is due to a sort of honesty and avoidance of what is disgraceful (for some seem, or at least profess, to hoard their money for this reason, that they may not some day be forced to do something disgraceful; to this class belong the cheeseparer and every one of the sort; he is so called from

[1] ll. 16–19.

his excess of unwillingness to give anything); while others again keep their hands off the property of others from fear, on the ground that it is not easy, if one takes the property of others oneself, to avoid having one's own taken by them; they are therefore content neither to take nor to give.

Others again exceed in respect of taking by taking anything and from any source, e.g. those who ply sordid trades, pimps and all such people, and those who lend small sums and at high rates. For all of these take more than they 1122a
ought and from wrong sources. What is common to them is evidently sordid love of gain; they all put up with a bad name for the sake of gain, and little gain at that. For those who make great gains but from wrong sources, and not the right gains, e.g. despots when they sack cities and spoil temples, we do not call mean but rather wicked, impious, and unjust. But the gamester and the footpad [and the highwayman][1] belong to the class of the mean, since they have a sordid love of gain. For it is for gain that both of them ply their craft and endure the disgrace of it, and the one faces the greatest dangers for the sake of the booty, while the other makes gain from his friends, to whom he ought to be giving. Both, then, since they are willing to make gain from wrong sources, are sordid lovers of gain; therefore all such forms of taking are mean.

And it is natural that meanness is described as the contrary of liberality; for not only is it a greater evil than prodigality, but men err more often in this direction than in the way of prodigality as we have described it.

So much, then, for liberality and the opposed vices.

2 It would seem proper to discuss magnificence next. For this[2] also seems to be a virtue concerned with wealth; but it does not like liberality extend to all the actions that are concerned with wealth, but only to those that involve expenditure; and in these it surpasses liberality in scale. For, as the name itself suggests, it is a fitting expenditure involving largeness of scale. But the scale is relative; for

[1] Omitting καὶ ὁ λῃστής, as Bywater suggests and as Aspasius seems to do.

[2] Reading αὕτη in l. 19, with Coraes.

the expense of equipping a trireme is not the same as that of heading a sacred embassy. It is what is fitting, then, in relation to the agent, and to the circumstances and the object. The man who in small or middling things spends according to the merits of the case is not called magnificent (e.g. the man who can say 'many a gift I gave the wanderer'),[1] but only the man who does so in great things. For the magnificent man is liberal, but the liberal man is not necessarily magnificent. The deficiency of this state of character is called niggardliness, the excess vulgarity, lack of taste, and the like, which do not go to excess in the amount spent on right objects, but by showy expenditure in the wrong circumstances and the wrong manner; we shall speak of these vices later.[2]

The magnificent man is like an artist; for he can see what is fitting and spend large sums tastefully. For, as we
1122b said at the beginning,[3] a state of character is determined by its activities and by its objects. Now the expenses of the magnificent man are large and fitting. Such, therefore, are also his results; for thus there will be a great expenditure and one that is fitting to its result. Therefore the result should be worthy of the expense, and the expense should be worthy of the result, or should even exceed it. And the magnificent man will spend such sums for honour's sake; for this is common to the virtues. And further he will do so gladly and lavishly; for nice calculation is a niggardly thing. And he will consider how the result can be made most beautiful and most becoming rather than for how much it can be produced and how it can be produced most cheaply. It is necessary, then, that the magnificent man be also liberal. For the liberal man also will spend what he ought and as he ought; and it is in these matters that the greatness implied in the name of the magnificent man—his bigness, as it were—is manifested, since liberality is concerned with these matters; and at an equal expense he will produce a more magnificent work of art. For a possession and a work of art have not the same excellence.

[1] *Od.* xvii. 420. [2] 1123a 19–33.
[3] Not in so many words, but cf. 1103b 21–23, 1104a 27–29.

The most valuable possession is that which is worth most, e.g. gold, but the most valuable work of art is that which is great and beautiful (for the contemplation of such a work inspires admiration, and so does magnificence); and a work has an excellence—viz. magnificence—which involves magnitude. Magnificence is an attribute of expenditures of the kind which we call honourable, e.g. those connected with the gods—votive offerings, buildings, and sacrifices—and similarly with any form of religious worship, and all those that are proper objects of public-spirited ambition, as when people think they ought to equip a chorus or a trireme, or entertain the city, in a brilliant way. But in all cases, as has been said,[1] we have regard to the agent as well and ask who he is and what means he has; for the expenditure should be worthy of his means, and suit not only the result but also the producer. Hence a poor man cannot be magnificent, since he has not the means with which to spend large sums fittingly; and he who tries is a fool, since he spends beyond what can be expected of him and what is proper, but it is *right* expenditure that is virtuous. But great expenditure is becoming to those who have suitable means to start with, acquired by their own efforts or from ancestors or connexions, and to people of high birth or reputation, and so on; for all these things bring with them greatness and prestige. Primarily, then, the magnificent man is of this sort, and magnificence is shown in expenditures of this sort, as has been said;[2] for these are the greatest and most honourable. Of *private* occasions of expenditure the most suitable are those that take place once for all, e.g. a wedding or anything of the kind, or anything that interests the whole city or the people 1123a
of position in it, and also the receiving of foreign guests and the sending of them on their way, and gifts and counter-gifts; for the magnificent man spends not on himself but on public objects, and gifts bear some resemblance to votive offerings. A magnificent man will also furnish his house suitably to his wealth (for even a house is a sort of public ornament), and will spend by preference on those works

[1] a 24–26. [2] ll. 19–23.

that are lasting (for these are the most beautiful), and on every class of things he will spend what is becoming; for the same things are not suitable for gods and for men, nor in a temple and in a tomb. And since each expenditure may be great of its kind, and what is most magnificent absolutely is great expenditure on a great object, but what is magnificent *here* is what is great in *these* circumstances, and greatness in the work differs from greatness in the expense (for the most beautiful ball or bottle is magnificent as a gift to a child, but the price of it is small and mean),—therefore it is characteristic of the magnificent man, whatever kind of result he is producing, to produce it magnificently (for such a result is not easily surpassed) and to make it worthy of the expenditure.

Such, then, is the magnificent man; the man who goes to excess and is vulgar exceeds, as has been said,[1] by spending beyond what is right. For on small objects of expenditure he spends much and displays a tasteless showiness; e. g. he gives a club dinner on the scale of a wedding banquet, and when he provides the chorus for a comedy he brings them on to the stage in purple, as they do at Megara. And all such things he will do not for honour's sake but to show off his wealth, and because he thinks he is admired for these things, and where he ought to spend much he spends little and where little, much. The niggardly man on the other hand will fall short in everything, and after spending the greatest sums will spoil the beauty of the result for a trifle, and whatever he is doing he will hesitate and consider how he may spend least, and lament even that, and think he is doing everything on a bigger scale than he ought.

These states of character, then, are vices; yet they do not bring *disgrace* because they are neither harmful to one's neighbour nor very unseemly.

Pride seems even from its name[2] to be concerned with 3
great things; what sort of great things, is the first question

[1] 1122[a] 31–33.
[2] 'Pride' of course has not the etymological associations of μεγαλοψυχία, but seems in other respects the best translation.

we must try to answer. It makes no difference whether we consider the state of character or the man characterized by it. Now the man is thought to be proud who thinks him- 1123a
self worthy of great things, being worthy of them; for he who does so beyond his deserts is a fool, but no virtuous man is foolish or silly. The proud man, then, is the man we have described. For he who is worthy of little and thinks himself worthy of little is temperate, but not proud; for pride implies greatness, as beauty implies a good-sized body, and little people may be neat and well-proportioned but cannot be beautiful. On the other hand, he who thinks himself worthy of great things, being unworthy of them, is vain; though not every one who thinks himself worthy of more than he really is worthy of is vain. The man who thinks himself worthy of less than he is really worthy of is unduly humble, whether his deserts be great or moderate, or his deserts be small but his claims yet smaller. And the man whose deserts are great would seem *most* unduly humble; for what would he have done if they had been less? The proud man, then, is an extreme in respect of the greatness of his claims, but a mean in respect of the rightness of them; for he claims what is in accordance with his merits, while the others go to excess or fall short.

If, then, he deserves and claims great things, and above all the greatest things, he will be concerned with one thing in particular. Desert is relative to external goods; and the greatest of these, we should say, is that which we render to the gods, and which people of position most aim at, and which is the prize appointed for the noblest deeds; and this is honour; that is surely the greatest of external goods. Honours and dishonours, therefore, are the objects with respect to which the proud man is as he should be. And even apart from argument it is with honour that proud men appear to be concerned; for it is honour that they chiefly claim, but in accordance with their deserts. The unduly humble man falls short both in comparison with his own merits and in comparison with the proud man's claims. The vain man goes to excess in comparison with his own merits, but does not exceed the proud man's claims.

Now the proud man, since he deserves most, must be good in the highest degree; for the better man always deserves more, and the best man most. Therefore the truly proud man must be good. And greatness in every virtue would seem to be characteristic of a proud man. And it would be most unbecoming for a proud man to fly from danger, swinging his arms by his sides, or to wrong another; for to what end should he do disgraceful acts, he to whom nothing is great? If we consider him point by point we shall see the utter absurdity of a proud man who is not good. Nor, again, would he be worthy of honour if he were bad; for honour is the prize of virtue, and it is to the good
1124a that it is rendered. Pride, then, seems to be a sort of crown of the virtues; for it makes them greater, and it is not found without them. Therefore it is hard to be truly proud; for it is impossible without nobility and goodness of character. It is chiefly with honours and dishonours, then, that the proud man is concerned; and at honours that are great and conferred by good men he will be moderately pleased, thinking that he is coming by his own or even less than his own; for there can be no honour that is worthy of perfect virtue, yet he will at any rate accept it since they have nothing greater to bestow on him; but honour from casual people and on trifling grounds he will utterly despise, since it is not this that he deserves, and dishonour too, since in his case it cannot be just. In the first place, then, as has been said,[1] the proud man is concerned with honours; yet he will also bear himself with moderation towards wealth and power and all good or evil fortune, whatever may befall him, and will be neither over-joyed by good fortune nor over-pained by evil. For not even towards honour does he bear himself as if it were a very great thing. Power and wealth are desirable for the sake of honour (at least those who have them wish to get honour by means of them); and for him to whom even honour is a little thing the others must be so too. Hence proud men are thought to be disdainful.

[1] 1123b 15–22.

The goods of fortune also are thought to contribute towards pride. For men who are well-born are thought worthy of honour, and so are those who enjoy power or wealth; for they are in a superior position, and everything that has a superiority in something good is held in greater honour. Hence even such things make men prouder; for they are honoured by some for having them; but in truth the good man alone is to be honoured; he, however, who has both advantages is thought the more worthy of honour. But those who without virtue have such goods are neither justified in making great claims nor entitled to the name of 'proud'; for these things imply perfect virtue. Disdainful and insolent, however, even those who have such goods become. For without virtue it is not easy to bear gracefully the goods of fortune; and, being unable to bear them, and thinking themselves superior to others, they 1124b
despise others and themselves do what they please. They imitate the proud man without being like him, and this they do where they can; so they do not act virtuously, but they do despise others. For the proud man despises justly (since he thinks truly), but the many do so at random.

He does not run into trifling dangers, nor is he fond of danger, because he honours few things; but he will face great dangers, and when he is in danger he is unsparing of his life, knowing that there are conditions on which life is not worth having. And he is the sort of man to confer benefits, but he is ashamed of receiving them; for the one is the mark of a superior, the other of an inferior. And he is apt to confer greater benefits in return; for thus the original benefactor besides being paid will incur a debt to him, and will be the gainer by the transaction. They seem also to remember any service they have done, but not those they have received (for he who receives a service is inferior to him who has done it, but the proud man wishes to be superior), and to hear of the former with pleasure, of the latter with displeasure; this, it seems, is why Thetis did not mention to Zeus the services she had done him,[1] and why the Spartans did not recount

[1] In fact she did, *Il.* i. 503.

their services to the Athenians, but those they had received.[1] It is a mark of the proud man also to ask for nothing or scarcely anything, but to give help readily, and to be dignified towards people who enjoy high position and good fortune, but unassuming towards those of the middle class; for it is a difficult and lofty thing to be superior to the former, but easy to be so to the latter, and a lofty bearing over the former is no mark of ill-breeding, but among humble people it is as vulgar as a display of strength against the weak. Again, it is characteristic of the proud man not to aim at the things commonly held in honour, or the things in which others excel; to be sluggish and to hold back except where great honour or a great work is at stake, and to be a man of few deeds, but of great and notable ones. He must also be open in his hate and in his love (for to conceal one's feelings, i.e. to care less for truth than for what people will think, is a coward's part), and must speak and act openly; for he is free of speech because he is contemptuous, and he is given to telling the truth, except when he speaks in irony to the vulgar. He must be unable to make his life revolve
1125[a] round another, unless it be a friend; for this is slavish, and for this reason all flatterers are servile and people lacking in self-respect are flatterers. Nor is he given to admiration; for nothing to him is great. Nor is he mindful of wrongs; for it is not the part of a proud man to have a long memory, especially for wrongs, but rather to overlook them. Nor is he a gossip; for he will speak neither about himself nor about another, since he cares not to be praised nor for others to be blamed; nor again is he given to praise; and for the same reason he is not an evil-speaker, even about his enemies, except from haughtiness. With regard to necessary or small matters he is least of all men given to lamentation or the asking of favours; for it is the part of one who takes such matters seriously to behave so with respect to them. He is one who will possess beautiful and profitless things rather than profitable and useful ones;

[1] The Aldine scholiast quotes Callisthenes as stating that the Spartans behaved in this way when they were asking for help from the Athenians on the occasion of an invasion by the Thebans. If the reference is to B.C. 369, it does not agree with Xen. *Hell.* vi. 5. 33 f.

for this is more proper to a character that suffices to itself.

Further, a slow step is thought proper to the proud man, a deep voice, and a level utterance; for the man who takes few things seriously is not likely to be hurried, nor the man who thinks nothing great to be excited, while a shrill voice and a rapid gait are the results of hurry and excitement.

Such, then, is the proud man; the man who falls short of him is unduly humble, and the man who goes beyond him is vain. Now even these are not thought to be bad (for they are not malicious), but only mistaken. For the unduly humble man, being worthy of good things, robs himself of what he deserves, and seems to have something bad about him from the fact that he does not think himself worthy of good things, and seems also not to know himself; else he would have desired the things he was worthy of, since these were good. Yet such people are not thought to be fools, but rather unduly retiring. Such a reputation, however, seems actually to make them worse; for each class of people aims at what corresponds to its worth, and these people stand back even from noble actions and undertakings, deeming themselves unworthy, and from external goods no less. Vain people, on the other hand, are fools and ignorant of themselves, and that manifestly; for, not being worthy of them, they attempt honourable undertakings, and then are found out; and they adorn themselves with clothing and outward show and such things, and wish their strokes of good fortune to be made public, and speak about them as if they would be honoured for them. But undue humility is more opposed to pride than vanity is; for it is both commoner and worse.

Pride, then, is concerned with honour on the grand scale, as has been said.[1]

4 There seems to be in the sphere of honour also, as was 1125^b
said in our first remarks on the subject,[2] a virtue which would appear to be related to pride as liberality is to magnificence. For neither of these has anything to do with the grand scale, but both dispose us as is right with

[1] 1107^b 26, 1123^a 34–^{b} 22. [2] Ib. 24–27.

regard to middling and unimportant objects; as in getting and giving of wealth there is a mean and an excess and defect, so too honour may be desired more than is right, or less, or from the right sources and in the right way. We blame both the ambitious man as aiming at honour more than is right and from wrong sources, and the unambitious man as not willing to be honoured even for noble reasons. But sometimes we praise the ambitious man as being manly and a lover of what is noble, and the unambitious man as being moderate and self-controlled, as we said in our first treatment of the subject.[1] Evidently, since 'fond of such and such an object' has more than one meaning, we do not assign the term 'ambition' or 'love of honour' always to the same thing, but when we praise the quality we think of the man who loves honour more than most people, and when we blame it we think of him who loves it more than is right. The mean being without a name, the extremes seem to dispute for its place as though that were vacant by default. But where there is excess and defect, there is also an intermediate; now men desire honour both more than they should and less; therefore it is possible also to do so as one should; at all events this is the state of character that is praised, being an unnamed mean in respect of honour. Relatively to ambition it seems to be unambitiousness, and relatively to unambitiousness it seems to be ambition, while relatively to both severally it seems in a sense to be both together. This appears to be true of the other virtues also. But in this case the extremes seem to be contradictories because the mean has not received a name.

Good temper is a mean with respect to anger; the middle 5
state being unnamed, and the extremes almost without a name as well, we place good temper in the middle position, though it inclines towards the deficiency, which is without a name. The excess might be called a sort of 'irascibility'. For the passion is anger, while its causes are many and diverse.

The man who is angry at the right things and with the right people, and, further, as he ought, when he ought, and as

[1] 1107^{b} 33.

long as he ought, is praised. This will be the good-tempered man, then, since good temper is praised. For the good-tempered man tends to be unperturbed and not to be led by passion, but to be angry in the manner, at the things, and for the length of time, that the rule dictates; but he is **1126[a]**
thought to err rather in the direction of deficiency; for the good-tempered man is not revengeful, but rather tends to make allowances.

The deficiency, whether it is a sort of 'inirascibility' or whatever it is, is blamed. For those who are not angry at the things they should be angry at are thought to be fools, and so are those who are not angry in the right way, at the right time, or with the right persons; for such a man is thought not to feel things nor to be pained by them, and, since he does not get angry, he is thought unlikely to defend himself; and to endure being insulted and put up with insult to one's friends is slavish.

The excess can be manifested in all the points that have been named (for one can be angry with the wrong persons, at the wrong things, more than is right, too quickly, or too long); yet *all* are not found in the same person. Indeed they could not; for evil destroys even itself, and if it is complete becomes unbearable. Now *hot-tempered* people get angry quickly and with the wrong persons and at the wrong things and more than is right, but their anger ceases quickly—which is the best point about them. This happens to them because they do not restrain their anger but retaliate openly owing to their quickness of temper, and then their anger ceases. By reason of excess *choleric* people are quick-tempered and ready to be angry with everything and on every occasion; whence their name. *Sulky* people are hard to appease, and retain their anger long; for they repress their passion. But it ceases when they retaliate; for revenge relieves them of their anger, producing in them pleasure instead of pain. If this does not happen they retain their burden; for owing to its not being obvious no one even reasons with them, and to digest one's anger in oneself takes time.[1] Such people are most troublesome to

[1] Reading in l. 25 δεῖται as Γ apparently does and Bywater suggests.

themselves and to their dearest friends. We call *bad-tempered* those who are angry at the wrong things, more than is right, and longer, and cannot be appeased until they inflict vengeance or punishment.

To good temper we oppose the excess rather than the defect; for not only is it commoner (since revenge is the more human), but bad-tempered people are worse to live with.

What we have said in our earlier treatment of the subject[1] is plain also from what we are now saying; viz. that it is not easy to define how, with whom, at what, and how long one should be angry, and at what point right action ceases and wrong begins. For the man who strays a little from the path, either towards the more or towards the less, is not blamed; since sometimes we praise those who exhibit the
1126b deficiency, and call them good-tempered, and sometimes we call angry people manly, as being capable of ruling. How far, therefore, and how a man must stray before he becomes blameworthy, it is not easy to state in words; for the decision depends on the particular facts and on perception. But so much at least is plain, that the middle state is praiseworthy—that in virtue of which we are angry with the right people, at the right things, in the right way, and so on, while the excesses and defects are blameworthy—slightly so if they are present in a low degree, more if in a higher degree, and very much if in a high degree. Evidently, then, we must cling to the middle state.—Enough of the states relative to anger.

In gatherings of men, in social life and the interchange 6
of words and deeds, some men are thought to be obsequious, viz. those who to give pleasure praise everything and never oppose, but think it their duty 'to give no pain to the people they meet'; while those who, on the contrary, oppose everything and care not a whit about giving pain are called churlish and contentious. That the states we have named are culpable is plain enough, and that the middle state is laudable—that in virtue of which a man will

[1] 1109b 14-26.

put up with, and will resent, the right things and in the right way; but no name has been assigned to it, though it most resembles friendship. For the man who corresponds to this middle state is very much what, with affection added, we call a good friend. But the state in question differs from friendship in that it implies no passion or affection for one's associates; since it is not by reason of loving or hating that such a man takes everything in the right way, but by being a man of a certain kind. For he will behave so alike towards those he knows and those he does not know, towards intimates and those who are not so, except that in each of these cases he will behave as is befitting; for it is not proper to have the same care for intimates and for strangers, nor again is it the same conditions that make it right to give pain to them. Now we have said generally that he will associate with people in the right way; but it is by reference to what is honourable and expedient that he will aim at not giving pain or at contributing pleasure. For he seems to be concerned with the pleasures and pains of social life; and wherever it is not honourable, or is harmful, for him to contribute pleasure, he will refuse, and will choose rather to give pain; also if his acquiescence in another's action would bring disgrace, and that in a high degree, or injury, *on that other*, while his opposition brings a little pain, he will not acquiesce but will decline. He will associate differently with people in high station and with ordinary people, with closer and more distant 1127a
acquaintances, and so too with regard to all other differences, rendering to each class what is befitting, and while for its own sake he chooses to contribute pleasure, and avoids the giving of pain, he will be guided by the consequences, if these are greater, i.e. honour and expediency. For the sake of a great future pleasure, too, he will inflict small pains.

The man who attains the mean, then, is such as we have described, but has not received a name; of those who contribute pleasure, the man who aims at being pleasant with no ulterior object is obsequious, but the man who does so in order that he may get some advantage in the direction of money or the things that money buys is a flatterer; while the man who quarrels with everything is, as has been said,[1] churlish and contentious. And the extremes seem to be contradictory to each other because the mean is without a name.

The mean opposed to boastfulness[2] is found in almost 7
the same sphere; and this[3] also is without a name. It will be no bad plan to describe these states as well; for we shall both know the facts about character better if we go through them in detail, and we shall be convinced that the virtues are means if we see this to be so in all cases. In the field of social life those who make the giving of pleasure or pain their object in associating with others have been described;[4] let us now describe those who pursue truth or falsehood alike in words and deeds and in the claims they put forward. The boastful man, then, is thought to be apt to claim the things that bring glory, when he has not got them, or to claim more of them than he has, and the mock-modest man on the other hand to disclaim what he has or belittle it, while the man who observes the mean is one who calls a thing by its own name, being truthful both in life and in word, owning to what he has, and neither more nor less. Now each of these courses may be adopted either with or without an object. But each man speaks and acts and lives in accordance with his character, if he is *not* acting for some ulterior object. And falsehood is *in itself*[5] mean and culpable, and truth noble and worthy of praise. Thus the truthful man is another case of a man who, being in the mean, is worthy of praise, and both forms of untruthful man are culpable, and particularly the boastful man.

Let us discuss them both, but first of all the truthful man. We are not speaking of the man who keeps faith in his agreements, i.e. in the things that pertain to justice or injustice (for this would belong to another virtue), but the
1127b man who in the matters in which nothing of this sort is at

[1] 1125b 14-16.

[2] Omitting in l. 13 καὶ εἰρωνείας, which as Burnet observes is not necessary according to Greek idiom.

[3] Reading αὕτη in l. 14, with L^b M^b.

[4] Ch. 6.

[5] I. e. apart from any ulterior object it may serve.

stake is true both in word and in life because his character is such. But such a man would seem to be as a matter of fact equitable. For the man who loves truth, and is truthful where nothing is at stake, will still more be truthful where something is at stake; he will avoid falsehood as something base, seeing that he avoided it even for its own sake; and such a man is worthy of praise. He inclines rather to understate the truth; for this seems in better taste because exaggerations are wearisome.

He who claims more than he has with no ulterior object is a contemptible sort of fellow (otherwise he would not have delighted in falsehood), but seems futile rather than bad; but if he does it for an object, he who does it for the sake of reputation or honour is (for a boaster [1]) not very much to be blamed, but he who does it for money, or the things that lead to money, is an uglier character (it is not the capacity that makes the boaster, but the purpose; for it is in virtue of his state of character and by being a man of a certain kind that he is a boaster); as one man is a liar because he enjoys the lie itself, and another because he desires reputation or gain. Now those who boast for the sake of reputation claim such qualities as win praise or congratulation, but those whose object is gain claim qualities which are of value to one's neighbours and one's lack of which is not easily detected, e.g. the powers of a seer, a sage, or a physician. For this reason it is such things as these that most people claim and boast about; for in them the above-mentioned qualities are found.

Mock-modest people, who understate things, seem more attractive in character; for they are thought to speak not for gain but to avoid parade; and here too it is qualities which bring reputation that they disclaim, as Socrates used to do. Those who disclaim trifling and obvious qualities are called humbugs and are more contemptible; and sometimes this seems to be boastfulness, like the Spartan dress; for both excess and great deficiency are boastful. But those who use understatement with moderation and understate about matters that do not very much force themselves

[1] Reading ὡς ἀλαζών in l. 12.

on our notice seem attractive. And it is the boaster that seems to be opposed to the truthful man; for he is the worse character.

Since life includes rest as well as activity, and in this is 8
included leisure and amusement, there seems here also to
1128a be a kind of intercourse which is tasteful; there is such a thing as saying—and again listening to—what one should and as one should. The kind of people one is speaking or listening to will also make a difference. Evidently here also there is both an excess and a deficiency as compared with the mean. Those who carry humour to excess are thought to be vulgar buffoons, striving after humour at all costs, and aiming rather at raising a laugh than at saying what is becoming and at avoiding pain to the object of their fun; while those who can neither make a joke themselves nor put up with those who do are thought to be boorish and unpolished. But those who joke in a tasteful way are called ready-witted, which implies a sort of readiness to turn this way and that; for such sallies are thought to be movements of the character, and as bodies are discriminated by their movements, so too are characters. The ridiculous side of things is not far to seek, however, and most people delight more than they should in amusement and in jesting, and so even buffoons are called ready-witted because they are found attractive; but that they differ from the ready-witted man, and to no small extent, is clear from what has been said.

To the middle state belongs also tact; it is the mark of a tactful man to say and listen to such things as befit a good and well-bred man; for there are some things that it befits such a man to say and to hear by way of jest, and the well-bred man's jesting differs from that of a vulgar man, and the joking of an educated man from that of an uneducated. One may see this even from the old and the new comedies; to the authors of the former indecency of language was amusing, to those of the latter innuendo is more so; and these differ in no small degree in respect of propriety. Now should we define the man who jokes well by his saying what is not unbecoming to a well-bred man, or by his not giving pain, or even giving delight, to the hearer? Or is the latter definition, at any rate, itself indefinite, since different things are hateful or pleasant to different people? The kind of jokes he will listen to will be the same; for the kind he can put up with are also the kind he seems to make. There are, then, jokes he will not make; for the jest is a sort of abuse, and there are things that lawgivers forbid us to abuse; and they should, perhaps, have forbidden us even to make a jest of such. The refined and well-bred man, therefore, will be as we have described, being as it were a law to himself.

Such, then, is the man who observes the mean, whether he be called tactful or ready-witted. The buffoon, on the other hand, is the slave of his sense of humour, and spares neither himself nor others if he can raise a laugh, and says things none of which a man of refinement would say, and to some of which he would not even listen. The boor, again, 1128b is useless for such social intercourse; for he contributes nothing and finds fault with everything. But relaxation and amusement are thought to be a necessary element in life.

The means in life that have been described, then, are three in number, and are all concerned with an interchange of words and deeds of some kind. They differ, however, in that one is concerned with truth, and the other two with pleasantness. Of those concerned with pleasure, one is displayed in jests, the other in the general social intercourse of life.

9 Shame should not be described as a virtue; for it is more like a feeling than a state of character. It is defined, at any rate, as a kind of fear of dishonour, and produces an effect similar to that[1] produced by fear of danger; for people who feel disgraced blush, and those who fear death turn pale. Both, therefore, seem to be in a sense bodily conditions, which is thought to be characteristic of feeling rather than of a state of character.

The feeling is not becoming to every age, but only

[1] Reading ἀποτελεῖ τι τῷ in l. 12.

to youth. For we think young people should be prone to the feeling of shame because they live by feeling and therefore commit many errors, but are restrained by shame; and we praise young people who are prone to this feeling, but an older person no one would praise for being prone to the sense of disgrace, since we think he should not do anything that need cause this sense. For the sense of disgrace is not even characteristic of a good man,[1] since it is consequent on bad actions (for such actions should not be done; and if some actions are disgraceful in very truth and others only according to common opinion, this makes no difference; for neither class of actions should be done, so that no disgrace should be felt); and it is a mark of a bad man even to be such as to do any disgraceful action. To be so constituted as to feel disgraced if one does such an action, and for this reason to think oneself good, is absurd; for it is for voluntary actions that shame is felt, and the good man will never voluntarily do bad actions. But shame may be said to be conditionally a good thing; *if* a good man does such actions, he will feel disgraced; but the virtues are not subject to such a qualification. And if shamelessness—not to be ashamed of doing base actions—is bad, that does not make it good to be ashamed of doing such actions. Continence too is not virtue, but a mixed sort of state; this will be shown later.[2] Now, however, let us discuss justice.

[1] *Sc.* still less is it itself a virtue.

[2] vii. 1–10.

BOOK V

1 WITH regard to justice and injustice we must consider 1129a (1) what kind of actions they are concerned with, (2) what sort of mean justice is, and (3) between what extremes the just act is intermediate. Our investigation shall follow the same course as the preceding discussions.

We see that all men mean by justice that kind of state of character which makes people disposed to do what is just and makes them act justly and wish for what is just; and similarly by injustice that state which makes them act unjustly and wish for what is unjust. Let us too, then, lay this down as a general basis. For the same is not true of the sciences and the faculties as of states of character. A faculty or a science which is one and the same is held to relate to contrary objects, but a state of character which is one of two contraries does *not* produce the contrary results; e. g. as a result of health we do not do what is the opposite of healthy, but only what is healthy; for we say a man walks healthily, when he walks as a healthy man would.

Now often one contrary state is recognized from its contrary, and often states are recognized from the subjects that exhibit them; for (A) if good condition is known, bad condition also becomes known, and (B) good condition is known from the things that are in good condition, and they from it. If good condition is firmness of flesh, it is necessary both that bad condition should be flabbiness of flesh and that the wholesome should be that which causes firmness in flesh. And it follows for the most part that if one contrary is ambiguous the other also will be ambiguous; e. g. if 'just' is so, that 'unjust' will be so too.

Now 'justice' and 'injustice' seem to be ambiguous, but because their different meanings approach near to one another the ambiguity escapes notice and is not obvious as it is, comparatively, when the meanings are far apart, e. g.

(for here the difference in outward form is great) as the ambiguity in the use of κλείς for the collar-bone of an animal and for that with which we lock a door. Let us take as a starting-point, then, the various meanings of 'an unjust man'. Both the lawless man and the grasping and unfair man are thought to be unjust, so that evidently both the law-abiding and the fair man will be just. The just, then, is the lawful and the fair, the unjust the unlawful and the unfair.

1129b Since the unjust man is grasping, he must be concerned with goods—not all goods, but those with which prosperity and adversity have to do, which taken absolutely are always good, but for a particular person are not always good. Now men pray for and pursue these things; but they should not, but should pray that the things that are good absolutely may also be good for them, and should choose the things that *are* good for them. The unjust man does not always choose the greater, but also the less—in the case of things bad absolutely; but because the lesser evil is itself thought to be in a sense good, and graspingness is directed at the good, therefore he is thought to be grasping. And he is unfair; for this contains and is common to both.

Since the lawless man was seen[1] to be unjust and the law-abiding man just, evidently all lawful acts are in a sense just acts; for the acts laid down by the legislative art are lawful, and each of these, we say, is just. Now the laws in their enactments on all subjects aim at the common advantage either of all or of the best or of those who hold power, or something of the sort; so that in one sense we call those acts just that tend to produce and preserve happiness and its components for the political society. And the law bids us do both the acts of a brave man (e.g. not to desert our post nor take to flight nor throw away our arms), and those of a temperate man (e.g. not to commit adultery nor to gratify one's lust), and those of a good-tempered man (e.g. not to strike another nor to speak evil), and similarly with regard to the other virtues and forms of wickedness, commanding some acts and forbidding others; and the

[1] a32–b1.

rightly-framed law does this rightly, and the hastily conceived one less well.

This form of justice, then, is complete virtue, but not absolutely, but in relation to our neighbour. And therefore justice is often thought to be the greatest of virtues, and 'neither evening nor morning star'[1] is so wonderful; and proverbially 'in justice is every virtue comprehended'.[2] And it is complete virtue in its fullest sense, because it is the actual exercise of complete virtue. It is complete because he who possesses it can exercise his virtue not only in himself but towards his neighbour also; for many men can exercise virtue in their own affairs, but not in their relations to their neighbour. This is why the saying of 1130[a]
Bias is thought to be true, that 'rule will show the man'; for a ruler is necessarily in relation to other men and a member of a society. For this same reason justice, alone of the virtues, is thought to be 'another's good',[3] because it is related to our neighbour; for it does what is advantageous to another, either a ruler or a copartner. Now the worst man is he who exercises his wickedness both towards himself and towards his friends, and the best man is not he who exercises his virtue towards himself but he who exercises it towards another; for this is a difficult task. Justice in this sense, then, is not part of virtue but virtue entire, nor is the contrary injustice a part of vice but vice entire. What the difference is between virtue and justice in this sense is plain from what we have said; they are the same but their essence is not the same; what, as a relation to one's neighbour, is justice is, as a certain kind of state without qualification, virtue.

2 But at all events what we are investigating is the justice which is a *part* of virtue; for there is a justice of this kind, as we maintain. Similarly it is with injustice in the particular sense that we are concerned.

That there is such a thing is indicated by the fact that

[1] Eur., fr. from *Melanippe* (Nauck[2], fr. 486). [2] Theog. 147.
[3] Pl. *Rep.* 343 c.

while the man who exhibits in action the other forms of wickedness acts wrongly indeed, but not graspingly (e.g. the man who throws away his shield through cowardice or speaks harshly through bad temper or fails to help a friend with money through meanness), when a man acts graspingly he often exhibits none of these vices,—no, nor all together, but certainly wickedness of some kind (for we blame him) and injustice. There is, then, another kind of injustice which is a part of injustice in the wide sense, and a use of the word 'unjust' which answers to a part of what is unjust in the wide sense of 'contrary to the law'. Again, if one man commits adultery for the sake of gain and makes money by it, while another does so at the bidding of appetite though he loses money and is penalized for it, the latter would be held to be self-indulgent rather than grasping, but the former is unjust, but not self-indulgent; evidently, therefore, he is unjust by reason of his making gain by his act. Again, all other unjust acts are ascribed invariably to some particular kind of wickedness, e.g. adultery to self-indulgence, the desertion of a comrade in battle to cowardice, physical violence to anger; but if a man makes gain, his action is ascribed to no form of wickedness but injustice. Evidently, therefore, there is apart from injustice in the wide sense another, 'particular', injustice which shares the name and nature of the first, because its
1130b definition falls within the same genus; for the significance of both consists in a relation to one's neighbour, but the one is concerned with honour or money or safety—or that which includes all these, if we had a single name for it—and its motive is the pleasure that arises from gain; while the other is concerned with all the objects with which the good man is concerned.

It is clear, then, that there is more than one kind of justice, and that there is one which is distinct from virtue entire; we must try to grasp its genus and differentia.

The unjust has been divided into the unlawful and the unfair, and the just into the lawful and the fair. To the unlawful answers the afore-mentioned sense of injustice. But since the unfair and the unlawful are not the same, but are different as a part is from its whole (for all that is unfair is unlawful, but not all that is unlawful is unfair), the unjust and injustice in the sense of the unfair are not the same as but different from the former kind, as part from whole; for injustice in this sense is a part of injustice in the wide sense, and similarly justice in the one sense of justice in the other. Therefore we must speak also about particular justice and particular injustice, and similarly about the just and the unjust. The justice, then, which answers to the whole of virtue, and the corresponding injustice, one being the exercise of virtue as a whole, and the other that of vice as a whole, towards one's neighbour, we may leave on one side. And how the meanings of 'just' and 'unjust' which answer to these are to be distinguished is evident; for practically the majority of the acts commanded by the law are those which are prescribed from the point of view of virtue taken as a whole; for the law bids us practise every virtue and forbids us to practise any vice. And the things that tend to produce virtue taken as a whole are those of the acts prescribed by the law which have been prescribed with a view to education for the common good. But with regard to the education of the individual as such, which makes him without qualification a good *man*, we must determine later[1] whether this is the function of the political art or of another; for perhaps it is not the same to be a good man and a good citizen of any state taken at random.

Of particular justice and that which is just in the corresponding sense, (A) one kind is that which is manifested in distributions of honour or money or the other things that fall to be divided among those who have a share in the constitution (for in these it is possible for one man to have a share either unequal or equal to that of another), and (B) one is that which plays a rectifying part in transactions between man and man. Of this there are two divisions; of 1131^{a}
transactions (1) some are voluntary and (2) others involuntary —voluntary such transactions as sale, purchase, loan for consumption, pledging, loan for use, depositing, letting (they

[1] 1179^{b} 20–1181^{b} 12. *Pol.* 1276^{b} 16–1277^{b} 32, 1278^{a} 40–^{b}5, 1288^{a} 32–^{b}2, 1333^{a} 11–16, 1337^{a} 11–14.

are called voluntary because the origin of these transactions is voluntary), while of the involuntary (*a*) some are clandestine, such as theft, adultery, poisoning, procuring, enticement of slaves, assassination, false witness, and (*b*) others are violent, such as assault, imprisonment, murder, robbery with violence, mutilation, abuse, insult.

(A) We have shown that both the unjust man and the 3
unjust act are unfair or unequal; now it is clear that there is also an intermediate between the two unequals involved in either case. And this is the equal; for in any kind of action in which there is a more and a less there is also what is equal. If, then, the unjust is unequal, the just is equal, as all men suppose it to be, even apart from argument. And since the equal is intermediate, the just will be an intermediate. Now equality implies at least two things. The just, then, must be both intermediate and equal and relative (i. e for certain persons). And *qua* intermediate it must be between certain things (which are respectively greater and less); *qua* equal, it involves *two* things; *qua* just, it is for certain people. The just, therefore, involves at least four terms; for the persons for whom it is in fact just are two, and the things in which it is manifested, the objects distributed, are two. And the same equality will exist between the persons and between the things concerned; for as the latter—the things concerned—are related, so are the former; if they are not equal, they will not have what is equal, but this is the origin of quarrels and complaints—when either equals have and are awarded unequal shares, or unequals equal shares. Further, this is plain from the fact that awards should be 'according to merit'; for all men agree that what is just in distribution must be according to merit in some sense, though they do not all specify the same sort of merit, but democrats identify it with the status of freeman, supporters of oligarchy with wealth (or with noble birth), and supporters of aristocracy with excellence.

The just, then, is a species of the proportionate (proportion being not a property only of the kind of number which consists of abstract units, but of number in general). For pro-

portion is equality of ratios, and involves four terms at least (that discrete proportion involves four terms is plain, but so does continuous proportion, for it uses one term as two and mentions it twice; e. g. 'as the line A is to the line B, so is 1131b
the line B to the line C'; the line B, then, has been mentioned twice, so that if the line B be assumed twice, the proportional terms will be four); and the just, too, involves at least four terms, and the ratio between one pair is the same as that between the other pair; for there is a similar distinction between the persons and between the things. As the term A, then, is to B, so will C be to D, and therefore, *alternando*, as A is to C, B will be to D. Therefore also the whole is in the same ratio to the whole;[1] and this coupling the distribution effects, and, if the terms are so combined, effects justly. The conjunction, then, of the term A with C and of B with D is what is just in distribution,[2] and this species of the just is intermediate, and the unjust is what violates the proportion; for the proportional is intermediate, and the just is proportional. (Mathematicians call this kind of proportion geometrical; for it is in geometrical proportion that it follows that the whole is to the whole as either part is to the corresponding part.) This proportion is not continuous; for we cannot get a single term standing for a person and a thing.

This, then, is what the just is—the proportional; the unjust is what violates the proportion. Hence one term becomes too great, the other too small, as indeed happens in practice; for the man who acts unjustly has too much, and the man who is unjustly treated too little, of what is good. In the case of evil the reverse is true; for the lesser evil is reckoned a good in comparison with the greater evil, since the lesser evil is rather to be chosen than the greater,

[1] Person A + thing C to person B + thing D.

[2] The problem of distributive justice is to divide the distributable honour or reward into parts which are to one another as are the merits of the persons who are to participate. If
A (first person) : B (second person) :: C (first portion) : D (second portion),
then (*alternando*) A : C :: B : D,
and therefore (*componendo*) A + C : B + D :: A : B.
In other words the position established answers to the relative merits of the parties.

and what is worthy of choice is good, and what is worthier of choice a greater good.

This, then, is one species of the just.

(B) The remaining one is the rectificatory, which arises in 4
connexion with transactions both voluntary and involuntary. This form of the just has a different specific character from the former. For the justice which distributes common possessions is always in accordance with the kind of proportion mentioned above[1] (for in the case also in which the distribution is made from the common funds of a partnership it will be according to the same ratio which the funds put into the business by the partners bear to one another); and the injustice opposed to this kind of justice is that which violates the proportion. But the justice in transactions between man and man is a sort of equality indeed,
1132a and the injustice a sort of inequality; not according to that kind of proportion, however, but according to arithmetical proportion.[2] For it makes no difference whether a good man has defrauded a bad man or a bad man a good one, nor whether it is a good or a bad man that has committed adultery; the law looks only to the distinctive character of the injury, and treats the parties as equal, if one is in the wrong and the other is being wronged, and if one inflicted injury and the other has received it. Therefore, this kind of injustice being an inequality, the judge tries to equalize it; for in the case also in which one has received and the other has inflicted a wound, or one has slain and the other been slain, the suffering and the action have been unequally distributed; but the judge tries to equalize things by means

[1] l. 12 f.

[2] The problem of 'rectificatory justice' has nothing to do with punishment proper but is only that of rectifying a wrong that has been done, by awarding damages; i.e. rectificatory justice is that of the civil, not that of the criminal courts. The parties are treated by the court as equal (since a law court is not a court of morals), and the wrongful act is reckoned as having brought equal gain to the wrongdoer and loss to his victim; it brings A to the position $A+C$, and B to the position $B-C$. The judge's task is to find the arithmetical mean between these, and this he does by transferring C from A to B. Thus (A being treated as = B) we get the arithmetical 'proportion'

$$(A+C)-(A+C-C) = (A+C-C)-(B-C)$$

or

$$(A+C)-(B-C+C) = (B-C+C)-(B-C).$$

of the penalty, taking away from the gain of the assailant. For the term 'gain' is applied generally to such cases, even if it be not a term appropriate to certain cases, e.g. to the person who inflicts a wound—and 'loss' to the sufferer; at all events when the suffering has been estimated, the one is called loss and the other gain. Therefore the equal is intermediate between the greater and the less, but the gain and the loss are respectively greater and less in contrary ways; more of the good and less of the evil are gain, and the contrary is loss; intermediate between them is, as we saw,[1] the equal, which we say is just; therefore corrective justice will be the intermediate between loss and gain. This is why, when people dispute, they take refuge in the judge; and to go to the judge is to go to justice; for the nature of the judge is to be a sort of animate justice; and they seek the judge as an intermediate, and in some states they call judges mediators, on the assumption that if they get what is intermediate they will get what is just. The just, then, is an intermediate, since the judge is so. Now the judge restores equality; it is as though there were a line divided into unequal parts, and he took away that by which the greater segment exceeds the half, and added it to the smaller segment. And when the whole has been equally divided, then they say they have 'their own'—i.e. when they have got what is equal. The equal is intermediate between the greater and the lesser line according to arithmetical proportion. It is for this reason also that it is called just (δίκαιον), because it is a division into two equal parts (δίχα), just as if one were to call it δίχαιον; and the judge (δικαστής) is one who bisects (διχαστής). For when something is subtracted from one of two equals and added to the other, the other is in excess by these two; since if what was taken from the one had not been added to the other, the latter would have been in excess by one only. It therefore exceeds the intermediate by one, and 1132b
the intermediate exceeds by one that from which something was taken. By this, then, we shall recognize both what we must subtract from that which has more, and what we must

[1] l. 14.

add to that which has less; we must add to the latter that by which the intermediate exceeds it, and subtract from the greatest that by which it exceeds the intermediate. Let the lines AA′, BB′, CC′ be equal to one another; from the line AA′ let the segment AE have been subtracted, and to the line CC′ let the segment CD[1] have been added, so that the whole line DCC′ exceeds the line EA′ by the segment CD and the segment CF; therefore it exceeds the line BB′ by the segment CD.

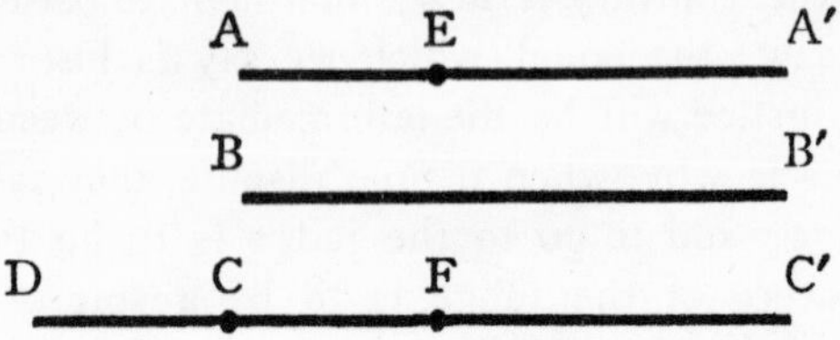

A E A′

B B′

D C F C′

These names, both loss and gain, have come from voluntary exchange; for to have more than one's own is called gaining, and to have less than one's original share is called losing, e.g. in buying and selling and in all other matters in which the law has left people free to make their own terms; but when they get neither more nor less but just what belongs to themselves, they say that they have their own and that they neither lose nor gain.

Therefore the just is intermediate between a sort of gain and a sort of loss, viz. those which are involuntary;[2] it consists in having an equal amount before and after the transaction.

Some think that *reciprocity* is without qualification just, 5
as the Pythagoreans said; for they defined justice without qualification as reciprocity.[3] Now 'reciprocity' fits neither distributive nor rectificatory justice—yet people *want* even the justice of Rhadamanthus to mean this:

> Should a man suffer what he did, right justice would be done[4]

—for in many cases reciprocity and rectificatory justice are not in accord; e.g. (1) if an official has inflicted a wound, he should not be wounded in return, and if some one has

[1] *Sc.* equal to AE.
[2] I.e. for the loser.
[3] Cf. Diels *Vors.* 45 B 4.
[4] Hes. fr. 174 Rzach.

wounded an official, he ought not to be wounded only but punished in addition. Further (2) there is a great difference between a voluntary and an involuntary act. But in associations for exchange this sort of justice does hold men together—reciprocity in accordance with a proportion and not on the basis of precisely equal return. For it is by proportionate requital that the city holds together. Men seek to return either evil for evil—and if they cannot do so, think their position mere slavery—or good for good— **1133a** and if they cannot do so there is no exchange, but it is by exchange that they hold together. This is why they give a prominent place to the temple of the Graces—to promote the requital of services; for this is characteristic of grace—we should serve in return one who has shown grace to us, and should another time take the initiative in showing it.

Now proportionate return is secured by cross-conjunction.[1] Let A be a builder, B a shoemaker, C a house, D a shoe. The builder, then, must get from the shoemaker the latter's work, and must himself give him in return his own. If, then, first there is proportionate equality of goods, and then reciprocal action takes place, the result we mention will be effected. If not, the bargain is not equal, and does not hold; for there is nothing to prevent the work of the one being better than that of the other; they must therefore be equated. (And this is true of the other arts also; for they would have been destroyed if what the patient suffered had not been just what the agent did, and of the same amount and kind.[2]) For it is not two doctors that associate for exchange, but a doctor and a farmer, or in

[1] The working of 'proportionate reciprocity' is not very clearly described by Aristotle, but seems to be as follows. A and B are workers in different trades, and will normally be of different degrees of 'worth'. Their products, therefore, will also have unequal worth, i.e. (though Aristotle does not expressly reduce the question to one of time) if $A = nB$, C (what A makes, say, in an hour) will be worth n times as much as D (what B makes in an hour). A fair exchange will then take place if A gets nD and B gets 1 C; i.e. if A gives what it takes him an hour to make, in exchange for what it takes B n hours to make.

[2] This sentence conveys a natural enough thought, and echoes closely the language of Pl. *Gorg.* 474 B–D. But it seems to have no relevance to the context, and probably here as in 1132b 9–11 we have the unsuccessful attempt of an early editor to find a suitable place for an isolated note of Aristotle's.

general people who are different and unequal; but these must be equated. This is why all things that are exchanged must be somehow comparable. It is for this end that money has been introduced, and it becomes in a sense an intermediate; for it measures all things, and therefore the excess and the defect—how many shoes are equal to a house or to a given amount of food. The number of shoes exchanged for a house [or for a given amount of food][1] must therefore correspond to the ratio of builder to shoemaker. For if this be not so, there will be no exchange and no intercourse. And this proportion will not be effected unless the goods are somehow equal. All goods must therefore be measured by some one thing, as we said before.[2] Now this unit is in truth demand, which holds all things together (for if men did not need one another's goods at all, or did not need them equally, there would be either no exchange or not the same exchange); but money has become by convention a sort of representative of demand; and this is why it has the name 'money' (*νόμισμα*)—because it exists not by nature but by law (*νόμος*) and it is in our power to change it and make it useless. There will, then, be reciprocity when the terms have been equated so that as farmer is to shoemaker, the amount of the shoemaker's work is to that of the farmer's work for which it exchanges.
1133b But we must not bring them into a figure of proportion when they have already exchanged (otherwise one extreme will have both excesses), but when they still have their own goods.[3] Thus they are equals and associates just because

[1] ἢ τροφήν will not do here, and must surely be the work of a copyist who has been misled by the occurrence of the farmer and his product, food, as additional examples in the context (a 17, 22, 32, b 4). So Ramsauer.

[2] l. 19.

[3] Aristotle's meaning, which has caused much difficulty, seems to be explained by a reference to ix. 1. That chapter concludes with the observation δεῖ δ' ἴσως οὐ τοσούτου τιμᾶν ὅσου ἔχοντι φαίνεται ἄξιον, ἀλλ' ὅσου πρὶν ἔχειν ἐτίμα. The reasoning in that chapter shows that Aristotle's meaning here must be that people must not exchange goods in random amounts and *then* bring themselves into a 'figure of proportion'. For each will then set an unduly high value on the goods he has parted with and an unduly low value on those he has received; and any adjustment that is made will be decided by their respective powers of bluff. One party will have 'both excesses' over the other, since what he gets will exceed the mean and what the other man gets

this equality can be effected in their case. Let A be a farmer, C food, B a shoemaker, D his product equated to C. If it had not been possible for reciprocity to be thus effected, there would have been no association of the parties. That demand holds things together as a single unit is shown by the fact that when men do not need one another, i. e. when neither needs the other or one does not need the other, they do not exchange, as we do when some one wants what one has oneself, e. g. when people permit the exportation of corn in exchange for wine.[1] This equation therefore must be established. And for the future exchange—that if we do not need a thing now we shall have it if ever we do need it—money is as it were our surety; for it must be possible for us to get what we want by bringing the money. Now the same thing happens to money itself as to goods—it is not always worth the same; yet it tends to be steadier. This is why all goods must have a price set on them; for then there will always be exchange, and if so, association of man with man. Money, then, acting as a measure, makes goods commensurate and equates them; for neither would there have been association if there were not exchange, nor exchange if there were not equality, nor equality if there were not commensurability. Now in truth it is impossible that things differing so much should become commensurate, but with reference to demand they may become so sufficiently. There must, then, be a unit, and that fixed by agreement (for which reason it is called money[2]); for it is this that makes all things commensurate, since all things are measured by money. Let A be a house, B ten minae, C a bed. A is half of B, if the house is worth five minae or equal to them; the bed, C, is a tenth of B; it is plain, then, how many beds are equal to a house, viz. five. That exchange took place thus before there was money is plain; for it makes no difference whether it is five beds that exchange for a house, or the money value of five beds.

will fall short of it (cf. 1132^{a} 32–^{b} 2). The only fair method is for each to set a value on his own and on the other's goods *before* they exchange, and come to an agreement if they can.

[1] Omitting the comma after *οἴνου* in l. 9.

[2] Cf. ^{a} 30.

We have now defined the unjust and the just. These having been marked off from each other, it is plain that just action is intermediate between acting unjustly and being unjustly treated; for the one is to have too much and the other to have too little. Justice is a kind of mean, but not in the same way as the other virtues, but because it relates to an intermediate amount, while injustice relates to the extremes.
1134a And justice is that in virtue of which the just man is said to be a doer, by choice, of that which is just, and one who will distribute either between himself and another or between two others not so as to give more of what is desirable to himself and less to his neighbour (and conversely with what is harmful), but so as to give what is equal in accordance with proportion; and similarly in distributing between two other persons. Injustice on the other hand is similarly related to the unjust, which is excess and defect, contrary to proportion, of the useful or hurtful. For which reason injustice is excess and defect, viz. because it is productive of excess and defect—in one's own case excess of what is in its own nature useful and defect of what is hurtful, while in the case of others it is as a whole like what it is in one's own case, but proportion may be violated in either direction. In the unjust act to have too little is to be unjustly treated; to have too much is to act unjustly.

Let this be taken as our account of the nature of justice and injustice, and similarly of the just and the unjust in general.

Since acting unjustly does not necessarily imply being 6
unjust, we must ask what sort of unjust acts imply that the doer is unjust with respect to each type of injustice, e.g. a thief, an adulterer, or a brigand. Surely the answer does not turn on the difference between these types. For a man might even lie with a woman knowing who she was, but the origin of his act might be not deliberate choice but passion. He acts unjustly, then, but is not unjust; e.g. a man is not a thief, yet he stole, nor an adulterer, yet he committed adultery; and similarly in all other cases.[1]

[1] This paragraph has no connexion with what follows; the subject of it is continued in ch. 8.

Now we have previously stated how the reciprocal is related to the just;[1] but we must not forget that what we are looking for is not only what is just without qualification but also political justice. This is found among men who share their life with a view to self-sufficiency, men who are free and either proportionately or arithmetically equal, so that between those who do not fulfil this condition there is no political justice but justice in a special sense and by analogy. For justice exists only between men whose mutual relations are governed by law; and law exists for men between whom there is injustice; for legal justice is the discrimination of the just and the unjust. And between men between whom there is injustice there is also unjust action (though there is not injustice between all between whom there is unjust action), and this is assigning too much to oneself of things good in themselves and too little of things evil in themselves. This is why we do not allow a *man* to rule, but *rational principle*, because a man behaves thus in his own interests and becomes a tyrant. The magistrate on the other hand is the guardian 1134b
of justice, and, if of justice, then of equality also. And since he is assumed to have no more than his share, if he is just (for he does not assign to himself more of what is good in itself, unless such a share is proportional to his merits—so that it is for others that he labours, and it is for this reason that men, as we stated previously,[2] say that justice is 'another's good'), therefore a reward must be given him, and this is honour and privilege; but those for whom such things are not enough become tyrants.

The justice of a master and that of a father are not the same as the justice of citizens, though they are like it; for there can be no injustice in the unqualified sense towards things that are one's own, but a man's chattel,[3] and his child until it reaches a certain age and sets up for itself, are as it were part of himself, and no one chooses to hurt himself (for which reason there can be no injustice towards oneself). Therefore the justice or injustice of citizens is not manifested in these relations; for it was as we saw[4] according to law, and

[1] 1132b 21–1133b 28.

[2] 1130a 3.

[3] I.e. his slave.

[4] a 30.

between people naturally subject to law, and these as we saw[1] are people who have an equal share in ruling and being ruled. Hence justice can more truly be manifested towards a wife than towards children and chattels, for the former is household justice; but even this is different from political justice.

Of political justice part is natural, part legal,—natural, 7
that which everywhere has the same force and does not exist by people's thinking this or that; legal, that which is originally indifferent, but when it has been laid down is not indifferent, e.g. that a prisoner's ransom shall be a mina, or that a goat and not two sheep shall be sacrificed, and again all the laws that are passed for particular cases, e.g. that sacrifice shall be made in honour of Brasidas,[2] and the provisions of decrees. Now some think that all justice is of this sort, because that which is by nature is unchangeable and has everywhere the same force (as fire burns both here and in Persia), while they see change in the things recognized as just. This, however, is not true in this unqualified way, but is true in a sense; or rather, with the gods it is perhaps not true at all, while with us there is something that is just even by nature, yet all of it is changeable; but still some is by nature, some not by nature. It is evident which sort of thing, among things capable of being otherwise, is by nature, and which is not but is legal and conventional, assuming that both are equally changeable. And in all other things the same distinction will apply; by nature the right hand is stronger, yet it is possible that all men should come to be ambidextrous. The things which are just by virtue of convention and
1135a expediency are like measures; for wine and corn measures are not everywhere equal, but larger in wholesale and smaller in retail markets. Similarly, the things which are just not by nature but by human enactment are not everywhere the same, since constitutions also are not the same, though there is but one which is everywhere by nature the best.

[1] a 26–8.

[2] Thuc. v. 11.

Of things just and lawful each is related as the universal to its particulars; for the things that are done are many, but of *them* each is one, since it is universal.

There is a difference between the act of injustice and what is unjust, and between the act of justice and what is just; for a thing is unjust by nature or by enactment; and this very thing, when it has been done, is an act of injustice, but before it is done is not yet that but is unjust. So, too, with an act of justice (though the general term is rather 'just action', and 'act of justice' is applied to the correction of the act of injustice).

Each of these must later[1] be examined separately with regard to the nature and number of its species and the nature of the things with which it is concerned.

8 Acts just and unjust being as we have described them, a man acts unjustly or justly whenever he does such acts voluntarily; when involuntarily, he acts neither unjustly nor justly except in an incidental way; for he does things which happen to be just or unjust. Whether an act is or is not one of injustice (or of justice) is determined by its voluntariness or involuntariness; for when it is voluntary it is blamed, and at the same time is then an act of injustice; so that there will be things that are unjust but not yet acts of injustice, if voluntariness be not present as well. By the voluntary I mean, as has been said before,[2] any of the things in a man's own power which he does with knowledge, i.e. not in ignorance either of the person acted on or of the instrument used or of the end that will be attained (e.g. whom he is striking, with what, and to what end), each such act being done not incidentally nor under compulsion (e.g. if A takes B's hand and therewith strikes C, B does not act voluntarily; for the act was not in his own power). The person struck may be the striker's father, and the striker may know that it is a man or one of the persons present, but not know that it is his father; a similar distinction may be made in the case of the end, and with

[1] Possibly a reference to an intended (or now lost) book of the *Politics* on laws.

[2] 1109^{b}35–1111^{a}24.

regard to the whole action. Therefore that which is done in ignorance, or though not done in ignorance is not in the agent's power, or is done under compulsion, is involuntary (for many natural processes, even, we knowingly both per-
1135b form and experience, none of which is either voluntary or involuntary; e.g. growing old or dying). But in the case of unjust and just acts alike the injustice or justice may be only incidental; for a man might return a deposit unwillingly and from fear, and then he must not be said either to do what is just or to act justly, except in an incidental way. Similarly the man who under compulsion and unwillingly fails to return the deposit must be said to act unjustly, and to do what is unjust, only incidentally. Of voluntary acts we do some by choice, others not by choice; by choice those which we do after deliberation, not by choice those which we do without previous deliberation. Thus there are three kinds of injury in transactions between man and man; those done in ignorance are *mistakes* when the person acted on, the act, the instrument, or the end that will be attained is other than the agent supposed; the agent thought either that he was not hitting any one or that he was not hitting with this missile or not hitting this person or to this end, but a result followed other than that which he thought likely (e.g. he threw not with intent to wound but only to prick), or the person hit or the missile was other than he supposed. Now when (1) the injury takes place contrary to reasonable expectation, it is a *misadventure*. When (2) it is not contrary to reasonable expectation, but does not imply vice, it is a *mistake* (for a man makes a mistake when the fault originates in him, but is the victim of accident when the origin lies outside him). When (3) he acts with knowledge but not after deliberation, it is an *act of injustice*—e.g. the acts due to anger or to other passions necessary or natural to man; for when men do such harmful and mistaken acts they act unjustly, and the acts are acts of injustice, but this does not imply that the doers are unjust or wicked; for the injury is not due to vice. But when (4) a man acts from choice, he is an *unjust man* and a vicious man.

Hence acts proceeding from anger are rightly judged not to be done of malice aforethought; for it is not the man who acts in anger but he who enraged him that starts the mischief. Again, the matter in dispute is not whether the thing happened or not, but its justice; for it is apparent injustice that occasions rage. For they do not dispute about the occurrence of the act—as in commercial transactions where one of the two parties *must* be vicious [1]—unless they do so owing to forgetfulness; but, agreeing about the fact, they dispute on which side justice lies (whereas a man who has deliberately injured another cannot help knowing that he has done so), so that the one thinks he is being treated unjustly and the other disagrees.[2]

But if a man harms another by choice, he acts unjustly; 1136[a]
and *these* are the acts of injustice which imply that the doer is an unjust man, provided that the act violates proportion or equality. Similarly, a man *is just* when he acts justly by choice; but he *acts justly* if he merely acts voluntarily.

Of involuntary acts some are excusable, others not. For the mistakes which men make not only in ignorance but also from ignorance are excusable, while those which men do not from ignorance but (though they do them *in* ignorance) owing to a passion which is neither natural nor such as man is liable to, are not excusable.

9 Assuming that we have sufficiently defined the suffering and doing of injustice, it may be asked (1) whether the truth in expressed in Euripides' paradoxical words:

'I slew my mother, that's my tale in brief.'
'Were you both willing, or unwilling both?' [3]

[1] The plaintiff, if he brings a false accusation; the defendant, if he denies a true one.

[2] With Bywater's punctuation *ὁ μέν* means the person who acted in anger, *ὁ δ'* the person who angered him. I should prefer to treat *ὁ δ' ἐπιβουλεύσας οὐκ ἀγνοεῖ* as not parenthetical, in which case *ὁ δ' οὔ* will mean 'while a deliberate aggressor does not think he is being treated unjustly'. In any case, *ὁ ἐπιβουλεύσας* is apparently not one of the parties in the dispute *περὶ τοῦ δικαίου*, i.e. neither the *θυμῷ ποιῶν* nor the *ὀργίσας*, but is the *μοχθηρός* party to the dispute *περὶ τοῦ γενέσθαι*, i.e. either the guilty defendant or the fraudulent plaintiff.

[3] Fr. 68 (from the *Alcmeon*), Nauck[2].

Is it truly possible to be willingly treated unjustly, or is all suffering of injustice on the contrary involuntary, as all unjust action is voluntary? And is all suffering of injustice of the latter kind or else all of the former, or is it sometimes voluntary, sometimes involuntary? So, too, with the case of being justly treated; all just action is voluntary, so that it is reasonable that there should be a similar opposition in either case—that both being unjustly and being justly treated should be either alike voluntary or alike involuntary. But it would be thought paradoxical even in the case of being justly treated, if it were always voluntary; for some are unwillingly treated justly. (2) One might raise this question also, whether every one who has suffered what is unjust is being unjustly treated, or on the other hand it is with suffering as with acting. In action and in passivity alike it is possible to partake of justice incidentally, and similarly (it is plain) of injustice; for to do what is unjust is not the same as to act unjustly, nor to suffer what is unjust as to be treated unjustly, and similarly in the case of acting justly and being justly treated; for it is impossible to be unjustly treated if the other does not act unjustly, or justly treated unless he acts justly. Now if to act unjustly is simply to harm some one voluntarily, and 'voluntarily' means 'knowing the person acted on, the instrument, and the manner of one's acting', and the incontinent man voluntarily harms himself, not only will he voluntarily be unjustly treated but it will be possible to treat oneself unjustly. (This also is one of the questions in doubt, whether a man
1136b can treat himself unjustly.) Again, a man may voluntarily, owing to incontinence, be harmed by another who acts voluntarily, so that it would be possible to be voluntarily treated unjustly. Or is our definition incorrect; must we to 'harming another, with knowledge both of the person acted on, of the instrument, and of the manner' add 'contrary to the wish of the person acted on'? Then a man may be voluntarily harmed and voluntarily suffer what is unjust, but no one is voluntarily treated unjustly; for no one wishes to be unjustly treated, not even the incontinent man. He acts contrary to his wish; for no one *wishes* for what he does

not think to be good, but the incontinent man does *do* things that he does not think he ought to do. Again, one who gives what is his own, as Homer says Glaucus gave Diomede

> Armour of gold for brazen, the price of a hundred beeves for nine,[1]

is not unjustly treated; for though to give is in his power, to be unjustly treated is not, but there must be some one to treat him unjustly. It is plain, then, that being unjustly treated is not voluntary.

Of the questions we intended to discuss two still remain for discussion; (3) whether it is the man who has assigned to another more than his share that acts unjustly, or he who has the excessive share, and (4) whether it is possible to treat oneself unjustly. The questions are connected; for if the former alternative is possible and the distributor acts unjustly and not the man who has the excessive share, then if a man assigns more to another than to himself, knowingly and voluntarily, he treats himself unjustly; which is what modest people seem to do, since the virtuous man tends to take less than his share. Or does this statement too need qualification? For (*a*) he perhaps gets more than his share of some other good, e.g. of honour or of intrinsic nobility. (*b*) The question is solved by applying the distinction we applied to unjust action;[2] for he suffers nothing contrary to his own wish, so that he is not unjustly treated as far as this goes, but at most only suffers harm.

It is plain too that the distributor acts unjustly, but not always the man who has the excessive share; for it is not he to whom what is unjust appertains that acts unjustly, but he to whom it appertains to do the unjust act voluntarily, i.e. the person in whom lies the origin of the action, and this lies in the distributor, not in the receiver. Again, since the word 'do' is ambiguous, and there is a sense in which lifeless things, or a hand, or a servant who obeys an order, may be said to slay, he who gets an excessive share does not act unjustly, though he 'does' what is unjust.

Again, if the distributor gave his judgement in ignorance,

[1] *Il.* vi. 236. [2] ll. 3-5.

he does not act unjustly in respect of legal justice, and his judgement is not unjust in this sense, but in a sense it *is* unjust (for legal justice and primordial justice are different);
1137a but if with knowledge he judged unjustly, he is himself aiming at an excessive share either of gratitude or of revenge. As much, then, as if he were to share in the plunder, the man who has judged unjustly for these reasons has got too much; the fact that what he gets is different from what he distributes makes no difference, for even if he awards land with a view to sharing in the plunder he gets not land but money.

Men think that acting unjustly is in their power, and therefore that being just is easy. But it is not; to lie with one's neighbour's wife, to wound another, to deliver a bribe, is easy and in our power, but to do these things as a result of a certain state of character is neither easy nor in our power. Similarly to know what is just and what is unjust requires, men think, no great wisdom, because it is not hard to understand the matters dealt with by the laws (though these are not the things that are just, except incidentally); but how actions must be done and distributions effected in order to be just, to know *this* is a greater achievement than knowing what is good for the health; though even there, while it is easy to know that honey, wine, hellebore, cautery, and the use of the knife are so, to know how, to whom, and when these should be applied with a view to producing health, is no less an achievement than that of being a physician. Again, for this very reason [1] men think that acting unjustly is characteristic of the just man no less than of the unjust, because he would be not less but even more capable of doing each of these unjust acts; [2] for he could lie with a woman or wound a neighbour; and the brave man could throw away his shield and turn to flight in this direction or in that. But to play the coward or to act unjustly consists not in doing these things, except incidentally, but in doing them as the result of a certain state of character, just as to practise medicine and healing consists not in applying or

[1] i.e. that stated in l. 4 f., that acting unjustly is in our own power.
[2] Cf. ll. 6–8.

not applying the knife, in using or not using medicines, but in doing so in a certain way.

Just acts occur between people who participate in things good in themselves and can have too much or too little of them; for some beings (e.g. presumably the gods) cannot have too much of them, and to others, those who are incurably bad, not even the smallest share in them is beneficial but all such goods are harmful, while to others they are beneficial up to a point; therefore justice is essentially something human.

10 Our next subject is equity and the equitable (τὸ ἐπιεικές), and their respective relations to justice and the just. For on examination they appear to be neither absolutely the same nor generically different; and while we sometimes praise what is equitable and the equitable man (so that we apply the name by way of praise even to instances of the other virtues, instead of 'good', meaning by ἐπιεικέστερον 1137b
that a thing is better[1]), at other times, when we reason it out, it seems strange if the equitable, being something different from the just, is yet praiseworthy; for either the just or the equitable is not good,[2] if they are different; or, if both are good, they are the same.

These, then, are pretty much the considerations that give rise to the problem about the equitable; they are all in a sense correct and not opposed to one another; for the equitable, though it is better than one kind of justice, yet is just, and it is not as being a different class of thing that it is better than the just. The same thing, then, is just and equitable, and while both are good the equitable is superior. What creates the problem is that the equitable is just, but not the legally just but a correction of legal justice. The reason is that all law is universal but about some things it is not possible to make a universal statement which shall be correct. In those cases, then, in which it is necessary to speak universally, but not possible to do so correctly, the law takes the usual case, though it is not ignorant of the

[1] Reading τῷ ἐπιεικέστερον in l. 1.

[2] The sense requires us to omit οὐ δίκαιον (with N[b] Γ) or read οὐ σπουδαῖον for it in ll. 4–5.

possibility of error. And it is none the less correct; for the error is not in the law nor in the legislator but in the nature of the thing, since the matter of practical affairs is of this kind from the start. When the law speaks universally, then, and a case arises on it which is not covered by the universal statement, then it is right, where the legislator fails us and has erred by over-simplicity, to correct the omission—to say what the legislator himself would have said had he been present, and would have put into his law if he had known. Hence the equitable is just, and better than one kind of justice—not better than absolute justice but better than the error that arises from the absoluteness of the statement. And this is the nature of the equitable, a correction of law where it is defective owing to its universality. In fact this is the reason why all things are not determined by law, viz. that about some things it is impossible to lay down a law, so that a decree is needed. For when the thing is indefinite the rule also is indefinite, like the leaden rule used in making the Lesbian moulding; the rule adapts itself to the shape of the stone and is not rigid, and so too the decree is adapted to the facts.

It is plain, then, what the equitable is, and that it is just and is better than one kind of justice. It is evident also from this who the equitable man is; the man who chooses and does such acts, and is no stickler for his rights in a bad
1138a sense but tends to take less than his share though he has the law on his side, is equitable, and this state of character is equity, which is a sort of justice and not a different state of character.

Whether a man can treat himself unjustly or not, is 11
evident from what has been said.[1] For (*a*) one class of just acts are those acts in accordance with any virtue which are prescribed by the law; e.g. the law does not expressly permit suicide, and what it does not expressly permit it forbids. Again, when a man in violation of the law harms another (otherwise than in retaliation) voluntarily, he acts unjustly, and a voluntary agent is one who knows both the

[1] Cf. 1129a 32–b 1, 1136a 10–1137a 4.

person he is affecting by his action and the instrument he is using; and he who through anger voluntarily stabs himself does this contrary to the right rule of life, and this the law does not allow; therefore he is acting unjustly. But towards whom? Surely towards the state, not towards himself. For he suffers voluntarily, but no one is voluntarily treated unjustly. This is also the reason why the state punishes; a certain loss of civil rights attaches to the man who destroys himself, on the ground that he is treating the state unjustly.

Further (*b*) in that sense of 'acting unjustly' in which the man who 'acts unjustly' is unjust only and not bad all round, it is not possible to treat oneself unjustly (this is different from the former sense; the unjust man in one sense of the term is wicked in a particularized way just as the coward is, not in the sense of being wicked all round, so that his 'unjust act' does not manifest wickedness in general). For (i) that would imply the possibility of the same thing's having been subtracted from and added to the same thing at the same time; but this is impossible—the just and the unjust always involve more than one person. Further, (ii) unjust action is voluntary and done by choice, and *takes the initiative* (for the man who because he has suffered does the same in return is not thought to act unjustly); but if a man harms himself he suffers and does the same things *at the same time*. Further, (iii) if a man could treat himself unjustly, he could be voluntarily treated unjustly. Besides, (iv) no one acts unjustly without committing particular acts of injustice; but no one can commit adultery with his own wife or housebreaking on his own house or theft on his own property.

In general, the question 'can a man treat himself unjustly?' is solved also by the distinction we applied to the question 'can a man be voluntarily treated unjustly?'[1]

(It is evident too that both are bad, being unjustly treated and acting unjustly; for the one means having less and the other having more than the intermediate amount, which plays the part here that the healthy does in the medical

[1] Cf. $1136^a 31-^b 5$.

art, and that good condition does in the art of bodily training. But still acting unjustly is the worse, for it involves vice and is blameworthy—involves vice which is either of the complete and unqualified kind or almost so (we must admit the latter alternative, because not all voluntary unjust action implies injustice as a state of character), while being unjustly treated does not involve vice and injustice in oneself. In itself, then, being unjustly
1138b treated is less bad, but there is nothing to prevent its being incidentally a greater evil. But theory cares nothing for this; it calls pleurisy a more serious mischief than a stumble; yet the latter may become incidentally the more serious, if the fall due to it leads to your being taken prisoner or put to death by the enemy.)

Metaphorically and in virtue of a certain resemblance there is a justice, not indeed between a man and himself, but between certain parts of him; yet not every kind of justice but that of master and servant or that of husband and wife.[1] For these are the ratios in which the part of the soul that has a rational principle stands to the irrational part; and it is with a view to these parts that people also think a man can be unjust to himself, viz. because these parts are liable to suffer something contrary to their respective desires; there is therefore thought to be a mutual justice between them as between ruler and ruled.

Let this be taken as our account of justice and the other, i.e. the other moral, virtues.

[1] Cf. 1134b 15–17.

BOOK VI

1 SINCE we have previously said that one ought to choose that which is intermediate, not the excess nor the defect,[1] and that the intermediate is determined by the dictates of the right rule,[2] let us discuss the nature of these dictates. In all the states of character we have mentioned,[3] as in all other matters, there is a mark to which the man who has the rule looks, and heightens or relaxes his activity accordingly, and there is a standard which determines the mean states which we say are intermediate between excess and defect, being in accordance with the right rule. But such a statement, though true, is by no means clear; for not only here but in all other pursuits which are objects of knowledge it is indeed true to say that we must not exert ourselves nor relax our efforts too much nor too little, but to an intermediate extent and as the right rule dictates; but if a man had only this knowledge he would be none the wiser—e. g. we should not know what sort of medicines to apply to our body if some one were to say 'all those which the medical art prescribes, and which agree with the practice of one who possesses the art'. Hence it is necessary with regard to the states of the soul also not only that this true statement should be made, but also that it should be determined what is the right rule and what is the standard that fixes it.

We divided the virtues of the soul and said that some are virtues of character and others of intellect.[4] Now we 1139a
have discussed in detail the moral virtues;[3] with regard to the others let us express our view as follows, beginning with some remarks about the soul. We said before[5] that there are two parts of the soul—that which grasps a rule

[1] 1104a 11–27, 1106a 26–1107a 27.
[2] 1107a 1, cf. 1103b 31, 1114b 29.
[3] In iii. 6–v. 11.
[4] 1103a 3–7.
[5] 1102a 26–8.

or rational principle, and the irrational; let us now draw a similar distinction within the part which grasps a rational principle. And let it be assumed that there are two parts which grasp a rational principle—one by which we contemplate the kind of things whose originative causes are invariable, and one by which we contemplate variable things; for where objects differ in kind the part of the soul answering to each of the two is different in kind, since it is in virtue of a certain likeness and kinship with their objects that they have the knowledge they have. Let one of these parts be called the scientific and the other the calculative; for to deliberate and to calculate are the same thing, but no one deliberates about the invariable. Therefore the calculative is one part of the faculty which grasps a rational principles. We must, then, learn what is the best state of each of these two parts; for this is the virtue of each.

The virtue of a thing is relative to its proper work.[1] Now 2
there are three things in the soul which control action and truth—sensation, reason, desire.

Of these sensation originates no action; this is plain from the fact that the lower animals have sensation but no share in action.

What affirmation and negation are in thinking, pursuit and avoidance are in desire; so that since moral virtue is a state of character concerned with choice, and choice is deliberate desire, therefore both the reasoning must be true and the desire right, if the choice is to be good, and the latter must pursue just what the former asserts. Now this kind of intellect and of truth is practical; of the intellect which is contemplative, not practical nor productive, the good and the bad state are truth and falsity respectively (for this is the work of everything intellectual); while of the part which is practical and intellectual the good state is truth in agreement with right desire.

The origin of action—its efficient, not its final cause—is choice, and that of choice is desire and reasoning with a view

[1] There should, as Greenwood observes, be a full stop after ἑκατέρου in l. 16. ἡ δ' ἀρετή, &c. is the beginning of the argument which occupies ch. 2.

to an end. This is why choice cannot exist either without reason and intellect or without a moral state; for good action and its opposite cannot exist without a combination of intellect and character. Intellect itself, however, moves nothing, but only the intellect which aims at an end and is practical; for this rules the productive intellect as well, since 1139b every one who makes makes for an end, and that which is made is not an end in the unqualified sense (but only an end in a particular relation, and the end of a particular operation)—only that which is *done* is that; for good action is an end, and desire aims at this. Hence choice is either desiderative reason or ratiocinative desire, and such an origin of action is a man. (It is to be noted that nothing that is past is an object of choice, e.g. no one chooses to have sacked Troy; for no one *deliberates* about the past, but about what is future and capable of being otherwise, while what is past is not capable of not having taken place; hence Agathon is right in saying [1]

For this alone is lacking even to God,
To make undone things that have once been done.)

The work of both the intellectual parts, then, is truth. Therefore the states that are most strictly those in respect of which each of these parts will reach truth are the virtues of the two parts.

3 Let us begin, then, from the beginning, and discuss these states once more. Let it be assumed that the states by virtue of which the soul possesses truth by way of affirmation or denial are five in number, i.e. art, scientific knowledge, practical wisdom, philosophic wisdom, intuitive reason; we do not include judgement and opinion because in these we may be mistaken.

Now what *scientific knowledge* is, if we are to speak exactly and not follow mere similarities, is plain from what follows. We all suppose that what we know is not even capable of being otherwise; of things capable of being otherwise we do not know, when they have passed outside our observation, whether they exist or not. Therefore the object

[1] Fr. 5, Nauck^2.

of scientific knowledge is of necessity. Therefore it is eternal; for things that are of necessity in the unqualified sense are all eternal;[1] and things that are eternal are ungenerated and imperishable. Again, every science is thought to be capable of being taught, and its object of being learned. And all teaching starts from what is already known, as we maintain in the *Analytics*[2] also; for it proceeds sometimes through induction and sometimes by syllogism. Now induction is the starting-point which knowledge even of the universal presupposes, while syllogism proceeds *from* universals. There are therefore starting-points from which syllogism proceeds, which are not reached by syllogism; it is therefore by induction that they are acquired. Scientific knowledge is, then, a state of capacity to demonstrate, and has the other limiting characteristics which we specify in the *Analytics*;[3] for it is when a man believes in a certain way and the starting-points are known to him that he has scientific knowledge, since if they are not better known to him than the conclusion, he will have his knowledge only incidentally.

Let this, then, be taken as our account of scientific knowledge.

1140a In the variable are included both things made and things 4
done; making and acting are different (for their nature we treat even the discussions outside our school as reliable); so that the reasoned state of capacity to act is different from the reasoned state of capacity to make. Hence too they are not included one in the other; for neither is acting making nor is making acting. Now since architecture is an art and is essentially a reasoned state of capacity to make, and there is neither any art that is not such a state nor any such state that is not an art, *art* is identical with a state of capacity to make, involving a true course of reasoning. All art is concerned with coming into being, i.e. with contriving and considering how something may come into being which is capable of either being or not being, and whose origin is

[1] A colon is required after πάντα ἀΐδια in l. 24.
[2] *An. Post.* 71a 1. [3] Ib. b 9–23.

in the maker and not in the thing made; for art is concerned neither with things that are, or come into being, by necessity, nor with things that do so in accordance with nature (since these have their origin in themselves). Making and acting being different, art must be a matter of making, not of acting. And in a sense chance and art are concerned with the same objects; as Agathon says,[1] 'art loves chance and chance loves art'. Art, then, as has been said,[2] is a state concerned with making, involving a true course of reasoning, and lack of art on the contrary is a state concerned with making, involving a false course of reasoning; both are concerned with the variable.

5 Regarding *practical wisdom* we shall get at the truth by considering who are the persons we credit with it. Now it is thought to be the mark of a man of practical wisdom to be able to deliberate well about what is good and expedient for himself, not in some particular respect, e.g. about what sorts of thing conduce to health or to strength, but about what sorts of thing conduce to the good life in general. This is shown by the fact that we credit men with practical wisdom in some particular respect when they have calculated well with a view to some good end which is one of those that are not the object of any art. It follows that in the general sense also the man who is capable of deliberating has practical wisdom. Now no one deliberates about things that are invariable, nor about things that it is impossible for him to do. Therefore, since scientific knowledge involves demonstration, but there is no demonstration of things whose first principles are variable (for all such things might actually be otherwise), and since it is impossible to deliberate about things that are of necessity, practical wisdom cannot be scientific knowledge nor art; not **1140b** science because that which can be done is capable of being otherwise, not art because action and making are different kinds of thing. The remaining alternative, then, is that it is a true and reasoned state of capacity to act with regard to the things that are good or bad for man. For while making

[1] Fr. 6, Nauck[2]. [2] l. 9.

has an end other than itself, action cannot; for good action itself is its end. It is for this reason that we think Pericles and men like him have practical wisdom, viz. because they can see what is good for themselves and what is good for men in general; we consider that those can do this who are good at managing households or states. (This is why we call temperance (σωφροσύνη) by this name; we imply that it preserves one's practical wisdom (σῴζουσα τὴν φρόνησιν). Now what it preserves is a judgement of the kind we have described. For it is not any and every judgement that pleasant and painful objects destroy and pervert, e. g. the judgement that the triangle has or has not its angles equal to two right angles, but only judgements about what is to be done. For the originating causes of the things that are done consist in the end at which they are aimed; but the man who has been ruined by pleasure or pain forthwith fails to see any such originating cause—to see that for the sake of this or because of this he ought to choose and do whatever he chooses and does; for vice is destructive of the originating cause of action.)

Practical wisdom, then, must be a reasoned and true state of capacity to act with regard to human goods. But further, while there is such a thing as excellence in art, there is no such thing as excellence in practical wisdom; and in art he who errs willingly is preferable, but in practical wisdom, as in the virtues, he is the reverse. Plainly, then, practical wisdom is a virtue and not an art. There being two parts of the soul that can follow a course of reasoning, it must be the virtue of one of the two, i. e. of that part which forms opinions; for opinion is about the variable and so is practical wisdom. But yet it is not only a reasoned state; this is shown by the fact that a state of that sort may be forgotten but practical wisdom cannot.

Scientific knowledge is judgement about things that are 6
universal and necessary, and the conclusions of demonstration, and all scientific knowledge, follow from first principles (for scientific knowledge involves apprehension of a rational ground). This being so, the first principle from which what

is scientifically known follows cannot be an object of scientific knowledge, of art, or of practical wisdom; for that which can be scientifically known can be demonstrated, and art and practical wisdom deal with things that are variable. Nor are these first principles the objects of philosophic wisdom, for it is a mark of the philosopher to have *demonstration* about some things. If, then, the states of mind by which we have truth and are never deceived about things invariable or even variable are scientific knowledge, practical wisdom, philosophic wisdom, and intuitive reason, and it cannot be any of the three (i. e. practical wisdom, scientific knowledge, or philosophic wisdom), the remaining alternative is that it is *intuitive reason* that grasps the first principles.

7 *Wisdom*[1] (1) in the arts we ascribe to their most finished exponents, e. g. to Phidias as a sculptor and to Polyclitus as a maker of portrait-statues, and here we mean nothing by wisdom except excellence in art; but (2) we think that some people are wise in general, not in some particular field or in any other limited respect, as Homer says in the *Margites*,[2]

Him did the gods make neither a digger nor yet a ploughman
Nor wise in anything else.

Therefore wisdom must plainly be the most finished of the forms of knowledge. It follows that the wise man must not only know what follows from the first principles, but must also possess truth about the first principles. Therefore wisdom must be intuitive reason combined with scientific knowledge—scientific knowledge of the highest objects which has received as it were its proper completion.

Of the highest objects, we say; for it would be strange to think that the art of politics, or practical wisdom, is the best knowledge, since man is not the best thing in the world. Now if what is healthy or good is different for men and for fishes, but what is white or straight is always

[1] In this chapter Aristotle restricts to a very definite meaning the word σοφία, which in ordinary Greek, as the beginning of the chapter points out, was used both of skill in a particular art or craft, and of wisdom in general.

[2] Fr. 2, Allen.

the same, any one would say that what is wise is the same but what is practically wise is different; for it is to that which observes well the various matters concerning itself that one ascribes practical wisdom, and it is to this that one will entrust such matters. This is why we say that some even of the lower animals have practical wisdom,[1] viz. those which are found to have a power of foresight with regard to their own life. It is evident also that philosophic wisdom and the art of politics cannot be the same; for if the state of mind concerned with a man's own interests is to be called philosophic wisdom, there will be many philosophic wisdoms; there will not be one concerned with the good of all animals (any more than there is one art of medicine for all existing things), but a different philosophic wisdom about the good of each species.

But if the argument be that man is the best of the animals, this makes no difference; for there are other things much
1141b more divine in their nature even than man, e.g., most conspicuously, the bodies of which the heavens are framed. From what has been said it is plain, then, that philosophic wisdom is scientific knowledge, combined with intuitive reason, of the things that are highest by nature. This is why we say Anaxagoras, Thales, and men like them have philosophic but not practical wisdom, when we see them ignorant of what is to their own advantage, and why we say that they know things that are remarkable, admirable, difficult, and divine, but useless; viz. because it is not human goods that they seek.[2]

Practical wisdom on the other hand is concerned with things human and things about which it is possible to deliberate; for we say this is above all the work of the man of practical wisdom, to deliberate well, but no one deliberates about things invariable, nor about things which have not an end, and that a good that can be brought about by action. The man who is without qualification good at deliberating is the man who is capable of aiming in accordance with calculation at the best for man of things attainable

[1] We do not say this in English; but we call them 'intelligent' or 'sagacious', which comes to the same thing.

[2] Cf. Diels, *Vors.* 46 A 30.

by action. Nor is practical wisdom concerned with universals only—it must also recognize the particulars; for it is practical, and practice is concerned with particulars. This is why some who do not know, and especially those who have experience, are more practical than others who know; for if a man knew that light meats are digestible and wholesome, but did not know which sorts of meat are light, he would not produce health, but the man who knows that chicken is wholesome is more likely to produce health.

Now practical wisdom is concerned with action; therefore one should have both forms of it, or the latter in preference to the former. But of practical as of philosophic wisdom there must be a controlling kind.

8 Political wisdom and practical wisdom are the same state of mind, but their essence is not the same. Of the wisdom concerned with the city, the practical wisdom which plays a controlling part is legislative wisdom, while that which is related to this as particulars to their universal is known by the general name 'political wisdom'; this has to do with action and deliberation, for a decree is a thing to be carried out in the form of an individual act. This is why the exponents of this art are alone said to 'take part in politics'; for these alone 'do things' as manual labourers 'do things'

Practical wisdom also is identified especially with that form of it which is concerned with a man himself—with the individual; and this is known by the general name 'practical wisdom'; of the other kinds one is called household management, another legislation, the third politics, and of the latter one part is called deliberative and the other judicial. Now knowing what is good for oneself will be one kind of knowledge, but it is very different from the other kinds; and the 1142a
man who knows and concerns himself with his own interests is thought to have practical wisdom, while politicians are thought to be busybodies; hence the words of Euripides,[1]

But how could I be wise, who might at ease,
Numbered among the army's multitude,
Have had an equal share? . . .
For those who aim too high and do too much . . . .

[1] Prologue to *Philoctetes* (Fr. 787, 782. 2, Nauck[2]).

Those who think thus seek their own good, and consider that one ought to do so. From this opinion, then, has come the view that such men have practical wisdom; yet perhaps one's own good cannot exist without household management, nor without a form of government. Further, how one should order one's own affairs is not clear and needs inquiry.

What has been said is confirmed by the fact that while young men become geometricians and mathematicians and wise in matters like these, it is thought that a young man of practical wisdom cannot be found. The cause is that such wisdom is concerned not only with universals but with particulars, which become familiar from experience, but a young man has no experience, for it is length of time that gives experience; indeed one might ask this question too, why a boy may become a mathematician, but not a philosopher or a physicist. Is it because the objects of mathematics exist by abstraction, while the first principles of these other subjects come from experience, and because young men have no conviction about the latter but merely use the proper language, while the essence of mathematical objects is plain enough to them?

Further, error in deliberation may be either about the universal or about the particular; we may fail to know either that all water that weighs heavy is bad, or that this particular water weighs heavy.

That practical wisdom is not scientific knowledge is evident; for it is, as has been said,[1] concerned with the ultimate particular fact, since the thing to be done is of this nature. It is opposed, then, to intuitive reason; for intuitive reason is of the limiting premisses, for which no reason can be given, while practical wisdom is concerned with the ultimate particular, which is the object not of scientific knowledge but of perception—not the perception of qualities peculiar to one sense but a perception akin to that by which we perceive that the particular figure before us is a triangle; for in that direction as well as in that of the major premiss there will be a limit. But this is rather

[1] 1141b 14–22.

perception than practical wisdom,[1] though it is another kind of perception than that of the qualities peculiar to each sense.

9 There is a difference between inquiry and deliberation; for deliberation is inquiry into a particular kind of thing. We must grasp the nature of excellence in deliberation as well—whether it is a form of scientific knowledge, or opinion, or skill in conjecture, or some other kind of thing. *Scientific knowledge* it is not; for men do not inquire about the things they know about, but good deliberation is a kind 1142b
of deliberation, and he who deliberates inquires and calculates. Nor is it *skill in conjecture*; for this both involves no reasoning and is something that is quick in its operation, while men deliberate a long time, and they say that one should carry out quickly the conclusions of one's deliberation, but should deliberate slowly. Again, *readiness of mind* is different from excellence in deliberation; it is a sort of skill in conjecture. Nor again is excellence in deliberation *opinion* of any sort. But since the man who deliberates badly makes a mistake, while he who deliberates well does so correctly, excellence in deliberation is clearly a kind of correctness, but neither of knowledge nor of opinion; for there is no such thing as correctness of knowledge (since there is no such thing as error of knowledge), and correctness of opinion is truth; and at the same time everything that is an object of opinion is already determined. But again excellence in deliberation involves reasoning. The remaining alternative, then, is that it is *correctness of thinking*; for this is not yet assertion, since, while even opinion is not inquiry but has reached the stage of assertion, the man who is deliberating, whether he does so well or ill, is searching for something and calculating.

But excellence in deliberation is a certain correctness of deliberation; hence we must first inquire what deliberation is and what it is about. And, there being more than one kind of correctness, plainly excellence in deliberation is not

[1] I should prefer to read in l. 30 ᾗ ἡ φρόνησις, 'this is more truly perception than practical wisdom is'.

any and every kind; for (1) the incontinent man and the bad man, if he is clever,[1] will reach as a result of his calculation what he sets before himself, so that he will have deliberated correctly, but he will have got for himself a great evil. Now to have deliberated well is thought to be a good thing; for it is this kind of correctness of deliberation that is excellence in deliberation, viz. that which tends to attain what is good. But (2) it is possible to attain even good by a false syllogism, and to attain what one ought to do but not by the right means, the middle term being false; so that this too is not yet excellence in deliberation—this state in virtue of which one attains what one ought but not by the right means. Again (3) it is possible to attain it by long deliberation while another man attains it quickly. Therefore in the former case we have not yet got excellence in deliberation, which is rightness with regard to the expedient—rightness in respect both of the end, the manner, and the time. (4) Further it is possible to have deliberated well either in the unqualified sense or with reference to a particular end. Excellence in deliberation in the unqualified sense, then, is that which succeeds with reference to what is the end in the unqualified sense, and excellence in deliberation in a particular sense is that which succeeds relatively to a particular end. If, then, it is characteristic of men of practical wisdom to have deliberated well, excellence in deliberation will be correctness with regard to what conduces to the end of which practical wisdom is the true apprehension.

Understanding, also, and goodness of understanding, in 10
virtue of which men are said to be men of understanding or
1143a of good understanding, are neither entirely the same as opinion or scientific knowledge (for at that rate all men would have been men of understanding), nor are they one of the particular sciences, such as medicine, the science of things connected with health, or geometry, the science of spatial magnitudes. For understanding is neither about things that are always and are unchangeable, nor about any and every one of the things that come into being, but

[1] Reading εἰ δεινός for ἰδεῖν in l. 19 as suggested by Apelt.

about things which may become subjects of questioning and deliberation. Hence it is about the same objects as practical wisdom; but understanding and practical wisdom are not the same. For practical wisdom issues commands, since its end is what ought to be done or not to be done; but understanding only judges. (Understanding is identical with goodness of understanding, men of understanding with men of good understanding.) Now understanding is neither the having nor the acquiring of practical wisdom; but as learning is called understanding when it means the exercise of the faculty of knowledge,[1] so 'understanding' is applicable to the exercise of the faculty of opinion for the purpose of judging of what some one else says about matters with which practical wisdom is concerned—and of judging soundly; for 'well' and 'soundly' are the same thing. And from this has come the use of the name 'understanding' in virtue of which men are said to be 'of good understanding', viz. from the application of the word to the grasping of scientific truth; for we often call such grasping understanding.

11 What is called judgement, in virtue of which men are said to 'be sympathetic judges' and to 'have judgement', is the right discrimination of the equitable. This is shown by the fact that we say the equitable man is above all others a man of sympathetic judgement, and identify equity with sympathetic judgement about certain facts. And sympathetic judgement is judgement which discriminates what is equitable and does so correctly; and correct judgement is that which judges what is true.

Now all the states we have considered converge, as might be expected, to the same point; for when we speak of judgement and understanding and practical wisdom and intuitive reason we credit the same people with possessing judgement and having reached years of reason and with having practical wisdom and understanding. For all these faculties deal with ultimates, i.e. with particulars; and being a man

[1] For this use of μανθάνειν (which is not shared by the English 'learn') cf. *Soph. El.* 165^b 32, and L. and S.[8] *s.v.* IV.

of understanding and of good or sympathetic judgement consists in being able to judge about the things with which practical wisdom is concerned; for the equities are common to all good men in relation to other men. Now all things which have to be done are included among particulars or ultimates; for not only must the man of practical wisdom know particular facts, but understanding and judgement are also concerned with things to be done, and these are ultimates. And intuitive reason is concerned with the ultimates in both directions; for both the first terms and the last are objects of intuitive reason and not of argument,
1143b and the intuitive reason which is presupposed by demonstrations grasps the unchangeable and first terms, while the intuitive reason involved in practical reasonings grasps the last and variable fact, i.e. the minor premiss. For these variable facts are the starting-points for the apprehension of the end, since the universals are reached from the particulars; of these therefore we must have perception, and this perception is intuitive reason.

This is why these states are thought to be natural endowments—why, while no one is thought to be a philosopher by nature, people are thought to have by nature judgement, understanding, and intuitive reason. This is shown by the fact that we think our powers correspond to our time of life, and that a particular age brings with it intuitive reason and judgement; this implies that nature is the cause. [Hence intuitive reason is both beginning and end; for demonstrations are from these and about these.[1]] Therefore we ought to attend to the undemonstrated sayings and opinions of experienced and older people or of people of practical wisdom not less than to demonstrations; for because experience has given them an eye they see aright.

We have stated, then, what practical and philosophic wisdom are, and with what each of them is concerned, and we have said that each is the virtue of a different part of the soul.

[1] This sentence should probably be read, as Bywater suggests, at the end of the previous paragraph.

12 Difficulties might be raised as to the utility of these qualities of mind. For (1) philosophic wisdom will contemplate none of the things that will make a man happy (for it is not concerned with any coming into being), and though practical wisdom has *this* merit, for what purpose do we need it? Practical wisdom is the quality of mind concerned with things just and noble and good for man, but these are the things which it is the mark of a *good* man to do, and we are none the more able to act for *knowing* them if the virtues are states of *character*, just as we are none the better able to act for knowing the things that are healthy and sound, in the sense not of producing but of issuing from the state of health; for we are none the more able to act for having the art of medicine or of gymnastics. But (2) if we are to say that a man should have practical wisdom not for the sake of knowing moral truths but for the sake of becoming good, practical wisdom will be of no use to those who *are* good; but again it is of no use to those who have *not* virtue; for it will make no difference whether they have practical wisdom themselves or obey others who have it, and it would be enough for us to do what we do in the case of health; though we wish to become healthy, yet we do not learn the art of medicine. (3) Besides this, it would be thought strange if practical wisdom, being inferior to philosophic wisdom, is to be put in authority over it, as seems to be implied by the fact that the art which produces anything rules and issues commands about that thing.

These, then, are the questions we must discuss; so far we have only stated the difficulties.

(1) Now first let us say that in themselves these states 1144a
must be worthy of choice because they are the virtues of the two parts of the soul respectively, even if neither of them produce anything.

(2) Secondly, they do produce something, not as the art of medicine produces health, however, but as health produces health;[1] so does philosophic wisdom produce happiness;

[1] i. e. as health, as an inner state, produces the activities which we know as constituting health.

for, being a part of virtue entire, by being possessed and by actualizing itself it makes a man happy.

(3) Again, the work of man is achieved only in accordance with practical wisdom as well as with moral virtue; for virtue makes us aim at the right mark, and practical wisdom makes us take the right means. (Of the fourth part of the soul—the nutritive[1]—there is no such virtue; for there is nothing which it is in its power to do or not to do.)

(4) With regard to our being none the more able to do because of our practical wisdom what is noble and just, let us begin a little further back, starting with the following principle. As we say that some people who do just acts are not necessarily just, i. e. those who do the acts ordained by the laws either unwillingly or owing to ignorance or for some other reason and not for the sake of the acts themselves (though, to be sure, they do what they should and all the things that the good man ought), so is it, it seems, that in order to be good one must be in a certain state when one does the several acts, i. e. one must do them as a result of choice and for the sake of the acts themselves. Now virtue makes the choice right, but the question of the things which should naturally be done to carry out our choice belongs not to virtue but to another faculty. We must devote our attention to these matters and give a clearer statement about them. There is a faculty which is called cleverness; and this is such as to be able to do the things that tend towards the mark we have set before ourselves, and to hit it. Now if the mark be noble, the cleverness is laudable, but if the mark be bad, the cleverness is mere smartness; hence we call even men of practical wisdom clever or smart. Practical wisdom is not the faculty, but it does not exist without this faculty. And this eye of the soul acquires its formed state not without the aid of virtue, as has been said[2] and is plain; for the syllogisms which deal with acts to be done are things which involve a starting-point, viz. 'since the

[1] The other three being the scientific (τὸ ἐπιστημονικόν), the calculative (τὸ λογιστικόν), and the desiderative (τὸ ὀρεκτικόν).

[2] ll. 6–26.

end, i. e. what is best, is of such and such a nature', whatever it may be (let it for the sake of argument be what we please); and this is not evident except to the good man; for wickedness perverts us and causes us to be deceived about the starting-points of action. Therefore it is evident that it is impossible to be practically wise without being good.

13 We must therefore consider virtue also once more; for 1144[b] virtue too is similarly related; as practical wisdom is to cleverness—not the same, but like it—so is natural virtue to virtue in the strict sense. For all men think that each type of character belongs to its possessors in some sense by nature; for from the very moment of birth we are just or fitted for self-control or brave or have the other moral qualities; but yet we seek something else as that which is good in the strict sense—we seek for the presence of such qualities in another way. For both children and brutes have the natural dispositions to these qualities, but without reason these are evidently hurtful. Only we seem to see this much, that, while one may be led astray by them, as a strong body which moves without sight may stumble badly because of its lack of sight, still, if a man once acquires reason, that makes a difference in action; and his state, while still like what it was, will then be virtue in the strict sense. Therefore, as in the part of us which forms opinions there are two types, cleverness and practical wisdom, so too in the moral part there are two types, natural virtue and virtue in the strict sense, and of these the latter involves practical wisdom. This is why some say that all the virtues are forms of practical wisdom, and why Socrates in one respect was on the right track while in another he went astray; in thinking that all the virtues were forms of practical wisdom he was wrong, but in saying they implied practical wisdom he was right. This is confirmed by the fact that even now all men, when they define virtue, after naming the state of character and its objects add 'that (state) which is in accordance with the right rule'; now the right rule is that which is in accordance with practical wisdom. All men, then, seem somehow to

divine that this kind of state is virtue, viz. that which is in accordance with practical wisdom. But we must go a little further. For it is not merely the state in accordance with the right rule, but the state that implies the *presence* of the right rule, that is virtue; and practical wisdom is a right rule about such matters. Socrates, then, thought the virtues were rules or rational principles (for he thought they were, all of them, forms of scientific knowledge), while we think they *involve* a rational principle.

It is clear, then, from what has been said, that it is not possible to be good in the strict sense without practical wisdom, nor practically wise without moral virtue. But in this way we may also refute the dialectical argument whereby it might be contended that the virtues exist in separation from each other; the same man, it might be said, is not best equipped by nature for all the virtues, so that he will have already acquired one when he has not yet acquired another. This is possible in respect of the natural virtues, but not in respect of those in respect of which a man
1145a is called without qualification good; for with the presence of the one quality, practical wisdom, will be given all the virtues. And it is plain that, even if it were of no practical value, we should have needed it because it is the virtue of the part of us in question; plain too that the choice will not be right without practical wisdom any more than without virtue; for the one determines the end and the other makes us do the things that lead to the end.

But again it is not *supreme* over philosophic wisdom, i.e. over the superior part of us, any more than the art of medicine is over health; for it does not use it but provides for its coming into being; it issues orders, then, for its sake, but not to it. Further, to maintain its supremacy would be like saying that the art of politics rules the gods because it issues orders about all the affairs of the state.

BOOK VII

1 LET us now make a fresh beginning and point out that of moral states to be avoided there are three kinds—vice, incontinence, brutishness. The contraries of two of these are evident—one we call virtue, the other continence; to brutishness it would be most fitting to oppose superhuman virtue, a heroic and divine kind of virtue, as Homer has represented Priam saying of Hector that he was very good,

> For he seemed not, he,
> The child of a mortal man, but as one that of God's seed came.[1]

Therefore if, as they say, men become gods by excess of virtue, of this kind must evidently be the state opposed to the brutish state; for as a brute has no vice or virtue, so neither has a god; his state is higher than virtue, and that of a brute is a different kind of state from vice.

Now, since it is rarely that a godlike man is found—to use the epithet of the Spartans, who when they admire any one highly call him a 'godlike man'—so too the brutish type is rarely found among men; it is found chiefly among barbarians, but some brutish qualities are also produced by disease or deformity; and we also call by this evil name those men who go beyond all ordinary standards by reason of vice. Of this kind of disposition, however, we must later make some mention,[2] while we have discussed vice before;[3] we must now discuss incontinence and softness (or effeminacy), and continence and endurance; for we must treat each of the two neither as identical with virtue 1145b
or wickedness, nor as a different genus. We must, as in all other cases, set the observed facts before us and, after first discussing the difficulties, go on to prove, if possible, the truth of all the common opinions about these affections

[1] *Il.* xxiv. 258 f. [2] Ch. 5. [3] Bks. II–V.

of the mind, or, failing this, of the greater number and the most authoritative; for if we both refute the objections and leave the common opinions undisturbed, we shall have proved the case sufficiently.

Now (1) both continence and endurance are thought to be included among things good and praiseworthy, and both incontinence and softness among things bad and blameworthy; and the same man is thought to be continent and ready to abide by the result of his calculations, or incontinent and ready to abandon them. And (2) the incontinent man, knowing that what he does is bad, does it as a result of passion, while the continent man, knowing that his appetites are bad, refuses on account of his rational principle to follow them. (3) The temperate man all men call continent and disposed to endurance, while the continent man some maintain to be always temperate but others do not; and some call the self-indulgent man incontinent and the incontinent man self-indulgent indiscriminately, while others distinguish them. (4) The man of practical wisdom, they sometimes say, cannot be incontinent, while sometimes they say that some who are practically wise and clever *are* incontinent. Again (5) men are said to be incontinent even with respect to anger, honour, and gain.—These, then, are the things that are said.

Now we may ask (1) how a man who judges rightly can 2
behave incontinently. That he should behave so when he has knowledge, some say is impossible; for it would be strange—so Socrates[1] thought—if when knowledge was in a man something else could master it and drag it about like a slave. For *Socrates* was entirely opposed to the view in question, holding that there is no such thing as incontinence; no one, he said, when he judges acts against what he judges best—people act so only by reason of ignorance. Now this view plainly contradicts the observed facts, and we must inquire about what happens to such a man; if he acts by reason of ignorance, what is the manner of his ignorance? For that the man who behaves

[1] Pl. *Prot.* 352 B, C.

incontinently does not, before he gets into this state, *think* he ought to act so, is evident. But there are *some* who concede certain of Socrates' contentions but not others; that nothing is stronger than knowledge they admit, but not that no one acts contrary to what has seemed to him the better course, and therefore they say that the incontinent man has not knowledge when he is mastered by his pleasures, but opinion. But *if* it is opinion and not knowledge, if it is not a strong conviction that resists but a weak one, as in men who hesitate, we sympathize with their 1146a failure to stand by such convictions against strong appetites; but we do not sympathize with wickedness, nor with any of the other blameworthy states. Is it then *practical wisdom* whose resistance is mastered? That is the strongest of all states. But this is absurd; the same man will be at once practically wise and incontinent, but *no one* would say that it is the part of a practically wise man to do willingly the basest acts. Besides, it has been shown before that the man of practical wisdom is one who will *act*[1] (for he is a man concerned with the individual facts)[2] and who has the other virtues.[3]

(2) Further, if continence involves having strong and bad appetites, the temperate man will not be continent nor the continent man temperate; for a temperate man will have neither excessive nor bad appetites. But the continent man *must*; for if the appetites are good, the state of character that restrains us from following them is bad, so that not all continence will be good; while if they are weak and not bad, there is nothing admirable in resisting them, and if they are weak and bad, there is nothing great in resisting these either.

(3) Further, if continence makes a man ready to stand by any and every opinion, it is bad, i.e. if it makes him stand even by a false opinion; and if incontinence makes a man apt to abandon any and every opinion, there will be a good incontinence, of which Sophocles' Neoptolemus in the *Philoctetes*[4] will be an instance; for he is to be

[1] 1140b 4-6.
[2] 1141b 16, 1142a 24.
[3] 1144b 30-1145a 2.
[4] ll. 895-916.

praised for not standing by what Odysseus persuaded him to do, because he is pained at telling a lie.

(4) Further, the sophistic argument presents a difficulty; the syllogism arising from men's wish to expose paradoxical results arising from an opponent's view, in order that they may be admired when they succeed, is one that puts us in a difficulty (for thought is bound fast when it will not rest because the conclusion does not satisfy it, and cannot advance because it cannot refute the argument). There is an argument from which it follows that folly coupled with incontinence is virtue; for a man does the opposite of what he judges, owing to incontinence, but judges what is good to be evil and something that he should not do, and in consequence he will do what is good and not what is evil.

(5) Further, he who on conviction does and pursues and chooses what is pleasant would be thought to be better than one who does so as a result not of calculation but of incontinence; for he is easier to cure since he may be persuaded to change his mind. But to the incontinent man may be applied the proverb 'when water chokes, what is one to wash it down with?' If he had been persuaded of the rightness of what he does, he would have desisted
1146b when he was persuaded to change his mind; but now he acts in spite of his being persuaded of something quite different.

(6) Further, if incontinence and continence are concerned with any and every kind of object, who is it that is incontinent in the unqualified sense? No one has all the forms of incontinence, but we say some people are incontinent without qualification.

Of some such kind are the difficulties that arise; some of these points must be refuted and the others left in possession of the field; for the solution of the difficulty
is the discovery of the truth. (1) We must consider first, 3
then, whether incontinent people act knowingly or not, and in what sense knowingly; then (2) with what sorts of object the incontinent and the continent man may be

said to be concerned (i. e. whether with any and every pleasure and pain or with certain determinate kinds), and whether the continent man and the man of endurance are the same or different; and similarly with regard to the other matters germane to this inquiry. The starting-point of our investigation is (*a*) the question whether the continent man and the incontinent are differentiated by their objects or by their attitude, i. e. whether the incontinent man is incontinent simply by being concerned with such and such objects, or, instead, by his attitude, or, instead of that, by both these things; (*b*) the second question is whether incontinence and continence are concerned with any and every object or not. The man who is incontinent in the unqualified sense is neither concerned with any and every object, but with precisely those with which the self-indulgent man is concerned, nor is he characterized by being simply related to these (for then his state would be the same as self-indulgence), but by being related to them in a certain way. For the one is led on in accordance with his own choice, thinking that he ought always to pursue the present pleasure; while the other does not think so, but yet pursues it.

(1) As for the suggestion that it is true opinion and not knowledge against which we act incontinently, that makes no difference to the argument; for some people when in a state of opinion do not hesitate, but think they know exactly. If, then, the notion is that owing to their weak conviction those who have opinion are more likely to act against their judgement than those who know, we answer that there need be no difference between knowledge and opinion in this respect; for some men are no less convinced of what they think than others of what they know; as is shown by the case of Heraclitus. But (*a*), since we use the word 'know' in two senses (for both the man who has knowledge but is not using it and he who is using it are said to know), it *will* make a difference whether, when a man does what he should not, he has the knowledge but is not exercising it, or *is* exercising it; for the latter seems strange, but not the former.

(*b*) Further, since there are two kinds of premisses, there
1147a is nothing to prevent a man's having both premisses and acting against his knowledge, provided that he is using only the universal premiss and not the particular; for it is particular acts that have to be done. And there are also two kinds of universal term; one is predicable of the agent, the other of the object; e. g. 'dry food is good for every man', and 'I am a man', or 'such and such food is dry'; but whether 'this food is such and such', of this the incontinent man either has not or is not exercising the knowledge.[1] There will, then, be, firstly, an enormous difference between these manners of knowing, so that to know in one way when we act incontinently would not seem anything strange, while to know in the other way would be extraordinary.

And further (*c*) the possession of knowledge in another sense than those just named is something that happens to men; for within the case of having knowledge but not using it we see a difference of state, admitting of the possibility of having knowledge in a sense and yet not having it, as in the instance of a man asleep, mad, or drunk. But now this is just the condition of men under the influence of passions; for outbursts of anger and sexual appetites and some other such passions, it is evident, actually alter our bodily condition, and in some men even produce fits of madness. It is plain, then, that incontinent people must be said to be in a similar condition to men asleep, mad, or drunk. The fact that men use the language that flows from knowledge proves nothing; for even men under the influence of these passions utter scientific proofs and verses of Empedocles, and those who have just begun to learn a science can string together its phrases, but do not yet know it; for it has to become part of themselves, and that takes time; so that we must suppose that the

[1] i.e., if I am to be able to deduce from (*a*) 'dry food is good for all men' that 'this food is good for me', I must have (*b*) the premiss 'I am a man' and (*c*) the premisses (i) '*x* food is dry', (ii) 'this food is *x*'. I cannot fail to know (*b*), and I may know (*c* i); but if I do not know (*c* ii), or know it only 'at the back of my mind', I shall not draw the conclusion.

use of language by men in an incontinent state means no more than its utterance by actors on the stage.

(*d*) Again, we may also view the cause as follows with reference to the facts of human nature. The one opinion is universal, the other is concerned with the particular facts, and here we come to something within the sphere of perception; when a single opinion results from the two, the soul must in one type of case[1] affirm the conclusion, while in the case of opinions concerned with production it must immediately act (e.g. if 'everything sweet ought to be tasted', and 'this is sweet', in the sense of being one of the particular sweet things, the man who can act and is not prevented must at the same time actually act accordingly). When, then, the universal opinion is present in us forbidding us to taste, and there is also the opinion that 'everything sweet is pleasant', and that 'this is sweet' (now this is the opinion that is active),[2] and when appetite happens to be present in us, the one opinion bids us avoid the object, but appetite leads us towards it (for it can move each of our bodily parts); so that it turns out that a man behaves incontinently under the influence (in a sense) of a rule and an opinion, and of one not contrary in itself, **1147b** but only incidentally—for the appetite is contrary, not the opinion—to the right rule. It also follows that this is the reason why the lower animals are not incontinent, viz. because they have no universal judgement but only imagination and memory of particulars.

The explanation of how the ignorance is dissolved and the incontinent man regains his knowledge, is the same as in the case of the man drunk or asleep and is not peculiar to this condition; we must go to the students of natural science for it. Now, the last premiss both being an opinion about a perceptible object, and being what determines our actions, this a man either has not when he is in the state of passion, or has it in the sense in which having knowledge did not mean knowing but only talking, as a drunken man may mutter the verses of Empedocles.[3] And because the

[1] I.e. in scientific reasoning. [2] I.e. determines action (cf. b10).
[3] Cf. a10–24.

last term is not universal nor equally an object of scientific knowledge with the universal term, the position that Socrates sought to establish[1] actually seems to result; for it is not in the presence of what is thought to be knowledge proper that the affection of incontinence arises (nor is it this that is 'dragged about' as a result of the state of passion), but in that of perceptual knowledge.[2]

This must suffice as our answer to the question of action with and without knowledge, and how it is possible to behave incontinently with knowledge.

(2) We must next discuss whether there is any one who 4
is incontinent without qualification, or all men who are incontinent are so in a particular sense, and if there is, with what sort of objects he is concerned. That both continent persons and persons of endurance, and incontinent and soft persons, are concerned with pleasures and pains, is evident.

Now of the things that produce pleasure some are necessary, while others are worthy of choice in themselves but admit of excess, the bodily causes of pleasure being necessary (by such I mean both those concerned with food and those concerned with sexual intercourse, i.e. the bodily matters with which we defined[3] self-indulgence and temperance as being concerned), while the others are not necessary but worthy of choice in themselves (e.g. victory, honour, wealth, and good and pleasant things of this sort). This being so, (*a*) those who go to excess with reference to the latter, contrary to the right rule which is in themselves, are not called incontinent simply, but incontinent with the qualification 'in respect of money, gain, honour, or anger', —not simply incontinent, on the ground that they are different from incontinent people and are called incontinent by reason of a resemblance. (Compare the case of Anthropos (Man), who won a contest at the Olympic games;

[1] 1145[b] 22–24.

[2] Even before the minor premiss of the practical syllogism has been obscured by passion, the incontinent man has not scientific knowledge in the strict sense, since his minor premiss is not universal but has for its subject a sensible particular, e.g. 'this glass of wine'.

[3] III. 10.

in his case the general definition of man differed little from the definition peculiar to *him*, but yet it *was* different.[1]) This is shown by the fact that incontinence either without qualification or in respect of some particular bodily pleasure is blamed not only as a fault but as a kind of vice, while none of the people who are incontinent in these other respects is so blamed. 1148a

But (*b*) of the people who are incontinent with respect to bodily enjoyments, with which we say the temperate and the self-indulgent man are concerned, he who pursues the excesses of things pleasant—and shuns those of things painful, of hunger and thirst and heat and cold and all the objects of touch and taste—not by choice but contrary to his choice and his judgement, is called incontinent, not with the qualification 'in respect of this or that', e.g. of anger, but just simply. This is confirmed by the fact that men are called 'soft' with regard to these pleasures, but not with regard to any of the others. And for this reason we group together the incontinent and the self-indulgent, the continent and the temperate man—but not any of these other types—because they are concerned somehow with the same pleasures and pains; but though these are concerned with the same objects, they are not similarly related to them, but some of them make a deliberate choice while the others do not.[2]

This is why we should describe as self-indulgent rather the man who without appetite or with but a slight appetite pursues the excesses of pleasure and avoids moderate pains, than the man who does so because of his strong appetites; for what would the former do, if he had in addition a vigorous appetite, and a violent pain at the lack of the 'necessary' objects?

Now of appetites and pleasures some belong to the class

[1] I.e. the definition appropriate to him was not 'rational animal' but 'rational animal who won the boxing contest at Olympia in 456 B.C.' The reading Ἄνθρωπος in l. 35 is confirmed not only by Alexander but by an Oxyrhynchus papyrus giving a list of Olympian victors; cf. *Class. Rev.* XIII (1899), 290 f.

[2] I.e. the temperate and the self-indulgent, not the continent and the incontinent.

of things generically noble and good—for some pleasant things are by nature worthy of choice, while others are contrary to these, and others are intermediate, to adopt our previous distinction[1]—e.g. wealth, gain, victory, honour. And with reference to all objects whether of this or of the intermediate kind men are not blamed for being affected by them, for desiring and loving them, but for doing so in a certain way, i.e. for going to excess. (This is why all those who contrary to the rule either are mastered by or pursue one of the objects which are naturally noble and good, e.g. those who busy themselves more than they ought about honour or about children and parents, ⟨are not wicked⟩; for these too are goods, and those who busy themselves about them are praised; but yet there is an excess even in them—if like Niobe one were to fight even against the gods, or were to be as much
1148b devoted to one's father as Satyrus nicknamed 'the filial', who was thought to be very silly on this point.[2]) There is no wickedness, then, with regard to these objects, for the reason named, viz. because each of them is by nature a thing worthy of choice for its own sake; yet excesses in respect of them are bad and to be avoided. Similarly there is no incontinence with regard to them; for incontinence is not only to be avoided but is also a thing worthy of blame; but owing to a similarity in the state of feeling people apply the name incontinence, adding in each case what it is in respect of, as we may describe as a bad doctor or a bad actor one whom we should not call bad, simply. As, then, in this case we do not apply the term without qualification because each of these conditions is not badness but only analogous to it, so it is clear that in the other case also that alone must be taken to be incontinence and continence which is concerned with the same objects as temperance and self-indulgence, but we apply the term to

[1] 1147b 23–31, where, however, the 'contraries' are not mentioned. It is better to end the parenthesis at *πρότερον*, l. 25, than at *αἱρετά*, l. 24, since *χρήματα κτλ* are instances of *τὰ τῷ γένει καλὰ καὶ σπουδαῖα*.

[2] Nothing is really known about the Satyrus referred to, but Prof. Burnet's suggestion that he was a king of Bosporus who deified his father seems probable.

anger by virtue of a resemblance; and this is why we say with a qualification 'incontinent in respect of anger' as we say 'incontinent in respect of honour, or of gain'.

5 (1) Some things are pleasant by nature, and of these (*a*) some are so without qualification, and (*b*) others are so with reference to particular classes either of animals or of men; while (2) others are not pleasant by nature, but (*a*) some of them become so by reason of injuries to the system, and (*b*) others by reason of acquired habits, and (*c*) others by reason of originally bad natures. This being so, it is possible with regard to each of the latter kinds to discover similar states of character to those recognized with regard to the former; I mean (A) the brutish states,[1] as in the case of the female who, they say, rips open pregnant women and devours the infants, or of the things in which some of the tribes about the Black Sea that have gone savage are said to delight—in raw meat or in human flesh, or in lending their children to one another to feast upon—or of the story told of Phalaris.[2]

These states are brutish, but (B) others arise as a result of disease[3] (or, in some cases, of madness, as with the man who sacrificed and ate his mother, or with the slave who ate the liver of his fellow), and others are morbid states (C) resulting from custom,[4] e. g. the habit of plucking out the hair or of gnawing the nails, or even coals or earth, and in addition to these paederasty; for these arise in some by nature and in others, as in those who have been the victims of lust from childhood, from habit.

Now those in whom nature is the cause of such a state no one would call incontinent, any more than one would apply the epithet to women because of the passive part they play in copulation; nor would one apply it to those who are in a morbid condition as a result of habit. To have these various types of habit is beyond the limits of vice, as brutishness is too; for a man who has them to 1149a
master or be mastered by them is not simple ⟨continence

[1] Answering to (2 *c*).
[2] Sc. and the bull. But cf. 1149a 14.
[3] Answering to (2 *a*).
[4] Answering to (2 *b*). Omit ἢ in l. 27, with Kb.

or) incontinence but that which is so by analogy, as the man who is in this condition in respect of fits of anger is to be called incontinent in respect of that feeling, but not incontinent simply.

For every excessive state whether of folly, of cowardice, of self-indulgence, or of bad temper, is either brutish or morbid; the man who is by nature apt to fear everything, even the squeak of a mouse, is cowardly with a brutish cowardice, while the man who feared a weasel did so in consequence of disease; and of foolish people those who by nature are thoughtless and live by their senses alone are brutish, like some races of the distant barbarians, while those who are so as a result of disease (e.g. of epilepsy) or of madness are morbid. Of these characteristics it is possible to have some only at times, and not to be mastered by them, e.g. Phalaris may have restrained a desire to eat the flesh of a child or an appetite for unnatural sexual pleasure; but it is also possible to be mastered, not merely to have the feelings. Thus, as the wickedness which is on the human level is called wickedness simply, while that which is not is called wickedness not simply but with the qualification 'brutish' or 'morbid', in the same way it is plain that some incontinence is brutish and some morbid, while only that which corresponds to *human* self-indulgence is incontinence simply.

That incontinence and continence, then, are concerned only with the same objects as self-indulgence and temperance and that what is concerned with other objects is a type distinct from incontinence, and called incontinence by a metaphor and not simply, is plain.

That incontinence in respect of anger is less disgraceful 6
than that in respect of the appetites is what we will now proceed to see. (1) Anger seems to listen to argument to some extent, but to mishear it, as do hasty servants who run out before they have heard the whole of what one says, and then muddle the order, or as dogs bark if there is but a knock at the door, before looking to see if it is a friend; so anger by reason of the warmth and hastiness of its

nature, though it hears, does not hear an order, and springs to take revenge. For argument or imagination informs us that we have been insulted or slighted, and anger, reasoning as it were that anything like this must be fought against, boils up straightway; while appetite, if argument or perception merely says that an object is pleasant, springs to
the enjoyment of it. Therefore anger obeys the argument 1149b
in a sense, but appetite does not. It is therefore more disgraceful; for the man who is incontinent in respect of anger is in a sense conquered by argument, while the other is conquered by appetite and not by argument.

(2) Further, we pardon people more easily for following natural desires, since we pardon them more easily for following such appetites as are common to all men, and in so far as they are common; now anger and bad temper are more natural than the appetites for excess, i. e. for unnecessary objects. Take for instance the man who defended himself on the charge of striking his father by saying 'yes, but *he* struck *his* father, and *he* struck *his*, and' (pointing to his child) 'this boy will strike *me* when he is a man; it runs in the family'; or the man who when he was being dragged along by his son bade him stop at the doorway, since he himself had dragged his father only as far as that.

(3) Further, those who are more given to plotting against others are more criminal. Now a passionate man is not given to plotting, nor is anger itself—it is open; but the nature of appetite is illustrated by what the poets call Aphrodite, 'guile-weaving daughter of Cyprus',[1] and by Homer's words about her 'embroidered girdle':

> And the whisper of wooing is there,
> Whose subtlety stealeth the wits of the wise, how prudent soe'er.[2]

Therefore if this form of incontinence is more criminal and disgraceful than that in respect of anger, it is both incontinence without qualification and in a sense vice.

(4) Further, no one commits wanton outrage with a feeling of pain, but every one who acts in anger acts with

[1] Author unknown.

[2] *Il.* xiv. 214, 217.

pain, while the man who commits outrage acts with pleasure. If, then, those acts at which it is most just to be angry are more criminal than others, the incontinence which is due to appetite is the more criminal; for there is no wanton outrage involved in anger.

Plainly, then, the incontinence concerned with appetite is more disgraceful than that concerned with anger, and continence and incontinence are concerned with bodily appetites and pleasures; but we must grasp the differences among the latter themselves. For, as has been said at the beginning,[1] some are human and natural both in kind and in magnitude, others are brutish, and others are due to organic injuries and diseases. Only with the first of these are temperance and self-indulgence concerned; this is why we call the lower animals neither temperate nor self-indulgent except by a metaphor, and only if some one[2] race of animals exceeds another as a whole in wantonness, destructiveness, and omnivorous greed; these have no power of choice or calculation, but they *are* departures from the natural norm,[3]
1150a as, among men, madmen are. Now brutishness is a less evil than vice, though more alarming; for it is not that the better part has been perverted, as in man,—they *have* no better part. Thus it is like comparing a lifeless thing with a living in respect of badness; for the badness of that which has no originative source of movement is always less hurtful, and reason is an originative source. Thus it is like comparing injustice in the abstract with an unjust man. Each is in some sense worse; for a bad man will do ten thousand times as much evil as a brute.[4]

[1] 1148b 15–31. [2] Reading τι in l. 32 as suggested by Bywater.

[3] And therefore cannot be called self-indulgent properly, but *can* be so called by a metaphor.

[4] The comparison between the badness of a brute and that of a bad man is illustrated (1) by a comparison between the badness of a lifeless and that of a living thing; a living thing can do more harm than a lifeless because it has in ψυχή an ἀρχὴ κινήσεως which the other has not; and a man can do more harm than a brute because he has in νοῦς an ἀρχὴ κινήσεως which the brute has not; (2) by a comparison between injustice in the abstract and an unjust man; injustice is in a sense worse—more terrible—because it is what makes the unjust man unjust, and in a sense less bad because it cannot operate except as realized in an unjust man; and a brute is more alarming than a bad man, but (owing to its lack of νοῦς) does much less harm. The

7 With regard to the pleasures and pains and appetites and aversions arising through touch and taste, to which both self-indulgence and temperance were formerly narrowed down,[1] it is possible to be in such a state as to be defeated even by those of them which most people master, or to master even those by which most people are defeated; among these possibilities, those relating to pleasures are incontinence and continence, those relating to pains softness and endurance. The state of most people is intermediate, even if they lean more towards the worse states.

Now, since some pleasures are necessary while others are not, and are necessary up to a point while the excesses of them are not, nor the deficiencies, and this is equally true of appetites and pains, the man who pursues the excesses of things pleasant, or pursues to excess necessary objects, and[2] does so by choice, for their own sake and not at all for the sake of any result distinct from them, is self-indulgent; for such a man is of necessity unlikely to repent, and therefore incurable, since a man who cannot repent cannot be cured.[3] The man who is deficient in his pursuit of them is the opposite of self-indulgent; the man who is intermediate is temperate. Similarly, there is the man who avoids bodily pains not because he is defeated by them but by choice. (Of those who do not *choose* such acts, one kind of man is led to them as a result of the pleasure involved, another because he avoids the pain arising from the appetite, so that these types differ from one another. Now any one would think worse of a man if with no appetite or with weak appetite he were to do something disgraceful, than if he did it under the influence of powerful appetite, and worse of him if he struck a blow not in anger than if he did it in anger; for what would he have done if he *had* been strongly affected? This is why the self-indulgent man is worse than the incontinent.) Of the states named, then,[4] the latter

second illustration is very far-fetched, and corruption may be suspected in l. 6.

[1] III. 10.

[2] Reading ἢ καθ' ὑπερβολὴν καί, with M^b and Aspasius, in ll. 19, 20.

[3] *ἀνάγκη . . . ἀνίατος* ll. 21–22 is a note to defend the use of the word ὁλαστος, lit. incorrigible.

[4] In ll. 19–25.

is rather a kind of softness;[1] the former is self-indulgence. While to the incontinent man is opposed the continent, to the soft is opposed the man of endurance; for endurance consists in resisting, while continence consists in conquering, and resisting and conquering are different, as not being beaten is different from winning; this is why continence
1150b is also more worthy of choice than endurance. Now the man who is defective in respect of resistance to the things which most men both resist and resist successfully is soft and effeminate; for effeminacy too is a kind of softness; such a man trails his cloak to avoid the pain of lifting it, and plays the invalid without thinking himself wretched, though the man he imitates is a wretched man.

The case is similar with regard to continence and incontinence. For if a man is defeated by violent and excessive pleasures or pains, there is nothing wonderful in that; indeed we are ready to pardon him if he has resisted, as Theodectes' Philoctetes does when bitten by the snake,[2] or Carcinus' Cercyon in the *Alope*,[3] and as people who try to restrain their laughter burst out in a guffaw, as happened to Xenophantus.[4] But it is surprising if a man is defeated by and cannot resist pleasures or pains which most men can hold out against, when this is not due to heredity or disease, like the softness that is hereditary with the kings of the Scythians, or that which distinguishes the female sex from the male.

The lover of amusement, too, is thought to be self-indulgent, but is really soft. For amusement is a relaxation, since it is a rest from work; and the lover of amusement is one of the people who go to excess in this.

Of incontinence one kind is impetuosity, another weakness. For some men after deliberating fail, owing to their emotion, to stand by the conclusions of their deliberation, others because they have not deliberated are led by their emotion; since some men (just as people who first tickle others are not tickled themselves), if they have first per-

[1] Not softness proper, which is non-deliberate avoidance of pain (ll. 13–15).

[2] Cf. Nauck[2], p. 803.

[3] Cf. ib. p. 797.

[4] Apparently a musician at Alexander's court.

ceived and seen what is coming and have first roused themselves and their calculative faculty, are not defeated by their emotion, whether it be pleasant or painful. It is keen and excitable people that suffer especially from the impetuous form of incontinence; for the former by reason of their quickness and the latter by reason of the violence of their passions do not await the argument, because they are apt to follow their imagination.

8 The self-indulgent man, as was said,[1] is not apt to repent; for he stands by his choice; but any incontinent man is likely to repent. This is why the position is not as it was expressed in the formulation of the problem,[2] but the self-indulgent man is incurable and the incontinent man curable; for wickedness is like a disease such as dropsy or consumption, while incontinence is like epilepsy; the former is a permanent, the latter an intermittent badness. And generally incontinence and vice are different in kind; vice is unconscious of itself, incontinence is not (of incontinent men themselves, **1151a**
those who become temporarily beside themselves are better than those who have the rational principle but do not abide by it, since the latter are defeated by a weaker passion, and do not act without previous deliberation like the others); for the incontinent man is like the people who get drunk quickly and on little wine,[3] i. e. on less than most people.

Evidently, then, incontinence is not vice (though perhaps it is so in a qualified sense); for incontinence is contrary to choice while vice is in accordance with choice; not but what they are similar in respect of the actions they lead to; as in the saying of Demodocus about the Milesians, 'the Milesians are not without sense, but they do the things that senseless people do', so too incontinent people are not criminal, but they will do criminal acts.

Now, since the incontinent man is apt to pursue, not on conviction, bodily pleasures that are excessive and contrary to the right rule, while the self-indulgent man is convinced because he is the sort of man to pursue them, it is on the

[1] a 21. [2] 1146a 31–b 2.

[3] To get a proper sense for this clause it seems necessary to treat ll. 1–3 as parenthetical.

contrary the former that is easily persuaded to change his mind, while the latter is not. For virtue andvice respectively preserve and destroy the first principle, and in actions the final cause is the first principle, as the hypotheses [1] are in mathematics; neither in that case is it argument that teaches the first principles, nor is it so here—virtue either natural or produced by habituation is what teaches right opinion about the first principle. Such a man as this, then, is temperate; his contrary is the self-indulgent.

But there is a sort of man who is carried away as a result of passion and contrary to the right rule—a man whom passion masters so that he does not act according to the right rule, but does not master to the extent of making him ready to believe that he ought to pursue such pleasures without reserve; this is the incontinent man, who is better than the self-indulgent man, and not bad without qualification; for the best thing in him, the first principle, is preserved. And contrary to him is another kind of man, he who abides by his convictions and is not carried away, at least as a result of passion. It is evident from these considerations that the latter is a good state and the former a bad one.

Is the man continent who abides by any and every rule 9
and any and every choice, or the man who abides by the right choice, and is he incontinent who abandons any and every choice and any and every rule, or he who abandons the rule that is not false and the choice that is right; this is how we put it before in our statement of the problem.[2] Or is it incidentally any and every choice but *per se* the true rule and the right choice by which the one abides and the other does not? If any one chooses or pursues this for the sake
1151b of that, *per se* he pursues and chooses the latter, but incidentally the former. But when we speak without qualification we mean what is *per se*. Therefore in a sense the one abides by, and the other abandons, any and every opinion; but without qualification, the true opinion.

There are some who are apt to abide by their opinion,

[1] i.e. the assumptions of the existence of the primary objects of mathematics, such as the straight line or the unit.

[2] 1146a 16–31.

who are called strong-headed, viz. those who are hard to persuade in the first instance and are not easily persuaded to change; these have in them something like the continent man, as the prodigal is in a way like the liberal man and the rash man like the confident man; but they are different in many respects. For it is to passion and appetite that the one will not yield, since on occasion the continent man *will* be easy to persuade; but it is to argument that the others refuse to yield, for they do form appetites and many of them are led by their pleasures. Now the people who are strong-headed are the opinionated, the ignorant, and the boorish—the opinionated being influenced by pleasure and pain; for they delight in the victory they gain if they are not persuaded to change, and are pained if their decisions become null and void as decrees sometimes do; so that they are liker the incontinent than the continent man.

But there are some who fail to abide by their resolutions, not as a result of incontinence, e.g. Neoptolemus in Sophocles' *Philoctetes*;[1] yet it was for the sake of pleasure that he did not stand fast—but a noble pleasure; for telling the truth was noble to him, but he had been persuaded by Odysseus to tell the lie. For not every one who does anything for the sake of pleasure is either self-indulgent or bad or incontinent, but he who does it for a disgraceful pleasure.

Since there is also a sort of man who takes less delight than he should in bodily things, and does not abide by the rule, he who is intermediate between him and the incontinent man is the continent man; for the incontinent man fails to abide by the rule because he delights too much in them, and this man because he delights in them too little; while the continent man abides by the rule and does not change on either account. Now if continence is good, both the contrary states must be bad, as they actually appear to be; but because the other extreme is seen in few people and seldom, as temperance is thought to be contrary only to self-indulgence, so is continence to incontinence.

Since many names are applied analogically, it is by

[1] ll. 895–916.

analogy that we have come to speak of the 'continence' of the temperate man; for both the continent man and the temperate man are such as to do nothing contrary to the
1152ª rule for the sake of the bodily pleasures, but the former has and the latter has not bad appetites, and the latter is such as not to feel pleasure contrary to the rule, while the former is such as to feel pleasure but not to be led by it. And the incontinent and the self-indulgent man are also like another; they are different, but both pursue bodily pleasures—the latter, however, also thinking that he ought to do so, while the former does not think this.

Nor can the same man have practical wisdom and be **10**
incontinent; for it has been shown[1] that a man is at the same time practically wise, and good in respect of character. Further, a man has practical wisdom not by knowing only but by being able to act; but the incontinent man is unable to act—there is, however, nothing to prevent a *clever* man from being incontinent; this is why it is sometimes actually thought that some people have practical wisdom but are incontinent, viz. because cleverness and practical wisdom differ in the way we have described in our first discussions,[2] and are near together in respect of their reasoning, but differ in respect of their purpose—nor yet is the incontinent man like the man who knows and is contemplating a truth, but like the man who is asleep or drunk. And he acts willingly (for he acts in a sense with knowledge both of what he does and of the end to which he does it), but is not wicked, since his purpose is good; so that he is half-wicked. And he is not a criminal; for he does not act of malice aforethought; of the two types of incontinent man the one does not abide by the conclusions of his deliberation, while the excitable man does not deliberate at all. And thus the incontinent man is like a city which passes all the right decrees and has good laws, but makes no use of them, as in Anaxandrides' jesting remark,[3]

'The city willed it, that cares nought for laws';

[1] 1144ª 11–ᵇ 32.

[2] 1144ª 23–ᵇ 4.

[3] Fr. 67 Kock.

but the wicked man is like a city that uses its laws, but has wicked laws to use.

Now incontinence and continence are concerned with that which is in excess of the state characteristic of most men; for the continent man abides by his resolutions more and the incontinent man less than most men can.

Of the forms of incontinence, that of excitable people is more curable than that of those who deliberate but do not abide by their decisions, and those who are incontinent through habituation are more curable than those in whom incontinence is innate; for it is easier to change a habit than to change one's nature; even habit is hard to change just because it is like nature, as Evenus says:[1]

> I say that habit 's but long practice, friend,
> And this becomes men's nature in the end.

We have now stated what continence, incontinence, endurance, and softness are, and how these states are related to each other.

11 The study of pleasure and pain belongs to the province 1152b
of the political philosopher; for he is the architect of the end, with a view to which we call one thing bad and another good without qualification. Further, it is one of our necessary tasks to consider them; for not only did we lay it down that moral virtue and vice are concerned with pains and pleasures,[2] but most people say that happiness involves pleasure; this is why the blessed man is called by a name derived from a word meaning enjoyment.[3]

Now (1) some people think that no pleasure is a good, either in itself or incidentally, since the good and pleasure are not the same; (2) others think that some pleasures are good but that most are bad. (3) Again there is a third view, that even if all pleasures are goods, yet the best thing in the world cannot be pleasure. (1) The reasons given for the view that pleasure is not a good at all are (*a*) that every pleasure is a perceptible process to a natural state, and that no process is of the same kind as its end, e.g. no process

[1] Fr. 9 Diehl. [2] 1104b 8–1105a 13.
[3] μακάριος from μάλα χαίρειν!

of building of the same kind as a house. (*b*) A temperate man avoids pleasures. (*c*) A man of practical wisdom pursues what is free from pain, not what is pleasant. (*d*) The pleasures are a hindrance to thought, and the more so the more one delights in them, e.g. in sexual pleasure; for no one could think of anything while absorbed in this. (*e*) There is no art of pleasure; but every good is the product of some art. (*f*) Children and the brutes pursue pleasures. (2) The reasons for the view that not all pleasures are good are that (*a*) there are pleasures that are actually base and objects of reproach, and (*b*) there are harmful pleasures; for some pleasant things are unhealthy. (3) The reason for the view that the best thing in the world is not pleasure is that pleasure is not an end but a process.

These are pretty much the things that are said. That it 12
does not follow from these grounds that pleasure is not a good, or even the chief good, is plain from the following considerations. (A)[1] (*a*) First, since that which is good may be so in either of two senses (one thing good simply and another good for a particular person), natural constitutions and states of being, and therefore also the corresponding movements and processes, will be correspondingly divisible. Of those which are thought to be bad some will be bad if taken without qualification but not bad for a particular person, but worthy of his choice, and some will not be worthy of choice even for a particular person, but only at a particular time and for a short period, though not without qualification; while others are not even pleasures, but seem to be so, viz. all those which involve pain and whose end is curative, e.g. the processes that go on in sick persons.

(*b*) Further, one kind of good being activity and another being state, the processes that restore us to our natural state are only incidentally pleasant; for that matter the activity at work in the appetites for them is the activity of so much of our state and nature as has remained unimpaired; for there are actually pleasures that involve *no*

[1] (A) is the answer to (1 *a*) and (3).

pain or appetite (e.g. those of contemplation), the nature in 1153a such a case not being defective at all. That the others are incidental is indicated by the fact that men do not enjoy the same pleasant objects when their nature is in its settled state as they do when it is being replenished, but in the former case they enjoy the things that are pleasant without qualification, in the latter the contraries of these as well; for then they enjoy even sharp and bitter things, none of which is pleasant either by nature or without qualification. The states they produce, therefore, are not pleasures naturally or without qualification; for as pleasant things differ, so do the pleasures arising from them.

(*c*) Again, it is not necessary that there should be something else better than pleasure, as some say the end is better than the process; for pleasures are not processes nor do they all involve process—they are activities and ends; nor do they arise when we are becoming something, but when we are exercising some faculty; and not all pleasures have an end different from themselves, but only the pleasures of persons who are being led to the perfecting of their nature. This is why it is not right to say that pleasure is perceptible process, but it should rather be called activity of the natural state, and instead of 'perceptible' 'unimpeded'. It is thought by *some* people to be process just because they think it is in the strict sense *good*; for they think that activity is process, which it is not.

(B)[1] The view that pleasures are bad because some pleasant things are unhealthy is like saying that healthy things are bad because some healthy things are bad for money-making; both are bad in the respect mentioned, but they are not *bad* for *that* reason—indeed, thinking itself is sometimes injurious to health.

Neither practical wisdom nor any state of being is impeded by the pleasure arising from it; it is foreign pleasures that impede, for the pleasures arising from thinking and learning will make us think and learn all the more.

(C)[2] The fact that no pleasure is the product of any art

[1] Answer to (2 *b*) and (1 *d*).

[2] Answer to (1 *e*).

arises naturally enough; there is no art of any other activity either, but only of the corresponding faculty; though for that matter the arts of the perfumer and the cook *are* thought to be arts of pleasure.

(D)[1] The arguments based on the grounds that the temperate man avoids pleasure and that the man of practical wisdom pursues the painless life, and that children and the brutes pursue pleasure, are all refuted by the same consideration. We have pointed out[2] in what sense pleasures are good without qualification and in what sense some are not good; now both the brutes and children pursue pleasures of the latter kind (and the man of practical wisdom pursues tranquil freedom from that kind), viz. those which imply appetite and pain, i. e. the bodily pleasures (for it is these that are of this nature) and the excesses of them, in respect of which the self-indulgent man is self-indulgent. This is why the temperate man avoids these pleasures; for even he *has* pleasures of his own.

1153b But further (E) it is agreed that pain is bad and to be 13
avoided; for some pain is without qualification bad, and other pain is bad because it is in some respect an impediment to us. Now the contrary of that which is to be avoided, *qua* something to be avoided and bad, is good. Pleasure, then, is necessarily a good. For the answer of Speusippus, that pleasure is contrary both to pain and to good, as the greater is contrary both to the less and to the equal, is not successful; since he would not say that pleasure is essentially just a species of evil.

And (F)[3] if certain pleasures are bad, that does not prevent the chief good from being some pleasure, just as the chief good may be some form of knowledge though certain kinds of knowledge are bad. Perhaps it is even necessary, if each disposition has unimpeded activities, that, whether the activity (if unimpeded) of all our dispositions or that of some one of them is happiness, this should be the thing most worthy of our choice; and this activity is pleasure.

[1] Answer to (1 *b*), (1 *c*), (1 *f*).
[2] 1152b 26–1153a 7.
[3] Answer to (2 *a*).

Thus the chief good would be some pleasure, though most pleasures might perhaps be bad without qualification. And for this reason all men think that the happy life is pleasant and weave pleasure into their ideal of happiness—and reasonably too; for no activity is perfect when it is impeded, and happiness is a perfect thing; this is why the happy man needs the goods of the body and external goods, i. e. those of fortune, viz. in order that he may not be impeded in these ways. Those who say that the victim on the rack or the man who falls into great misfortunes is happy if he is good, are, whether they mean to or not, talking nonsense. Now because we need fortune as well as other things, some people think good fortune the same thing as happiness; but it is not that, for even good fortune itself when in excess is an impediment, and perhaps should then be no longer called good fortune; for its limit is fixed by reference to happiness.

And indeed the fact that all things, both brutes and men, pursue pleasure is an indication of its being somehow the chief good:

> No voice is wholly lost that many peoples[1]. . .

But since no one nature or state either is or is thought the best for all, neither do all pursue the same pleasure; yet all pursue pleasure. And perhaps they actually pursue not the pleasure they think they pursue nor that which they would say they pursue, but the same pleasure; for all things have by nature something divine in them. But the bodily pleasures have appropriated the name both because we oftenest steer our course for them and because all men share in them; thus because they alone are familiar, men think there are no others.

It is evident also that if pleasure, i. e. the activity of our 1154a
faculties, is not a good, it will not be the case that the happy man lives a pleasant life; for to what end should he need pleasure, if it is not a good but the happy man may even live a painful life? For pain is neither an evil nor a good, if pleasure is not; why then should he avoid it?

[1] Hes. *Op.* 763.

Therefore, too, the life of the good man will not be pleasanter than that of any one else, if his activities are not more pleasant.

(G)[1] With regard to the bodily pleasures, those who say 14
that *some* pleasures are very much to be chosen, viz. the noble pleasures, but not the bodily pleasures, i. e. those with which the self-indulgent man is concerned, must consider why,[2] then, the contrary pains are bad. For the contrary of bad is good. Are the necessary pleasures good in the sense in which even that which is not bad is good? Or are they good up to a point? Is it that where you have states and processes of which there cannot be too much, there cannot be too much of the corresponding pleasure, and that where there can be too much of the one there can be too much of the other also? Now there can be too much of bodily goods, and the bad man is bad by virtue of pursuing the excess, not by virtue of pursuing the necessary pleasures (for *all* men enjoy in some way or other both dainty foods and wines and sexual intercourse, but not all men do so as they ought). The contrary is the case with pain; for he does not avoid the excess of it, he avoids it altogether; and this is peculiar to him, for the alternative to excess of pleasure is not pain, except to the man who pursues this excess.[3]

Since we should state not only the truth, but also the cause of error—for this contributes towards producing conviction, since when a reasonable explanation is given of why the false view appears true, this tends to produce belief in the true view—therefore we must state why the bodily pleasures appear the more worthy of choice. (*a*) Firstly, then, it is because they expel pain; owing to the excesses of pain that men experience, they pursue excessive and in general bodily pleasure as being a cure for the pain. Now curative agencies produce intense feeling—which is the

[1] Answer to (2).
[2] Reading a comma after ἀκόλαστος in l. 10.
[3] I have expanded this sentence slightly to bring out the rather obscure connexion of thought. To the voluptuary, and to him alone, pain and violent bodily pleasure appear exhaustive alternatives, and because he always pursues the latter he always shuns the former.

reason why they are pursued—because they show up against the contrary pain. (Indeed pleasure is thought not to be good for these two reasons, as has been said,[1] viz. that (α) some of them are activities belonging to a bad nature—either congenital, as in the case of a brute, or due to habit, i. e. those of bad men; while (β) others are meant to cure a defective nature, and it is better to be in a healthy state than to be getting into it, but these arise during the 1154b process of being made perfect and are therefore only incidentally good.) (*b*) Further, they are pursued because of their violence by those who cannot enjoy other pleasures. (At all events they go out of their way to manufacture thirsts somehow for themselves. When these are harmless, the practice is irreproachable; when they are hurtful, it is bad.) For they have nothing else to enjoy, and, besides, a neutral state is painful to many people because of their nature. For the animal nature is always in travail, as the students of natural science also testify, saying that sight and hearing are painful; but we have become used to this, as they maintain. Similarly, while, in youth, people are, owing to the growth that is going on, in a situation like that of drunken men, and youth is pleasant,[2] on the other hand people of excitable nature[3] always need relief; for even their body is ever in torment owing to its special composition, and they are always under the influence of violent desire; but pain is driven out both by the contrary pleasure, and by any chance pleasure if it be strong; and for these reasons they become self-indulgent and bad. But the pleasures that do not involve pains do not admit of excess; and these are among the things pleasant by nature and not incidentally. By things pleasant incidentally I mean those that act as cures (for because as a result people are cured, through some action of the part that remains healthy, for this reason the process is thought pleasant); by things naturally pleasant I mean those that stimulate the action of the healthy nature.

[1] 1152b 26–33.

[2] i. e. the growth or replenishment that is going on produces exhilaration and pleasure. Read a comma after νεότης.

[3] Lit., melancholic people, those characterized by an excess of black bile.

There is no one thing that is always pleasant, because our nature is not simple but there is another element in us as well, inasmuch as we are perishable creatures, so that if the one element does something, this is unnatural to the other nature, and when the two elements are evenly balanced, what is done seems neither painful nor pleasant; for if the nature of anything were simple, the same action would always be most pleasant to it. This is why God always enjoys a single and simple pleasure; for there is not only an activity of movement but an activity of immobility, and pleasure is found more in rest than in movement. But 'change in all things is sweet', as the poet says,[1] because of some vice; for as it is the vicious man that is changeable, so the nature that needs change is vicious; for it is not simple nor good.

We have now discussed continence and incontinence, and pleasure and pain, both what each is and in what sense some of them are good and others bad; it remains to speak of friendship.

[1] Eur. *Or.* 234.

BOOK VIII

1 AFTER what we have said, a discussion of friendship 1155a would naturally follow, since it is a virtue or implies virtue, and is besides most necessary with a view to living. For without friends no one would choose to live, though he had all other goods; even rich men and those in possession of office and of dominating power are thought to need friends most of all; for what is the use of such prosperity without the opportunity of beneficence, which is exercised chiefly and in its most laudable form towards friends? Or how can prosperity be guarded and preserved without friends? The greater it is, the more exposed is it to risk. And in poverty and in other misfortunes men think friends are the only refuge. It helps the young, too, to keep from error; it aids[1] older people by ministering to their needs and supplementing the activities that are failing from weakness; those in the prime of life it stimulates to noble actions—'two going together'[2]—for with friends men are more able both to think and to act. Again, parent seems by nature to feel it for offspring and offspring for parent, not only among men but among birds and among most animals; it is felt mutually by members of the same race, and especially by men, whence we praise lovers of their fellow-men. We may see even in our travels how near and dear every man is to every other. Friendship seems too to hold states together, and lawgivers to care more for it than for justice; for unanimity seems to be something like friendship, and this they aim at most of all, and expel faction as their worst enemy; and when men are friends they have no need of justice, while when they are just they need friendship as well, and the truest form of justice is thought to be a friendly quality.

But it is not only necessary but also noble; for we praise those who love their friends, and it is thought to be a fine

[1] Reading βοήθεια in l. 14 with M[b].

[2] *Il.* x. 224.

thing to have many friends; and again we think it is the same people that are good men and are friends.

Not a few things about friendship are matters of debate. Some define it as a kind of likeness and say like people are friends, whence come the sayings 'like to like',[1] 'birds of a feather flock together',[2] and so on; others on the
1155b contrary say 'two of a trade never agree'.[3] On this very question they inquire for deeper and more physical causes, Euripides saying that 'parched earth loves the rain, and stately heaven when filled with rain loves to fall to earth',[4] and Heraclitus that 'it is what opposes that helps' and 'from different tones comes the fairest tune' and 'all things are produced through strife';[5] while Empedocles, as well as others, expresses the opposite view that like aims at like.[6] The physical problems we may leave alone (for they do not belong to the present inquiry); let us examine those which are human and involve character and feeling, e.g. whether friendship can arise between any two people or people cannot be friends if they are wicked, and whether there is one species of friendship or more than one. Those who think there is only one because it admits of degrees have relied on an inadequate indication; for even things different in species admit of degree. We have discussed this matter previously.[7]

The kinds of friendship may perhaps be cleared up if 2
we first come to know the object of love. For not everything seems to be loved but only the lovable, and this is good, pleasant, or useful; but it would seem to be that by which some good or pleasure is produced that is useful, so that it is the good and the pleasant that are lovable as ends. Do men love, then, *the* good, or what is good for *them*? These sometimes clash. So too with regard to the pleasant. Now it is thought that each loves what is

[1] *Od.* xvii. 218.
[2] Lit. 'jackdaw to jackdaw'. The source is unknown.
[3] Lit. 'all such men (i.e. all those who resemble one another) are potters to one another', an allusion to Hes. *Op.* 25, καὶ κεραμεὺς κεραμεῖ κοτέει καὶ τέκτονι τέκτων.
[4] Fr. 898. 7–10 Nauck[2].
[5] Fr. 8 Diels.
[6] Fr. 22. 5, 62. 6, 90. 1–2 Diels.
[7] Place unknown.

good for himself, and that the good is without qualification lovable, and what is good for each man is lovable for him; but each man loves not what is good for him but what seems good. This however will make no difference; we shall just have to say that this is 'that which seems lovable'. Now there are three grounds on which people love; of the love of lifeless objects we do not use the word 'friendship'; for it is not mutual love, nor is there a wishing of good to the other (for it would surely be ridiculous to wish wine well; if one wishes anything for it, it is that it may keep, so that one may have it oneself); but to a friend we say we ought to wish what is good for his sake. But to those who thus wish good we ascribe only goodwill, if the wish is not reciprocated; goodwill when it *is* reciprocal being friendship. Or must we add 'when it is recognized'? For many people have goodwill to those whom they have not seen but judge to be good or useful; and one of these might return this feeling. These people seem to bear goodwill to each other; but how could one call them friends when they do not know their mutual feelings? To be friends, then, they must be mutually recognized as bearing goodwill and wishing well to each other for one of the aforesaid reasons.

3 Now these reasons differ from each other in kind; so, therefore, do the corresponding forms of love and friendship. There are therefore three kinds of friendship, equal in number to the things that are lovable; for with respect to each there is a mutual and recognized love, and those who love each other wish well to each other in that respect in which they love one another. Now those who love each other for their utility do not love each other for themselves but in virtue of some good which they get from each other. So too with those who love for the sake of pleasure; it is not for their character that men love ready-witted people, but because they find them pleasant. Therefore those who love for the sake of utility love for the sake of what is good for *themselves*, and those who love for the sake of pleasure do so for the sake of what is pleasant to *themselves*, and

not in so far as the other is the person loved [1] but in so far as he is useful or pleasant. And thus these friendships are only incidental; for it is not as being the man he is that the loved person is loved, but as providing some good or pleasure. Such friendships, then, are easily dissolved, if the parties do not remain like themselves; for if the one party is no longer pleasant or useful the other ceases to love him.

Now the useful is not permanent but is always changing. Thus when the motive of the friendship is done away, the friendship is dissolved, inasmuch as it existed only for the ends in question. This kind of friendship seems to exist chiefly between old people (for at that age people pursue not the pleasant but the useful) and, of those who are in their prime or young, between those who pursue utility. And such people do not live much with each other either; for sometimes they do not even find each other pleasant; therefore they do not need such companionship unless they are useful to each other; for they are pleasant to each other only in so far as they rouse in each other hopes of something good to come. Among such friendships people also class the friendship of host and guest. On the other hand the friendship of young people seems to aim at pleasure; for they live under the guidance of emotion, and pursue above all what is pleasant to themselves and what is immediately before them; but with increasing age their pleasures become different. This is why they quickly become friends and quickly cease to be so; their friendship changes with the object that is found pleasant, and such pleasure alters
1156b quickly. Young people are amorous too; for the greater part of the friendship of love depends on emotion and aims at pleasure; this is why they fall in love and quickly fall out of love, changing often within a single day. But these people do wish to spend their days and lives together; for it is thus that they attain the purpose of their friendship.

Perfect friendship is the friendship of men who are good, and alike in virtue; for these wish well alike to each other *qua* good, and they are good in themselves. Now those

[1] The MS. reading seems to be sufficiently supported by *E.E.* 1237b 1.

who wish well to their friends for their sake are most truly friends; for they do this by reason of their own nature and not incidentally; therefore their friendship lasts as long as they are good—and goodness is an enduring thing. And each is good without qualification and to his friend, for the good are both good without qualification and useful to each other. So too they are pleasant; for the good are pleasant both without qualification and to each other, since to each his own activities and others like them are pleasurable, and the actions of the good *are* the same or like. And such a friendship is as might be expected permanent, since there meet in it all the qualities that friends should have. For all friendship is for the sake of good or of pleasure—good or pleasure either in the abstract or such as will be enjoyed by him who has the friendly feeling—and is based on a certain resemblance; and to a friendship of good men all the qualities we have named belong in virtue of the nature of the friends themselves; for in the case of this kind of friendship the other qualities also[1] are alike in both friends, and that which is good without qualification is also without qualification pleasant, and these are the most lovable qualities. Love and friendship therefore are found most and in their best form between such men.

But it is natural that such friendships should be infrequent; for such men are rare. Further, such friendship requires time and familiarity; as the proverb says, men cannot know each other till they have 'eaten salt together'; nor can they admit each other to friendship or be friends till each has been found lovable and been trusted by each. Those who quickly show the marks of friendship to each other wish to be friends, but are not friends unless they both are lovable and know the fact; for a wish for friendship may arise quickly, but friendship does not.

4 This kind of friendship, then, is perfect both in respect of duration and in all other respects, and in it each gets from each in all respects the same as, or something like

[1] i. e. absolute pleasantness, relative goodness, and relative pleasantness, as well as absolute goodness.

what, he gives; which is what ought to happen between friends. Friendship for the sake of pleasure bears a resem-
1157a blance to this kind; for good people too *are* pleasant to each other. So too does friendship for the sake of utility; for the good are also useful to each other. Among men of these inferior sorts too, friendships are most permanent when the friends get the same thing from each other (e.g. pleasure), and not only that but also from the same source, as happens between ready-witted people, not as happens between lover and beloved. For these do not take pleasure in the same things, but the one in seeing the beloved and the other in receiving attentions from his lover; and when the bloom of youth is passing the friendship sometimes passes too (for the one finds no pleasure in the sight of the other, and the other gets no attentions from the first); but many lovers on the other hand are constant, if familiarity has led them to love each other's characters, these being alike. But those who exchange not pleasure but utility in their amour are both less truly friends and less constant. Those who are friends for the sake of utility part when the advantage is at an end; for they were lovers not of each other but of profit.

For the sake of pleasure or utility, then, even bad men may be friends of each other, or good men of bad, or one who is neither good nor bad may be a friend to any sort of person, but for their own sake clearly only good men can be friends; for bad men do not delight in each other unless some advantage come of the relation.

The friendship of the good too and this alone is proof against slander; for it is not easy to trust any one's talk about a man who has long been tested by oneself; and it is among good men that trust and the feeling that 'he would never wrong me' and all the other things that are demanded in true friendship are found. In the other kinds of friendship, however, there is nothing to prevent these evils arising.

For men apply the name of friends even to those whose motive is utility, in which sense states are said to be friendly (for the alliances of states seem to aim at advantage), and to those who love each other for the sake of pleasure, in which sense children are called friends. Therefore we too ought perhaps to call such people friends, and say that there are several kinds of friendship—firstly and in the proper sense that of good men *qua* good, and by analogy the other kinds; for it is in virtue of something good and something akin to what is found in true friendship that they are friends, since even the pleasant is good for the lovers of pleasure. But these two kinds of friendship are not often united, nor do the same people become friends for the sake of utility and of pleasure; for things that are only incidentally connected are not often coupled together.

Friendship being divided into these kinds, bad men will 1157[b]
be friends for the sake of pleasure or of utility, being in this respect like each other, but good men will be friends for their own sake, i. e. in virtue of their goodness. These, then, are friends without qualification; the others are friends incidentally and through a resemblance to these.

5 As in regard to the virtues some men are called good in respect of a state of character, others in respect of an activity, so too in the case of friendship; for those who live together delight in each other and confer benefits on each other, but those who are asleep or locally separated are not performing, but are disposed to perform, the activities of friendship; distance does not break off the friendship absolutely, but only the activity of it. But if the absence is lasting, it seems actually to make men forget their friendship; hence the saying 'out of sight, out of mind'.[1] Neither old people nor sour people seem to make friends easily; for there is little that is pleasant in them, and no one can spend his days with one whose company is painful, or not pleasant, since nature seems above all to avoid the painful and to aim at the pleasant. Those, however, who approve of each other but do not live together seem to be well-disposed rather than actual friends. For there is nothing so characteristic of friends as living together

[1] Lit. 'many a friendship has lack of converse broken'. The source is unknown.

(since while it is people who are in need that desire benefits, even those who are supremely happy desire to spend their days together; for solitude suits such people least of all); but people cannot live together if they are not pleasant and do not enjoy the same things, as friends who are companions seem to do.

The truest friendship, then, is that of the good, as we have frequently said;[1] for that which is without qualification good or pleasant seems to be lovable and desirable, and for each person that which is good or pleasant to him; and the good man is lovable and desirable to the good man for both these reasons. Now it looks as if love were a feeling, friendship a state of character; for love may be felt just as much towards lifeless things, but mutual love involves choice and choice springs from a state of character; and men wish well to those whom they love, for their sake, not as a result of feeling but as a result of a state of character. And in loving a friend men love what is good for themselves; for the good man in becoming a friend becomes a good to his friend. Each, then, both loves what is good for himself, and makes an equal return in goodwill and in pleasantness; for friendship is said to be equality, and both of these are found most in the friendship of the good.

1158a Between sour and elderly people friendship arises less 6
readily, inasmuch as they are less good-tempered and enjoy companionship less; for these are thought to be the greatest marks of friendship and most productive of it. This is why, while young men become friends quickly, old men do not; it is because men do not become friends with those in whom they do not delight; and similarly sour people do not quickly make friends either. But such men may bear goodwill to each other; for they wish one another well and aid one another in need; but they are hardly *friends* because they do not spend their days together nor delight in each other, and these are thought the greatest marks of friendship.

One cannot be a friend to many people in the sense of

[1] 1156b 7, 23, 33, 1157a 30, b 4.

having friendship of the perfect type with them, just as one cannot be in love with many people at once (for love is a sort of excess of feeling, and it is the nature of such only to be felt towards one person); and it is not easy for many people at the same time to please the same person very greatly, or perhaps even to be good in his eyes. One must, too, acquire some experience of the other person and become familiar with him, and that is very hard. But with a view to utility or pleasure it is possible that many people should please one; for many people are useful or pleasant, and these services take little time.

Of these two kinds that which is for the sake of pleasure is the more like friendship, when both parties get the same things from each other and delight in each other or in the same things, as in the friendships of the young; for generosity is more found in such friendships. Friendship based on utility is for the commercially minded. People who are supremely happy, too, have no need of useful friends, but do need pleasant friends; for they wish to live with *some one* and, though they can endure for a short time what is painful, no one could put up with it continuously, nor even with the Good itself if it were painful to him; this is why they look out for friends who are pleasant. Perhaps they should look out for friends who, being pleasant, are also good, and good for them too; for so they will have all the characteristics that friends should have.

People in positions of authority seem to have friends who fall into distinct classes; some people are useful to them and others are pleasant, but the same people are rarely both; for they seek neither those whose pleasantness is accompanied by virtue nor those whose utility is with a view to noble objects, but in their desire for pleasure they seek for ready-witted people, and their other friends they choose as being clever at doing what they are told, and these characteristics are rarely combined. Now we have said that the *good* man *is* at the same time pleasant and useful;[1] but such a man does not become the friend of one who surpasses him in station, unless he is surpassed also in

[1] 1156b 13-15, 1157a 1-3.

virtue; if this is not so, he does not establish equality by being proportionally exceeded in both respects. But people who surpass him in both respects are not so easy to find.

1158b However that may be, the aforesaid friendships involve equality; for the friends get the same things from one another and wish the same things for one another, or exchange one thing for another, e.g. pleasure for utility; we have said,[1] however, that they are both less truly friendships and less permanent. But it is from their likeness and their unlikeness to the same thing that they are thought both to be and not to be friendships. It is by their likeness to the friendship of virtue that they seem to be friendships (for one of them involves pleasure and the other utility, and these characteristics belong to the friendship of virtue as well); while it is because the friendship of virtue is proof against slander and permanent, while these quickly change (besides differing from the former in many other respects), that they appear *not* to be friendships; i.e. it is because of their unlikeness to the friendship of virtue.

But there is another kind of friendship, viz. that which 7
involves an inequality between the parties, e.g. that of father to son and in general of elder to younger, that of man to wife and in general that of ruler to subject. And these friendships differ also from each other; for it is not the same that exists between parents and children and between rulers and subjects, nor is even that of father to son the same as that of son to father, nor that of husband to wife the same as that of wife to husband. For the virtue and the function of each of these is different, and so are the reasons for which they love; the love and the friendship are therefore different also. Each party, then, neither gets the same from the other, nor ought to seek it; but when children render to parents what they ought to render to those who brought them into the world, and parents render what they should to their children, the friendship of such persons will be abiding and excellent.

[1] 1156a 16–24, 1157a 20–33.

In all friendships implying inequality the love also should be proportional, i. e. the better should be more loved than he loves, and so should the more useful, and similarly in each of the other cases; for when the love is in proportion to the merit of the parties, then in a sense arises equality, which is certainly held to be characteristic of friendship.

But equality does not seem to take the same form in acts of justice and in friendship; for in acts of justice what is equal in the primary sense is that which is in proportion to merit, while quantitative equality is secondary, but in friendship quantitative equality is primary and proportion to merit secondary. This becomes clear if there is a great interval in respect of virtue or vice or wealth or anything else between the parties; for then they are no longer friends, and do not even expect to be so. And this is most manifest in the case of the gods; for they surpass us most decisively in all good things. But it is clear also in the case of kings; for with them, too, men who are much their 1159a
inferiors do not expect to be friends; nor do men of no account expect to be friends with the best or wisest men. In such cases it is not possible to define exactly up to what point friends can remain friends; for much can be taken away and friendship remain, but when one party is removed to a great distance, as God is, the possibility of friendship ceases. This is in fact the origin of the question whether friends really wish for their friends the greatest goods, e. g. that of being gods; since in that case their friends will no longer be friends to them, and therefore will not be good things for them (for friends *are* good things). The answer is that if we were right in saying that friend wishes good to friend for his sake,[1] his friend must remain the sort of being he is, whatever that may be; therefore it is for him only so long as he remains a man that he will wish the greatest goods. But perhaps not *all* the greatest goods; for it is for himself most of all that each man wishes what is good.

8 Most people seem, owing to ambition, to wish to be loved rather than to love; which is why most men love

[1] 1155b 31.

flattery; for the flatterer is a friend in an inferior position, or pretends to be such and to love more than he is loved; and being loved seems to be akin to being honoured, and this is what most people aim at. But it seems to be not for its own sake that people choose honour, but incidentally. For most people enjoy being honoured by those in positions of authority because of their hopes (for they think that if they want anything they will get it from them; and therefore they delight in honour as a token of favour to come); while those who desire honour from good men, and men who know, are aiming at confirming their own opinion of themselves; they delight in honour, therefore, because they believe in their own goodness on the strength of the judgement of those who speak about them. In being loved, on the other hand, people delight for its own sake; whence it would seem to be better than being honoured, and friendship to be desirable in itself. But it seems to lie in loving rather than in being loved, as is indicated by the delight mothers take in loving; for some mothers hand over their children to be brought up, and so long as they know their fate they love them and do not seek to be loved in return (if they cannot have both), but seem to be satisfied if they see them prospering; and they themselves love their children even if these owing to their ignorance give them nothing of a mother's due. Now since friendship depends more on loving, and it is those who love their friends that are praised, loving seems to be the characteristic virtue of friends, so that it is only those in whom this is found in due measure that are lasting friends, and only their friendship that endures.

1159b It is in this way more than any other that even unequals can be friends; they can be equalized. Now equality and likeness are friendship, and especially the likeness of those who are like in virtue; for being steadfast in themselves they hold fast to each other, and neither ask nor give base services, but (one may say) even prevent them; for it is characteristic of good men neither to go wrong themselves nor to let their friends do so. But wicked men have no steadfastness (for they do not remain even like to themselves), but become friends for a short time because they delight in each other's wickedness. Friends who are useful or pleasant last longer; i. e. as long as they provide each other with enjoyments or advantages. Friendship for utility's sake seems to be that which most easily exists between contraries, e.g. between poor and rich, between ignorant and learned; for what a man actually lacks he aims at, and one gives something else in return. But under this head, too, might bring lover and beloved, beautiful and ugly. This is why lovers sometimes seem ridiculous, when they demand to be loved as they love; if they are equally lovable their claim can perhaps be justified, but when they have nothing lovable about them it is ridiculous. Perhaps, however, contrary does not even aim at contrary by its own nature, but only incidentally, the desire being for what is intermediate; for that is what is good, e.g. it is good for the dry not to become wet[1] but to come to the intermediate state, and similarly with the hot and in all other cases. These subjects we may dismiss; for they are indeed somewhat foreign to our inquiry.

9 Friendship and justice seem, as we have said at the outset of our discussion,[2] to be concerned with the same objects and exhibited between the same persons. For in every community there is thought to be some form of justice, and friendship too; at least men address as friends their fellow-voyagers and fellow-soldiers, and so too those associated with them in any other kind of community. And the extent of their association is the extent of their friendship, as it is the extent to which justice exists between them. And the proverb 'what friends have is common property' expresses the truth; for friendship depends on community. Now brothers and comrades have all things in common, but the others to whom we have referred have definite things in common—some more things, others fewer; for of friendships, too, some are more and others less truly friendships. And the claims of justice differ too; the
duties of parents to children and those of brothers to 1160a

[1] Cf. 1155b 3.

[2] 1155a 22–28.

each other are not the same, nor those of comrades and those of fellow-citizens, and so, too, with the other kinds of friendship. There is a difference, therefore, also between the acts that are unjust towards each of these classes of associates, and the injustice increases by being exhibited towards those who are friends in a fuller sense; e.g. it is a more terrible thing to defraud a comrade than a fellow-citizen, more terrible not to help a brother than a stranger, and more terrible to wound a father than any one else. And the demands of justice also seem to increase with the intensity of the friendship, which implies that friendship and justice exist between the same persons and have an equal extension.

Now all forms of community are like parts of the political community; for men journey together with a view to some particular advantage, and to provide something that they need for the purposes of life; and it is for the sake of advantage that the political community too seems both to have come together originally and to endure, for this is what legislators aim at, and they call just that which is to the common advantage. Now the other communities aim at advantage bit by bit, e.g. sailors at what is advantageous on a voyage with a view to making money or something of the kind, fellow-soldiers at what is advantageous in war, whether it is wealth or victory or the taking of a city that they seek, and members of tribes and demes act similarly [Some communities seem to arise for the sake of pleasure, viz. religious guilds and social clubs; for these exist respectively for the sake of offering sacrifice and of companionship. But all these seem to fall under the political community; for it aims not at present advantage but at what is advantageous for life as a whole],[1] offering sacrifices and arranging gatherings for the purpose, and assigning honours to the gods, and providing pleasant relaxations for themselves. For the ancient sacrifices and gatherings seem to take place after the harvest as a sort of firstfruits, because it was at these seasons that people had most

[1] It seems best to treat ll. 19–23 as an insertion from an alternative version. So J. Cook Wilson in *Class. Rev.* xvi. (1902), 28.

leisure. All the communities, then, seem to be parts of the political community; and the particular kinds of friendship will correspond to the particular kinds of community.

10 There are three kinds of constitution, and an equal number of deviation-forms—perversions, as it were, of them. The constitutions are monarchy, aristocracy, and thirdly that which is based on a property qualification, which it seems appropriate to call timocratic, though most people are wont to call it polity. The best of these is monarchy, the worst timocracy. The deviation from monarchy is tyranny; for both are forms of one-man rule, but there is the greatest difference between them; the tyrant looks to his own advantage, the king to that of his subjects. For a man is not a king unless he is sufficient to himself and excels his subjects in all good things; and such a man needs nothing further; therefore he will not look to his own interests but to those of his subjects; for a king who is not like that would be a mere titular king. Now tyranny is the very contrary of this; the tyrant pursues his own good. And it is clearer in the case of tyranny that it is the worst deviation-form;[1] but it is the contrary of the best that is worst.[2] Monarchy passes over into tyranny; for tyranny is the evil form of one-man rule and the bad king becomes a tyrant. Aristocracy passes over into oligarchy by the badness of the rulers, who distribute contrary to equity what belongs to the city—all or most of the good things to themselves, and office always to the same people, paying most regard to wealth; thus the rulers are few and are bad men instead of the most worthy. Timocracy passes over into democracy; for these are coterminous, since it is the ideal even of timocracy to be the rule of the majority, and all who have the property qualification count as equal. Democracy is the least bad of the deviations; for in its case the form of constitution is but a slight deviation. These then are the changes to which constitutions are most subject; for these are the smallest and easiest transitions.

[1] Than it is that monarchy is the best genuine form (a 35).

[2] Therefore monarchy must be the best.

One may find resemblances to the constitutions and, as it were, patterns of them even in households. For the association of a father with his sons bears the form of monarchy, since the father cares for his children; and this is why Homer calls Zeus 'father';[1] it is the ideal of monarchy to be paternal rule. But among the Persians the rule of the father is tyrannical; they use their sons as slaves. Tyrannical too is the rule of a master over slaves; for it is the advantage of the master that is brought about in it. Now this seems to be a correct form of government, but the Persian type is perverted; for the modes of rule appropriate to different relations are diverse. The association of man and wife seems to be aristocratic; for the man rules in accordance with his worth, and in those matters in which a man should rule, but the matters that befit a woman he hands over to her. If the man rules in everything the relation passes over into oligarchy; for in doing so he is not acting in accordance with their respective worth, and not ruling in virtue of his superiority. Sometimes, however, women rule,
1161a because they are heiresses; so their rule is not in virtue of excellence but due to wealth and power, as in oligarchies. The association of brothers is like timocracy; for they are equal, except in so far as they differ in age; hence if they differ *much* in age, the friendship is no longer of the fraternal type. Democracy is found chiefly in masterless dwellings (for here every one is on an equality), and in those in which the ruler is weak and every one has licence to do as he pleases.

Each of the constitutions may be seen to involve friend- II
ship just in so far as it involves justice. The friendship between a king and his subjects depends on an excess of benefits conferred; for he confers benefits on his subjects if being a good man he cares for them with a view to their well-being, as a shepherd does for his sheep (whence Homer called Agamemnon 'shepherd of the peoples').[2] Such too is the friendship of a father, though this exceeds the other in the greatness of the benefits conferred; for he is responsible for the existence of his

[1] E.g. *Il.* i. 503.

[2] E.g. *Il.* ii. 243.

children, which is thought the greatest good, and for their nurture and upbringing. These things are ascribed to ancestors as well. Further, by nature a father tends to rule over his sons, ancestors over descendants, a king over his subjects. These friendships imply superiority of one party over the other, which is why ancestors are honoured. The justice therefore that exists between persons so related is not the same on both sides but is in every case proportioned to merit; for that is true of the friendship as well. The friendship of man and wife, again, is the same that is found in an aristocracy; for it is in accordance with virtue—the better gets more of what is good, and each gets what befits him; and so, too, with the justice in these relations. The friendship of brothers is like that of comrades; for they are equal and of like age, and such persons are for the most part like in their feelings and their character. Like this, too, is the friendship appropriate to timocratic government; for in such a constitution the ideal is for the citizens to be equal and fair; therefore rule is taken in turn, and on equal terms; and the friendship appropriate here will correspond.

But in the deviation-forms, as justice hardly exists, so too does friendship. It exists least in the worst form; in tyranny there is little or no friendship. For where there is nothing common to ruler and ruled, there is not friendship either, since there is not justice; e.g. between craftsman and tool, soul and body, master and slave; the latter in each case is benefited by that which uses it, but there is 1161b
no friendship nor justice towards lifeless things. But neither is there friendship towards a horse or an ox, nor to a slave *qua* slave. For there is nothing common to the two parties; the slave is a living tool and the tool a lifeless slave. *Qua* slave then, one cannot be friends with him. But *qua* man one can; for there seems to be some justice between any man and any other who can share in a system of law or be a party to an agreement; therefore there can also be friendship with him in so far as he is a man. Therefore while in tyrannies friendship and justice hardly exist, in democracies they exist more fully; for where the citizens are equal they have much in common.

Every form of friendship, then, involves association, as has been said.[1] One might, however, mark off from the rest both the friendship of kindred and that of comrades. Those of fellow-citizens, fellow-tribesmen, fellow-voyagers, and the like are more like mere friendships of association; for they seem to rest on a sort of compact. With them we might class the friendship of host and guest. 12

The friendship of kinsmen itself, while it seems to be of many kinds, appears to depend in every case on parental friendship; for parents love their children as being a part of themselves, and children their parents as being something originating from them. Now (1) parents know their offspring better than their children know that they are their children, and (2) the originator feels his offspring to be his own more than the offspring do their begetter; for the product belongs to the producer (e.g. a tooth or hair or anything else to him whose it is), but the producer does not belong to the product, or belongs in a less degree. And (3) the length of time produces the same result; parents love their children as soon as these are born, but children love their parents only after time has elapsed and they have acquired understanding or the power of discrimination by the senses. From these considerations it is also plain why mothers love more than fathers do. Parents, then, love their children as themselves (for their issue are by virtue of their separate existence a sort of other selves), while children love their parents as being born of them, and brothers love each other as being born of the same parents; for their identity with them makes them identical with each other (which is the reason why people talk of 'the same blood', 'the same stock', and so on). They are, therefore, in a sense the same thing, though in separate individuals. Two things that contribute greatly to friendship are a common upbringing and similarity of age; for 'two of an age take to each other',[2] and people brought up together tend to be comrades; whence the friendship of brothers is
1162a akin to that of comrades. And cousins and other kinsmen are bound up together by derivation from brothers, viz. by

[1] 1159b 29–32.

[2] Source unknown.

being derived from the same parents. They come to be closer together or farther apart by virtue of the nearness or distance of the original ancestor.

The friendship of children to parents, and of men to gods, is a relation to them as to something good and superior; for they have conferred the greatest benefits, since they are the causes of their being and of their nourishment, and of their education from their birth; and this kind of friendship possesses pleasantness and utility also, more than that of strangers, inasmuch as their life is lived more in common. The friendship of brothers has the characteristics found in that of comrades (and especially when these are good), and in general between people who are like each other, inasmuch as they belong more to each other and start with a love for each other from their very birth, and inasmuch as those born of the same parents and brought up together and similarly educated are more akin in character; and the test of time has been applied most fully and convincingly in their case.

Between other kinsmen friendly relations are found in due proportion. Between man and wife friendship seems to exist by nature; for man is naturally inclined to form couples—even more than to form cities, inasmuch as the household is earlier and more necessary than the city, and reproduction is more common to man with the animals. With the other animals the union extends only to this point, but human beings live together not only for the sake of reproduction but also for the various purposes of life; for from the start the functions are divided, and those of man and woman are different; so they help each other by throwing their peculiar gifts into the common stock. It is for these reasons that both utility and pleasure seem to be found in this kind of friendship. But this friendship may be based also on virtue, if the parties are good; for each has its own virtue and they will delight in the fact. And children seem to be a bond of union (which is the reason why childless people part more easily); for children are a good common to both and what is common holds them together.

How man and wife and in general friend and friend ought

mutually to behave seems to be the same question as how it is just for them to behave; for a man does not seem to have the same duties to a friend, a stranger, a comrade, and a schoolfellow.

There are three kinds of friendship, as we said at the 13
outset of our inquiry,[1] and in respect of each some are friends on an equality and others by virtue of a superiority (for not only can equally good men become friends but
1162[b] a better man can make friends with a worse, and similarly in friendships of pleasure or utility the friends may be equal or unequal in the benefits they confer). This being so, equals must effect the required equalization on a basis of equality in love and in all other respects, while unequals must render what is in proportion to their superiority or inferiority.

Complaints and reproaches arise either only or chiefly in the friendship of utility, and this is only to be expected. For those who are friends on the ground of virtue are anxious to do well by each other (since that is a mark of virtue and of friendship), and between men who are emulating each other in this there cannot be complaints or quarrels; no one is offended by a man who loves him and does well by him—if he is a person of nice feeling he takes his revenge by doing well by the other. And the man who excels the other in the services he renders will not complain of his friend, since he gets what he aims at; for each man desires what is good. Nor do complaints arise much even in friendships of pleasure; for both get at the same time what they desire, if they enjoy spending their time together; and even a man who complained of another for *not* affording him pleasure would seem ridiculous, since it is in his power not to spend his days with him.

But the friendship of utility is full of complaints; for as they use each other for their own interests they always want to get the better of the bargain, and think they have got less than they should, and blame their partners because they do not get all they 'want and deserve'; and those who do well by others cannot help them as much as those whom they benefit want.

[1] 1156[a] 7.

Now it seems that, as justice is of two kinds, one unwritten and the other legal, one kind of friendship of utility is moral and the other legal. And so complaints arise most of all when men do not dissolve the relation in the spirit of the same type of friendship in which they contracted it. The *legal* type is that which is on fixed terms; its purely commercial variety is on the basis of immediate payment, while the more liberal variety allows time but stipulates for a definite *quid pro quo*. In this variety the debt is clear and not ambiguous, but in the postponement it contains an element of friendliness; and so some states do not allow suits arising out of such agreements, but think men who have bargained on a basis of credit ought to accept the consequences. The *moral* type is not on fixed terms; it makes a gift, or does whatever it does, as to a friend; but one expects to receive as much or more, as having not given but lent; and if a man is worse off when the relation is dissolved than he was when it was contracted he will complain. This happens because all or most men, while they wish for what is noble, choose what is advantageous; now it is noble to do well by another without a view to repayment, but it is the receiving of benefits that is advantageous.

Therefore if we can we should return the equivalent of 1163a
what we have received (for we must not make a man our friend against his will; we must recognize that we were mistaken at the first and took a benefit from a person we should not have taken it from—since it was not from a friend, nor from one who did it just for the sake of acting so—and we must settle up just as if we had been benefited on fixed terms). Indeed, one would agree to repay [1] if one could (if one could not, even the giver would not have expected one to do so); therefore if it is possible we must repay. But at the outset we must consider the man by whom we are being benefited and on what terms he is acting, in order that we may accept the benefit on these terms, or else decline it.

[1] It seems possible to keep the MS. reading, and suppose Aristotle to mean that in such a case, though we made no promise when we got the service, we should be willing, if we were asked, to promise to repay if we could.

It is disputable whether we ought to measure a service by its utility to the receiver and make the return with a view to that, or by the benevolence of the giver. For those who have received say they have received from their benefactors what meant little to the latter and what they might have got from others—minimizing the service; while the givers, on the contrary, say it was the biggest thing they had, and what could not have been got from others, and that it was given in times of danger or similar need. Now if the friendship is one that aims at *utility*, surely the advantage to the receiver is the measure. For it is he that asks for the service, and the other man helps him on the assumption that he will receive the equivalent; so the assistance has been precisely as great as the advantage to the receiver, and therefore he must return as much as he has received, or even more (for that would be nobler). In friendships based on *virtue* on the other hand, complaints do not arise, but the purpose of the doer is a sort of measure; for in purpose lies the essential element of virtue and character.

Differences arise also in friendships based on superiority; 14
for each expects to get more out of them, but when this happens the friendship is dissolved. Not only does the better man think he ought to get more, since more should be assigned to a good man, but the more useful similarly expects this; they say a useless man should not get as much as they should, since it becomes an act of public service and not a friendship if the proceeds of the friendship do not answer to the worth of the benefits conferred. For they think that, as in a commercial partnership those who put more in get more out, so it should be in friendship. But the man who is in a state of need and inferiority makes the opposite claim; they think it is the part of a good friend to help those who are in need; what, they say, is the use of being the friend of a good man or a powerful man, if one is to get nothing out of it?

1163b At all events it seems that each party is justified in his
claim, and that each should get more out of the friendship

than the other—not more of the same thing, however, but the superior more honour and the inferior more gain; for honour is the prize of virtue and of beneficence, while gain is the assistance required by inferiority.

It seems to be so in constitutional arrangements also; the man who contributes nothing good to the common stock is not honoured; for what belongs to the public is given to the man who benefits the public, and honour does belong to the public. It is not possible to get wealth from the common stock and at the same time honour. For no one puts up with the smaller share in *all* things; therefore to the man who loses in wealth they assign honour and to the man who is willing to be paid, wealth, since the proportion to merit equalizes the parties and preserves the friendship, as we have said.[1]

This then is also the way in which we should associate with unequals; the man who is benefited in respect of wealth or virtue must give honour in return, repaying what he can. For friendship asks a man to do what he can, not what is proportional to the merits of the case; since that cannot always be done, e.g. in honours paid to the gods or to parents; for no one could ever return to them the equivalent of what he gets, but the man who serves them to the utmost of his power is thought to be a good man.

This is why it would not seem open to a man to disown his father (though a father may disown his son); being in debt, he should repay, but there is nothing by doing which a son will have done the equivalent of what he has received, so that he is always in debt. But creditors can remit a debt; and a father can therefore do so too. At the same time it is thought that presumably no one would repudiate a son who was not far gone in wickedness; for apart from the natural friendship of father and son it is human nature not to reject a son's assistance. But the son, if he *is* wicked, will naturally avoid aiding his father, or not be zealous about it; for most people wish to get benefits, but avoid doing them, as a thing unprofitable.—So much for these questions.

[1] 1162a 34–b 4, cf. 1158b 27, 1159a 35–b 3.

BOOK IX

In all friendships between dissimilars it is, as we have I
said,[1] proportion that equalizes the parties and preserves the friendship; e. g. in the political form of friendship the shoemaker gets a return for his shoes in proportion to his worth,
1164[a] and the weaver and all other craftsmen do the same. Now here a common measure has been provided in the form of money, and therefore everything is referred to this and measured by this; but in the friendship of lovers sometimes the lover complains that his excess of love is not met by love in return (though perhaps there is nothing lovable about him), while often the beloved complains that the lover who formerly promised everything now performs nothing. Such incidents happen when the lover loves the beloved for the sake of pleasure while the beloved loves the lover for the sake of utility, and they do not both possess the qualities expected of them. If these be the objects of the friendship it is dissolved when they do not get the things that formed the motives of their love; for each did not love the other person himself but the qualities he had, and these were not enduring; that is why the friendships also are transient. But the love of characters, as has been said, endures because it is self-dependent.[2] Differences arise when what they get is something different and not what they desire; for it is like getting nothing at all when we do not get what we aim at; compare the story of the person who made promises to a lyre-player, promising him the more, the better he sang, but in the morning, when the other demanded the fulfilment of his promises, said that he had given pleasure [3] for pleasure. Now if this had been what each wanted, all would have been well; but if the one wanted enjoyment but the other gain, and the one has

[1] This has not been said precisely of friendship between dissimilars, but cf. 1132[b] 31–33, 1158[b] 27, 1159[a] 35–[b] 3, 1162[a] 34–[b] 4, 1163[b] 11.

[2] 1156[b] 9–12.

[3] i. e. the pleasure of expectation.

what he wants while the other has not, the terms of the association will not have been properly fulfilled; for what each in fact wants is what he attends to, and it is for the sake of that that he will give what he has.

But who is to fix the worth of the service; he who makes the sacrifice or he who has got the advantage? At any rate the other seems to leave it to him. This is what they say Protagoras used to do;[1] whenever he taught anything whatsoever, he bade the learner assess the value of the knowledge, and accepted the amount so fixed. But in such matters some men approve of the saying 'let a man have his fixed reward'.[2]

Those who get the money first and then do none of the things they said they would, owing to the extravagance of their promises, naturally find themselves the objects of complaint; for they do not fulfil what they agreed to. The sophists are perhaps compelled to do this because no one would give money for the things they *do* know. These people then, if they do not do what they have been paid for, are naturally made the objects of complaint.

But where there is *no* contract of service, those who give up something for the sake of the other party cannot (as we have said[3]) be complained of (for that is the nature of the friendship of virtue), and the return to them must be made **1164b** on the basis of their purpose (for it is purpose that is the characteristic thing in a friend and in virtue). And so too, it seems, should one make a return to those with whom one has studied philosophy; for their worth cannot be measured against money, and they can get no honour which will balance their services, but still it is perhaps enough, as it is with the gods and with one's parents, to give them what one can.

If the gift was not of this sort, but was made with a view to a return, it is no doubt preferable that the return made should be one that seems fair to both parties, but if this cannot be achieved, it would seem not only necessary that the person who gets the first service should fix the reward,

[1] Cf. Pl. *Prot.* 328 B, C.

[2] Hes. *Op.* 370 Rzach.

[3] 1162b 6–13.

but also just; for if the other gets in return the equivalent of the advantage the beneficiary has received, or the price he would have paid for the pleasure, he will have got what is fair as from the other.

We see this happening too with things put up for sale, and in some places there are laws providing that no actions shall arise out of voluntary contracts, on the assumption that one should settle with a person to whom one has given credit, in the spirit in which one bargained with him. The law holds that it is more just that the person to whom credit was given should fix the terms than that the person who gave credit should do so. For most things are not assessed at the same value by those who have them and those who want them; each class values highly what is its own and what it is offering; yet the return is made on the terms fixed by the receiver. But no doubt the receiver should assess a thing not at what it seems worth when he has it, but at what he assessed it at before he had it.

A further problem is set by such questions as, whether 2
one should in all things give the preference to one's father and obey him, or whether when one is ill one should trust a doctor, and when one has to elect a general should elect a man of military skill; and similarly whether one should render a service by preference to a friend or to a good man, and should show gratitude to a benefactor or oblige a friend, if one cannot do both.

All such questions are hard, are they not, to decide with precision? For they admit of many variations of all sorts in respect both of the magnitude of the service and of its nobility and necessity. But that we should not give the preference in all things to the same person is plain enough; and we must for the most part return benefits rather than oblige friends, as we must pay back a loan to a creditor rather than make one to a friend. But perhaps even this is not always true; e.g. should a man who has been ransomed out of the hands of brigands ransom his ransomer in return, whoever he may be (or pay him if he has not been captured
1165a but demands payment), or should he ransom his father? It

would seem that he should ransom his father in preference even to himself. As we have said,[1] then, generally the debt should be paid, but if the gift is exceedingly noble or exceedingly necessary, one should defer to these considerations. For sometimes it is not even fair to return the equivalent of what one has received, when the one man has done a service to one whom he knows to be good, while the other makes a return to one whom he believes to be bad. For that matter, one should sometimes not lend in return to one who has lent to oneself; for the one person lent to a good man, expecting to recover his loan, while the other has no hope of recovering from one who is believed to be bad. Therefore if the facts really are so, the demand is not fair; and if they are not, but people think they are, they would be held to be doing nothing strange in refusing. As we have often pointed out,[2] then, discussions about feelings and actions have just as much definiteness as their subject-matter.

That we should not make the same return to every one, nor give a father the preference in everything, as one does not sacrifice everything to Zeus,[3] is plain enough; but since we ought to render different things to parents, brothers, comrades, and benefactors, we ought to render to each class what is appropriate and becoming. And this is what people seem in fact to do; to marriages they invite their kinsfolk; for these have a part in the family and therefore in the doings that affect the family; and at funerals also they think that kinsfolk, before all others, should meet, for the same reason. And it would be thought that in the matter of food we should help our parents before all others, since we owe our own nourishment to them, and it is more honourable to help in this respect the authors of our being even before ourselves; and honour too one should give to one's parents as one does to the gods, but not any and every honour; for that matter one should not give the same honour to one's father and one's mother, nor again should one give them the honour due to a philosopher or to a

[1] 1164^b 31–1165^a 2.
[2] 1094^b 11–27, 1098^a 26–29, 1103^b 34–1104^a 5.
[3] Cf. 1134^b 18–24.

general, but the honour due to a father, or again to a mother. To all older persons, too, one should give honour appropriate to their age, by rising to receive them and finding seats for them and so on; while to comrades and brothers one should allow freedom of speech and common use of all things. To kinsmen, too, and fellow-tribesmen and fellow-citizens and to every other class one should always try to assign what is appropriate, and to compare the claims of each class with respect to nearness of relation and to virtue or usefulness. The comparison is easier when the persons belong to the same class, and more laborious when they are different. Yet we must not on *that* account shrink from the task, but decide the question as best we can.

Another question that arises is whether friendships should 3
or should not be broken off when the other party does not
1165b remain the same. Perhaps we may say that there is nothing strange in breaking off a friendship based on utility or pleasure, when our friends no longer have these attributes. For it was of these attributes that we were the friends; and when these have failed it is reasonable to love no longer. But one might complain of another if, when he loved us for our usefulness or pleasantness, he pretended to love us for our character. For, as we said at the outset,[1] most differences arise between friends when they are not friends in the spirit in which they think they are. So when a man has deceived himself and has thought he was being loved for his character, when the other person was doing nothing of the kind, he must blame himself; but when he has been deceived by the pretences of the other person, it is just that he should complain against his deceiver; he will complain with more justice than one does against people who counterfeit the currency, inasmuch as the wrongdoing is concerned with something more valuable.

But if one accepts another man as good, and he turns out badly and is seen to do so, must one still love him? Surely it is impossible, since not everything can be loved, but only what is good. What is evil neither can nor should be loved;

[1] 1162b 23–25.

for it is not one's duty to be a lover of evil, nor to become like what is bad; and we have said[1] that like is dear to like. Must the friendship, then, be forthwith broken off? Or is this not so in all cases, but only when one's friends are incurable in their wickedness? If they are capable of being reformed one should rather come to the assistance of their character or their property, inasmuch as this is better and more characteristic of friendship. But a man who breaks off such a friendship would seem to be doing nothing strange; for it was not to a man of this sort that he was a friend; when his friend has changed, therefore, and he is unable to save him, he gives him up.

But if one friend remained the same while the other became better and far outstripped him in virtue, should the latter treat the former as a friend? Surely he cannot. When the interval is great this becomes most plain, e.g. in the case of childish friendships; if one friend remained a child in intellect while the other became a fully developed man, how could they be friends when they neither approved of the same things nor delighted in and were pained by the same things? For not even with regard to each other will their tastes agree, and without this (as we saw[2]) they cannot be friends; for they cannot live together. But we have discussed these matters.[3]

Should he, then, behave no otherwise towards him than he would if he had never been his friend? Surely he should keep a remembrance of their former intimacy, and as we think we ought to oblige friends rather than strangers, so to those who have been our friends we ought to make some allowance for our former friendship, when the breach has not been due to excess of wickedness.

4 Friendly relations with one's neighbours, and the marks 1166a
by which friendships are defined, seem to have proceeded from a man's relations to himself. For (1) we define a friend as one who wishes and does what is good, or seems so, for the sake of his friend, or (2) as one who wishes his

[1] 1156b 19-21, 1159b 1. [2] 1157b 22-24.
[3] Ib. 17-24, 1158b 33-35.

friend to exist and live, for his sake; which mothers do to their children, and friends do who have come into conflict. And (3) others define him as one who lives with and (4) has the same tastes as another, or (5) one who grieves and rejoices with his friend; and this too is found in mothers most of all. It is by some one of these characteristics that friendship too is defined.

Now each of these is true of the good man's relation to himself (and of all other men in so far as they think themselves good; virtue and the good man seem, as has been said,[1] to be the measure of every class of things). For[2] his opinions are harmonious, and he desires the same things with all his soul; and therefore[3] he wishes for himself what is good and what seems so, and does it (for it is characteristic of the good man to work out the good), and does so for his own sake (for he does it for the sake of the intellectual element in him, which is thought to be the man himself); and[4] he wishes himself to live and be preserved, and especially the element by virtue of which he thinks. For existence is good to the virtuous man, and each man wishes himself what is good, while no one chooses to possess the whole world if he has first to become some one else (for that matter, even now God possesses the good[5]); he wishes for this only on condition of being whatever he is; and the element that thinks would seem to be the individual man, or to be so more than any other element in him. And[6] such a man wishes to live with himself; for he does so with pleasure, since the memories of his past acts are delightful and his hopes for the future are good, and therefore pleasant. His mind is well stored too with subjects of contemplation. And[7] he grieves and rejoices, more than any other, with himself; for the same thing is always painful, and the same thing always pleasant, and not one thing at one time and another at another; he has, so to speak, nothing to repent of.

[1] 1113^a 22–33, cf. 1099^a 13.
[2] (4) above.
[3] (1) above.
[4] (2) above.
[5] *Sc.* but as no one gains by God's now having the good, he would not gain if a new person which was no longer himself were to possess it. Cf. 1159^a 5–11.
[6] (3) above.
[7] (5) above.

Therefore, since each of these characteristics belongs to the good man in relation to himself, and he is related to his friend as to himself (for his friend is another self), friendship too is thought to be one of these attributes, and those who have these attributes to be friends. Whether there is or is not friendship between a man and himself is a question we may dismiss for the present;[1] there would seem to be friendship in so far as he is two or more, to judge from the afore-mentioned attributes of friendship, and 1166b
from the fact that the extreme of friendship is likened to one's love for oneself.

But the attributes named seem to belong even to the majority of men, poor creatures though they may be. Are we to say then that in so far as they are satisfied with themselves and think they are good, they share in these attributes? Certainly no one who is thoroughly bad and impious has these attributes, or even seems to do so. They hardly belong even to inferior people; for they[2] are at variance with themselves, and have appetites for some things and rational desires for others. This is true, for instance, of incontinent people; for they choose, instead of the things they themselves think good, things that are pleasant but hurtful; while others again, through cowardice and laziness, shrink from doing what they think best for themselves. And[3] those who have done many terrible deeds and are hated for their wickedness even shrink from life and destroy themselves. And[4] wicked men seek for people with whom to spend their days, and shun themselves; for they remember many a grievous deed, and anticipate others like them, when they are by themselves, but when they are with others they forget. And[5] having nothing lovable in them they have no feeling of love to themselves. Therefore[6] also such men do not rejoice or grieve with themselves; for their soul is rent by faction, and one element in it by reason of its wickedness grieves when it abstains from certain acts, while the other part is pleased, and one draws them this way and the other that, as if they were pulling them in

[1] Cf. 1168a 28–1169b 2.
[2] (4) above.
[3] (2) above.
[4] (3) above.
[5] (1) above.
[6] (5) above.

pieces. If a man cannot at the same time be pained and pleased, at all events after a short time he is pained *because* he was pleased, and he could have wished that these things had not been pleasant to him; for bad men are laden with repentance.

Therefore the bad man does not seem to be amicably disposed even to himself, because there is nothing in him to love; so that if to be thus is the height of wretchedness, we should strain every nerve to avoid wickedness and should endeavour to be good; for so and only so can one be either friendly to oneself or a friend to another.

Goodwill is a friendly sort of relation, but is not *identical* 5
with friendship; for one may have goodwill both towards people whom one does not know, and without their knowing it, but not friendship. This has indeed been said already.[1] But goodwill is not even friendly feeling. For it does not involve intensity or desire, whereas these accompany friendly feeling; and friendly feeling implies intimacy while goodwill may arise of a sudden, as it does towards competitors in
1167a a contest; we come to feel goodwill for them and to share in their wishes, but we would not *do* anything with them; for, as we said, we feel goodwill suddenly and love them only superficially.

Goodwill seems, then, to be a beginning of friendship, as the pleasure of the eye is the beginning of love. For no one loves if he has not first been delighted by the form of the beloved, but he who delights in the form of another does not, for all that, love him, but only does so when he also longs for him when absent and craves for his presence; so too it is not possible for people to be friends if they have not come to feel goodwill for each other, but those who feel goodwill are not for all that friends; for they only *wish* well to those for whom they feel goodwill, and would not do anything with them nor take trouble for them. And so one might by an extension of the term friendship say that goodwill is inactive friendship, though when it is prolonged and reaches the point of intimacy it becomes

[1] 1155b 32–1156a 5.

friendship—not the friendship based on utility nor that based on pleasure; for goodwill too does not arise on those terms. The man who has received a benefit bestows goodwill in return for what has been done to him, but in doing so is only doing what is just; while he who wishes some one to prosper because he hopes for enrichment through him seems to have goodwill not to him but rather to himself, just as a man is not a friend to another if he cherishes him for the sake of some use to be made of him. In general, goodwill arises on account of some excellence and worth, when one man seems to another beautiful or brave or something of the sort, as we pointed out in the case of competitors in a contest.

6 Unanimity also seems to be a friendly relation. For this reason it is not identity of opinion; for that might occur even with people who do not know each other; nor do we say that people who have the same views on any and every subject are unanimous, e.g. those who agree about the heavenly bodies (for unanimity about these is not a friendly relation), but we do say that a city is unanimous when men have the same opinion about what is to their interest, and choose the same actions, and do what they have resolved in common. It is about things to be done, therefore, that people are said to be unanimous, and, among these, about matters of consequence and in which it is possible for both or all parties to get what they want; e.g. a city is unanimous when all its citizens think that the offices in it should be elective, or that they should form an alliance with Sparta, or that Pittacus should be their ruler—at a time when he himself was also willing to rule. But when each of two people wishes himself to have the thing in question, like the captains in the *Phoenissae*,[1] they are in a state of faction; for it is not unanimity when each of two parties thinks of the same thing, whatever that may be, but only when they think of the same thing in the same hands, e.g. when both the common people and those of the better class wish the best men to rule; for thus 1167b

[1] Eteocles and Polynices (Eur. *Phoen.* 588 ff.).

and thus alone do all get what they aim at. Unanimity seems, then, to be political friendship, as indeed it is commonly said to be; for it is concerned with things that are to our interest and have an influence on our life.

Now such unanimity is found among good men; for they are unanimous both in themselves and with one another, being, so to say, of one mind (for the wishes of such men are constant and not at the mercy of opposing currents like a strait of the sea), and they wish for what is just and what is advantageous, and these are the objects of their common endeavour as well. But bad men cannot be unanimous except to a small extent, any more than they can be friends, since they aim at getting more than their share of advantages, while in labour and public service they fall short of their share; and each man wishing for advantage to himself criticizes his neighbour and stands in his way; for if people do not watch it carefully the common weal is soon destroyed. The result is that they are in a state of faction, putting compulsion on each other but unwilling themselves to do what is just.

Benefactors are thought to love those they have benefited, 7
more than those who have been well treated love those that have treated them well, and this is discussed as though it were paradoxical. Most people think it is because the latter are in the position of debtors and the former of creditors; and therefore as, in the case of loans, debtors wish their creditors did not exist, while creditors actually take care of the safety of their debtors, so it is thought that benefactors wish the objects of their action to exist since they will then get their gratitude, while the beneficiaries take no interest in making this return. Epicharmus would perhaps declare that they say this because they 'look at things on their bad side',[1] but it is quite like human nature; for most people are forgetful, and are more anxious to be well treated than to treat others well. But the cause would seem to be more deeply rooted in the nature of things; the case of those who have lent money is not even analogous.

[1] Fr. 146 Kaibel.

For they have no friendly feeling to their debtors, but only a wish that they may be kept safe with a view to what is to be got from them; while those who have done a service to others feel friendship and love for those they have served even if these are not of any use to them and never will be. This is what happens with craftsmen too; every man loves his own handiwork better than he would be loved by it
if it came alive; and this happens perhaps most of all with 1168a
poets; for they have an excessive love for their own poems, doting on them as if they were their children. This is what the position of benefactors is like; for that which they have treated well is their handiwork, and therefore they love this more than the handiwork does its maker. The cause of this is that existence is to all men a thing to be chosen and loved, and that we exist by virtue of activity (i. e. by living and acting), and that the handiwork *is* in a sense, the producer in activity; he loves his handiwork, therefore, because he loves existence. And this is rooted in the nature of things; for what he is in potentiality, his handiwork manifests in activity.

At the same time to the benefactor that is noble which depends on his action, so that he delights in the object of his action, whereas to the patient there is nothing noble in the agent, but at most something advantageous, and this is less pleasant and lovable. What *is* pleasant is the activity of the present, the hope of the future, the memory of the past; but most pleasant is that which depends on activity, and similarly this is most lovable. Now for a man who has made something his work remains (for the noble is lasting), but for the person acted on the utility passes away. And the memory of noble things is pleasant, but that of useful things is not likely to be pleasant, or is less so; though the reverse seems true of expectation.

Further, love is like activity, being loved like passivity; and loving and its concomitants are attributes of those who are the more active.[1]

Again, all men love more what they have won by labour; e.g. those who have made their money love it more than

[1] I. e. benefactors.

those who have inherited it; and to be well treated seems to involve no labour, while to treat others well is a laborious task. These are the reasons, too, why mothers are fonder of their children than fathers; bringing them into the world costs them more pains, and they know better that the children are their own. This last point, too, would seem to apply to benefactors.

8 The question is also debated, whether a man should love himself most, or some one else. People criticize those who love themselves most, and call them self-lovers, using this as an epithet of disgrace, and a bad man seems to do everything for his own sake, and the more so the more wicked he is—and so men reproach him, for instance, with doing nothing of his own accord—while the good man acts for honour's sake, and the more so the better he is, and acts for his friend's sake, and sacrifices his own interest.

But the facts clash with these arguments, and this is not 1168b surprising. For men say that one ought to love best one's best friend, and a man's best friend is one who wishes well to the object of his wish for his sake, even if no one is to know of it; and these attributes are found most of all in a man's attitude towards himself, and so are all the other attributes by which a friend is defined; for, as we have said,[1] it is from this relation that all the characteristics of friendship have extended to our neighbours. All the proverbs, too, agree with this, e.g. 'a single soul',[2] and 'what friends have is common property', and 'friendship is equality', and 'charity begins at home';[3] for all these marks will be found most in a man's relation to himself; he is his own best friend and therefore ought to love himself best. It is therefore a reasonable question, which of the two views we should follow; for both are plausible.

Perhaps we ought to mark off such arguments from each other and determine how far and in what respects each view is right. Now if we grasp the sense in which each school uses the phrase 'lover of self', the truth may become evident. Those who use the term as one of reproach

[1] Ch. 4.
[2] Eur. *Or.* 1046.
[3] Lit. 'the knee is nearer than the shin'.

ascribe self-love to people who assign to themselves the greater share of wealth, honours, and bodily pleasures; for these are what most people desire, and busy themselves about as though they were the best of all things, which is the reason, too, why they become objects of competition. So those who are grasping with regard to these things gratify their appetites and in general their feelings and the irrational element of the soul; and most men are of this nature (which is the reason why the epithet has come to be used as it is—it takes its meaning from the prevailing type of self-love, which is a bad one); it is just, therefore, that men who are lovers of self in this way are reproached for being so. That it is those who give themselves the preference in regard to objects of this sort that most people usually call lovers of self is plain; for if a man were always anxious that he himself, above all things, should act justly, temperately, or in accordance with any other of the virtues, and in general were always to try to secure for himself the honourable course, no one will call such a man a lover of self or blame him.

But such a man would seem more than the other a lover of self; at all events he assigns to himself the things that are noblest and best, and gratifies the most authoritative element in himself and in all things obeys this; and just as a city or any other systematic whole is most properly identified with the most authoritative element in it, so is a man; and therefore the man who loves this and gratifies it is most of all a lover of self. Besides, a man is said to have or not to have self-control according as his reason has or has not the control, on the assumption that this is the man himself; and the things men have done on
a rational principle are thought most properly their own 1169a
acts and voluntary acts. That this is the man himself, then, or is so more than anything else, is plain, and also that the good man loves most this part of him. Whence it follows that he is most truly a lover of self, of another type than that which is a matter of reproach, and as different from that as living according to a rational principle is from living as passion dictates, and desiring what is noble

from desiring what seems advantageous. Those, then, who busy themselves in an exceptional degree with noble actions all men approve and praise; and if *all* were to strive towards what is noble and strain every nerve to do the noblest deeds, everything would be as it should be for the common weal, and every one would secure for himself the goods that are greatest, since virtue is the greatest of goods.

Therefore the good man should be a lover of self (for he will both himself profit by doing noble acts, and will benefit his fellows), but the wicked man should not; for he will hurt both himself and his neighbours, following as he does evil passions. For the wicked man, what he does clashes with what he ought to do, but what the good man ought to do he does; for reason in each of its possessors chooses what is best for itself, and the good man obeys his reason. It is true of the good man too that he does many acts for the sake of his friends and his country, and if necessary dies for them; for he will throw away both wealth and honours and in general the goods that are objects of competition, gaining for himself nobility; since he would prefer a short period of intense pleasure to a long one of mild enjoyment, a twelvemonth of noble life to many years of humdrum existence, and one great and noble action to many trivial ones. Now those who die for others doubtless attain this result; it is therefore a great prize that they choose for themselves. They will throw away wealth too on condition that their friends will gain more; for while a man's friend gains wealth he himself achieves nobility; he is therefore assigning the greater good to himself. The same too is true of honour and office; all these things he will sacrifice to his friend; for this is noble and laudable for himself. Rightly then is he thought to be good, since he chooses nobility before all else. But he may even give up actions to his friend; it may be nobler to become the cause of his friend's acting than to act himself. In all the actions, therefore, that men are praised for, the good man is seen to assign to himself the greater share
1169b in what is noble. In this sense, then, as has been said,

a man should be a lover of self; but in the sense in which most men are so, he ought not.

9 It is also disputed whether the happy man will need friends or not. It is said that those who are supremely happy and self-sufficient have no need of friends; for they have the things that are good, and therefore being self-sufficient they need nothing further, while a friend, being another self, furnishes what a man cannot provide by his own effort; whence the saying 'when fortune is kind, what need of friends?'[1] But it seems strange, when one assigns all good things to the happy man, not to assign friends, who are thought the greatest of external goods. And if it is more characteristic of a friend to do well by another than to be well done by, and to confer benefits is characteristic of the good man and of virtue, and it is nobler to do well by friends than by strangers, the good man will need people to do well by. This is why the question is asked whether we need friends more in prosperity or in adversity, on the assumption that not only does a man in adversity need people to confer benefits on him, but also those who are prospering need people to do well by. Surely it is strange, too, to make the supremely happy man a solitary; for no one would choose the whole world on condition of being alone, since man is a political creature and one whose nature is to live with others. Therefore even the happy man lives with others; for he has the things that are by nature good. And plainly it is better to spend his days with friends and good men than with strangers or any chance persons. Therefore the happy man needs friends.

What then is it that the first school means, and in what respect is it right? Is it that most men identify friends with useful people? Of such friends indeed the supremely happy man will have no need, since he already has the things that are good; nor will he need those whom one makes one's friends because of their pleasantness, or he will need them only to a small extent (for his life, being

[1] Eur. *Or.* 667.

pleasant, has no need of adventitious pleasure); and because he does not need *such* friends he is thought not to need friends.

But that is surely not true. For we have said at the outset[1] that happiness is an activity; and activity plainly comes into being and is not present at the start like a piece of property. If (1) happiness lies in living and being active, and the good man's activity is virtuous and pleasant in itself, as we have said at the outset,[2] and (2) a thing's being one's own is one of the attributes that make it pleasant, and (3) we can contemplate our neighbours better than ourselves and their actions better than our own, and if the actions of virtuous men who are their friends are
1170^{a} pleasant to good men (since these have both the attributes that are naturally pleasant[3]),—if this be so, the supremely happy man will need friends of this sort, since his purpose is to contemplate worthy actions and actions that are his own, and the actions of a good man who is his friend have both these qualities.

Further, men think that the happy man ought to live pleasantly. Now if he were a solitary, life would be hard for him; for by oneself it is not easy to be continuously active; but with others and towards others it is easier. With others therefore his activity will be more continuous, and it is in itself pleasant, as it ought to be for the man who is supremely happy; for a good man *qua* good delights in virtuous actions and is vexed at vicious ones, as a musical man enjoys beautiful tunes but is pained at bad ones. A certain training in virtue arises also from the company of the good, as Theognis has said before us.[4]

If we look deeper into the nature of things, a virtuous friend seems to be naturally desirable for a virtuous man. For that which is good by nature, we have said,[5] is for the virtuous man good and pleasant in itself. Now life is defined in the case of animals by the power of perception, in that of man by the power of perception or thought; and

[1] 1098^{a} 16^{b}, 31–1099^{a} 7.
[2] 1099^{a} 14, 21.
[3] I. e. the attribute of goodness and that of being their own.
[4] Theog. 35.
[5] 1099^{a} 7–11, 1113^{a} 25–33.

a power is defined by reference to the corresponding activity, which is the essential thing; therefore life seems to be essentially the act of perceiving or thinking. And life is among the things that are good and pleasant in themselves, since it is determinate and the determinate is of the nature of the good; and that which is good by nature is also good for the virtuous man (which is the reason why life seems pleasant to all men); but we must not apply this to a wicked and corrupt life nor to a life spent in pain; for such a life is indeterminate, as are its attributes. The nature of pain will become plainer in what follows.[1] But if life itself is good and pleasant (which it seems to be, from the very fact that all men desire it, and particularly those who are good and supremely happy; for to such men life is most desirable, and their existence is the most supremely happy); and if he who sees perceives that he sees, and he who hears, that he hears, and he who walks, that he walks, and in the case of all other activities similarly there is something which perceives that we are active, so that if we perceive, we perceive that we perceive, and if we think, that we think; and if to perceive that we perceive or think is to perceive that we exist (for existence was defined as perceiving or thinking); and if perceiving that one lives 1170b
is in itself one of the things that are pleasant (for life is by nature good, and to perceive what is good present in oneself is pleasant); and if life is desirable, and particularly so for good men, because to them existence is good and pleasant (for they are pleased at the consciousness of the presence in them of what is in itself good); and if as the virtuous man is to himself, he is to his friend also (for his friend is another self):—if all this be true, as his own being is desirable for each man, so, or almost so, is that of his friend. Now his being was seen to be desirable because he perceived his own goodness, and such perception is pleasant in itself. He needs, therefore, to be conscious of the existence of his friend as well, and this will be realized in their living together and sharing in discussion and thought; for this is what living together would seem to

[1] x. 1–5.

mean in the case of man, and not, as in the case of cattle, feeding in the same place.

If, then, being is in itself desirable for the supremely happy man (since it is by its nature good and pleasant), and that of his friend is very much the same, a friend will be one of the things that are desirable. Now that which is desirable for him he must have, or he will be deficient in this respect. The man who is to be happy will therefore need virtuous friends.[1]

[1] The argument in 1170^{a} 14–^{b} 19 is admirably analysed by Prof. Burnet, whom I follow, with variations:—

Pro-syllogism A (1170^{a} 16–19):
Capacity is defined by reference to activity.
Human life is defined by the capacity of perception or thought.
∴ Human life is defined by the activity of perception or thought.

Pro-syllogism B (^{a} 19–21):
The determinate is good by nature.
Life is determinate.
∴ Life is good by nature.

Pro-syllogism C (implied):
What is good by nature is good and pleasant for the good man (^{a} 14–16, 21–22).
Life is good by nature (conclusion of B).
∴ Life is good and pleasant for the good man.

Pro-syllogism D (implied):
Life is good and pleasant for the good man (conclusion of C).
Perception and thought are life (conclusion of A).
∴ Perception and thought are good and pleasant for the good man.

Pro-syllogism E (^{a} 25–29):
What is desired by all men and particularly by the good and supremely happy man is good in itself.
Life is so desired.
∴ Life is good in itself.

Lemma (^{a} 29–32):
Perception and thought are accompanied by consciousness of themselves.

Argument F (^{a} 32–^{b} 1);
Perception and thought are life (conclusion of A).
∴ Consciousness of perception and thought is consciousness of life.

Argument G (^{b} 1–3):
Consciousness of having something good is pleasant.
Life is good in itself (conclusion of B and E).
∴ Consciousness of life is pleasant.

Argument H (implied):
Consciousness of life is pleasant (conclusion of G).
Consciousness of perception and thought is consciousness of life (conclusion of F).
∴ Consciousness of perception and thought is pleasant.

Lemma (^{b} 3–5):
The existence of the good man is specially desirable because the activities of which he is conscious are good.

10 Should we, then, make as many friends as possible, or—as in the case of hospitality it is thought to be suitable advice, that one should be 'neither a man of many guests nor a man with none[1]'—will that apply to friendship as well; should a man neither be friendless nor have an excessive number of friends?

To friends made with a view to *utility* this saying would seem thoroughly applicable; for to do services to many people in return is a laborious task and life is not long enough for its performance. Therefore friends in excess of those who are sufficient for our own life are superfluous, and hindrances to the noble life; so that we have no need of them. Of friends made with a view to *pleasure*, also, few are enough, as a little seasoning in food is enough.

But as regards *good* friends, should we have as many as possible, or is there a limit to the number of one's friends, as there is to the size of a city? You cannot make a city of ten men, and if there are a hundred thousand it is a city no longer. But the proper number is presumably not a single number, but anything that falls between certain fixed points. So for friends too there is a fixed number—perhaps the largest number with whom one can live together (for that, we found,[2] is thought to be very characteristic of friendship); and that one cannot live with many people and divide oneself up among them is plain. Further, they too must be friends of one another, if they are all to spend their days together; and it is a hard business for this condition to

Argument I (^{b} 5–8):
The good man is related to his friend as he is to himself (conclusion of ch. 4).
His own existence is desirable to him (conclusion of C).
∴ That of his friend is desirable to him.

Argument K (^{b} 8–11):
His own existence is desirable because of his consciousness of his good activities (stated in ^{b} 3–5).
∴ Consciousness of his friend's good activities is also desirable to him.

Summary (^{b} 14–17).

Argument L (^{b} 17–19):
If a man is to be happy, he must have all that is desirable for him.
Friends are desirable for a man (conclusion of I).
∴ If a man is to be happy, he must have friends.

1 Hes. *Op.* 715 Rzach.

2 1157^{b} 19, 1158^{a} 3, 10.

be fulfilled with a large number. It is found difficult, too, to rejoice and to grieve in an intimate way with many people, for it may likely happen that one has at once to be happy with one friend and to mourn with another. Presumably, then, it is well not to seek to have as many friends as possible, but as many as are enough for the purpose of living together; for it would seem actually impossible to be a great friend to many people. This is why one cannot love several people; love is ideally a sort of excess of friendship, and that can only be felt towards one person; therefore great friendship too can only be felt towards a few people. This seems to be confirmed in practice; for we do not find many people who are friends in the comradely way of friendship, and the famous friendships of this sort are always between two people. Those who have many friends and mix intimately with them all are thought to be no one's friend, except in the way proper to fellow-citizens, and such people are also called obsequious. In the way proper to fellow-citizens, indeed, it is possible to be the friend of many and yet not be obsequious but a genuinely good man; but one cannot have with many people the friendship based on virtue and on the character of our friends themselves, and we must be content if we find even a few such.

Do we need friends more in good fortune or in bad? II
They are sought after in both; for while men in adversity need help, in prosperity they need people to live with and to make the objects of their beneficence; for they wish to do well by others. Friendship, then, is more necessary in bad fortune, and so it is useful friends that one wants in this case; but it is more noble in good fortune, and so we also seek for good men as our friends, since it is more desirable to confer benefits on these and to live with these. For the very presence of friends is pleasant both in good fortune and also in bad, since grief is lightened when friends sorrow with us. Hence one might ask whether they share as it were our burden, or—without that happening—their presence by its pleasantness, and the thought of their grieving with us, make our pain less. Whether it is for

these reasons or for some other that our grief is lightened, is a question that may be dismissed ; at all events what we have described appears to take place.

But their presence seems to contain a mixture of various factors. The very seeing of one's friends is pleasant, especially if one is in adversity, and becomes a safeguard against 1171b grief (for a friend tends to comfort us both by the sight of him and by his words, if he is tactful, since he knows our character and the things that please or pain us); but to see him pained at our misfortunes is painful; for every one shuns being a cause of pain to his friends. For this reason people of a manly nature guard against making their friends grieve with them, and, unless he be exceptionally insensible to pain, such a man cannot stand the pain that ensues for his friends, and in general does not admit fellow-mourners because he is not himself given to mourning; but women and womanly men enjoy sympathisers in their grief, and love them as friends and companions in sorrow. But in all things one obviously ought to imitate the better type of person.

On the other hand, the presence of friends in our *prosperity* implies both a pleasant passing of our time and the pleasant thought of their pleasure at our own good fortune. For this cause it would seem that we ought to summon our friends readily to share our good fortunes (for the beneficent character is a noble one), but summon them to our bad fortunes with hesitation ; for we ought to give them as little a share as possible in our evils—whence the saying 'enough is *my* misfortune'.[1] We should summon friends to us most of all when they are likely by suffering a few inconveniences to do us a great service.

Conversely, it is fitting to go unasked and readily to the aid of those in adversity (for it is characteristic of a friend to render services, and especially to those who are in need and have not demanded them; such action is nobler and pleasanter for both persons); but when our friends are prosperous we should join readily in their activities (for they need friends for these too), but be tardy in coming

[1] Fr. adesp. 76 Nauck[2].

forward to be the objects of their kindness; for it is not noble to be keen to receive benefits. Still, we must no doubt avoid getting the reputation of kill-joys by repulsing them; for that sometimes happens.

The presence of friends, then, seems desirable in all circumstances.

Does it not follow, then, that, as for lovers the sight of the 12
beloved is the thing they love most, and they prefer this sense to the others because on it love depends most for its being and for its origin, so for friends the most desirable thing is living together? For friendship is a partnership, and as a man is to himself, so is he to his friend; now in his own case the consciousness of his being is desirable, and so therefore is the consciousness of his friend's being, and the
1172a activity of this consciousness is produced when they live together, so that it is natural that they aim at this. And whatever existence means for each class of men, whatever it is for whose sake they value life, in *that* they wish to occupy themselves with their friends; and so some drink together, others dice together, others join in athletic exercises and hunting, or in the study of philosophy, each class spending their days together in whatever they love most in life; for since they wish to live with their friends, they do and share in those things which give them the sense of living together. Thus the friendship of bad men turns out an evil thing (for because of their instability they unite in bad pursuits, and besides they become evil by becoming like each other), while the friendship of good men is good, being augmented by their companionship; and they are thought to become better too by their activities and by improving each other; for from each other they take the mould of the characteristics they approve—whence the saying 'noble deeds from noble men'.[1]—So much, then, for friendship; our next task must be to discuss pleasure.

[1] Theog. 35.

BOOK X

1 AFTER these matters we ought perhaps next to discuss pleasure. For it is thought to be most intimately connected with our human nature, which is the reason why in educating the young we steer them by the rudders of pleasure and pain; it is thought, too, that to enjoy the things we ought and to hate the things we ought has the greatest bearing on virtue of character. For these things extend right through life, with a weight and power of their own in respect both to virtue and to the happy life, since men choose what is pleasant and avoid what is painful; and such things, it will be thought, we should least of all omit to discuss, especially since they admit of much dispute. For some[1] say pleasure is the good, while others,[2] on the contrary, say it is thoroughly bad—some no doubt being persuaded that the facts are so, and others thinking it has a better effect on our life to exhibit pleasure as a bad thing even if it is not; for most people (they think) incline towards it and are the slaves of their pleasures, for which reason they ought to lead them in the opposite direction, since thus they will reach the middle state. But surely this is not correct. For arguments about matters concerned with feelings and actions are less reliable than facts: and so when they clash with the facts of perception they are despised, and discredit the truth as well; if a man who runs down pleasure is once 1172b
seen to be aiming at it, his inclining towards it is thought to imply that it is all worthy of being aimed at; for most people are not good at drawing distinctions. True arguments seem, then, most useful, not only with a view to knowledge, but with a view to life also; for since they harmonize with the facts they are believed, and so they stimulate those who understand them to live according to

[1] The school of Eudoxus, cf. ^{b}9. Aristippus is perhaps also referred to.

[2] The school of Speusippus, cf. 1153^{b} 5.

them.—Enough of such questions; let us proceed to review the opinions that have been expressed about pleasure.

Eudoxus thought pleasure was the good because he saw all 2
things, both rational and irrational, aiming at it, and because in all things that which is the object of choice is what is excellent, and that which is most the object of choice the greatest good; thus the fact that all things moved towards the same object indicated that this was for all things the chief good (for each thing, he argued, finds its own good, as it finds its own nourishment); and that which is good for all things and at which all aim was *the* good. His arguments were credited more because of the excellence of his character than for their own sake; he was thought to be remarkably self-controlled, and therefore it was thought that he was not saying what he did say as a friend of pleasure, but that the facts really were so. He believed that the same conclusion followed no less plainly from a study of the contrary of pleasure; pain was in itself an object of aversion to all things, and therefore its contrary must be similarly an object of choice. And again that is most an object of choice which we choose not because or for the sake of something else, and pleasure is admittedly of this nature; for no one asks to what end he is pleased, thus implying that pleasure is in itself an object of choice. Further, he argued that pleasure when added to any good, e.g. to just or temperate action, makes it more worthy of choice, and that it is only by itself that the good can be increased.

This argument seems to show it to be one of the goods, and no more a good than any other; for every good is more worthy of choice along with another good than taken alone. And so it is by an argument of this kind that Plato[1] proves the good *not* to be pleasure; he argues that the pleasant life is more desirable with wisdom than without, and that if the mixture is better, pleasure is not the good; for the good cannot become more desirable by the addition of anything to it. Now it is clear that nothing else, any more than pleasure, can be the good if it is made more

[1] *Phil.* 60 B–E.

desirable by the addition of any of the things that are good in themselves. What, then, is there that satisfies this criterion, which at the same time we can participate in? It is something of this sort that we are looking for.

Those who object that that at which all things aim is not necessarily good are, we may surmise, talking nonsense. For we say that that which every one thinks really is so; and the 1173a
man who attacks this belief will hardly have anything more credible to maintain instead. If it is senseless creatures that desire the things in question, there might be something in what they say; but if intelligent creatures do so as well, what sense can there be in this view? But perhaps even in inferior creatures there is some natural good stronger than themselves which aims at their proper good.

Nor does the argument about the contrary of pleasure seem to be correct. They say that if pain is an evil it does not follow that pleasure is a good; for evil is opposed to evil and at the same time both are opposed to the neutral state—which is correct enough but does not apply to the things in question. For if both pleasure and pain belonged to the class of evils they ought both to be objects of aversion, while if they belonged to the class of neutrals neither should be an object of aversion or they should both be equally so; but in fact people evidently avoid the one as evil and choose the other as good; that then must be the nature of the opposition between them.

3 Nor again, if pleasure is not a quality, does it follow that it is not a good; for the activities of virtue are not qualities either, nor is happiness.

They say,[1] however, that the good is determinate, while pleasure is indeterminate, because it admits of degrees. Now if it is from the feeling of pleasure that they judge thus, the same will be true of justice and the other virtues, in respect of which we plainly say that people of a certain character are so more or less, and act more or less in accordance with these virtues; for people may be more just or brave, and it is possible also to act justly or temperately

[1] Ib. 24 E–25 A, 31 A.

more or less. But if their judgement is based on the various pleasures, surely they are not stating the real cause,[1] if in fact some pleasures are unmixed and others mixed. Again, just as health admits of degrees without being indeterminate, why should not pleasure? The same proportion is not found in all things, nor a single proportion always in the same thing, but it may be relaxed and yet persist up to a point, and it may differ in degree. The case of pleasure also may therefore be of this kind.

Again, they assume [2] that the good is perfect while movements and comings into being are imperfect, and try to exhibit pleasure as being a movement and a coming into being. But they do not seem to be right even in saying that it is a movement. For speed and slowness are thought to be proper to every movement, and if a movement, e.g. that of the heavens, has not speed or slowness in itself, it has it in relation to something else; but of pleasure neither of these things is true. For while we may *become* pleased quickly as
1173b we may become angry quickly, we cannot *be* pleased quickly, not even in relation to some one else, while we *can* walk, or grow, or the like, quickly. While, then, we can change quickly or slowly into a state of pleasure, we cannot quickly exhibit the activity of pleasure, i.e. be pleased. Again, how can it be a coming into being? It is not thought that any chance thing can come out of any chance thing, but that a thing is dissolved into that out of which it comes into being; and pain would be the destruction of that of which pleasure is the coming into being.

They say, too,[3] that pain is the lack of that which is according to nature, and pleasure is replenishment. But these experiences are bodily. If then pleasure is replenishment with that which is according to nature, that which feels pleasure will be that in which the replenishment takes place, i.e. the body; but that is not thought to be the case; therefore the replenishment is not pleasure, though one would be pleased when replenishment was taking place,

[1] *Sc.*, of the badness of (some) pleasures. [2] Pl. *Phil.* 53 C–54 D.
[3] Ib. 31 E–32 B, 42 C D.

just as one would be pained if one was being operated on.[1] This opinion seems to be based on the pains and pleasures connected with nutrition; on the fact that when people have been short of food and have felt pain beforehand they are pleased by the replenishment. But this does not happen with all pleasures; for the pleasures of learning and, among the sensuous pleasures, those of smell, and also many sounds and sights, and memories and hopes, do not presuppose pain. Of what then will these be the coming into being? There has not been lack of anything of which they could be the supplying anew.

In reply to those who bring forward the disgraceful pleasures one may say that these are not pleasant; if things are pleasant to people of vicious constitution, we must not suppose that they are also pleasant to others than these, just as we do not reason so about the things that are wholesome or sweet or bitter to sick people, or ascribe whiteness to the things that seem white to those suffering from a disease of the eye. Or one might answer thus—that the pleasures are desirable, but not from *these* sources, as wealth is desirable, but not as the reward of betrayal, and health, but not at the cost of eating anything and everything. Or perhaps pleasures differ in kind; for those derived from noble sources are different from those derived from base sources, and one cannot get the pleasure of the just man without being just, nor that of the musical man without being musical, and so on.

The fact, too, that a friend is different from a flatterer seems to make it plain that pleasure is not a good or that pleasures are different in kind; for the one is thought to consort with us with a view to the good, the other with a view to our pleasure, and the one is reproached for his conduct while the other is praised on the ground that he consorts with us for different ends. And no one would 1174a
choose to live with the intellect of a child throughout his life, however much he were to be pleased at the things that children are pleased at, nor to get enjoyment by doing

[1] The point being that the being replenished no more *is* pleasure than the being operated on *is* pain. For the instance, cf. Pl. *Tim.* 65 B.

some most disgraceful deed, though he were never to feel any pain in consequence. And there are many things we should be keen about even if they brought no pleasure, e.g. seeing, remembering, knowing, possessing the virtues. If pleasures necessarily do accompany these, that makes no odds; we should choose these even if no pleasure resulted. It seems to be clear, then, that neither is pleasure the good nor is all pleasure desirable, and that some pleasures *are* desirable in themselves, differing in kind or in their sources from the others. So much for the things that are said about pleasure and pain.

What pleasure is, or what kind of thing it is, will become 4
plainer if we take up the question again from the beginning. Seeing seems to be at any moment complete, for it does not lack anything which coming into being later will complete its form; and pleasure also seems to be of this nature. For it is a whole, and at no time can one find a pleasure whose form will be completed if the pleasure lasts longer. For this reason, too, it is not a movement. For every movement (e.g. that of building) takes time and is for the sake of an end, and is complete when it has made what it aims at. It is complete, therefore, only in the whole time or at that final moment. In their parts and during the time they occupy, all movements are incomplete, and are different in kind from the whole movement and from each other. For the fitting together of the stones is different from the fluting of the column, and these are both different from the making of the temple; and the making of the temple is complete (for it lacks nothing with a view to the end proposed), but the making of the base or of the triglyph is incomplete; for each is the making of only a part. They differ in kind, then, and it is not possible to find at any and every time a movement complete in form, but if at all, only in the whole time. So, too, in the case of walking and all other movements. For if locomotion is a movement from here to there, it, too, has differences in kind—flying, walking, leaping, and so on. And not only so, but in walking itself there are such differences; for the whence

and whither are not the same in the whole racecourse and in a part of it, nor in one part and in another, nor is it the same thing to traverse this line and that; for one traverses 1174[b] not only a line but one which is in a place, and this one is in a different place from that. We have discussed movement with precision in another work,[1] but it seems that it is not complete at any and every time, but that the many movements are incomplete and different in kind, since the whence and whither give them their form. But of pleasure the form is complete at any and every time. Plainly, then, pleasure and movement must be different from each other, and pleasure must be one of the things that are whole and complete. This would seem to be the case, too, from the fact that it is not possible to move otherwise than in time, but it *is* possible to be pleased; for that which takes place in a moment is a whole.

From these considerations it is clear, too, that these thinkers are not right in saying there is a movement or a coming into being *of* pleasure.[2] For these cannot be ascribed to all things, but only to those that are divisible and not wholes; there is no coming into being of seeing nor of a point nor of a unit, nor is any of these a movement or coming into being; therefore there is no movement or coming into being of pleasure either; for it is a whole.

Since every sense is active in relation to its object, and a sense which is in good condition acts perfectly in relation to the most beautiful of its objects (for perfect activity seems to be ideally of this nature; whether we say that *it* is active, or the organ in which it resides, may be assumed to be immaterial), it follows that in the case of each sense the best activity is that of the best-conditioned organ in relation to the finest of its objects. And this activity will be the most complete and pleasant. For, while there is pleasure in respect of any sense, and in respect of thought and contemplation no less, the most complete is pleasantest, and that of a well-conditioned organ in relation to the worthiest of its objects is the most complete; and the

[1] *Phys.* vi–viii.
[2] Reading τῆς ἡδονῆς in l. 10 with Ramsauer.

pleasure completes the activity. But the pleasure does not complete it in the same way as the combination of object and sense, both good, just as health and the doctor are not in the same way the cause of a man's being healthy. (That pleasure is produced in respect to each sense is plain; for we speak of sights and sounds as pleasant. It is also plain that it arises most of all when both the sense is at its best and it is active in reference to an object which corresponds; when both object and perceiver are of the best there will always be pleasure, since the requisite agent and patient are both present.) Pleasure completes the activity not as the corresponding permanent state does, by its immanence, but as an end which supervenes as the bloom of youth does on those in the flower of their age. So long, then, as both the intelligible or sensible object and the discriminating or contemplative faculty are as they should be, the pleasure will be
1175[a] involved in the activity; for when both the passive and the active factor are unchanged and are related to each other in the same way, the same result naturally follows.

How, then, is it that no one is continuously pleased? Is it that we grow weary? Certainly all human things are incapable of continuous activity. Therefore pleasure also is not continuous; for it accompanies activity. Some things delight us when they are new, but later do so less, for the same reason; for at first the mind is in a state of stimulation and intensely active about them, as people are with respect to their vision when they look hard at a thing, but afterwards our activity is not of this kind, but has grown relaxed; for which reason the pleasure also is dulled.

One might think that all men desire pleasure because they all aim at life; life is an activity, and each man is active about those things and with those faculties that he loves most; e.g. the musician is active with his hearing in reference to tunes, the student with his mind in reference to theoretical questions, and so on in each case; now pleasure completes the activities, and therefore life, which they desire. It is with good reason, then, that they aim at pleasure too, since for every one it completes life, which is desirable.

But whether we choose life for the sake of pleasure or pleasure for the sake of life is a question we may dismiss for the present. For they seem to be bound up together and not to admit of separation, since without activity pleasure does not arise, and every activity is completed by the attendant pleasure.

5 For this reason pleasures seem, too, to differ in kind. For things different in kind are, we think, completed by different things (we see this to be true both of natural objects and of things produced by art, e.g. animals, trees, a painting, a sculpture, a house, an implement); and, similarly, we think that activities differing in kind are completed by things differing in kind. Now the activities of thought differ from those of the senses, and both differ among themselves, in kind; so, therefore, do the pleasures that complete them.

This may be seen, too, from the fact that each of the pleasures is bound up with the activity it completes. For an activity is intensified by its proper pleasure, since each class of things is better judged of and brought to precision by those who engage in the activity with pleasure; e.g. it is those who enjoy geometrical thinking that become geometers and grasp the various propositions better, and, similarly, those who are fond of music or of building, and so on, make progress in their proper function by enjoying it; so[1] the pleasures intensify the activities, and what intensifies a thing is proper to it, but things different in kind have properties different in kind.

This will be even more apparent from the fact that 1175b
activities are hindered by pleasures arising from other sources. For people who are fond of playing the flute are incapable of attending to arguments if they overhear some one playing the flute, since they enjoy flute-playing more than the activity in hand; so the pleasure connected with flute-playing destroys the activity concerned with argument. This happens, similarly, in all other cases, when one is active about two things at once; the more

[1] Reading συναύξουσι δή in l. 36 with Par. 1417.

pleasant activity drives out the other, and if it is much more pleasant does so all the more, so that one even ceases from the other. This is why when we enjoy anything very much we do not throw ourselves into anything else, and do one thing only when we are not much pleased by another; e.g. in the theatre the people who eat sweets do so most when the actors are poor. Now since activities are made precise and more enduring and better by their proper pleasure, and injured by alien pleasures, evidently the two kinds of pleasure are far apart. For alien pleasures do pretty much what proper pains do, since activities are destroyed by their proper pains; e.g. if a man finds writing or doing sums unpleasant and painful, he does not write, or does not do sums, because the activity is painful. So an activity suffers contrary effects from its proper pleasures and pains, i.e. from those that supervene on it in virtue of its own nature. And alien pleasures have been stated to do much the same as pain; they destroy the activity, only not to the same degree.

Now since activities differ in respect of goodness and badness, and some are worthy to be chosen, others to be avoided, and others neutral, so, too, are the pleasures; for to each activity there is a proper pleasure. The pleasure proper to a worthy activity is good and that proper to an unworthy activity bad; just as the appetites for noble objects are laudable, those for base objects culpable. But the pleasures involved in activities are more proper to them than the desires; for the latter are separated both in time and in nature, while the former are close to the activities, and so hard to distinguish from them that it admits of dispute whether the activity is not the same as the pleasure. (Still, pleasure does not seem to *be* thought or perception—that would be strange; but because they are not found apart they appear to some people the same.) As activities are different, then, so are the corresponding pleasures. Now sight is
1176a superior to touch in purity, and hearing and smell to taste; the pleasures, therefore, are similarly superior, and those of thought superior to these, and within each of the two kinds some are superior to others.

Each animal is thought to have a proper pleasure, as it has a proper function; viz. that which corresponds to its activity. If we survey them species by species, too, this will be evident; horse, dog, and man have different pleasures, as Heraclitus says 'asses would prefer sweepings to gold';[1] for food is pleasanter than gold to asses. So the pleasures of creatures different in kind differ in kind, and it is plausible to suppose that those of a single species do not differ. But they vary to no small extent, in the case of men at least; the same things delight some people and pain others, and are painful and odious to some, and pleasant to and liked by others. This happens, too, in the case of sweet things; the same things do not seem sweet to a man in a fever and a healthy man—nor hot to a weak man and one in good condition. The same happens in other cases. But in all such matters that which appears to the good man is thought to be really so. If this is correct, as it seems to be, and virtue and the good man as such are the measure of each thing, those also will be pleasures which appear so to him, and those things pleasant which he enjoys. If the things he finds tiresome seem pleasant to some one, that is nothing surprising; for men may be ruined and spoilt in many ways; but the things are not pleasant, but only pleasant to these people and to people in this condition. Those which are admittedly disgraceful plainly should not be said to be pleasures, except to a perverted taste; but of those that are thought to be good what kind of pleasure or what pleasure should be said to be that proper to man? Is it not plain from the corresponding activities? The pleasures follow these. Whether, then, the perfect and supremely happy man has one or more activities, the pleasures that perfect these will be said in the strict sense to be pleasures proper to man, and the rest will be so in a secondary and fractional way, as are the activities.

6 Now that we have spoken of the virtues, the forms of friendship, and the varieties of pleasure, what remains is to discuss in outline the nature of happiness, since this is what

[1] Fr. 9 Diels.

we state the end of human nature to be. Our discussion will be the more concise if we first sum up what we have said already. We said,[1] then, that it is not a disposition; for if it were it might belong to some one who was asleep throughout his life, living the life of a plant, or, again, to some one who was suffering the greatest misfortunes. If 1176b these implications are unacceptable, and we must rather class happiness as an activity, as we have said before,[2] and if some activities are necessary, and desirable for the sake of something else, while others are so in themselves, evidently happiness must be placed among those desirable in themselves, not among those desirable for the sake of something else; for happiness does not lack anything, but is self-sufficient. Now those activities are desirable in themselves from which nothing is sought beyond the activity. And of this nature virtuous actions are thought to be; for to do noble and good deeds is a thing desirable for its own sake.

Pleasant amusements also are thought to be of this nature; we choose them not for the sake of other things; for we are injured rather than benefited by them, since we are led to neglect our bodies and our property. But most of the people who are deemed happy take refuge in such pastimes, which is the reason why those who are ready-witted at them are highly esteemed at the courts of tyrants; they make themselves pleasant companions in the tyrants' favourite pursuits, and that is the sort of man they want. Now these things are thought to be of the nature of happiness because people in despotic positions spend their leisure in them, but perhaps such people prove nothing; for virtue and reason, from which good activities flow, do not depend on despotic position; nor, if these people, who have never tasted pure and generous pleasure, take refuge in the bodily pleasures, should these for that reason be thought more desirable; for boys, too, think the things that are valued among themselves are the best. It is to be expected, then, that, as different things seem valuable to boys and to men, so they

[1] 1095b 31–1096a 2, 1098b 31–1099a 7.

[2] 1098a 5–7.

should to bad men and to good. Now, as we have often maintained,[1] those things are both valuable and pleasant which are such to the good man; and to each man the activity in accordance with his own disposition is most desirable, and, therefore, to the good man that which is in accordance with virtue. Happiness, therefore, does not lie in amusement; it would, indeed, be strange if the end were amusement, and one were to take trouble and suffer hardship all one's life in order to amuse oneself. For, in a word, everything that we choose we choose for the sake of something else—except happiness, which is an end. Now to exert oneself and work for the sake of amusement seems silly and utterly childish. But to amuse oneself in order that one may exert oneself, as Anacharsis[2] puts it, seems right; for amusement is a sort of relaxation, and we need relaxation because we cannot work continuously. Relaxation, then, is not an end; for it is taken for the sake of activity.

The happy life is thought to be virtuous; now a virtuous **1177a**
life requires exertion, and does not consist in amusement. And we say that serious things are better than laughable things and those connected with amusement, and that the activity of the better of any two things—whether it be two elements of our being or two men—is the more serious; but the activity of the better is *ipso facto* superior and more of the nature of happiness. And any chance person —even a slave—can enjoy the bodily pleasures no less than the best man; but no one assigns to a slave a share in happiness—unless he assigns to him also a share in human life. For happiness does not lie in such occupations, but, as we have said before,[3] in virtuous activities.

7 If happiness is activity in accordance with virtue, it is reasonable that it should be in accordance with the highest virtue; and this will be that of the best thing in us. Whether it be reason or something else that is this element which is thought to be our natural ruler and guide and to take

[1] 1099a 13, 1113a 22–33, 1166a 12, 1170a 14–16, 1176a 15–22.

[2] A Scythian prince who was believed to have travelled in Greece, and to have been the author of many aphorisms.

[3] 1098a 16, 1176a 35–b9.

thought of things noble and divine, whether it be itself also divine or only the most divine element in us, the activity of this in accordance with its proper virtue will be perfect happiness. That this activity is contemplative we have already said.[1]

Now this would seem to be in agreement both with what we said before[2] and with the truth. For, firstly, this activity is the best (since not only is reason the best thing in us, but the objects of reason are the best of knowable objects); and, secondly, it is the most continuous, since we can contemplate truth more continuously than we can *do* anything. And we think happiness has pleasure mingled with it, but the activity of philosophic wisdom is admittedly the pleasantest of virtuous activities; at all events the pursuit of it is thought to offer pleasures marvellous for their purity and their enduringness, and it is to be expected that those who know will pass their time more pleasantly than those who inquire. And the self-sufficiency that is spoken of must belong most to the contemplative activity. For while a philosopher, as well as a just man or one possessing any other virtue, needs the necessaries of life, when they are sufficiently equipped with things of that sort the just man needs people towards whom and with whom he shall act justly, and the temperate man, the brave man, and each of the others is in the same case, but the philosopher, even when by himself, can contemplate truth, and the better the wiser he is; he can perhaps do so better if he has fellow-
1177b workers, but still he is the most self-sufficient. And this activity alone would seem to be loved for its own sake; for nothing arises from it apart from the contemplating, while from practical activities we gain more or less apart from the action. And happiness is thought to depend on leisure; for we are busy that we may have leisure, and make war that we may live in peace. Now the activity of the practical virtues is exhibited in political or military affairs, but the actions concerned with these seem

[1] This has not been said, but cf. 1095b 14–1096a 5, 1141a 18–b 3, 1143b 33–1144a 6, 1145a 6–11.

[2] 1097a 25–b 21, 1099a 7–21, 1173b 15–19, 1174b 20–23, 1175b 36–1176a 3.

to be unleisurely. Warlike actions are completely so (for no one chooses to be at war, or provokes war, for the sake of being at war; any one would seem absolutely murderous if he were to make enemies of his friends in order to bring about battle and slaughter); but the action of the statesman is also unleisurely, and—apart from the political action itself—aims at despotic power and honours, or at all events happiness, for him and his fellow citizens—a happiness different from political action, and evidently sought as being different. So if among virtuous actions political and military actions are distinguished by nobility and greatness, and these are unleisurely and aim at an end and are not desirable for their own sake, but the activity of reason, which is contemplative, seems both to be superior in serious worth and to aim at no end beyond itself, and to have its pleasure proper to itself (and this augments the activity), and the self-sufficiency, leisureliness, unweariedness (so far as this is possible for man), and all the other attributes ascribed to the supremely happy man are evidently those connected with this activity, it follows that this will be the complete happiness of man, if it be allowed a complete term of life (for none of the attributes of happiness is *in*complete).

But such a life would be too high for man; for it is not in so far as he is man that he will live so, but in so far as something divine is present in him; and by so much as this is superior to our composite nature is its activity superior to that which is the exercise of the other kind of virtue. If reason is divine, then, in comparison with man, the life according to it is divine in comparison with human life. But we must not follow those who advise us, being men, to think of human things,[1] and, being mortal, of mortal things,[2] but must, so far as we can, make ourselves immortal, and strain every nerve to live in accordance with the best thing in us; for even if it be small in bulk, much more does it in 1178a power and worth surpass everything. This would seem, too, to be each man himself, since it is the authoritative and better

[1] Eur. fr. 1040 Nauck[2].
[2] Pind. *Isthm.* 5. 16 Schroeder; Soph. (*Tereus*) fr. 531 Nauck[2]; Antiphanes fr. 289 Kock.

part of him. It would be strange, then, if he were to choose not the life of his self but that of something else. And what we said before[1] will apply now; that which is proper to each thing is by nature best and most pleasant for each thing; for man, therefore, the life according to reason is best and pleasantest, since reason more than anything else *is* man. This life therefore is also the happiest.

But in a secondary degree the life in accordance with the **8**
other kind of virtue is happy; for the activities in accordance with this befit our human estate. Just and brave acts, and other virtuous acts, we do in relation to each other, observing our respective duties with regard to contracts and services and all manner of actions and with regard to passions; and all of these seem to be typically human. Some of them seem even to arise from the body, and virtue of character to be in many ways bound up with the passions. Practical wisdom, too, is linked to virtue of character, and this to practical wisdom, since the principles of practical wisdom are in accordance with the moral virtues and rightness in morals is in accordance with practical wisdom. Being connected with the passions also, the moral virtues must belong to our composite nature; and the virtues of our composite nature are human; so, therefore, are the life and the happiness which correspond to these. The excellence of the reason is a thing apart; we must be content to say this much about it, for to describe it precisely is a task greater than our purpose requires. It would seem, however, also to need external equipment but little, or less than moral virtue does. Grant that both need the necessaries, and do so equally, even if the statesman's work is the more concerned with the body and things of that sort; for there will be little difference there; but in what they need for the exercise of their activities there will be much difference. The liberal man will need money for the doing of his liberal deeds, and the just man too will need it for the returning of services (for wishes are hard to discern, and even people who are not just pretend to wish to act justly); and the brave man will

[1] 1169^b 33, 1176^b 26.

need power if he is to accomplish any of the acts that correspond to his virtue, and the temperate man will need opportunity; for how else is either he or any of the others to be recognized? It is debated, too, whether the will or the deed is more essential to virtue, which is assumed to involve both; it is surely clear that its perfection involves both; but 1178b
for deeds many things are needed, and more, the greater and nobler the deeds are. But the man who is contemplating the truth needs no such thing, at least with a view to the exercise of his activity; indeed they are, one may say, even hindrances, at all events to his contemplation; but in so far as he is a man and lives with a number of people, he chooses to do virtuous acts; he will therefore need such aids to living a human life.

But that perfect happiness is a contemplative activity will appear from the following consideration as well. We assume the gods to be above all other beings blessed and happy; but what sort of actions must we assign to them? Acts of justice? Will not the gods seem absurd if they make contracts and return deposits, and so on? Acts of a brave man, then, confronting[1] dangers and running risks because it is noble to do so? Or liberal acts? To whom will they give? It will be strange if they are really to have money or anything of the kind. And what would their temperate acts be? Is not such praise tasteless, since they have no bad appetites? If we were to run through them all, the circumstances of action would be found trivial and unworthy of gods. Still, every one supposes that they *live* and therefore that they are active; we cannot suppose them to sleep like Endymion. Now if you take away from a living being action, and still more production, what is left but contemplation? Therefore the activity of God, which surpasses all others in blessedness, must be contemplative; and of human activities, therefore, that which is most akin to this must be most of the nature of happiness.

This is indicated, too, by the fact that the other animals have no share in happiness, being completely deprived of such activity. For while the whole life of the gods is

[1] Reading ἀνδρείου ὑπομένοντος in l. 12 as suggested by Bywater.

blessed, and that of men too in so far as some likeness of such activity belongs to them, none of the other animals is happy, since they in no way share in contemplation. Happiness extends, then, just so far as contemplation does, and those to whom contemplation more fully belongs are more truly happy, not as a mere concomitant but in virtue of the contemplation; for this is in itself precious. Happiness, therefore, must be some form of contemplation.

But, being a man, one will also need external prosperity; for our nature is not self-sufficient for the purpose of contemplation, but our body also must be healthy and must
1179a have food and other attention. Still, we must not think that the man who is to be happy will need many things or great things, merely because he cannot be supremely happy without external goods; for self-sufficiency and action do not involve excess, and we can do noble acts without ruling earth and sea; for even with moderate advantages one can act virtuously (this is manifest enough; for private persons are thought to do worthy acts no less than despots—indeed even more); and it is enough that we should have so much as that; for the life of the man who is active in accordance with virtue will be happy. Solon, too, was perhaps sketching well the happy man when he described him [1] as moderately furnished with externals but as having done (as Solon thought) the noblest acts, and lived temperately; for one can with but moderate possessions do what one ought. Anaxagoras also seems to have supposed the happy man not to be rich nor a despot, when he said [2] that he would not be surprised if the happy man were to seem to most people a strange person; for they judge by externals, since these are all they perceive. The opinions of the wise seem, then, to harmonize with our arguments. But while even such things carry some conviction, the truth in practical matters is discerned from the facts of life; for these are the decisive factor. We must therefore survey what we have already said, bringing it to the test of the facts of life, and if it harmonizes with the facts we must accept it, but if it clashes with them we must suppose it to be mere theory. Now he

[1] Hdt. i. 30,

[2] Diels, *Vors.* 46 A 30.

who exercises his reason and cultivates it seems to be both in the best state of mind and most dear to the gods. For if the gods have any care for human affairs, as they are thought to have, it would be reasonable both that they should delight in that which was best and most akin to them (i. e. reason) and that they should reward those who love and honour this most, as caring for the things that are dear to them and acting both rightly and nobly. And that all these attributes belong most of all to the philosopher is manifest. He, therefore, is the dearest to the gods. And he who is that will presumably be also the happiest; so that in this way too the philosopher will more than any other be happy.

9 If these matters and the virtues, and also friendship and pleasure, have been dealt with sufficiently in outline, are we to suppose that our programme has reached its end? Surely, as the saying goes, where there are things to be done the end is not to survey and recognize the various things, but rather to do them; with regard to virtue, then, 1179b
it is not enough to know, but we must try to have and use it, or try any other way there may be of becoming good. Now if arguments were in themselves enough to make men good, they would justly, as Theognis says,[1] have won very great rewards, and such rewards should have been provided; but as things are, while they seem to have power to encourage and stimulate the generous-minded among our youth, and to make a character which is gently born, and a true lover of what is noble, ready to be possessed by virtue, they are not able to encourage the many to nobility and goodness. For these do not by nature obey the sense of shame, but only fear, and do not abstain from bad acts because of their baseness but through fear of punishment; living by passion they pursue their own pleasures and the means to them, and avoid the opposite pains, and have not even a conception of what is noble and truly pleasant, since they have never tasted it. What argument would remould such people? It is hard, if not impossible, to remove by

[1] Theog. 432–434.

argument the traits that have long since been incorporated in the character; and perhaps we must be content if, when all the influences by which we are thought to become good are present, we get some tincture of virtue.

Now some think that we are made good by nature, others by habituation, others by teaching. Nature's part evidently does not depend on us,[1] but as a result of some divine causes is present in those who are truly fortunate; while argument and teaching, we may suspect, are not powerful with all men, but the soul of the student must first have been cultivated by means of habits for noble joy and noble hatred, like earth which is to nourish the seed. For he who lives as passion directs will not hear argument that dissuades him, nor understand it if he does; and how can we persuade one in such a state to change his ways? And in general passion seems to yield not to argument but to force. The character, then, must somehow be there already with a kinship to virtue, loving what is noble and hating what is base.

But it is difficult to get from youth up a right training for virtue if one has not been brought up under right laws; for to live temperately and hardily is not pleasant to most people, especially when they are young. For this reason their nurture and occupations should be fixed by law; for they will not be painful when they have become customary.
1180a But it is surely not enough that when they are young they should get the right nurture and attention; since they must, even when they are grown up, practise and be habituated to them, we shall need laws for this as well, and generally speaking to cover the whole of life; for most people obey necessity rather than argument, and punishments rather than the sense of what is noble.

This is why some think[2] that legislators ought to stimulate men to virtue and urge them forward by the motive of the noble, on the assumption that those who have been well advanced by the formation of habits will attend to such influences; and that punishments and penalties should be imposed on those who disobey and are of inferior nature,

[1] Omitting ὑπάρχει in l. 22, with Richards.
[2] Pl. *Laws* 722 D ff.

while the incurably bad should be completely banished.[1] A good man (they think), since he lives with his mind fixed on what is noble, will submit to argument, while a bad man, whose desire is for pleasure, is corrected by pain like a beast of burden. This is, too, why they say the pains inflicted should be those that are most opposed to the pleasures such men love.

However that may be, if (as we have said)[2] the man who is to be good must be well trained and habituated, and go on to spend his time in worthy occupations and neither willingly nor unwillingly do bad actions, and if this can be brought about if men live in accordance with a sort of reason and right order, provided this has force,—if this be so, the paternal command indeed has not the required force or compulsive power (nor in general has the command of one man, unless he be a king or something similar), but the law *has* compulsive power, while it is at the same time a rule proceeding from a sort of practical wisdom and reason. And while people hate *men* who oppose their impulses, even if they oppose them rightly, the law in its ordaining of what is good is not burdensome.

In the Spartan state alone, or almost alone, the legislator seems to have paid attention to questions of nurture and occupations; in most states such matters have been neglected, and each man lives as he pleases, Cyclops-fashion, 'to his own wife and children dealing law'.[3] Now it is best that there should be a public and proper care for such matters; but if they are neglected by the community it would seem right for each man to help his children and friends towards virtue, and that they should have the power, or at least the will, to do this.[4]

It would seem from what has been said that he can do this better if he makes himself capable of legislating. For public control is plainly effected by laws, and good control by good laws; whether written or unwritten would seem to make no difference, nor whether they are laws providing for 1180b

[1] Pl. *Prot.* 325 A.

[2] 1179^{b} 31–1180^{a} 5.

[3] *Od.* ix. 114 f.

[4] Placing καὶ δρᾶν αὐτὸ δύνασθαι after συμβάλλεσθαι in l. 32, as Bywater suggests.

the education of individuals or of groups—any more than it does in the case of music or gymnastics and other such pursuits. For as in cities laws and prevailing types of character have force, so in households do the injunctions and the habits of the father, and these have even more because of the tie of blood and the benefits he confers; for the children start with a natural affection and disposition to obey. Further, private education has an advantage over public, as private medical treatment has; for while in general rest and abstinence from food are good for a man in a fever, for a particular man they may not be; and a boxer presumably does not prescribe the same style of fighting to all his pupils. It would seem, then, that the detail is worked out with more precision if the control is private; for each person is more likely to get what suits his case.

But the details can be best looked after, one by one, by a doctor or gymnastic instructor or any one else who has the general knowledge of what is good for every one or for people of a certain kind (for the sciences both are said to be, and are, concerned with what is universal); not but what some particular detail may perhaps be well looked after by an unscientific person, if he has studied accurately in the light of experience what happens in each case, just as some people seem to be their own best doctors, though they could give no help to any one else. None the less, it will perhaps be agreed that if a man does wish to become master of an art or science he must go to the universal, and come to know it as well as possible; for, as we have said, it is with this that the sciences are concerned.

And surely he who wants to make men, whether many or few, better by his care must try to become capable of legislating, if it is through laws that we can become good. For to get any one whatever—any one who is put before us—into the right condition is not for the first chance comer; if any one can do it, it is the man who knows, just as in medicine and all other matters which give scope for care and prudence.

Must we not, then, next examine whence or how one can

learn how to legislate? Is it, as in all other cases, from statesmen? Certainly it was thought to be a part of statesmanship.[1] Or is a difference apparent between statesmanship and the other sciences and arts? In the others the same people are found offering to teach the arts and practising them, e.g. doctors or painters; but while the sophists profess to teach politics, it is practised not by any **1181a** of them but by the politicians, who would seem to do so by dint of a certain skill and experience rather than of thought; for they are not found either writing or speaking about such matters (though it were a nobler occupation perhaps than composing speeches for the law-courts and the assembly), nor again are they found to have made statesmen of their own sons or any other of their friends. But it was to be expected that they should if they could; for there is nothing better than such a skill that they could have left to their cities, or could prefer to have for themselves, or, therefore, for those dearest to them. Still, experience seems to contribute not a little; else they could not have become politicians by familiarity with politics; and so it seems that those who aim at knowing about the art of politics need experience as well.

But those of the sophists who profess the art seem to be very far from teaching it. For, to put the matter generally, they do not even know what kind of thing it is nor what kinds of things it is about; otherwise they would not have classed it as identical with rhetoric or even inferior to it,[2] nor have thought it easy to legislate by collecting the laws that are thought well of;[3] they say it is possible to select the best laws, as though even the selection did not demand intelligence and as though right judgement were not the greatest thing, as in matters of music. For while people experienced in any department judge rightly the works produced in it, and understand by what means or how they are achieved, and what harmonizes with what, the inexperienced must be content if they do not fail to see whether the work has been well or ill made—as in the case

[1] 1141b 24.

[2] Isoc. *Antid.* § 80.

[3] Ib. §§ 82, 83.

of painting. Now laws are as it were the 'works' of the 1181b political art; how then can one learn from them to be a legislator, or judge which are best? Even medical men do not seem to be made by a study of text-books. Yet people try, at any rate, to state not only the treatments, but also how particular classes of people can be cured and should be treated—distinguishing the various habits of body; but while this seems useful to experienced people, to the inexperienced it is valueless. Surely, then, while collections of laws, and of constitutions also, may be serviceable to those who can study them and judge what is good or bad and what enactments suit what circumstances, those who go through such collections without a practised faculty will not have right judgement (unless it be as a spontaneous gift of nature), though they may perhaps become more intelligent in such matters.

Now our predecessors have left the subject of legislation to us unexamined; it is perhaps best, therefore, that we should ourselves study it, and in general study the question of the constitution, in order to complete to the best of our ability our philosophy of human nature. First, then, if anything has been said well in detail by earlier thinkers, let us try to review it; then in the light of the constitutions we have collected let us study what sorts of influence preserve and destroy states, and what sorts preserve or destroy the particular kinds of constitution, and to what causes it is due that some are well and others ill administered. When these have been studied we shall perhaps be more likely to see with a comprehensive view, which constitution is best, and how each must be ordered, and what laws and customs it must use, if it is to be at its best.[1] Let us make a beginning of our discussion.

[1] 1181b 12–23 is a programme for the *Politics*, agreeing to a large extent with the existing contents of that work.

INDEX

94^{a}–99^{b} = 1094^{a}–1099^{b}, 0^{a}–81^{b} = 1100^{a}–1181^{b}

INDEX

INDEX

INDEX

MAGNA MORALIA

ETHICA EUDEMIA

DE VIRTUTIBUS ET VITIIS

IN bringing out this part of the translation, I wish to acknowledge my many obligations to my fellow members of the Oxford Aristotelian Society. The Society has recently read the *Eudemian Ethics*, and while (owing to my occasional absence from the meetings) the translation has not profited as much by this as it might have done, yet I have been able to transmit to Mr. Solomon, and he has accepted, not a few readings and renderings which were suggested at meetings of the Society. Readings the authority for which is not given in the notes come as a rule from this source.

The introduction, the tables of contents, and the indices to the three works contained in this part have all been prepared by Mr. St. George Stock.

Mr. Stock and Mr. Solomon have for the most part rendered λόγος in the traditional way, as 'reason'. Personally I doubt whether this rendering is ever required, but the final choice in such a question rests with the translators.

W. D. ROSS.

CONTENTS OF INTRODUCTION

INTRODUCTION

§ 1. The three moral treatises that go under the name of Aristotle present a problem somewhat analogous to that of the three Synoptic Gospels. All three used once to be ascribed to the direct authorship of Aristotle with the same simple-heartedness, or the same absence of reflection, with which all three Gospels used to be ascribed to the Holy Ghost. We may see that some advance, or at all events some movement, has been made in the Aristotelian problem, if we remember that it was once possible for so great a critic as Schleiermacher to maintain that the *Magna Moralia* was the original treatise from which the two others were derived. Nowadays the opinion of Spengel is generally accepted, namely, that the *Nicomachean Ethics* emanates directly from the mind of Aristotle himself, that the *Eudemian Ethics* contains the same matter recast by another hand, and that the *Magna Moralia* is the work of a later writer who had both the other treatises before him. Whether the three books which are common to the *Nicomachean* and *Eudemian Ethics* (*E.N.* v, vi, vii: *E.E.* iv, v, vi) proceed from the writer of the former or of the latter work is a point which is still under debate. To an Oxford man indeed who has been nurtured on the *Nicomachean Ethics*, and to whom that treatise has become, mentally speaking, 'bone of his bone and flesh of his flesh', it seems too self-evident to require discussion that the *Nicomachean Ethics* is the substance of which the others are the shadow. But this confidence may be born of prejudice, and it is possible that, if the same person had had the *Eudemian Ethics* equally carefully instilled into him in his youth, he might on making acquaintance with the *Nicomachean* find nothing more in that than a less literary rearrangement of the *Eudemian*. There is no doubt a prejudice in favour of the familiar, which has to be guarded against, but we may encourage ourselves by remembering that the preference for the *Nicomachean Ethics* is not confined to Oxford, or to English or foreign Universities, or to modern times, since, as Grant points out, there have been many commentaries by Greek and Latin writers on the *Nicomachean*, but not one on the *Eudemian Ethics*. Herein we have an unconscious testimony to the superior value of the Nicomachean work.

§ 2. But why 'Nicomachean'? There is no certain tradition on this subject. Our earliest information is derived from the well-known passage in Cicero,[1] from which we gather that the *Nicomachean Ethics* was commonly ascribed to Aristotle himself, whereas Cicero thought that it might well have been written by his son Nicomachus. But what we are otherwise told about Nicomachus rather goes against this. Aristocles the Peripatetic, who is said to have been teacher to Alexander Aphrodisiensis, is thus quoted by Eusebius in his *Praeparatio Evangelica*, xv. 2 § 10: 'After the death of Pytheas, daughter of Hermeias, Aristotle married Epyllis of Stagira, by whom he had a son Nicomachus. He is said to have been brought up as an orphan in the house of Theophrastus and died, while a mere lad, in war.' On the other hand Diogenes Laertius at about the same date as Aristocles (A. D. 200) evidently shared Cicero's opinion that Nicomachus, the son of Aristotle, wrote the work which bears his name.[2]

A different tradition, which appears in some of the commentators, is to the effect that Aristotle himself wrote three treatises on morals, one of which he addressed to his disciple Eudemus, another to his father Nicomachus, and yet a third to his son of the same name. The two latter

[1] *Fin.* v. § 12 'qua re teneamus Aristotelem et eius filium Nicomachum, cuius accurate scripti de moribus libri dicuntur illi quidem esse Aristoteli, sed non video, cur non potuerit patris similis esse filius.'

[2] D. L. viii. § 88 *φησὶ δ' αὐτὸν* (i. e. Eudoxus) Νικόμαχος ὁ Ἀριστοτέλους τὴν ἡδονὴν λέγειν τὸ ἀγαθόν. Cp. *E. N.* 1101^b 27 and 1172^b 9.

were distinguished from one another by the one addressed to the father being called 'the great Nicomacheans', while that addressed to the son was called 'the little Nicomacheans'.[1]

That all three works were by Aristotle himself is assumed by Atticus the Platonist, who lived in the time of Marcus Aurelius, and who is the first writer to mention the *Magna Moralia*,[2] while the common authorship of the last-mentioned and of the *Nicomachean Ethics* is similarly assumed by the Scholiast on Plato, *Rep.* 495 E.[3] It seems to be only by Aspasius in a note on *E.N.* viii. 8 that Eudemus is recognized as being himself the author of the treatise which bears his name.[4]

§ 3. Let us now inquire what is known about Eudemus. First of all he is called by Simplicius[5] 'the most genuine among the followers of Aristotle', which may be taken to mean that he followed him most closely, as indeed we are expressly told elsewhere that of all the interpreters he was best acquainted with the mind of Aristotle. We are sometimes informed that Theophrastus deviated from Aristotle, but we never hear this of Eudemus. Then there is the charming story told by Aulus Gellius[6] of how Aristotle elected his successor by indicating his preference for the wine of Lesbos over that of Rhodes. 'Both are good,' pronounced the philosopher after tasting them, 'but ἡδίων ὁ Λέσβιος'. It was clearly understood by all that the suavity of Theophrastus of Lesbos had been preferred to the more austere excellence of Eudemus of Rhodes.

Further we are told by Ammonius[7] that 'the disciples of Aristotle, Eudemus and Phanias and Theophrastus, in

[1] Comm. Porphyr. Prolegg. in Categ. Schol. in Arist. 9[b] 20 sqq.: David in Cat. Schol. 25[a] 40.

[2] Eus. *Pr. Ev.* xv. 4 § 6 Heinechen αἱ γοῦν Ἀριστοτέλους περὶ ταῦτα πραγματεῖαι, Εὐδήμειοί τε καὶ Νικομάχειοι καὶ μεγάλων ἠθικῶν ἐπιγραφόμενοι.

[3] He points out that the contrary of μικροπρέπεια is called by Aristotle βαναυσία or ἀπειροκαλία in the Nicomachean Ethics, but σαλακωνία ἐν τοῖς μεγάλοις.

[4] λέγει δὲ καὶ Εὔδημος καὶ Θεόφραστος, ὅτι καὶ αἱ καθ' ὑπεροχὴν φιλίαι κτλ. See *E.E.* vii. 10 § 9, 1242[b] 4.

[5] Ar. *Phys.* fol. 93[b] Εὔδημος ὁ γνησιώτατος τῶν Ἀριστοτέλους ἑταίρων.

[6] *N.A.* xiii. 5.

[7] Brandis, *Scholia in Aristot.* p. 28, note.

rivalry with their master, wrote *Categories* and *On Interpretation* and *Analytics*'. As to *Categories* or *de Interpretatione* written by Eudemus nothing more seems to be known, but the following works at least are ascribed to him by ancient writers :—

On the Angle . . .	(περὶ γωνίας).
Researches in Geometry .	(γεωμετρικαὶ ἱστορίαι).
Researches in Arithmetic .	(ἀριθμητικὴ ἱστορία).
Researches in Astronomy .	(ἀστρολογικαὶ ἱστορίαι).
Analytics	(ἀναλυτικά).
On Diction	(περὶ λέξεως).
On Physics	(φυσικά).[1]

It would appear from this list that, apart from Ethics, the chief interest of Eudemus lay in Mathematics. But Fritzsche has made it appear probable that Eudemus of Rhodes is identical with the author of a work *On Animals*, which was used by Aelian, and also with the famous anatomist of the same name who is often mentioned by Galen. However this may be—and Fritzsche himself abstains from pronouncing judgement—the composition of his treatise on Physics was no mere by-work with Eudemus, for we know that while he was engaged on the task he wrote to Theophrastus to send him a correct copy of the fifth book of Aristotle's *Physics*, because his own copy was vitiated by clerical errors. It would be a boon to us if some later member of the School had taken the like care with regard to the *Eudemian Ethics*; for as the text of that work now stands a reader or translator has to conjecture his way through a great part of it. That the opinion of Eudemus on general questions of philosophy was held in high esteem appears from the statement made by the Greek commentators that Aristotle before publishing his *Metaphysics* sent the work to Eudemus, and that in consequence of some difficulties raised by him its publication was delayed, so that it did not appear until after the

[1] References for the above writings are given by Fritzsche in his edition of the *Eudemian Ethics*.

author's death. It is said that the appendix to Book I known as *α′ ἔλαττον* was the work of Pasicles, the nephew of Eudemus, son of his brother Boethus.

§ 4. We turn now to the work known as the *Eudemian Ethics*. The first thing that must strike any one who reads it is its general resemblance to the *Nicomachean Ethics*. This, following Grant, we may exhibit as follows:—

E.E.	i, ii	=	*E.N.*	i–iii. 5.
—	iii	=	—	iii. 6–end of iv.
—	iv, v, vi	=	—	v, vi, vii.
—	vii	=	—	viii, ix.
—	viii new.			

Further we may notice that in both treatises there is first a scheme of the moral virtues with some brief remarks followed by a more detailed treatment of each of the virtues in particular. Both treatises also are in what may be called a half-baked state, presenting now the appearance of mere lecture-notes, now that of finished literary work. Thus in *E.E.* 1220ᵇ 10 the words *ἡ διαίρεσις ἐν τοῖς ἀπηλλαγμένοις* may be a memorandum for personal guidance, which had a meaning for the author, but has none for us. The same explanation perhaps applies to 1218ᵃ 36 *τὸ ἐν τῷ λόγῳ γεγραμμένον* and to 1244ᵇ 30, 31 *ὥσπερ ἐν τῷ λόγῳ γέγραπται*. In using the words *ἐν τοῖς λόγοις* in 1240ᵃ 23, 1244ᵃ 20 the writer may be referring to his own lectures, while in 1233ᵃ 1, the words 'But there's left there' are suggestive of the lecturer pointing to some diagram which he has just set before the eyes of his class.

§ 5. Grant has noticed how the greater precision of statement which we sometimes find in *E.E.* as compared with *E.N.* is suggestive of a commentator improving on the original author. Instances of this may be seen in connexion with the Delian inscription (1214ᵃ 1–6: *E.N.* 1299ᵃ 24–29), the saying of Anaxagoras (1216ᵃ 11–16; *E.N.* 1179ᵃ 13), Heraclitus on anger (1223ᵇ 22: *E.N.* 1105ᵃ 8), Socrates on courage (1229ᵃ 16, 1230ᵃ 7: *E.N.* 1116ᵇ 4), Philoxenus (1231ᵃ 17).

§ 6. Another thing which tends to show that the *Eudemian*

Ethics is the later work is that while it creates an impression of less power than the *Nicomachean*, it at the same time presents a more developed form of doctrine. Thus the division of impulse (ὄρεξις) into its three species, which is latent in *E.N.*, becomes patent in *E.E.*[1]

Again the true nature of the σώφρων of *E.N.* 1223^b 5, or sober-minded man, who estimates himself at his true worth, comes out more clearly in *E.E.* 1233^a 16–25, where it appears that he is of the same nature as the man of great mind, who is in fact only a particular instance of sober-minded man, namely one whose merits happen to be superlative. Eudemus too is not content to enumerate the ways in which Happiness may conceivably be acquired, but adds some inducements to believe that the division is exhaustive.[2] He also states explicitly that Happiness must consist mainly in three things, Wisdom, Virtue, and Pleasure, which is only implied in *E.N.*[3] Generally the connexion of moral virtue with pleasure and pain comes out more clearly in *E.E.* than in *E.N.*, insomuch that this connexion is made to form part of the definition of moral virtue in *E.E.* (1227^b 5–10). The frank rejection also in *E.E.* of the Platonic ideas altogether as 'mere empty logical fictions' reflects weariness of a controversy which has been threshed out sufficiently 'both in the exoteric and in the philosophical treatises'.[4]

The method of arriving at a definition of Purpose is the same in both treatises, but in *E.E.* it is worked out with more consciousness of logic than in *E.N.* For instance in *E.E.* we have the explicit assumption that Purpose is one of two things, either opinion or impulse,[5] which in *E.N.* we have to extract for ourselves from the seemingly loose assertion—'Those who say that it is appetite or anger or wish or opinion of some kind do not seem to speak rightly'.[6]

The question why we should do what is right is not touched in *E.N.* or *E.E.*; in both it is assumed that τὸ καλόν shines by its own light. But while *E.N.* leaves

[1] 1223^a 26. Cp. *E.N.* 1111^b 11.
[2] 1214^a 26–30.
[3] 1214^a 30–^{b} 5, 1218^b 31–35.
[4] 1217^b 16–23.
[5] *E.E.* 1225^b 22, 23.
[6] 1111^b 10–12.

the matter so, *E. E.* gives us the explicit declaration that there is no λόγος of the σκοπός,[1] that is, no rational account to be given of an end. It is in fact a question of values. This is what *E. N.* leads up to, but does not say. Aristotle often speaks of λόγος as a faculty which supplies us with ends. Eudemus coming after him is inclined to think that it ought to be confined to means, though in 1229ᵃ 2 he says ὁ δὲ λόγος τὸ καλὸν αἱρεῖσθαι κελεύει. This latter is the orthodox view, which imports a moral meaning into λόγος, just as a moral meaning was imported into προαίρεσις, so that, strictly speaking, there was no such thing as a bad will (προαίρεσις). When Eudemus in a different context[2] asserts that 'Virtue is an instrument of the intellect' he has managed by anticipation exactly to reverse the famous saying of Comte that 'The intellect is the servant of the heart'.

§ 7. The *Nicomachean Ethics* might have emanated from a pure intelligence, but there are some touches of personal feeling about Eudemus. He is inclined to Pessimism. There is about him that note of melancholy which seems inseparable from the Asiatic Greek from Homer downwards. He has not got far in his treatise before we find him involved in a discussion of the question—'Is life worth living?' Eudemus, it is a relief to find, has not such a good conceit of himself as most of the Greek philosophers, whose tall talk about the sage seems to have incapacitated them from facing the rather sordid realities of the actual moral life. Eudemus speaks as one who has felt, when he includes the attractions of ignoble pleasures among the things which make it 'better not to be'.[3]

§ 8. Even with the *Eudemian Ethics* before us it is difficult to pronounce judgement on the literary merits of the writer, so corrupt is the text in many passages. Some parts of the treatise, especially the first book, show that he can write well and clearly; but at the same time there are signs here and there of a certain muddle-headedness, displayed among other things in his lugging in recognized

[1] *E. E.* 1227ᵇ 24, 25.

[2] 1248ᵃ 29 ἡ γὰρ ἀρετὴ τοῦ νοῦ ὄργανον.

[3] 1215ᵇ 25, 26.

doctrines of the School in inappropriate places, e. g. the two uses of anything from the *Politics*, when he is discussing the virtue of liberality.[1]

The close correspondence in the subject-matter between *E. E.* and *E. N.* is quite in accordance with what we are told by the commentators as to the fidelity of Eudemus to his master's doctrines. We find no deviations in the main outlines, though there are some on minor points, for instance, the writer of *E. E.* deliberately rejects the definition of wit proposed in *E. N.*, which shows that he must have had this work before him.[2]

On the whole the estimate that we form of this writer is that he is a man of sound judgement, but destitute of originality. Like the writer of *E. N.*, he has passages on Method[3] and is frequent in his appeal to Induction.[4] But personally he is more interested in the form than in the matter of knowledge. He has an unseasonable fondness for definition,[5] is over-addicted to distinction,[6] and likes to guard his statements in a way which seems due to long polemical habit.[7] In one word he is somewhat of a formalist. This is in keeping with the list of works which we have seen ascribed to Eudemus, which deal with Mathematics, Logic, and Diction, with the one exception of his work on Physics.

§ 9. The last point to notice about the writer of *E. E.*, whom we may as well frankly call Eudemus, is his religious tone, which differentiates him from Aristotle as we conceive of him. But the difference seems to be in the tone, not really in the utterance. For perhaps it is not true to say with Grant that Eudemus does not identify θεωρία with the highest good. Is not this just what he means by saying that the right limit with regard to health, wealth, friends, and all natural goods is whatever promotes most the contemplation of God? And when he alters his phrase into 'worshipping and contemplating God', we need not

1 *E. E.* 1231^b 38–^{a}9 : *Pol.* 1257^a 6–14.
2 *E. E.* 1234^a 21 : *E. N.* 1128^a 26.
3 1216^b 26–1217^a 17 : 1235^b 12–18.
4 1219^a 1, 1220^a 28, ^{b}30, 1248^b 26.
5 1215^a 29–32.
6 1249^b 15.
7 1221^b 4–7.

suppose that by 'worshipping' he means a Semitic prostration of the body, but rather the earnest prosecution by the mind of the search for truth. That Eudemus' conception of the divine nature was really no less abstract than that of Aristotle seems to follow from the hint which he throws out in passing that the things which admit not of change may perhaps be the highest in their nature.[1]

§ 10. We come now to the vexed question of the three disputed books. But let it be observed to begin with that the question is not one of any great importance. For in any case the doctrine is Aristotle's. The point in dispute is whether the three books come directly from the hand that wrote the *Nicomachean Ethics*, which we assume to be that of Aristotle himself, or indirectly through the most faithful of his followers, Eudemus.

§ 11. Neither the *Nicomachean* nor the *Eudemian Ethics*[2] would be complete without some treatment of the queen of virtues, Justice, of the Intellectual Virtues, or of that half-way house on the road to virtue, which is known as Self-control. There are therefore two gaps which have been filled up by the same three books. But if on inquiry it should turn out that these books fit into one of the gaps more neatly than into the other, it will be reasonable to conclude that that is the hole for which they were originally intended.

§ 12. Now if these books be assigned to *E. N.*, we have on the one hand two treatments of Pleasure in the same volume[3] which entirely ignore each other's presence, and on the other no treatment of Pleasure by Eudemus, though that is a subject on the importance of which he is specially insistent. This argument has authority as well as reason to support it. Aspasius ascribed the treatment of Pleasure in Book VII to Eudemus on the ground that Aristotle in the *Nicomachean Ethics* speaks as though he had never yet said anything on the subject.[4] The double treatment of

[1] 1217^a 32–34.
[2] By *E. N.* will now be meant *Ethica Nicomachea* i–iv, viii–x, and by *E. E. Ethica Eudemia* i–iii, vii, viii.
[3] *E. N.* 1152^b 1–1154^b 31, 1172^a 16–1176^a 29.
[4] Aspasius on *E. N.* vii. 14, p. 151, ll. 21–26.

Pleasure is a difficulty, or rather an impossibility, on the hypothesis of Aristotelian authorship of the doubtful books, whereas on the hypothesis of Eudemian authorship things fall into their place. We have, as might be expected, a treatment of pleasure from the hand of Aristotle himself and another in close imitation of it from Eudemus.

§ 13. Another argument which certainly carries weight is that in the summary which is given at the beginning of the ninth chapter of Book X the writer enumerates the topics of *E. N.*, but ignores the contents of the doubtful books, Pleasure alone excepted. 'Having therefore' the passage runs, 'said enough in outline about these things (i. e. θεωρία), and about the virtues, and further about friendship and pleasure, are we to suppose that our purpose is accomplished?' Here we seem to have Aristotle himself telling us what were originally the exact contents of *E. N.*

§ 14. The mathematical character of Book V seems in favour of Eudemian authorship, though Professor Burnet gives this argument a curious twist the other way. He says in effect [1] that the fifth book must be by Aristotle, because it is so bad. 'Mathematics', he tells us, 'was just the one province of human knowledge in which Aristotle did not show himself a master, while Eudemus was one of the foremost mathematicians of an age in which that science made more progress than it ever did again till the seventeenth century.' But is not this reducible to the fact that Eudemus wrote on mathematics? And have we independent evidence that Aristotle was weak in this department?

§ 15. One obvious line of argument as to the authorship of the disputed books is to inquire whether there are any differences of doctrine between them and *E. N.* or *E. E.* It would be natural to assign the three books to that treatise with which they are least in disagreement.

Now the writer of Book V speaks of actions due to anger as being done knowingly, whereas in *E. N.* we are told that they are not.[2]

Again in Book VII it is proved that incontinence of

[1] Introd. pp. xiii, xiv.
[2] v. 8 § 8, 1135^b 20: *E. N.* iii. 1 § 14, 1110^b 27.

anger is less disgraceful than incontinence of appetite.[1] But in *E. N.* it is laid down that it is more difficult to contend against pleasure than against anger, and that virtue is always concerned with the more difficult,[2] whence it follows that incontinence of anger is more disgraceful than incontinence of appetite.

Similarly in Book VII we have the statement that continence or self-control is more choiceworthy than endurance.[3] Now endurance consists in resisting pain and self-control in abstaining from pleasure; and we are told in *E. N.* that it is more difficult to resist pain than to abstain from pleasure;[4] whence it follows, on the principle of the more difficult being the more virtuous, that endurance is more choiceworthy than self-control.

§ 16. Another line of argument which naturally presents itself is that based on references. But here the ground is a quagmire. For the works ascribed to Aristotle have been as 'heavily edited' as the Sacred Books of the Jews. Nevertheless we must try to see in what direction this argument points. There are three questions which present themselves.

1. Are there references in *E. N.* to the doubtful books?

2. Are there references in *E. E.* to the doubtful books?

3. Do the references in the doubtful books point rather to a connexion with *E. N.* or with *E. E.*?

1. In *E. N.* ii. 7 § 16, 1108^b 5–10 there is an anticipation of Books V and VI. But it is singularly out of place and is for well-known reasons open to the gravest suspicion on the score of genuineness.

Again in *E. N.* iv. 9 § 8, 1128^b 33–35 there is an anticipation of Books VII and V in a tag appended to the treatment of Shame.

Further *E. N.* x. 6 § 1, 1176^a 30, 31, like *E. N.* x. 9 § 1, 1179^a 33, 34, which has been already spoken of, is a good summary of the contents of *E. N.* minus the doubtful books. We may notice that in both these passages pleasure is mentioned *after* friendship.

[1] vii. 6 §§ 1–5, 1149^a 24–^{b}25.

[2] ii. 3 § 10, 1105^a 7–9.

[3] vii. 7 § 4, 1150^a 36.

[4] iii. 9 § 2, 1117^a 34, 35.

2. In *E.E.* 1216ᵃ 37 Eudemus promises to inquire later into pleasure, which is done in Book VII, while the subject is again touched on in *E.E.* 1249ᵃ 17–20.

In *E.E.* 1218ᵇ 16 Eudemus makes a promise which is considered by Fischer and Fritzsche to be fulfilled in Book VI. 1141ᵇ 23.

E.E. 1227ᵃ 2, 3 is a reference to Book V. 8 § 1, 1135ᵃ 15–36ᵃ 9.

E.E. 1227ᵇ 16 contains a promise which is fulfilled in Book VI. See especially 1144ᵃ 35.

E.E. 1231ᵇ 2–4 contains a promise which may be regarded as fulfilled in vii. 4, though some doubt this.

E.E. 1234ᵃ 28. The promise here made is fulfilled in vi. 13 § 1, 1144ᵇ 1–17.

E.E. 1234ᵇ 14 is a transition formula to Book V, like that in *E.N.* 1128ᵃ 35 with only the difference of ἤδη for νῦν.

E.E. 1249ᵃ 17 looks back on Pleasure as a subject treated of. But where is this done, if we refuse to Eudemus the treatise on Pleasure in Book VII?

It will be seen from the above that the references, actual or possible, in *E.E.* to the doubtful books are much more numerous than those in *E.N.* They also come in much more naturally.

Now let us shift our point of view and see how things look from the other side. As *E.E.* is so like *E.N.* there will naturally be many references which are satisfied by either treatise.

v. 1 § 2, 1129ᵃ 5, 6. A reference to previous method, which is much the same in both.

v. 4 § 6, 1132ᵃ 17. There is mention here of 'gain' and 'loss', 'between which the equal is, as we found (ἦν), a mean.' There is nothing in *E.N.* for this to refer to, but we find it in *E.E.* 1221ᵃ 4, 23.

v. 7 § 7, 1135ᵃ 15. This is not satisfied by either treatise.

v. 8 § 3, 1135ᵃ 23–25. 'I call that voluntary, as has been said before.' The substance of the definition here given is to be found in *E.N.* iii. 1 § 20, 1111ᵃ 23, 24, but the language is rather that of *E.E.* ii. 9 § 2, 1225ᵇ 8, 9.

vii. 1 § 4, 1145^a 34. 'And about Vice we have spoken previously' (in both treatises).

vii. 2 § 5, 1146^a 8. The previous passage here referred to must be vi. 8 §§ 8, 9, 1142^a 25–30. But all that this goes to show is that Books VI and VII are by the same writer.

vii. 4 § 2, 1147^b 28. Neutral.

vii. 7 § 1, 1150^a 11. Neutral.

§ 17. We now come to the argument from language.

Grant used the word ὅρος as a striking instance of 'the agreement of philosophical phraseology between the Disputed Books and the *Eudemian Ethics*. In the sense of 'standard' or 'determining principle' this word occurs three times in these books.[1] It is not to be found in *E. N.*,[2] but it is used by Eudemus. But we must not insist very strongly on this argument, for, if pressed, it would prove the Eudemian authorship of the *Politics*, in which this use of ὅρος abounds.[3]

The way of speaking of the goods of fortune as being ἁπλῶς ἀγαθά, which presents itself in the fifth book,[4] is not to be found in *E. N.*, but reappears at the end of *E. E.*[5]

Fritzsche noted the use of the word μεταμελητικός in the disputed books[6] as a sign of Eudemian authorship. It occurs in *E. E.* 1240^b 23, but not in *E. N.*

In vi. 12 § 5, 1144^a 5 we find the phrase τῆς ὅλης ἀρετῆς, which Professor Stewart notices does not occur in *E. N.*, but is used by Eudemus.[7]

Professor Stewart has also pointed out that the peculiar phrase ἐπιθυμίας λαμβάνειν, which appears in vii. 9 § 2, 1151^b 11 is to be found also in *E. E.* 1231^a 29.

There is hardly anything more distinctive of Eudemus than his fondness for the formula ἀληθὲς μέν, οὐ σαφὲς δέ.[8]

[1] vi. 1 § 1, 1138^b 23, vi. 1 § 3, 1138^b 34, vii. 13 § 4, 1153^b 25.

[2] *E. N.* i. 7 § 7, 1097^b 12 is different.

[3] For contending views on this subject see Grant, Essay I, pp. 60, 61 Burnet, pp. 250, 251.

[4] v. 1 § 9, 1129^b 3, v. 6 § 6, 1134^b 4, v. 9 § 17 1137^a 26.

[5] 1249^b 25. See Grant, Essay I, p. 62.

[6] vii. 7 § 2, 1150^a 21, vii. 8 § 1 (*bis*), 1150^b 29, 30.

[7] *E. E.* ii. 1 § 14, 1219^b 21.

[8] *E. E.* 1216^b 22, 23, 1217^a 19, 1220^a 16, 17, 1249^b 6.

Now in vi. 1 § 2, 1138b 26 we find the same formula, which nowhere occurs in *E. N.*

It certainly looks as if the phrase ἡ κατὰ διάμετρον σύζευξις in v. 5 § 8 came from the same hand as the words κατὰ διάμετρον συζεύγνυσιν in *E. E.* 1242b 16. But the latter were written by the mathematician Eudemus. Therefore it is likely that the former were so also.

In v. 8 § 3, 1135a 27 we find the words ὥσπερ εἴ τις λαβὼν τὴν χεῖρα αὐτοῦ τύπτοι ἕτερον. In *E. E.* 1224b 13 we find them again with the substitution of τινά for ἕτερον.

In Book VII[1] there is a contrast drawn between the θρασύς and the θαρραλέος, where θαρραλέος as a substitute for ἀνδρεῖος comes as rather a surprise upon the reader familiar with *E. N.*, but it fits in nicely with the distinction drawn by Eudemus between θάρσος as a good quality and θράσος as a bad.[2]

εὐθύς in the sense of *ipso facto* occurs in the disputed books[3] and in *E. E.*,[4] but not in *E. N.*

In *E. N.* the abstract noun used as the contrary of πραότης is ὀργιλότης;[5] that used in *E. E.* is χαλεπότης.[6] In the disputed books χαλεπότης is used.[7]

In vi. 1 § 14, 1129b 22 μὴ τύπτειν μηδὲ κακηγορειν are what occur to the writer as attributes of the πρᾶος. This would have a special appropriateness, if it came from the same writer who made the πλήκτης καὶ λοιδορητικός into a species co-ordinate with the ὀξύθυμος, χαλεπός, and πικρός,[8] to which species there is nothing to correspond in *E. N.*

The use of the neuter plural with a plural verb is not, I believe, to be found in *E. N.* It appears, however, in the disputed books and also in *E. E.*[9]

Lastly the use of the relative for the interrogative in v. 8 § 3, 1135a 25 tallies with the practice of *E. E.*, and not with that of *E. N.*[10]

1 vii. 9 § 2, 1151b 7, 8.

2 *E. E.* 1234b 12.

3 v. 10 § 4, 1137b 19, vi. 5 § 6, 1140b 17.

4 1237a 28.

5 1108a 7, 1125b 29.

6 1231b 6.

7 v. 2 § 2, 1130a 18, vii. 5 § 5, 1149a 6, vii. 6 § 2, 1149b 7.

8 *E. E.* ii. 3 § 12, 1221b 14.

9 v. 4 § 2, 1131b 30: *E. E.* 1231b 35, 1232a 10. It is common in the *Metaphysics*.

10 *E. E.* 1225b 2, 5: *E. N.* iii. 1 § 16, 1111a 3–5.

§ 18. So far everything seems to go in favour of assigning the disputed books to *E. E.* But there is evidence from the *Politics*, which must be taken account of. The writer of that treatise, who has always been regarded as Aristotle himself, refers to the *Ethics* with all the modesty of an author.[1] In this of course there is nothing to surprise us. But out of six references in the *Politics* to the *Ethics* three are to Book V. We seem therefore to have the warrant of Aristotle himself for ascribing this book to him. And his it undoubtedly is, so far as the thought goes. Even the illustrations come from him. For instance an example given of the conventionally just is the hero-worship paid to Brasidas at Amphipolis. How natural this is in the mouth of Aristotle himself, who had lived near the place! But would it have occurred to Eudemus of Rhodes?

While, however, we regard Book V, and with it Books VI and VII, as the genuine outcome of the mind of Aristotle, there is no need to suppose that, in the form in which we have these books, they were written by him. The references in the *Politics* are not necessarily to a written work. They may be only to the author's lectures on Ethics. Part of these lectures have come down to us in the written form into which they were put either by Aristotle himself or possibly by his son. But part we have only as worked up by Eudemus and adjusted to his own treatise. That seems to be all that can be said with safety.

§ 19. The *Magna Moralia* justifies its name by its containing in a succinct form the whole course of Aristotle's lectures on Ethics, both what we get from *E. N.* and what we get from *E. E.*, and further what is contained in the doubtful books. At starting we find the writer distinguishing like Eudemus between the two questions of what virtue is and from what it comes, while towards the end he brings in the Eudemian discussion of Good Luck[2] and that on Nobility and Goodness,[3] which have no counterparts in

[1] *Pol.* iv. 11 § 3, 1295^a 37, vii. 13 § 5, 1332^a 8.
[2] *M. M.* ii. 8 = *E. E.* viii. 14.
[3] *M. M.* ii. 9 = *E. E.* viii. 15, 1248^b 8–49^a 16.

E.N. The writer's treatment of pleasure displays affinity both with that of Book VII and that of *E.N.* x. How close is the correspondence between *M.M.* and *E.N.* may be illustrated by the following striking instance. In *E.N.* 1109ᵃ 15, 16 it is written—'and so we are more prone to intemperance than to sobriety' (κοσμιότητα). Here the natural word to employ would be 'stolidity' (ἀναισθησία)[1] which is, in fact, employed by the Paraphrast, but which Aristotle seems to have avoided because of its being unusual,[2] even at the cost of a slight impropriety; but when the writer of the *Magna Moralia* comes to the same subject we find him also using 'sobriety' instead of 'stolidity'.

§ 20. Who was this writer? He pronounces judgement in the first person as to what 'appears to me' (1181ᵇ 28); he poses as the representative of the school (1198ᵃ 20); and he claims to have written the *Analytics* (1201ᵇ 25). This last pretension is peculiarly inconvenient. Aristotle's *Analytics* we know, and Eudemus' *Analytics* we know of: but who is this? We seem to be reduced to this alternative. Either we have here Aristotle himself, as Schleiermacher thought (but against this there are at all events linguistic objections), or else we have some student who has attended the whole course of lectures on Ethics, and written them out as coming from the Master. One thing seems certain, namely, that there is no allusion in the treatise which might not well have been made by Aristotle. Mention is made of Clearchus, tyrant of Heraclea Pontica, in whom Aristotle would have a special interest, as he had, like Aristotle himself, been a pupil of Plato's. The transformation of one whom he probably knew personally from 'a most generous, kind, and gentle student', such as he is described by Isocrates (423 d) as being, into a monster of iniquity[3] must have presented a curious psychological problem to the philosopher. Clearchus was assassinated in B.C. 353, when Aristotle himself would have just turned

[1] See *E.N.* 1109ᵃ 4, 1119ᵃ 7.
[2] See *E.N.* ii. 7 § 3, 1107ᵇ 7, 8.
[3] See Justin xvi. 4 § 5.

thirty. Eight years later, in B.C. 345, there occurred an event which Aristotle was not likely to forget, namely, the treacherous seizure of his friend Hermeias, the autocrat of Atarneus, and his delivery to Artaxerxes, who put him to death. The Greek who perpetrated this crime was Mentor, the very person who is selected by the writer as an illustration of the man who is clever, but not wise (1197^a 21). The last historical event alluded to is the death of Darius in B.C. 330, when Aristotle was 54 years old. We may notice that the writer of *M. M.* agrees with Eudemus in taking the Indians instead of the Scythians[1] as the type of a far-away people, with whom we have no practical concern. The exploits of Alexander in India would make it extremely appropriate for Aristotle himself to say—'For we often think about things in India, but it does not follow that we purpose them' (1189^a 20).

§ 21. As regards the subject-matter of *M. M.* the most important point to notice is that here we get the crowning word of Peripatetic Ethics, for which we wait in vain in *E. N.* or even in *E. E.*—'Speaking generally, it is not the case, as the rest of the world think, that reason is the principle of and guide to virtue, but rather the feelings.'[2] It has been thought that 'the rest of the world' (*οἱ ἄλλοι*) here is meant for the Stoics, but they only carried on the doctrine of Plato and Speusippus. Professor Burnet, rightly, I think, declares that the *Magna Moralia* 'shows no trace of Stoic influence'.

On the subject of the self-contemplation of God the writer of *M. M.* dissents both from Aristotle and Eudemus; but he leaves the question undetermined.[3]

In one passage of this treatise[4] we find the statement that intellectual virtue is not praised. This, though it is in accordance with modern ideas, contradicts both *E. N.*[5] and *E. E.*[6] It is, however, itself contradicted in another passage.[7]

The poison case in the Areopagus, which is obscure in

[1] *M. M.* 1189^a 20: *E. E.* 1226^a 29: *E. N.* 1112^a 28.
[2] 1206^b 17–19.
[3] 1212^b 37–1213^a 7.
[4] 1185^b 9.
[5] i. 13 § 20, 1103^a 8.
[6] ii. i. § 18, 1220^a 5.
[7] 1197^a 17.

E. E.[1] and which escaped notice altogether in *E. N.*, until it was revealed by Bernays and by Bywater's text,[2] comes out clearly in *M. M.*

The meaning put upon ἐνέργεια by this writer, namely, that it implies ὁρμή,[3] is confined to himself.

§ 22. Certain peculiarities of diction have been noticed in *M. M.*, such as the phrase τὸ ἄριστον ἀγαθόν,[4] the use of ἐπιστήμη for τέχνη, of τὸ ὅλον in an adverbial sense for ὅλως, and above all the persistent employment of ὑπέρ for περί.[5] Further there are forty words in *M. M.* which occur neither in *E. N.* nor *E. E.* Lastly the utmost laxity is displayed as to the rule of syntax that a neuter plural should have its verb in the singular.

§ 23. The tract on Virtues and Vices, which closes the ethical works attributed to Aristotle, appears to be later than his time. The elaborate way in which the virtues and vices are divided and subdivided reminds one of Stoic work, which the writer may have wished to rival. But perhaps the tract may be later still. For the fixed place assigned to daemons, as intermediate between gods and men,[6] is suggestive of neo-Platonic times, while the eclectic nature of the work seems to point to the same period of the blending of philosophic brands.

Assuming, to start with, Plato's threefold division of the soul, the writer makes Wisdom the virtue of the rational part, Gentleness and Courage those of the passionate part, and Temperance and Self-restraint those of the appetitive part. Justice, Liberality and Magnanimity are declared to be virtues of the whole soul. The Vices are arranged on precisely parallel lines. After the Virtues and Vices have been duly defined we have a statement of the characteristics and concomitants of both, which occupies most of the treatise. The conclusion consists in a brief view of the general effect of virtue. The treatment is not purely Peripatetic. There is not a word about the Doctrine of

[1] 1225[b] 5.
[2] *E. N.* iii. 1 § 17, 1111[a] 14.
[3] 1185[a] 28.
[4] 1183[a] 6–1185[a] 1.
[5] This last usage appears as early as Plato, *Apol.* 39 e.
[6] 1250[b] 20, 1251[a] 31.

the Mean. The assignment of the two virtues of Gentleness and Courage to the passionate part of the soul carries us back to Plato with his comparison of the Guardians to dogs. Self-restraint is exalted into a virtue in spite of Aristotle's regarding it as a mixed state. There is no mention of the Aristotelian virtue of Magnificence, but, by way of compensation, the liberal man has absorbed into himself some of the attributes of the magnificent man.[1]

[1] 1250^{b} 28–31.

MAGNA MORALIA

BY

ST. GEORGE STOCK, M.A.

LECTURER ON GREEK IN THE UNIVERSITY OF BIRMINGHAM

OXFORD UNIVERSITY PRESS

PREFACE

In these sad times it gives me special pleasure to acknowledge my indebtedness to eminent German scholars, past and present. In composing the Introduction to this volume I have availed myself of the learned labours of Fritzsche. The text of the *M. M.* which has been followed in the translation is that of Susemihl, from whose valuable Index and References I have also derived great advantage. Further I have to thank Mr. W. D. Ross, the Editor, and Mr. Charles Cannan, the Secretary to the Delegates, for their acute and searching criticisms.

ST. GEORGE STOCK.

PREFACE

In these sad times it gives me special pleasure to acknowledge my indebtedness to eminent German scholars, past and present. In composing the Introduction to this volume I have availed myself of the learned labours of [illegible]. The text [illegible] which has been followed in the translation is that of [illegible] Index and References I have also derived great advantage. Further I have to thank Mr. W. D. Ross, the Editor, and Mr. Charles Cannan, the Secretary to the Delegates, for their acute and searching criticisms.

ST. GEORGE STOCK.

CONTENTS

BOOK I

CHAPTER 3.

§§ 1, 2. Fifth Division. (1) Goods of the soul (wisdom, virtue, pleasure), (2) goods of the body, (3) external goods. 1184^b 1–6.

2. Happiness is identical with doing well and living well. 1184^b 7–9.

3, 4. Having is only for the sake of using. 1184^b 9–17.

5. The virtue of an agent makes him do his work well. 1184^b 17–21.

CHAPTER 4.

§§ 1–4. Happiness consists in living virtuously. 1184^b 22–1185^a 1.

5. Corollaries from the completeness of Happiness. (1) Children are not happy, (2) Happiness requires a full lifetime. 1185^a 1–9.

6. Further proof that Happiness is an activity. 1185^a 9–13.

7–9. The nutritive part of the soul has no bearing on Happiness. 1185^a 14–35.

10. What is virtue? It is the best state. 1185^a 36–39.

CHAPTER 5.

§§ 1, 2. Division of the Soul into—(1) rational, (2) irrational. 1185^b 1–12.

3–5. Moral virtue is destroyed by excess or defect. 1185^b 13–32.

CHAPTER 6.

§ 1. Moral virtue is concerned with pleasures and pains. 1185^b 33–37.

2. Etymology of 'ethical'. 1185^b 38–1186^a 2.

3. Moral virtues do not come by nature. 1186^a 2–8.

CHAPTER 7.

§§ 1–3. Things in the soul are three—(1) feelings, (2) capacities, (3) states. 1186^a 9–19.

3, 4. Virtue is a mean with respect to feelings. 1186^a 19–27.

CHAPTER 8.

§§ 1, 2. The same continued. 1186^a 27–33.

2. Feelings are attended with pain or pleasure.

∴ Virtue is concerned with pains and pleasures. 1186^a 33–35.

3. Not every feeling admits of a mean. 1186^a 36–^{b} 3.

CHAPTER 9.

§ 1. Sometimes one extreme is more opposed to the mean than the other. 1186^b 4–11.

2. Both the extremes are opposed to the mean. 1186^b 11–17.

3, 4. Two reasons for the excess or defect being opposed to the mean—(1) owing to the nature of the thing, (2) owing to our nature. 1186^b 17–32.

5, 6. Difficulty of Virtue. 1186^b 33–1187^a 4.

CONTENTS

CHAPTER 16.

For an act to be voluntary it must have been premeditated. 1188^b 25–38.

CHAPTER 17.

§ 1. What is Purpose? It is not identical with Impulse in general. 1189^a 1–5.

2, 3. Nor yet with Wish in particular. 1189^a 5–12.

3. Purpose is the choice of the better instead of the worse. 1189^a 12–16.

4. As Purpose is not any form of Impulse, so neither is it Thought. 1189^a 16–22.

5. But there is nothing else in the soul.

∴ Purpose must be the combination of both.

Purpose is the impulse to act which follows upon deliberation. 1189^a 22–31.

6, 7. ∴ Purpose is not coextensive with the Voluntary. This is recognized by some legislators. 1189^a 31–^{b} 6.

8. Purpose is confined to acts in our own power, where we can know the reason why. 1189^b 6–8.

9. In matters of action the reason is not definite, as in Geometry. 1189^b 9–17.

10. In such matters we deliberate as to the how, but not in the sciences. 1189^b 18–25.

11. Twofold error in matters of action. 1189^b 25–32.

CHAPTER 18.

§ 1 Thought has not one definite function like the senses. 1189^b 32–37.

2. When we err, it is not in the ends, but in the means. 1190^a 1–7.

3. Has Virtue to do with the end or with the means? 1190^a 8–10.

4. With both, like Science. 1190^a 10–15.

5, 6. But more with the end than with the means. 1190^a 15–28.

CHAPTER 19.

§ 1. ∴ Virtue aims at the right. 1190^a 28–33.

2, 3. This is not inconsistent with saying that the activity is better than the state. 1190^a 34–^{b} 6.

CHAPTER 20. COURAGE.

§§ 1, 2. Determination of the Sphere of Courage. 1190^b 7–20.

3–9. Spurious forms of Courage. 1190^b 21–1191^a 16.

3, 4. The Courage of Experience. 1190^b 21–32.

5. The Courage of Inexperience. 1190^b 32–35.

6, 7. The Courage of Passion. 1190^b 35–1191^a 4.

8. Civic Courage. 1191^a 5–13.

9. The Courage of Hope. 1191^a 13–16.

§ 28. To forgo one's rights for honour or praise or glory or friendship is not to be injured. 1195^{b} 9–17.

29. Men pride themselves on such things as these, but no one prides himself on being injured. 1195^{b} 17–24.

30. The incontinent man hurts himself voluntarily, but no one wishes to be injured. 1195^{b} 25–34.

31. Difficulty. Can a man be unjust to himself? Arguments for. 1195^{b} 35–1196^{a} 6.

32. Counter arguments. (1) The same man would at the same time have more and less. 1196^{a} 6–13.

33. (2) He would at the same time be acting voluntarily and involuntarily. 1196^{a} 13–17.

34. (3) No particular act of injustice can be committed by a man against himself. 1196^{a} 17–25.

35. There may be injustice or justice of a kind between the several parts of oneself. 1196^{a} 25–33.

36. In an unfair award does the injustice lie with the giver or the receiver? 1196^{a} 34–^{b} 3.

CHAPTER 34. ABOUT RIGHT REASON.

§§ 1, 2. What is Right Reason? 1196^{b} 4–11.

3–6. The Soul and its Parts. 1196^{b} 12–33.

7. What are the respective objects of—Science, Wisdom, Intellect, Philosophy, Supposition? 1196^{b} 34–37.

8. Science and Wisdom. 1196^{b} 37–1197^{a} 3.

9, 10. Difference between Making and Doing. Wisdom distinguished from Art. 1197^{a} 3–13.

11. Definition of Wisdom. 1197^{a} 13–16.

12. Proof that Wisdom is a Virtue, not a Science. 1197^{a} 16–20.

13. How Intellect is distinguished from Science. 1197^{a} 20–23.

14. Philosophy is a compound of Science and Intellect. 1197^{a} 23–30.

15. Supposition. 1197^{a} 30, 31.

16. Wisdom and Philosophy not the same. 1197^{a} 32–^{b} 2.

17. Is Philosophy a virtue? 1197^{b} 3–10.

18. Intelligence distinguished from Wisdom. 1197^{b} 11–17.

19, 20. How Cleverness differs from Wisdom. 1197^{b} 18–26.

21, 22. Reasons for discussing Philosophy in a treatise on Ethics. 1197^{b} 27–35.

23, 24. Cleverness : Wisdom :: Natural Virtue : Virtue. 1197^{b} 36–1198^{a} 6.

24, 25. Neither natural impulse nor rational purpose is complete without the other. 1198^{a} 6–9.

25, 26. The true relation of Reason to Virtue. 1198^{a} 10–21.

27. Is Wisdom a virtue? Yes: for it is praiseworthy, inasmuch as it enjoins what Virtue does. 1198^{a} 22–31.

28, 29. It is therefore practical in the architectonic sense. 1198^{a} 32–^{b} 8.

30–32. But this does not make it superior to philosophy. 1198^{b} 9–20.

CONTENTS

BOOK II

§§ 27, 28. Distinction between Self-control and Endurance and their Contraries. 1202b 29–37.

29. Distinction between the intemperate and the incontinent. 1202b 38–1203a 5.

30–34. Which is the better, the incontinent or the intemperate? 1203a 6–29.

35, 36. Two species of Incontinence—(1) from precipitancy, (2) from weakness. 1203a 30–b 11.

37, 38. The temperate man is also self-controlled, but not vice versa. 1203b 12–23.

39–42. Contrast between the intemperate and the incontinent. 1203b 24–1204a 4.

43, 44. Wisdom cannot consist with Lack of Self-control, but Cleverness may. 1204a 5–18.

CHAPTER 7.

§§ 1–27. Pleasure. 1204a 19–1206a 35.

1, 2. Introduction. 1204a 19–30.

3. Arguments to prove that Pleasure is not a good. 1204a 31–b 3.

4–10. Attack on the position that Pleasure is a becoming. 1204b 4–1205a 6.

4–6. (1) Some pleasures are not becomings. 1204b 4–20.

7–10. (2) No pleasure is a becoming. 1204b 20–36.

10. Pleasure not rightly defined as a conscious restoration to a normal state. 1204b 36–1205a 6.

11. All pleasures are good. 1205a 7–15.

12. Corollary. Pleasures differ in kind. 1205a 16–25.

13–18. Answer to the argument 'Some pleasures are bad.' 1205a 26–b 28.

13, 14. A thing must be judged at its best, not at its worst. 1205a 26–37.

15, 16. There are bad natures, and pleasure is the restoration of an animal to its proper nature. 1205b 1–13.

17. The view that Pleasure is not a good is based solely on bodily pleasures. 1205b 13–20.

18. The pleasures of a restored nature are superior to those of restoration. 1205b 20–28.

19, 20. Answer to the argument that 'Pleasure is common to all'.

This rather proves that Pleasure is good. 1205b 29–37.

21–25. Answer to the argument that 'Pleasure is an impediment'. 1206a 1–25.

21–23. The pleasure that comes from the action itself is not an impediment, but an incentive. 1206a 1–12.

23. Such pleasure is a sign of Virtue. 1206a 12–16.

24, 25. Proof that Virtue is attended with Pleasure. 1206a 17–25.

§§ 18–20. Importance of distinguishing between these different forms. 1209^{a} 37–^{b} 10.

21, 22. Superiority of the Friendship based on Virtue. 1209^{b} 11–19.

23–25. It is unreasonable to expect from the lower forms what can only be had from the higher. 1209^{b} 20–37.

26, 27. Must the Friendship of the serious be pleasant? 1209^{b} 38–1210^{a} 5.

28–30. While perfect friendship is based on likeness, the friendship of utility is based on unlikeness. 1210^{a} 6–22.

31–33. Defect in friendship is more obvious when the object aimed at on either side is different. 1210^{a} 23–^{b} 2.

34–37. It is better to love than to be loved. 1210^{b} 3–13.

38, 39. But men are ambitious of the superiority that is implied in being loved. 1210^{b} 13–22.

40, 41. Characteristics of perfect Friendship. 1210^{b} 23–32.

42–44. They are all found in a man's relations towards himself. 1210^{b} 32–1211^{a} 5.

45, 46. The fields of Justice and of Friendship are co-extensive. 1211^{a} 6–15.

47–50. In what sense there can be Friendship towards oneself. 1211^{a} 16–^{b} 3.

51–53. Actual and proportional equality in Friendship. 1211^{b} 4–17.

CHAPTER 12.

§§ 1–5. Why does the father love the son more than the son loves the father? 1211^{b} 18–39.

6–10. How Goodwill is related to Friendship. 1211^{b} 40–1212^{a} 13.

11–13. Unanimity is a unity of purpose with regard to rule in matters of action. 1212^{a} 14–27.

CHAPTER 13. SELF-LOVE.

The good man's love of self will be displayed in the choice of the noble for himself. 1212^{a} 28–^{b} 8.

CHAPTER 14. SELF-LOVE, CONTINUED.

The good man is not so much a lover of self as a lover of good. 1212^{b} 8–23.

CHAPTER 15. SELF-SUFFICINGNESS.

Will the self-sufficing man need Friendship? 1212^{b} 24–1213^{b} 2.

CHAPTER 16. OUGHT ONE TO HAVE MANY FRIENDS? 1213^{b} 3–17.

CHAPTER 17. HOW TO TREAT A FRIEND. 1213^{b} 18–30.

BOOK I

I SINCE our purpose is to speak about ethics, we must 1181a first inquire of what moral character is a branch. To speak concisely, then, it would seem to be a branch of nothing else than statecraft. For it is not possible to act at all in affairs of state unless one is of a certain kind, to wit, good. Now to be good is to possess the virtues. If therefore one is to act successfully in affairs of state, 1181b one must be of a good moral character. The treatment of moral character then is, as it seems, a branch and starting-point of statecraft. And as a whole it seems to me that the subject ought rightly to be called, not Ethics, but Politics.

We must therefore, as it seems, first say about virtue 1182a both what it is and from what it comes. For it is perhaps of no use to know virtue without understanding how or from what it is to arise. We must not limit our inquiry to knowing what it is, but extend it to how it is to be produced. For we wish not only to know but also ourselves to be such; and this will be impossible for us, unless we know from what and how it is to be produced. Of course, it is indispensable to know what virtue is (for it is not easy to know the source and manner of its production, if one does not know what it is, any more than in the sciences); but we ought to be aware also of what others have said before us on this subject.

Pythagoras first attempted to speak about virtue, but not successfully; for by reducing the virtues to numbers he submitted the virtues to a treatment which was not proper to them. For justice is not a square number.[1]

1181a 24–1182a 1 = *E.N.* 1094a 26–b 11. 1–7 = *E.E.* 1216b 10–25. 4–6 = *E.N.* 1103b 27–29.

---

[1] Plat. *Theaet.* 147 E, 148 A; *Rep.* 546 C. Philo, *de Mund. Op.* § 16 οὐδ' ἐκεῖνο ἀγνοητέον, ὅτι πρῶτος ἀριθμῶν ὁ τέτταρα τετράγωνός ἐστιν ἰσάκις ἴσος, μέτρον δικαιοσύνης καὶ ἰσότητος.

After him came Socrates, who spoke better and further about this subject, but even he was not successful. For he used to make the virtues sciences, and this is impossible. For the sciences all involve reason, and reason is to be found in the intellectual part of the soul. So that all the virtues, according to him, are to be found in the rational part of the soul. The result is that in making the virtues sciences he is doing away with the irrational part of the soul, and is thereby doing away also both with passion and moral character; so that he has not been successful in this respect in his treatment of the virtues.

After this Plato divided the soul into the rational and the irrational part—and in this he was right—assigning appropriate virtues to each. So far so good. But after this he went astray. For he mixed up virtue with the treatment of the good, which cannot be right, not being appropriate. For in speaking about the truth of things he ought not to have discoursed upon virtue; for there is nothing common to the two.

The above-mentioned, then, have touched upon the subject so far and in the way above described. The next thing will be to see what we ought to say ourselves upon the subject.

First of all, then, we must see that every science and art has an end, and that too a good one; for no science or art exists for the sake of evil. Since then in all the arts the end is good, it is plain that the end of the best art
1182b will be the best good. But statecraft is the best art, so that the end of this will be the good.[1] It is about good, then, as it seems, that we must speak, and about good not without qualification, but relatively to ourselves. For we have not to do with the good of the Gods. To speak about that is a different matter, and the inquiry is foreign to our present purpose. It is therefore about the good of the state that we must speak.

24, 25: cf. *E.N.* 1102a 26–28. 33–35 = *E.N.* 1094a 1, 2. 35–38 = *E.N.* 1094a 26–28. 1182b 2, 3: cf. *E.N.* 1094b 7, 1102a 13–15. 4 = *E.E.* 1217a 21–24.

[1] Reading τἀγαθόν with Casaubon.

But we must distinguish different meanings in the word 'good' itself. About good in what sense of the term have we to speak? For the word is not univocal. For 'good' is used either of what is best in the case of each being, that is, what is choiceworthy because of its own nature, or of that by partaking in which all other things are good, that is, the Idea of Good.

Are we, then, to speak of the Idea of Good? Or not of that, but of good as the element common to all goods? For this would seem to be different from the Idea. For the Idea is a thing apart and by itself, whereas the common element exists in all: it therefore is not identical with what is apart. For that which is apart and whose nature it is to be by itself cannot possibly exist in all. Are we then to speak about this indwelling good? Surely not![1] And why? Because the common element is that which is got by definition or by induction. Now the aim of defining is to state the essence of each thing, either what good is[2] or what evil is, or whatever else it may be. But the definition states that whatever thing is of such a kind as to be choiceworthy for its own sake is good in all cases. And the common element in all goods is much the same as the definition. And the definition says what is good, whereas no science or art whatsoever states of its own end that it is good,[3] but it is the province of another art to speculate as to this (for neither the physician nor the mason says that health or a house is good, but that one thing produces health, and how it produces it, and another thing a house). It is evident then that neither has statecraft to do with the common element of good. For it is itself only one science among the rest, and we have seen that it is not the business of any art or science to talk of this as end. It is not

10–1183b 8 = *E.E.* 1217b 1–1218b 24 = *E.N.* 1096a 11–1097a 14. 22: cf. *E.N.* 1097a 18. 23–27 = *E.E.* 1218b 22–24: cf. *E.N.* 1112b 12–16.

[1] Susemihl, addenda p. 100, corrects his punctuation.

[2] Printing thus—ὅ τι ἀγαθὸν ἢ ὅ τι κακόν.

[3] It is difficult here to follow the argument, which presents the appearance of an elementary fallacy—

The definition λέγει ὅ τι ἀγαθόν.

No art or science λέγει ὅτι ἀγαθὸν τὸ τέλος.

therefore the business of statecraft any more than of any other art to speak of the common element of good corresponding to the definition.

But neither has it to speak of the common element as arrived at by induction. Why so? Because when we wish to show some particular[1] good, we either show by defining that the same description applies to the good and to the thing which we wish to show to be good, or else have recourse to induction; for instance, when we wish to show
1183^{a} that magnanimity is a good, we say that justice is a good and courage is a good, and so of the virtues generally, and that magnanimity is a virtue, so that magnanimity also is a good. Neither then will statecraft have to speak of the common good arrived at by induction, because the same impossible consequences will ensue in this case as in that of the common good conformable to the definition. For here also one will be saying that the end is good. It is clear therefore that what it has to speak about is the best good, and the best in the sense of 'the best for us'.

And generally one can see that it is not the part of any one science or art to consider the question of good in general. Why so? Because good occurs in all the categories—in that of substance, quality, quantity, time, relation, [instrument], and generally in all. But what is good at a given time is known in medicine by the doctor, in navigation by the pilot, and in each art by the expert in that art. For it is the doctor who knows when one ought to amputate, and the pilot when one ought to sail. And in each art each expert will know the time of the good which concerns himself. For neither will the doctor know the time of the good in navigation nor the pilot that in medicine. It follows then from this point of view also that we have not to speak about the common good: for time is common to all the arts. Similarly the relative good and the good which corresponds to other categories is common to all, and it does not belong to any art or science to speak

1183^{a} 7–23 = *E.E.* 1217^{b} 25–1218^{a} 1: cf. *E.N.* 1096^{a} 23–34.

[1] Reading κατὰ μέρος (κατά is omitted by accident in Susemihl's text).

of what is good in each at a given time, nor, we may add, is it the part of statecraft to speak about the common element of good. Our subject then is the good, in the sense of the best, and that the best for us.

Perhaps when one wishes to show something, one ought not to employ illustrations that are not manifest, but to illustrate the obscure by the manifest, and the things of mind by the things of sense, for the latter are more manifest. When, therefore, one takes in hand to speak about the good, one ought not to speak about the Idea. And yet they think it quite necessary, when they are speaking about the good, to speak about the Idea. For they say that it is necessary to speak about what is most good, and the very thing in each kind has the quality of that kind in the highest degree, so that the Idea will be the most good, as they think. Possibly there is truth in such a contention: but all the same the science or art of statecraft, about which we are now speaking, does not inquire about this good, but about that which is good for us. [For no science or art pronounces its end to be good, so that statecraft does not do so either.] Wherefore it does not concern itself to speak about the good in the sense of the Idea.

But, it may be said, one may employ this good as a first principle to start from in speaking about particular goods. Even this is not correct. For the first principles that one 1183b
assumes ought to be appropriate. How absurd it would be if, when one wished to show that the three angles of a triangle are equal to two right angles, one were to assume as a principle that the soul is immortal! For it is not appropriate, and the first principle ought to be appropriate and connected. As a matter of fact, one can prove that the three angles of a triangle are equal to two right angles quite as well without the immortality of the soul. In the same way in the case of goods, one can speculate about the rest without the Ideal Good. Wherefore we declare[1] such a good is not an appropriate principle.

24–27 = *E. N.* 1104a 13, 14: cf. *E. E.* 1218a 15–19. 35–36 = *E. E.* 1218b 22–24. 39, b 1: cf. *E. N.* 1096b 35–1097a 14.

[1] Reading εἶναι λέγομεν (Spengel) τοῦτο τἀγαθόν (Bonitz).

Neither was Socrates right in making the virtues sciences. For he used to think that nothing ought to be in vain, but from the virtues being sciences he met with the result that the virtues were in vain. Why so? Because in the case of the sciences, as soon as one knows the essence of a science, it results that one is scientific (for any one who knows the essence of medicine is forthwith a physician, and so with the other sciences[1]). But this result does not follow in the case of the virtues. For any one who knows the essence of justice is not forthwith just, and similarly in the case of the rest. It follows then both that the virtues are in vain and that they are not sciences.

Now that we have settled these points, let us try to say 2
in how many senses the term 'good' is used. For goods may be divided into the honourable, the praiseworthy, and potencies. By the 'honourable' I mean such a thing as the divine, the more excellent (for instance, soul, intellect), the more ancient, the first principle, and so on. For those things are honourable which attract honour, and all such things as these are attended with honour. Virtue then also is a thing that is honourable, at least when[2] some one has become a good man in consequence of it; for already such a one has come into the form of virtue. Other goods are praiseworthy, as virtues; for praise is bestowed in consequence of the actions[3] which are prompted by them. Others are potencies, for instance, office, wealth, strength, beauty; for these are things which the good man can use well and the bad man ill. Wherefore such goods are called potencies. Goods indeed they are (for everything is judged

b 9–18 = *E. E.* 1216b 3–25. 20–35 = *E. N.* 1101b 10–1102a 4: cf. *E. E.* 1219b 8–16.

---

[1] *τῶν ἄλλων ἐπιστημῶν* seems to depend on *ἐπιστήμονες* understood, but it looks as if *καί* ought to be *κἀπί*. See line 17.

[2] The writer is doubtless aware that he is running counter to *E. N.* 1101b 15 and *E. E.* 1219b 8. Hence the distinction drawn between *ἀρετή* and *ἀρεταί*. *ἀρετή* implies complete virtue, which is happiness, and above praise.

[3] According to Plat. *Rep.* 607 A, *E. N.* 1101b 33, and *E. E.* 1219b 15 *ἐγκώμιον* is appropriate to actual achievements, while *ἔπαινος* (praise) is bestowed upon meritorious qualities.

by the use made of it by the good man, not by that of the bad); and it is incidental to these same goods that fortune is the cause of their production. For from fortune comes wealth, and also office, and generally all the things which rank as potencies. The fourth and last class of goods is that which is preservative and productive of good,[1] as exercise of health, and other things of that sort.

But goods admit of another division, to wit, some goods are everywhere and absolutely choiceworthy, and some are not. For instance, justice and the other virtues are every- 1184a
where and absolutely choiceworthy, but strength, and wealth, and power, and the like, are not so everywhere nor absolutely.

Again, take another division. Some goods are ends and some are not; for instance, health is an end, but the means to health are not ends. And wherever things stand in this relation, the end is always better; for instance, health is better than the means to health, and without exception, always and universally, that thing is better for the sake of which the rest are.

Again, among ends themselves the complete is always better than the incomplete. A 'complete' good is one the presence of which leaves us in need of nothing;[2] an 'incomplete' good is one which may be present while yet we need something further; for instance, we may have justice and yet need many things besides, but when we have happiness we need nothing more. This then is the best thing of which we are in search, which is the complete end. The complete end then is the good and end of goods.

The next point is how we are to look for the best good. Is it itself to be reckoned in with other goods? Surely that is absurd. For the best is the final end, and the final end, roughly speaking, would seem to be nothing else than

35–37 = *E. N.* 1096b 11–13. 1184a 3–6: cf. *E. N.* 1096b 13, 14. 8, 9: cf. *E. N.* 1097b 14, 15. 15–38 = *E. N.* 1097b 16–20.

[1] Cp. the Stoic division of goods into δι' αὑτὰ αἱρετά and ποιητικά given in Stob. *Ecl.* ii. 126.

[2] In *E. N.* a good is τέλειον when you desire nothing beyond it; it is αὔταρκες when you desire nothing beside it. The definition here given of τέλειον is equivalent to that of τὸ αὔταρκες in *E. N.* 1097b 14.

happiness, and happiness we regard as made up of many goods; so that if, in looking for the best, you reckon in itself also, it will be better than itself, because it is itself the best thing. For instance, take the means to health, and health, and raise the question which is the best of all these. The answer is that health is the best. If then this is the best of all, it is also better than itself:[1] so that an absurdity ensues. Perhaps then this is not the way in which we ought to look for the best. Are the other goods then to be separated from it?[2] Is not this also absurd? For happiness is composed of certain goods. But to raise the question whether a given thing is better than its own components is absurd. For happiness is not something else apart from these, but just these.

But perhaps the right method of inquiry may be by comparison of the best somewhat as follows. I mean by comparing happiness itself, which is made up of these goods, with others which are not contained in it. But the best of which we are now in search is not of a simple nature. For instance, one might say that wisdom is the best of all goods when they are compared one by one. But perhaps this is not the way in which we ought to seek for the best good. For it is the complete good whereof we are in search, and wisdom by itself is not complete. It is not, therefore, the best in this sense, nor in this way, of which we are in search.

1184b After this, then, goods admit of another division. For 3
some goods are in the soul—for instance, the virtues; some in the body—for instance, health, beauty; and some outside of us—wealth, office, honour, and such like. Of these those in the soul are best. But the goods in the soul are divided into three—wisdom, virtue, and pleasure.

Now we come to happiness, which we all declare to be, and which seems in fact to be, the final good and the most

1184b 1–5 = *E.N.* 1098b 12–15 = *E.E.* 1218b 32–35.

[1] Reading βέλτιον with Spengel.

[2] Something seems wrong with the text here. Perhaps we should read αὐτό or αὐτῶν for αὐτοῦ.

complete thing, and this we maintain to be identical with[1] doing well and living well. But the end is not single but twofold. For the end of some things is the activity and use itself—for instance, of sight; and the using is more choiceworthy than the having; for the using is the end. For no one would care to have sight, if he were destined never to see, but always to have his eyes shut. And the same with hearing and the like. When then a thing may be both used and had, the using is always better and more choiceworthy than the having. For the use and exercise are the end, whereas the having is with a view to the using.

Next, then, if one examines this point in the case of all the arts, he will see that it is not one art that makes a house and another that makes a good house, but simply the art of housebuilding; and what the housebuilder makes, that same thing his virtue enables him to make well. Similarly in all other cases.

4 After this, then, we see that it is by nothing else than soul that we live. Virtue is in the soul. We maintain that the soul and the virtue of the soul do the same thing. But virtue in each thing does that well of which it is the virtue, and, among the other functions of the soul, it is by it we live. It is therefore owing to the virtue of the soul that we shall live well. But to live well and do well we say is nothing else than being happy. Being happy, then, and happiness, consist in living well, and living well is living in accordance with the virtues. This, then, is the end and happiness and the best thing. [Happiness therefore will consist in a kind of use and activity. For we found[2] that where there was having and using, the use and exercise are the end. Now virtue is a habit of the soul. And

9, 10: cf. *E. N.* 1098b 21. 9–17 = *E. N.* 1094a 3–16 = *E. E.* 1219a 13–18: cf. *E. N.* 1098a 5, 6. 17–21 = *E. N.* 1098a 7–12 = *E. E.* 1219a 18–23. 22–1185a 1 = *E. E.* 1219a 23–35.

[1] Reading τῷ, for which τό in Susemihl's text seems to be a misprint.

[2] 1184b 15. The passage in brackets belongs in sense to that context.

there is such a thing as the exercise and use of it;[1] so that the end will be its activity and use. Happiness therefore will consist in living in accordance with the virtues.] Since then the best good is happiness, and this is the end, and the final end is an activity,[2] it follows that it is by living in accordance with the virtues that we shall be happy
1185a and shall have the best good.

Since, then, happiness is a complete good and end, we must not fail to observe that it will be found in that which is complete. For it will not be found in a child (for a child is not happy), but in a man; for he is complete. Nor will it be found in an incomplete, but in a complete, period. And a complete period of time will be as long as a man lives. For it is rightly said among the many that one ought to judge of the happy man in the longest time of his life, on the assumption that what is complete ought to be in a complete period and a complete person. But that it is an activity can be seen also from the following consideration. For supposing some one to be asleep all his life, we should hardly consent to call such a man happy. Life indeed he has, but life in accordance with the virtues he has not, and it was in this that we made the activity to consist.[3]

The topic that is next about to be treated of is neither very intimately connected with our main subject nor yet quite alien from it. I mean, since there is, as it seems, a part of the soul whereby we are nourished, which we call 'nutritive' (for it is reasonable to suppose that this exists; at all events we see that stones are incapable of being nourished, so that it is evident that to be nourished is a property of living things; and, if so, the soul will be the cause of it; but none of these parts of the soul will be the cause of nourishment, to wit, the rational or spirited

1–4 = *E. N.* 1100a 1–5 = *E. E.* 1219a 35–39. 4–9 = *E. N.* 1098a 18 = *E. E.* 1219b 6–8. 10–13 = *E. N.* 1099a 1, 2 = *E. E.* 1219a 23–27. 14–35 = *E. N.* 1102a 32–b 12 = *E. E.* 1219b 20–25, 36–40.

[1] Omitting τῶν ἀρετῶν (Spengel).

[2] Reading ἐνέργεια for ἐνεργείᾳ.

[3] 1184b 34–36.

or appetitive, but something else besides these, to which we can apply no more appropriate name than 'nutritive'), one might say, 'Very well, has this part of the soul also a virtue? For if it has, it is plain that we ought to act with this also. For happiness is the exercise of perfect virtue.' Now, whether there is or is not a virtue of this part is another question; but, if there is, it has no activity. For those things which have no impulse will not have any activity either; and there does not seem to be any impulse in this part, but it seems to be on a par with fire. For that also will consume whatever you throw in, but if you do not throw anything in, it has no impulse to get it. So it is also with this part of the soul; for, if you throw in food, it nourishes, but, if you fail to throw in food, it has no impulse to nourish. Wherefore it has no activity, being devoid of impulse. So that this part in no way co-operates towards happiness.

After this, then, we must say what virtue is, since it is the exercise of this which is happiness. Speaking generally, then, virtue is the best state. But perhaps it is not sufficient to speak thus generally, but it is necessary to define more clearly.

5 First, then, we ought to speak about the soul in which 1185b
it resides, not to say what the soul is (for to speak about that is another matter), but to divide it in outline. Now the soul is, as we say,[1] divided into two parts, the rational and the irrational. In the rational part, then, there resides wisdom, readiness of wit, philosophy, aptitude to learn, memory, and so on; but in the irrational those which are called the virtues—temperance, justice, courage, and such other moral states as are held to be praiseworthy. For it is in respect of these that we are called praiseworthy; but no one is praised for the virtues of the rational part. For no one is praised for being philosophical nor for being wise, nor generally on the ground of anything of that

38 = *E.N.* 1103a 9. b 1–12 = *E.N.* 1102a 18–28 = *E.E.* 1219b 26–30.

[1] Cf. 1182a 23–26.

sort.[1] Nor indeed is the irrational part praised, except in so far as it is capable of subserving or actually subserves the rational part.

Moral virtue is destroyed by defect and excess. Now, that defect and excess destroy can be seen from moral instances,[2] but we must use what we can see as an illustration of what we cannot see. For one can see this at once in the case of gymnastic exercises. If they are overdone, the strength is destroyed, while if they are deficient, it is so also. And the same is the case with food and drink. For if too much is taken health is destroyed, and also if too little, but by the right proportion strength and health are preserved. The same is the case with temperance and courage and the rest of the virtues. For if you make a man too fearless, so as not even to fear the Gods, he is not brave but mad, but if you make him afraid of everything, he is a coward. To be brave, then, a man must not either fear everything or nothing. The same things, then, both increase and destroy virtue. For undue and indiscriminate fears destroy, and so does the lack of fear about anything at all. And courage has to do with fears, so that moderate fears increase courage. Courage, then, is both increased and destroyed by the same things. For men are liable to this effect owing to fears. And the same holds true of the other virtues.

In addition to the preceding, virtue may also be deter- 6
mined by pleasure and pain. For it is owing to pleasure that we commit base actions, and owing to pain that we abstain from noble ones. And generally it is not possible

13-26 = *E. N.* 1104^{a} 11–^{b} 3. 26–32 = *E. N.* 1103^{b} 7–22 = *E. E.* 26–32. 33–37 = *E. N.* 1104^{b} 3–1105^{a} 14 = *E. E.* 1220^{a} 34–39.

---

[1] This contradicts *E. N.* 1103^{a} 8 ἐπαινοῦμεν δὲ καὶ τὸν σοφὸν κατὰ τὴν ἕξιν, and also *E. E.* 1220^{a} 5 ἐπαινοῦμεν γὰρ οὐ μόνον τοὺς δικαίους, ἀλλὰ καὶ τοὺς συνετοὺς καὶ τοὺς σοφούς. The author of this treatise himself reverts to the older view in 1197^{a} 17.

[2] The text makes sense as it stands, if the brackets are removed. ἐκ τῶν ἠθικῶν may be an anticipation of ὁμοίως δὲ τούτοις κτλ. in line 21. But ἐκτὸς τῶν ἠθικῶν would be a great improvement.

to achieve virtue or vice without pain and pleasure. Virtue then has to do with pleasures and pains.

The word 'ethical' (or 'moral') virtue is derived as follows, if etymology has any bearing upon truth, as perhaps 1186a
it has. From *ĕthos* comes *ēthos*, and so moral virtue is called 'ethical', as being attained by practice. Whereby it is evident that no one of the virtues of the irrational part springs up in us by nature. For nothing that is by nature becomes other by training. For instance, a stone, and heavy things in general, naturally go downwards. If any one, then, throws them up repeatedly, and tries to train them to go up, all the same they never would go up, but always down. Similarly in all other such cases.

7 After this, then, as we wish to say what virtue is, we must know what are the things that there are in the soul. They are these—feelings, capacities, states; so that it is evident that virtue will be some one of these. Now feelings are anger, fear, hate, regret, emulation, pity, and the like, which are usually attended by pain or pleasure. Capacities are those things in virtue of which we are said to be capable of these feelings; for instance, those things in virtue of which we are capable of feeling anger or pain or pity, and so on. States are those things in virtue of which we stand in a good or bad relation to these feelings; for instance, towards being angered; if we are angry overmuch, we stand in a bad relation towards anger, whereas if we are not angry at all where we ought to be, in that case also we stand in a bad relation towards anger.

The mean state, then, is neither to be pained overmuch nor to be absolutely insensible. When, then, we stand thus, we are in a good disposition. And similarly as regards other like things. For good temper and gentleness are in a mean between anger and insensibility to anger. Similarly in the case of boastfulness and mock-humility. For to pretend to more than one has shows boastfulness,

38–1186a 2 = *E. N.* 1103a 17, 18 = *E. E.* 1220a 39–b 1. 2–8 = *E. N.* 1103a 18–26 = *E. E.* 1220b 2–5. 9–22 = *E. N.* 1105b 19–28 = *E. E.* 1220b 10–20.

while to pretend to less shows mock-humility. The mean state, then, between these is truthfulness.

Similarly in all other cases. For this is what marks the 8
state, to stand in a good or bad relation towards these feelings, and to stand in a good relation towards them is neither to incline towards the excess nor towards the defect. The state, then, which implies a good relation is directed towards the mean of such things, in respect of which we are called praiseworthy, whereas that which implies a bad relation inclines towards excess or defect.

Since, then, virtue is a mean of these feelings, and the feelings are either pains or pleasures or impossible apart from pain or pleasure, it is evident from this that virtue has to do with pains and pleasures.[1]

But there are other feelings, as one might think, in the case of which the vice does not lie in any excess or defect; for instance, adultery and the adulterer. The adulterer is
1186b not the man who corrupts free women too much; but both this and anything else of the kind which is comprised under the pleasure of intemperance, whether it be something in the way of excess or of defect,[2] is blamed.

After this, then, it is perhaps necessary to have it stated 9
what is opposed to the mean, whether it is the excess or the defect. For to some means the defect is opposed and to some the excess; for instance, to courage it is not rashness, which is the excess, that is opposed, but cowardice, which is the defect; and to temperance, which is a mean between intemperance and insensibility to pleasures, it does not seem that insensibility, which is the defect, is opposed, but intemperance, which is the excess. But both are opposed to the mean, excess and defect. For the mean is in defect of the excess and in excess of the defect. Hence it is that prodigals call the liberal illiberal, while

33–36 = *E. N.* 1104b 13–16. 36–b 3 = *E. N.* 1107a 8–17 = *E. E.* 1221b 18–26. 4–13 = *E. N.* 1108b 35–1109a 5. 14–16 = *E. N.* 1108b 23–26.

[1] Reading ἀρετὴ ὅτι ἐστίν (Sylburg).

[2] The meaning is plain, though the text at this point is corrupt, the ἤ not being wanted.

the illiberal call the liberal prodigals, and the rash and headlong call the brave cowards, while cowards call the brave headlong and mad.

There would seem to be two reasons for our opposing the excess or the defect to the mean. Either people look at the matter from the point of view of the thing itself, to see which is nearer to, or further from, the mean; for instance, in the case of liberality, whether prodigality or illiberality is further from it. For prodigality would seem more to be liberality than illiberality is. Illiberality, then, is further off. But things which are further distant from the mean would seem to be more opposed to it. From the point of view, then, of the thing itself the defect presents itself as more opposed. But there is also another way, to wit, those things are more opposed to the mean to which we have a greater natural inclination. For instance, we have a greater natural inclination to be intemperate than sober in our conduct. The tendency, therefore, occurs rather towards the things to which nature inclines us; and the things to which we have a greater tendency are more opposed; and our tendency is towards intemperance rather than towards sobriety; so that the excess of the mean will be the more opposed; for intemperance is the excess in the case of temperance.

What virtue is, then, has been examined (for it seems to be a mean of the feelings, so that it will be necessary for the man who is to obtain credit for moral character to observe the mean with regard to each of the feelings; for which reason it is a difficult matter to be good; for to seize the mean in anything is a difficult matter; for instance, any one can draw a circle, but to fix upon the mean point in it is hard; and in the same way to be angry indeed is easy, and so is the opposite of this, but to be in **1187a**
the mean is hard; and generally in each of the feelings one can see that what surrounds the mean is easy, but the mean is hard, and this is the point for which we are praised; for which reason the good is rare).

17–32 = *E. N.* 1109a 5–19 = *E. E.* 1222a 36–43. 33–1187a 4 = *E. N.* 1109a 20–29.

Since, then, virtue has been spoken of . . . we must next inquire whether it is possible of attainment or is not, but, as Socrates[1] said, to be virtuous or vicious does not rest with us to come about. For if, he says, one were to ask any one whatever whether he would wish to be just or unjust, no one would choose injustice. Similarly in the case of courage and cowardice, and so on always with the rest of the virtues. And it is evident that any who are vicious will not be vicious voluntarily; so that it is evident that neither will they be voluntarily virtuous[2].

Such a statement is not true. For why does the lawgiver forbid the doing of wrong acts, and bid the doing of right and virtuous ones? And why does he appoint a penalty for wrong acts, if one does them, and for right acts, if one fails to do them? Yet it would be absurd to legislate about those things which are not in our power to do. But, as it seems, it is in our power to be virtuous or vicious.

Again, we have evidence in the praise and blame that are accorded. For there is praise for virtue and blame for vice. But praise and blame are not bestowed upon things involuntary. So it is evident that it is equally in our power to do virtuous and vicious acts.

They used also to employ some such comparison as this in their desire to show that vice is not voluntary. For why, they say, when we are ill or ugly, does no one blame us for things of this sort? But this is not true. For we do blame people for things of this sort, when we think that they themselves are the causes of their being ill or of their having their body in a bad state, on the assumption that there is voluntary action even there. It seems, then, that there is voluntariness in being virtuous and vicious.

14–18 = *E. N.* 1113b 20–30. 19–22 = *E. N.* 1109b 30–33.

[1] See, for instance, *Meno* 78 A, *Rep.* 589 C, *Soph.* 228 C, *Tim.* 86 D, E. But the strongest expression given to the doctrine of the involuntariness of vice is in *Laws* 731 C, 860 D, E, the latter of which passages seems to be directed against Aristotle.

[2] This is an inference drawn by the writer, not by Plato. In Plato's view, vice was involuntary because it was ignorance, and virtue was voluntary for the opposite reason. Aristotle's main contention in *E. N.* iii. 5 against Plato is that the one is as voluntary as the other.

10 One can see this still more clearly from the following considerations. Every natural kind is given to begetting a being like itself, i. e. plants and animals; for both are apt to beget. And they are given to beget from their first principles—for instance, the tree from the seed; for this is a kind of principle. And what follows the principles stands thus: as are the principles, so is what comes from the principles.

This can be seen more clearly in matters of geometry. For there also, when certain principles are assumed, as are the principles, so are what follow the principles; for instance, if the triangle has its angles equal to two right angles, and the quadrilateral to four, then according as 1187b
the triangle changes, so does the quadrilateral share in its changes (for it is convertible), and if the quadrilateral has not its angles equal to four right angles, neither will the triangle have its angles equal to two right angles.

11 So, then, and in the like way with this, is it in the case of man. For since man is apt to produce being, he tends to produce the actions which he does from certain principles. How else could it be? For we do not say that any of the things without life acts, nor any other of the things with life, except men. It is evident, then, that man is the begetter of his acts.

Since, then, we see that the acts change, and we never do the same things, and the acts have been brought into being from certain principles, it is evident that, since the acts change, the principles from which the acts proceed also change, as we said in our comparison was the case with geometrical properties.

Now the principle of an act, whether virtuous or vicious, is purpose and wish, and all that accords with reason. It is evident, then, that these also change. But we change in our actions voluntarily. So that the principle also, purpose, changes voluntarily. So that it is plain that it will be in our power to be either virtuous or vicious.

Perhaps, then, some one may say, 'Since it is in my power to be just and good, if I wish I shall be the best of all men'. This, of course, is not possible. Why so? Because in the case of the body it is not so either. For if one wishes to bestow attention upon his body, it does not follow that he will have the best body that any one has. For it is necessary not merely for attention to be bestowed, but also for the body to be beautiful and good by nature. He will then have his body better, but best of all men, No. And so we must suppose it to be also in the case of soul. For he who wills to be best will not be so, unless Nature also be presupposed; better, however, he will be.

Since, then, it appears that to be good is in our power, **12**
it is necessary next to say what the voluntary is. For this is what chiefly determines virtue, to wit, the voluntary. Roughly speaking, that is voluntary which we do when not under compulsion. But perhaps we ought to speak more clearly about it.

What prompts us to action is impulse; and impulse has three forms—appetite, passion, wish.

First of all, then, we must inquire into the act which is in accordance with appetite. Is that voluntary or in-
1188a voluntary? That it is involuntary would not seem to be the case. Why so? And on what ground? Because wherever we do not act voluntarily, we act under compulsion, and all acts done under compulsion are attended with pain, whereas acts due to appetite are attended with pleasure, so that on this way of looking at the matter acts due to appetite will not be involuntary, but voluntary.

But, again, there is another argument opposed to this, which makes its appeal to incontinence. No one, it is maintained, does evil voluntarily, knowing it to be evil. But yet the incontinent, knowing that what he does is vicious, nevertheless does it, and does it in accordance with appetite; he is not therefore acting voluntarily; therefore he is under compulsion. There again the old answer will

b 32 = *E.N.* 1109b 33. 37, 38 = *E.E.* 1223a 26, 27. 39–1188a 5 = *E.N.* 1111a 32, 33 = *E.E.* 1223a 29–35. 6–12 = *E.E.* 1223b 5–8.

meet this argument. For if the act be in accordance with appetite, it is not of compulsion; for appetite is attended with pleasure, and acts due to pleasure are not of compulsion.

There is another way in which this conclusion may be made plain; I mean, that the incontinent acts voluntarily. For those who commit injustice do so voluntarily, and the incontinent are unjust and act unjustly. So that the incontinent man will voluntarily commit his acts of incontinence.

13 But, again, there is another argument opposed to this, which maintains that action due to appetite is not voluntary. For the self-restrained man voluntarily performs his acts of self-restraint. For he is praised, and people are praised for voluntary acts. But if that which is in accordance with appetite is voluntary, that which runs counter to appetite is involuntary. But the man of self-restraint acts contrary to his appetite. So that the man of self-restraint will not be self-restrained voluntarily. But this conclusion does not commend itself. Therefore the act which is in accordance with appetite is not voluntary.

Again, the same thing holds of acts prompted by passion. For the same arguments apply as to appetite, so that they will cause the difficulty. For it is possible to be incontinent or continent of anger.

Among the impulses in our division we have still to inquire about wish, whether it is voluntary. But assuredly the incontinent wish for the time being the things to which their impulse is directed. Therefore the incontinent perform their vicious acts with their own wish. But no one voluntarily does evil, knowing it to be evil. But the incontinent man, knowing evil to be evil, does it with his own wish. Therefore he is not a voluntary agent, and wish therefore is not a voluntary thing. But this argument annuls incontinence and the incontinent man. For, if he is not a voluntary agent, he is not blameworthy. But the incontinent is blameworthy. Therefore he is a voluntary agent. Therefore wish is voluntary.

12–16 = *E. E.* 1223a 36–b 3.

Since, then, certain arguments seem opposed, we must speak more clearly about the voluntary.

Before doing so, however, we must speak about force 14
1188b and about necessity. Force may occur even in the case of things without life. For things without life have each their proper place assigned to them—to fire the upper region and to earth the lower. It is, however, possible to force a stone to go up and fire to go down. It is also possible to apply force to an animal; for instance, when a horse is galloping straight ahead, one may take hold of him and divert his course. Now whenever the cause of men's doing something contrary to their nature or contrary to their wish is outside of them, we will say that they are forced[1] to do what they do. But when the cause is in themselves, we will not in that case say that they are forced. Otherwise the incontinent man will have his answer ready, in denying that he is vicious. For he will say that he is forced by his appetite to perform the vicious acts.

Let this, then, be our definition of what is due to force— 15
those things of which the cause by which men are forced to do them is external (but where the cause is internal and in themselves there is no force).

But now we must speak about necessity and the necessary. The term 'necessary' must not be used in all circumstances nor in every case—for instance, of what we do for the sake of pleasure. For if one were to say 'I was necessitated by pleasure to debauch my friend's wife', he would be a strange person. For 'necessary' does not apply to everything, but only to externals; for instance, whenever a man receives some damage by way of alternative to some other greater, when compelled by circumstances. For instance, 'I found it necessary to hurry my steps to the country; otherwise I should have found my stock destroyed.' Such, then, are the cases in which we have the necessary.

38–b 14 = *E. E.* 1224a 12–b 5. 13, 14 = *E. N.* 1110a 1–3.

[1] 1188b 8 reading βιαζομένους. βιαζομένοις in Susemihl is a misprint.

16 But since the voluntary lies in no impulse, there will remain what proceeds from thought.[1] For the involuntary is what is done from necessity or from force, and, thirdly, what is not accompanied by thought. This is plain from facts. For whenever a man has struck or killed a man, or has done something of that sort without having thought about it beforehand, we say that he has acted involuntarily, implying that the voluntariness lies in the having thought about it. For instance, they say that once on a time a woman gave a love-potion to somebody; then the man died from the effects of the love-potion, and the woman was put on her trial before the Areopagus; on her appearance before which she was acquitted, just for the reason that she did not do it with design. For she gave it in love, but missed her mark; wherefore it was not held to be voluntary, because in giving the love-potion she did not give it with the thought of killing. In that case, therefore, the voluntary falls under the head of what is accompanied with thought.

17 It now remains for us to inquire into purpose. Is purpose 1189^a
impulse or is it not? Now impulse is found in the lower animals, but not purpose; for purpose is attended with reason, and none of the lower animals has reason. Therefore it will not be impulse.

Is it then wish? Or is it not this either? For wish is concerned even with the impossible; for instance, we wish that we may live for ever, but we do not purpose it. Again, purpose is not concerned with the end but with

32–38 = *E.N.* 1111^a 14 = *E.E.* 1225^b 5. 1189^a 1–4 = *E.N.* 1111^b 12, 13. 5–12 = *E.N.* 1111^b 19–30 = *E.E.* 1226^a 6–17.

[1] The distinction drawn in *E.N.* between a merely voluntary act and an act done on purpose is here rather blurred. Ἐκ διανοίας must not be taken to mean more than εἰδότι τὰ καθ' ἕκαστα ἐν οἷς ἡ πρᾶξις in *E.N.* 1111^a 23. This is evident from the words which follow here in 1189^a 33, where it is recognized that instinctive acts are voluntary. When the jury acquitted the woman of design, they pronounced that she was ignorant of the ἕνεκα τίνος (*E.N.* 1111^a 5) of her act, an ignorance which rendered it involuntary. The words μετὰ διανοίας, which are used in this chapter of a voluntary act, are in the next (1189^a 36) made to be the differentia of an act done on purpose.

the means; for instance, no one purposes to be in health, but we purpose what leads to health, e. g. walking, running; but we wish for the ends. For we wish to be in health. So that it is evident in this way also that wish and purpose are not the same thing.

But purpose seems to be what its name suggests; I mean, we choose one thing instead of another; for instance, the better instead of the worse. Whenever, then, we take the better in exchange for the worse as a matter of choice, there the verb 'to purpose' would seem to be appropriate.

Since, then, purpose is none of these things, can it be thought that constitutes purpose? Or is this not so either? For we entertain many thoughts and opinions in our minds. Do we then purpose whatever we think? Or is this not so? For often we think about things in India, but it does not follow that we purpose them. Purpose therefore is not thought either.

Since, then, purpose is not any of these singly, and these are the things that there are in the soul, purpose must result from the combination of some of them.

Since, then, purpose, as was said before,[1] is concerned with the goods that are means and not with the end, and with the things that are possible to us, and with such as afford ground for controversy as to whether this or that is choiceworthy, it is evident that one must have thought and deliberated about them beforehand; then when a thing appears best to us after having thought it over, there ensues an impulse to act, and it is when we act in this way that we are held to act on purpose.

Since, then, purpose is a deliberate impulse attended with thought, the voluntary is not necessarily done on purpose. For there are many acts which we do voluntarily before thinking and deliberating about them; for instance, we sit down and rise up, and do many other things of the

13–16 = *E. N.* 1112^a 16, 17 = *E. E.* 1226^b 14–17. 17–22 = *E. N.* 1111^b 30–34 = *E. E.* 1226^a 1–6. 32 = *E. N.* 1113^a 11 = *E. E.* 1226^b 9. 33–^{b}6 = *E. N.* 1111^b 6–10 = *E. E.* 1226^b 30–1227^a 1.

[1] ll. 7–10.

same sort voluntarily but without having thought about them, whereas every act done on purpose was found to be attended with thought. The voluntary, therefore, is not 1189b necessarily done on purpose, but the act done on purpose is voluntary; for if we purpose to do anything after deliberation, we act voluntarily. And a few legislators, even, appear to distinguish the voluntary act from the act done on purpose as being something different, in making the penalties that they appoint for voluntary acts less than for those that are done on purpose.

Purpose, then, lies in matters of action, and in those in which it is in our power to do or not to do, and to act in this way or in that, and where we can know the reason why.

But the reason why is not always of the same kind. For in geometry, when one says that the quadrilateral has its angles equal to four right angles, and one asks the reason why, one says, 'Because the triangle has its angles equal to two right angles.' Now in such cases they reached the reason why from a definite principle; but in matters of action, with which purpose has to do, it is not so (for there is no definite principle laid down), but if one asks, 'Why did you do this?' the answer is, 'Because it was the only thing possible,' or 'Because it was better so.' It is from the consequences themselves, according as they appear to be better, that one forms one's purpose, and these are the reason why.

Wherefore in such matters the deliberation is as to the how, but not so in the sciences. For no one deliberates how he ought to write the name Archicles, because it is a settled matter how one ought to write the name Archicles. The error, then, does not arise in the thought, but in the act of writing. For where the error is not in the thought, neither do people deliberate about those things. But wherever there is an indefiniteness about the how, there error comes in.

Now there is the element of indefiniteness in matters of action, and in those matters in which the errors are two-

18–24 = *E.N.* 1112a 34–b 9 = *E.E.* 1226a 33–b 2.

fold. We err, then, in matters of action and in what pertains to the virtues in the same way. For in aiming at virtue we err in the natural directions. For there is error both in defect and in excess, and we are carried in both these directions through pleasure and pain. For it is owing to pleasure that we do base deeds, and owing to pain that we abstain from noble ones.

Again, thought is not like the senses; for instance, with **18**
sight one could not do anything else than see, nor with hearing anything else than hear. So also we do not deliberate whether we ought to hear with hearing or see. But thought is not like this, but it is able to do one thing
1190^{a} and others also. That is why deliberation comes in there.

The error, then, in the choice of goods is not about the ends (for as to these all are at one in their judgement, for instance, that health is a good), but only about those which lead to the ends; for instance, whether a particular food is good for health or not. The chief cause of our going wrong in these matters is pleasure and pain; for we avoid the one and choose the other.

Since, then, it has been settled in what error takes place and how, it remains to ask what it is that virtue aims at. Does it aim at the end or at the means; for instance, at what is right or at what conduces thereto?

How, then, is it with science? Does it belong to the science of housebuilding to design the end rightly, or to see the means that conduce to it? For if the design be right—I mean, to make a beautiful house—it is no other than the housebuilder who will discover and provide the means. And similarly in the case of all the other sciences.

So, then, it would seem to be also in the case of virtue, that its aim is rather the end, which it must design rightly, than the means. And no one else will provide the materials for this or discover the means that are required. And it is reasonable to suppose that virtue should have this in view. For both design and execution always belong to that with

27–32 = *E.N.* 1104^{b} 9–11 = *E.E.* 1227^{a} 36–41. 1190^{a} 8–33 = *E.E.* 1227^{b} 12–1228^{a} 2.

which the origination of the best lies. Now there is nothing better than virtue; for it is for its sake that all other things are, and the origination looks to this, and the means are rather for the sake of it; now the end seems to be a kind of principle, and everything is for the sake of it. But this will be as it ought to be. So that it is plain also in the case of virtue, since it is the best mode of causation, that it aims at the end rather than at the means.

19 Now the end of virtue is the right. This, then, is what virtue aims at rather than the things from which it will be produced. But it has to do also with these. But to make these its whole concern is manifestly absurd. For perhaps in painting one might be a good imitator and yet not be praised, if one does not make it his aim to imitate the best subjects. This, therefore, is quite the business of virtue, to design the right.

Why, then, some one may say, did we say before[1] that the activity was better than the corresponding state, whereas now we are assigning to virtue as nobler not the material for activity, but something in which there is no activity? Yes, but now also we assert this just the same, that the activity is better than the state. For his fellow men in viewing the good man judge him from his acts, owing to its not being possible to make clear the purpose which each has, since if it were possible to know how the judgement of each man stands towards the right, he would have been thought good even without acting.

But since we reckoned up certain means of the feelings, we must say with what sort of feelings they are concerned.[2]

20 . . . Since, then, courage has to do with feelings of confidence and fear, we must examine with what sort of fears and confidences it has to do. If, then, any one is afraid

24: cf. *E.N.* 1102^a 2, 3: *E.E.* 1227^b 25. 26: cf. *E.N.* 1099^b 23. ^{b}2–6: cf. *E.N.* 1111^b 5, 6, 1178^a 34, 35: *E.E.* 1228^a 2–19. 9–20 = *E.N.* 1115^a 6–21.

[1] 1184^b 11–17, 32–36.

[2] The author has mentioned various μεσότητες, 1185^b 21–30, 1186^a 17–35, ^{b}5–32, but has not enumerated them.

of losing his property, is he a coward? And if any one is confident about these matters, is he brave? Surely not! And in the same way if one is afraid of or confident about illness, one ought not to say that the man who fears is a coward or that the man who does not fear is brave. It is not, therefore, in such fears and confidences as these that courage consists. Nor yet in such as follow; for instance, if one is not afraid of thunder or lightning or any other superhuman terror, he is not brave but a sort of madman. It is with human fears and confidences, then, that the brave man has to do; I mean to say that whoso is confident under circumstances in which most people or all are afraid, he is a brave man.

These points having been settled, we must inquire, since there are many ways in which men are brave, which is the truly brave man. For you may have a man who is brave from experience, like professional soldiers. For they know, owing to experience, that in such a place or time or condition it is impossible to suffer any damage. But the man who knows these things and for this reason stands his ground against the enemy is not brave; for if none of these things be the case, he does not stand his ground. Wherefore one ought not to call those brave whose courage is due to experience. Nor indeed was Socrates right in asserting that courage was knowledge.[1] For knowledge becomes knowledge by getting experience from habit. But of those whose endurance is due to experience we do not say, nor would men in general say, that they are brave. Courage, therefore, will not consist in knowledge.

But again, on the other hand, there are some who are brave from the opposite of experience. For those who have no experience of the probable results are free from

16–20 = *E.N.* 1115^b 7–15, 26–28. 23–32 = *E.N.* 1116^b 3–23 = *E.E.* 1229^a 14–16. 33–35 = *E.N.* 1117^a 22–24 = *E.E.* 1229^a 16–18.

[1] Cp. *E.N.* 1116^b 4. It is true that Socrates thought courage to be a branch of knowledge, but, at least as represented by Plato, he meant thereby the knowledge that death is not really to be feared, if it comes in the course of duty. See the definition suggested in the *Laches*, 195 a.

fear owing to their inexperience. Neither, then, must we call these brave.

Again, there are others who appear brave owing to their passions; for instance, those who are in love or are inspired by religion. We must not call these brave either. For if their passion be taken away, they are not brave any **1191a** more, whereas the truly brave man must always be brave. Wherefore one would not call wild beasts like boars brave, owing to their defending themselves when they have been pained by a wound, nor ought the brave man to be brave through passion.

Again, there is another form of courage, which we may call civic; for instance, if men endure dangers out of shame before their fellow citizens, and so appear to be brave. In illustration of this we may take the way in which Homer has represented Hector as saying—

Then were Polydamas first to pile reproaches upon me;[1]

for which reason he thinks that he ought to fight. We must not call this sort courage either. For the same definition will apply to each of these. For he whose courage does not endure on the deprivation of something cannot properly be considered brave; if, then, I take away the shame owing to which he was brave, he will no longer be brave.

There is yet another way of appearing brave, namely, through hope and anticipation of good. We must not say that these are brave either, since it appears absurd to call those brave who are of such a character and under such circumstances.

No one, then, of the above kinds must be put down as brave.

We have then to ask who is to be so put down, and who is the really brave man. Broadly speaking, then, it is he who is brave owing to none of the things above-men-

36–1191a 4 = *E.N.* 1116b 23–1117a 9 = *E.E.* 1229a 20–30. 5–13 = *E.N.* 1116a 17–35 = *E.E.* 1229a 13, 14, 19. 14–16 = *E.N.* 1117a 9–22 = *E.E.* 1229a 18–20. 17–21: cf. *E.N.* 1115a 33, 34: *E.E.* 1230a 29–33.

[1] *Il.* xxii. 100.

tioned, but owing to his thinking it to be right, and who acts bravely whether any one be present or not.

Not, indeed, that courage arises in one entirely without passion and impulse. But the impulse must proceed from reason and be directed to the right. He, then, who is carried by a rational impulse to face danger for the sake of right, being free from fear about these things, is brave; and these are the things with which courage has to do.

When we say 'free from fear', it is not to be understood that the brave man feels no fear at all. For such a person is not brave, for whom nothing at all has any terrors. For in that way a stone and other things without life would be brave. But it is necessary that while he feels fear he should still face the danger; for if, on the other hand, he faces it without feeling fear, he will not be brave.

Further, according to the distinction that we made above,[1] it is not concerned with all fears and dangers, but only with those which threaten existence. Moreover, not at any and every time, but when the fears and the dangers are near. For if one is void of fear with regard to a danger that is ten years off, it does not follow that he is brave. For some are confident owing to its being far away, but, if they come near it, are ready to die with fear. Such, then, are courage and the brave man.

21 Temperance is a mean between intemperance and insensibility to pleasures. For temperance and generally every virtue is the best state, and the best state lies in
1191b the attainment of the best thing, and the best thing is the mean between excess and defect; for people are blameworthy on both grounds, both on that of excess and on that of defect. So that, since the mean is best, temperance will be a mean state between intemperance and insensibility. These, then, are the vices between which it will be a mean.

Temperance is concerned with pleasures and pains, but

25–30 = *E.N.* 1150b 10–13 = *E.E.* 1229a 1–11. 37–b 22 = *E.N.* 1117b 27–1118a 26 = *E.E.* 1230a 36–1231b 4.

---

[1] 1190b 9–20.

not with all, nor with those that have to do with all objects. For one is not intemperate if one takes pleasure in beholding a painting or a statue or something of that sort, and in the same way not so in the case of hearing or smell; but only in the pleasures which have to do with touch and taste.

Nor yet with regard to these will a man be temperate who is in such a state as not to be affected at all by any pleasures of this sort (for such a person is devoid of feeling), but rather he who feels them and yet does not let himself be led away into enjoying them to excess and regarding everything else as of secondary consideration; and, we must add, the man who acts for the sake of right and nothing else. . . . For whoever abstains from the excess of such pleasures either from fear or some other such motive is not temperate. For neither do we call the other animals temperate except man, because there is not reason in them whereby they test and choose the right. For every virtue is concerned with and aims at the right. So temperance will be concerned with pleasures and pains, and these those that occur in touch and taste.

22 Next to this it behoves us to speak about the definition and sphere of gentleness. Gentleness, then, is in a mean between irascibility and a want of anger. And generally the virtues seem to be a kind of means. One can show that they are so in this way as well. For if the best is in the mean, and virtue is the best state [and the mean is best], virtue will be the mean. But it will be more plain as we inquire into them separately. For since he is irascible who gets angry with everybody and under all circumstances and to too great an extent, and such a one is blameworthy (for one ought not to be angry with everybody nor at everything nor under all circumstances and always, nor yet again on the other hand[1] ought one to be in such a state as never to be angry with anybody; for this character also is blameworthy, as being insensible),

23–41 = *E.N.* 1125^{b} 26–1126^{a} 8 = *E.E.* 1231^{b} 5–26.

[1] Reading αὖ for οὖ, which is evidently a misprint.

since then both he who is in the excess is blameworthy and he who is in the defect, the man who is in the mean between them will be gentle and praiseworthy. For neither he who is in defect in anger nor he who is in excess is praiseworthy, but he who stands in a mean with regard to these things. He is gentle; and gentleness will be a mean state with regard to these feelings.[1]

Liberality is a mean state between prodigality and 23
1192^a illiberality. Feelings of this sort have to do with property. The prodigal is he who spends on wrong objects and more than he ought and at wrong times, while the illiberal man, in the opposite way to him, is he who does not spend on right objects and as much as he ought and when he ought. And both these characters are blameworthy. And one of them is characterized by defect and the other by excess. The liberal man, therefore, since he is praiseworthy, will be in a mean between them. Who, then, is he? He who spends on right objects and right amounts and at right times.

There are several forms of illiberality; for instance, we 24
call some people *niggards* and *cheese-parers*, and *lovers of base gain*, and *penurious*. Now all these fall under the head of illiberality. For evil is multiform, but good uniform; for instance, health is single, but disease has many shapes. In the same way virtue is single, but vice has many shapes. For all these characters are blameworthy in relation to property.

Is it, then, the business of the liberal man also to get and procure property? Surely not! That sort of thing is not the business of any virtue at all. It is not the business of courage to make weapons, but of something else, but it is the business of this when it has got them to make a right use of them; and so in the case of temperance and the other virtues. This, then, is not the

42–1192^a 20 = *E. N.* 1119^b 22–1122^a 17 = *E. E.* 1231^b 28–1232^a 18.
8–10 = *E. N.* 1121^b 21–28 = *E. E.* 1232^a 10–18. 11–14 = *E. N.* 1106^b 29–31.

[1] Putting the full stop after ταῦτα instead of after πρᾶος.

business of liberality, but rather of the art of procuring property.

25 Greatness of soul is a mean between vanity and littleness of soul, and it has to do with honour and dishonour, not so much with honour from the many as with that from the good, and more indeed with this. For the good will bestow honour with knowledge and good judgement. He will wish then rather to be honoured by those who know as he does himself that he deserves honour. For he will not be concerned with every honour, but with the best, and with the good that is honourable and ranks as a principle. Those, then, who are despicable and bad, but who deem themselves worthy of great things, and besides that think that they ought to be honoured, are vain. But those who deem themselves worthy of less than befits them are men of little soul. The man, therefore, who is in the mean between these is he who neither deems himself worthy of less honour than is befitting to him, nor of greater than he deserves, nor of all. And he is the man of great soul. So that it is evident that greatness of soul is a mean between vanity and littleness of soul.

26 Magnificence is a mean between ostentation and shabbiness. Now magnificence has to do with expenses which are proper to be incurred by a man of eminence. Who- **1192^{b}**
ever therefore spends on the wrong occasions is ostentatious; for instance, one who feasts his dinner-club as though he were giving a wedding-banquet, such a person is ostentatious (for the ostentatious man is the sort of person who shows off his own means on the wrong occasion). But the shabby man is the opposite of this, who fails to make a great expenditure when he ought;[1] or if, without going to that length, when, for instance, he is spending money on a wedding-feast or the mounting of

21–36 = *E.N.* 1123^{a} 34–1125^{a} 35 = *E.E.* 1232^{a} 19–1233^{a} 30. 37–^{b} 17 = *E.N.* 1122^{a} 18–1123^{a} 33.

[1] The meaning would be better expressed by saying, 'who, when he ought to make a great expenditure, fails to spend at all'. This, however, would require us to read ὃς οὗ δεῖ μεγαλείως, μὴ δαπανήσει.

a play, he does it in an unworthy and deficient way, such a person is shabby. Magnificence from its very name shows itself to be such as we are describing. For since it spends the great amount on the fitting occasion, it is rightly called magnificence. Magnificence, then, since it is praiseworthy, is a mean between defect and excess with regard to proper expenses on the right occasions.

But there are, as people think, more kinds of magnificence than one; for instance, people say, 'his gait was magnificent,' and there are of course other uses of the term 'magnificent' in a metaphorical, not in a strict sense. For it is not in those things that magnificence lies, but in those which we have mentioned.

Righteous indignation is a mean state between envious- **27**
ness and malice.[1] For both these states are blameworthy, but the man who shows righteous indignation is praiseworthy. Now righteous indignation is a kind of pain with regard to good things which are found to attach to the undeserving. The man, then, who feels righteous indignation is he who is apt to feel pain at such things. And this same person again will feel pain, if he sees a man faring ill, who does not deserve it. Righteous indignation, then, and the person who feels it, are perhaps of this sort, but the envious man is the opposite of this. For he will feel pain without distinction as to whether one deserves the good fortune or not. In the same way with him the malicious man will be pleased at ill-fortune, whether deserved or

18–29 = *E. N.* 1108^{b} 1–6 = *E. E.* 1233^{b} 18–26.

---

[1] This is in verbal agreement with *E. N.* ii. 1108^{b} 1, but the ἐπιχαιρέκακος there is the man who is so far in the defect of being pained at the prosperity of the wicked, that he even feels pleasure at it, having a disinterested delight in evil. This strained meaning of ἐπιχαιρέκακος is discarded in the *Rhetoric* (ii. 1386^{b} 34), but it is the one which is required by the theory of the mean. Here, instead of an excess and defect, we have two different forms of excess over νέμεσις. The νεμεσητικός is pained at the good fortune of the bad, and in this he is exceeded by the φθονερός, who is pained at any one's good fortune; on the other hand, the νεμεσητικός is pleased at the ill-fortune of the bad, and in this he is exceeded by the ἐπιχαιρέκακος, who is pleased at any one's ill-fortune.

undeserved. Not so with the man who feels righteous indignation, but he is in the mean between these.

28 Reserve is in a mean between pride[1] and complaisance, and has to do with social intercourse. For the proud man is inclined not to meet or talk to anybody (but his name seems to be given to him from his character; for it means self-pleasing, from his gratifying himself); but the complaisant is ready to associate with every one under all circumstances and in all places. Neither of these characters, then, is praiseworthy, but the reserved man, being in the mean between them, is praiseworthy. For he does not lay himself out to please everybody, but only those who are worthy, nor yet nobody, for he does so to these same.

29 Modesty is a mean between shamelessness and bashful- 1193a
ness, and it has to do with deeds and words. For the shameless man is he who says and does anything on any occasion or before any people; but the bashful man is the opposite of this, who is afraid to say or do anything before anybody (for such a man is incapacitated for action, who is bashful about everything); but modesty and the modest man are a mean between these. For he will not say and do anything under any circumstances, like the shameless man, nor, like the bashful man, be afraid on every occasion and under all circumstances, but will say and do what he ought, where he ought, and when he ought.

30 Wit is a mean state between buffoonery and boorishness, and it is concerned with jests. For the buffoon is he who thinks fit to jest at every one and everything, and the boor is he who neither thinks fit to make jests nor to have them made at him, but gets angry. But the witty man is midway between these, who neither jests at all persons and

30–41 = *E.E.* 1233b 34–38. 1193a 1–10 = *E.N.* 1108a 31–35, 1128b 10–35 = *E.E.* 1233b 26–29. 11–19 = *E.N.* 1127b 33–1128b 4 = *E.E.* 1234a 4–23.

[1] Neither reserve (σεμνότης) nor pride (αὐθάδεια) is to be found in *E.N.* They come from *E.E.* (iii. 1233b 34–8). The ἄρεσκος in *E.N.* ii. 1108a 28, 29 is the κόλαξ minus his interested motive.

under all circumstances, nor on the other hand is a boor. But wit has two sides to it. For both he who is able to jest in good taste and he who can stand being jested at may be called a man of wit. Such, then, is wit.

Friendliness is a mean state between flattery and un- 31
friendliness,[1] and it has to do with acts and words. For the flatterer is he who adds more than is proper and true, while the unfriendly man is hostile and detracts from the truth. Neither of them, then, can rightly be praised, but the friendly man is between the two. For he will not add more than the facts, nor praise what is not proper, nor on the other hand will he represent things as less than they are, nor oppose in all cases even contrary to what he thinks. Such, then, is the friendly man.

Truthfulness is a mean between self-depreciation and 32
boastfulness. It has to do, of course, with words, but not with all words. For the boaster is he who pretends to have more than he has, or to know what he does not know; while the self-depreciator, on the other hand, lays claim to less than he really has and does not declare what he knows, but tries to hide his knowledge. But the truthful man will do neither of these things. For he will not pretend either to more than he has or less, but will say that he has and knows what as a matter of fact he does have and does know.

Whether, then, these are virtues or not is another question. But that they are means of the above-mentioned states is plain. For those who live according to them are praised.

1193^b It remains to speak about justice—what it is, in what, 33
and about what.

20–28 = *E.N.* 1126^b 11–1127^a 12 = *E.E.* 1233^b 29–34. 28–35 = *E.N.* 1127^a 13–^{b} 32 = *E.E.* 1233^b 38–1234^a 3. 36–38 = *E.E.* 1234^a 24–30. 39–^{b} 3 = *E.N.* 1129^a 3–5.

[1] This term (ἔχθρα) comes from Eudemus (iii. 1233^b 30), who, in his table (ii. 1220^b 38–1221^a 12), splits up Aristotle's φιλία into two qualities, thus—

Excess.	Mean.	Defect.
κολακεία	φιλία	ἀπέχθεια
ἀρέσκεια	σεμνότης	αὐθάδεια

First, then, if we could fix upon what justice is. Justice is twofold, of which one kind is legal justice. For people say that what the law commands is just. Now the law commands us to act bravely and temperately, and generally to perform the actions which come under the head of the virtues. For which reason also, they say, justice appears to be a kind of perfect virtue. For if the things which the law commands us to do are just, and the law ordains what is in accordance with all virtues, it follows that he who abides by legal justice will be perfectly virtuous, so that the just man and justice are a kind of perfect virtue.

The just, then, in one sense is in these things and about these things. But it is not the just in this sense, nor the justice which deals with these things, of which we are in search. For in respect of just conduct of this sort it is possible to be just when one is alone (for the temperate and the brave and the self-controlled is so each of them when alone). But what is just towards one's neighbour is different from the legal justice that has been spoken of. For in things just towards one's neighbour it is not possible to be just when alone. But it is the just in this sense of which we are in search, and the justice which has to do with these things.

The just, then, in relation to one's neighbour is, speaking generally, the equal. For the unjust is the unequal. For when people assign more of the goods to themselves and less of the evils, this is unequal, and in that case they think that injustice is done and suffered. It is evident, therefore, that since injustice implies unequal things, justice and the just will consist in an equality of contracts. So that it is evident that justice will be a mean between excess and defect, between too much and too little. For the unjust man by doing wrong has more, and his victim by being wronged has less; but the mean between these is just. And the mean is equal. So that the equal between more and less will be just, and he will be just who wishes to have what is

3–18 = *E.N.* 1129^a 26–^{b} 1. 19–32 = *E.N.* 1129^a 32–^{b} 10, 1131^a 10–15.

equal. But the equal implies two things at least. To be equal therefore in relation to one's neighbour is just, and a man of this sort will be just.

Since, then, justice consists in just and equal dealing and in a mean, we must notice that the just is said to be just as between certain persons, and the equal is a relation between certain persons, and the mean is a mean for certain persons; so that justice and the just will have relation to certain persons and be between certain persons.

Since, then, the just is equal, the proportionally equal will be just. Now proportion implies four terms at least: A : B :: C : D. For instance, it is proportional that he who
1194a has much should contribute much, and that he who has little should contribute little; again, in the same way, that he who has worked much should receive much, and that he who has worked little should receive little. But as the man who has worked is to the man who has not worked, so is the much to the little; and as the man who has worked is to the much, so is the man who has not worked to the little. Plato also seems to employ proportional justice in his *Republic*.[1] For the farmer, he says, produces food, and the housebuilder a house, and the weaver a cloak, and the shoemaker a shoe. Now the farmer gives the housebuilder food, and the housebuilder gives the farmer a house; and in the same way all the rest exchange their products against those of others. And this is the proportion. As the farmer is to the housebuilder, so is the housebuilder to the farmer. In the same way with the shoemaker, the weaver, and all the rest, the same proportion holds towards one another. And this proportion holds the commonwealth together. So that the just seems to be the proportional. For the just holds commonwealths together, and the just is the same thing as the proportional.

But since the work which the housebuilder produces is of more value than that of the shoemaker, and the shoe-

33–38 = *E.N.* 1131a 14–20. 1194a 18–25 = *E.N.* 1133a 19–29.

[1] 369 D.

maker had to exchange[1] his work with the housebuilder, but it was not possible to get a house for shoes; under these circumstances they had recourse to using something for which all these things are purchasable, to wit silver, which they called money, and to effecting their mutual exchanges by each paying the worth of each product, and thereby holding the political communion together.

Since, then, the just is in those things and in what was mentioned before, the justice which is concerned with these things will be an habitual impulse[2] attended with purpose about and in these things.

Retaliation also is just; not, however, as the Pythagoreans maintained. For they thought that it was just that a man should suffer in return what he had done. But this cannot be the case in relation to all persons. For the same thing is not just for a domestic as for a freeman. For if the domestic has struck the freeman, it is not just that he should merely be struck in return, but many times. And retaliatory justice, also, consists in proportion. For as the freeman is to the slave in being superior, so is retaliation to aggression. It will be the same with one freeman in relation to another. For it is not just, if a man has knocked out somebody's eye, merely that he should have his own knocked out, but that he should suffer more, if he is to observe the proportion. For he was the first to begin and did a wrong, and is in the wrong in both ways, so that the acts of injustice are proportional, and for him to suffer more than he did is just.

But since the term 'just' is used in more senses than one, we must determine what kind of justice it is about which our inquiry is.

There is, then, a sort of justice, as they say, for a domestic as against his master, and a son as against his

29–^{b}2 = *E. N.* 1133^{a}24–1134^{b}18.

[1] ἦν with the dative seems here to be equivalent to ἔδει with the accusative. ἔργον in such a context can hardly be anything but the object after ἀντικαταλλάττεσθαι.

[2] Lit. 'possessed by habit of an impulse'. But perhaps we should read τις ἕξις (Spengel).

father. But the just in these cases would seem only to share the name of political justice without sharing the nature (for the justice about which we are inquiring is political justice); for this above all consists in equality (for citizens are a sort of partners, and tend to be on a par by nature, though they differ in character), but a son as against his father or a domestic against his master would not seem to have any rights at all, any more than my foot or my hand has any rights against me, and in the same way with each of the members. The same, then, would seem to be the case with the son as against his father. For the son is, as it were, a part of his father, except when he has already attained to the position of a man and has been separated from him; then, and not till then, is he the equal and peer of his father. Now citizens are supposed to be on that footing. And in the same way neither has a domestic any rights as against his master for the same reason. For the domestic is a part of his master. Or if he has any rights as against him, it is in the way of economic justice. But this is not what we are in search of, but political justice; for political justice seems to lie in equality and peerdom. Though, indeed, the justice that there is in the intercourse between wife and husband comes near to political justice. For the wife is inferior to the husband, but more intimately connected with him, and partakes in a way more of equality, because their life is an approximation to political society, so that justice between man and wife is more than any other like that between citizens. Since, then, the just is that which is found in political society, justice also and the just man will be concerned with the politically just.

Things are just either by nature or by law. But we must not regard the natural as being something which cannot by any possibility change; for even the things which are by nature partake of change. I mean, for instance, if we were all to practise always throwing with the left hand, we should become ambidextrous. But still by nature left is left, and the right is none the less naturally superior to the left hand, even if we do everything with

the left as we do with the right. Nor because things change does it follow that they are not by nature. But if for the most part and for the greater length of time the left continues thus to be left and the right right, this is by nature. The same is the case with things just by 1195a
nature. Do not suppose that, if things change owing to our use, there is not therefore a natural justice; because there is. For that which continues for the most part can plainly be seen to be naturally just. As to what we establish for ourselves and practise, that is thereby just, and we call it just according to law. Natural justice, then, is better than legal. But what we are in search of is political justice. Now the politically just is the legal, not the natural.

The unjust and the unjust act might seem on first hearing to be the same, but they are not. For the unjust is that which is determined by law; for instance, it is unjust to steal a deposit, but the unjust act is the actual doing of something unjustly. And in the same way the just is not the same with a piece of just conduct. For the just is what is determined by law, but a piece of just conduct is the doing of just deeds.

When, therefore, have we the just, and when not? Generally speaking, when one acts in accordance with purpose and voluntarily (what was meant by the voluntary has been stated by us above[1]), and when one does so knowing the person, the means, and the end, those are the conditions of a just act. In the very same way the unjust man will be he who knows the person, the means, and the end. But when without knowing any of these things one has done something that is unjust, one is not unjust oneself, but unfortunate. For if a man has slain his father under the idea that he was slaying an enemy, though he has done something that is unjust, still he is not doing injustice to anybody, but is unfortunate.

The possibility, then, of not committing injustice when

1195a 8–14 = *E. N.* 1135a 5–15. 15–22 = *E. N.* 1135a 15–31.

---

[1] See chs. 12–16.

one does things that are unjust lies in being ignorant of what was mentioned a little above, viz. when one does not know whom one is hurting, nor with what, nor to what end. But we must now define the ignorance, and say how the ignorance must arise if a man is not to be doing an injustice to the person whom he hurts. Let this, then, be the definition. When the ignorance is the cause of his doing something, he does not do this voluntarily, so that he does not commit injustice; but when he is himself the cause of his ignorance and does something in accordance with the ignorance of which he is himself the cause, then he is guilty of injustice, and such a person will justly be called unjust. Take for instance people who are drunk. Those who are drunk and have done something bad commit injustice. For they are themselves the causes of their ignorance. For they need not have drunk so much as not to know that they were beating their father. Similarly with the other sorts of ignorance which are due to men themselves, the people who commit injustice from them are unjust. But where they are not themselves the causes, but their ignorance is the cause of their doing what they do, they are not unjust. This sort of ignorance is that which comes from nature; for instance, children strike
1195b their parents in ignorance, but the ignorance which is in them being due to nature does not make the children to be called unjust owing to this conduct. For it is ignorance which is the cause of their behaving thus, and they are not themselves to blame for their ignorance, for which reason they are not called unjust either.

But how about being injured? Can a man be injured voluntarily? Surely not! We do indeed voluntarily perform just and unjust acts, but we cannot be said to be injured voluntarily. For we avoid being punished, so that it is evident that we would not voluntarily let ourselves be injured. For no one voluntarily endures to be hurt. Now to be injured is to be hurt.

Yes, but there are some who, when they ought to have an equal share, give way to others, so that if, as we have

32–38: cf. *E.N.* 1113^{b}30–1114^{a}3. ^{b}5–34 = *E.N.* 1136^{a}15–^{b}14.

seen,[1] to have the equal is just, and to have less is to be injured, and a man voluntarily has less, it follows, it is maintained, that he is injured voluntarily. But from the following consideration it is evident, on the other hand, that this is not so. For all who accept less get compensation for it in the way of honour, or praise, or glory, or friendship, or something of that sort. But he who takes compensation of some kind for what he forgoes cannot be said to be injured; and if he is not injured at all, then he is not injured voluntarily.

Yet again, those who get less and are injured in so far as they do not get what is equal, pride and plume themselves on such things, for they say, 'Though I might have had my share, I did not take it, but gave way to an elder' or 'to a friend'. But no one prides himself on being injured. But if they do not pride themselves upon suffering acts of injustice and do pride themselves upon such things, it follows generally that they will not be injured by thus getting less. And if they are not injured at all, then they will not be injured voluntarily.

But as against these and the like arguments[2] we have a counter-argument in the case of the incontinent man. For the incontinent man hurts himself by doing bad acts, and these acts he does voluntarily; he therefore hurts himself knowingly, so that he is voluntarily injured by himself. But here if we add the distinction,[3] it will impede the force of the argument. And the distinction is this, that no one wishes to be injured. The incontinent man does with his own wish[4] what is prompted by his incontinence, so that he injures himself; he therefore wishes to do to himself what is bad. But no one wishes to be injured, so that even the incontinent man will not voluntarily be doing an injury to himself.

But here again one might perhaps raise a difficulty. Is

35–1196a 24 = *E. N.* 1136a 34, 1138a 4–28.

---

[1] 1193b 19–24.

[2] Reading τοὺς τοιούτους λόγους (MSS.).

[3] 1195a 29 keeping ὁ, with the MSS.

[4] This is said only for the sake of argument. Contrast *E. N.* v. 1136b 6 οὐδεὶς γὰρ βούλεται, οὐδ' ὁ ἀκρατής.

it possible for a man to be unjust to himself? Judging from the incontinent man it would seem possible. And, again, in this way. If it is just to do those things which the law ordains to be done, he who does not do these is
1196a committing injustice; and if when he does not do them to him to whom the law commands, he is doing an injustice to that person, but the law commands one to be temperate, to possess property, to take care of one's body, and all other such things, then he who does not do these things is doing an injustice to himself. For it is not possible to refer such acts of injustice to any one else.

But these statements can hardly have been true, nor is it possible for a man to be unjust to himself. For it is not possible for the same man at the same time to have more and less, nor at once to act voluntarily and involuntarily. But yet he who does injustice, in so far as he does it, has more, and he who suffers it, in so far as he suffers it, has less. If therefore a man does injustice to himself, it is possible for the same man at the same time to have more and less. But this is impossible. It is not therefore possible for a man to be unjust to himself.

Again, he who does injustice does it voluntarily, and he who suffers it suffers it involuntarily, so that, if it is possible for a man to be unjust to himself, it would be possible at the same time to do something involuntarily and voluntarily. But this is impossible. So in this way also it is not possible for a man to be unjust to himself.

Again, one might look at the question from the point of view of particular acts of injustice. Whenever men commit injustice, it is either by stealing a deposit, or committing adultery, or thieving, or doing some other particular act of injustice; but no one ever robbed himself of a deposit, or committed adultery with his own wife, or stole his own property; so that if the commission of injustice lies in such things, and it is not possible to do any of them to oneself, it will not be possible to commit injustice against oneself.

Or if so, it will not be an act of injustice of the political,

25–33 = *E.N.* 1138b 9–14.

but rather of the family type. For the soul being divided into several parts has in itself a something better and a something worse, so that if there is any act of injustice within the soul, it will be done by the parts against one another. Now we distinguished[1] the economic act of injustice by its being directed against the better or worse, so that in this sense a man may be unjust or just to himself. But this is not what we are investigating, but the political act of injustice. So that in such acts of injustice as form the subject of our inquiry, it is not possible for a man to commit injustice against himself.

Which of the two, again, commits injustice, and with which of the two does the act of injustice lie, when a man has anything unjustly? Is it not with him who has judged and made the award, as in the games? For he who takes the palm from the president who has adjudged it to him is not committing injustice, even if it be wrongly awarded to him; but without doubt it is he who has judged badly and given it who is in the wrong. And he is in a way com- 1196b
mitting injustice, while in a way he is not. For in that he has not judged what is really and naturally just, he is committing an injustice, while in that he has judged what appears to him to be just, he is not committing an injustice.

34 Now since we have spoken about the virtues in general, saying what they are and in what and about what, and about each of them in particular, how that we must do the best in accordance with right reason,[2] to say no more than this, namely, 'to act in accordance with right reason,' would be much the same as if one were to say that health would be best secured, if one were to adopt the means of health. Such a statement is of course obscure. I shall have it said to me, 'Explain what are the means of health.' So also in the case of reason, 'What is reason and which is right reason?'

34–^{b}3 = *E. N.* 1136^{b}15–1137^{a}4. 4–11 = *E. N.* 1138^{b}18–34.

[1] 1194^{b}5–29.
[2] The author has not mentioned 'right reason' before.

Perhaps it is necessary first of all to make a division of that in which reason is found. A distinction, indeed, was made in outline[1] about soul before, how that one part of it is possessed of reason, while there is another part of the soul that is irrational. But the part of the soul which is possessed of reason has two divisions, of which one is the deliberative faculty, the other the faculty by which we know. That they are different from one another will be evident from their subject-matter. For as colour and flavour and sound and smell are different from one another, so also nature has rendered the senses whereby we perceive them different (for sound we cognise by hearing, flavour by taste, and colour by sight), and in like manner we must suppose it to be the same with all other things. When, then, the subject-matters are different, we must suppose that the parts of the soul whereby we cognise these are also different. Now there is a difference between the object of thought and the object of sense; and these we cognise by soul. The part of the soul, therefore, which is concerned with objects of sense will be different from that which is concerned with objects of thought. But the faculty of deliberation and purpose has to do with objects of sense that are liable to change, and generally all that is subject to generation and destruction. For we deliberate about those things which depend upon us and our purpose to do or not to do, about which there is deliberation and purpose as to whether to do them or not. And these are sensible objects which are in process of change. So that the part of the soul in which purpose resides will correspond to sensible objects.

These points having been settled, we must go on as follows. The question is one of truth, and the subject of our inquiry is how the truth stands, and we have to do with science, wisdom, intellect, philosophy, supposition. What, then, is the object of each of these?

Now science deals with the object of science, and this

12–33 = *E.N.* 1138^{b} 35–1139^{a} 15. 34–38 = *E.N.* 1139^{b} 15–17. 38–1197^{a} 2 = *E.N.* 1139^{b} 31–36.

[1] 1185^{b} 1–12.

through a process accompanied with demonstration and reason, but wisdom with matters of action, in which there is choice and avoidance, and it is in our power to do or not to do. 1197^{a}

When things are made and done, that which makes and that which does them are not the same. For the arts of making have some other end beyond the making; for instance, beyond housebuilding, since that is the art of making a house, there is a house as its end beyond the making, and similarly in the case of carpentry and the other arts of making; but in the processes of doing there is no other end beyond the doing; for instance, beyond playing the harp there is no other end, but just this is the end, the activity and the doing. Wisdom, then, is concerned with doing and things done, but art with making and things made; for it is in things made rather than in things done that artistic contrivance is displayed.

So that wisdom will be a state of purposing and doing things which it is in our own power to do or not to do, so far as they are of actual importance to welfare.

Wisdom is a virtue, it would seem, not a science. For the wise are praiseworthy, and praise is bestowed on virtue. Again, every science has its virtue, but wisdom has no virtue, but, as it seems, is itself[1] a virtue.

Intellect has to do with the first principles of things intelligible and real. For science has to do with things that admit of demonstration, but the principles are indemonstrable, so that it will not be science but intellect that is concerned with the principles.

Philosophy is compounded of science and intellect. For philosophy has to do both with the principles and with what can be proved from the principles, with which science deals. In so far, then, as it deals with the principles, it itself partakes of intellect, but in so far as it deals with demonstrative conclusions from the principles, it partakes

3–13 = *E.N.* 1140^{a} 1–6, ^{b} 1–4. 14–16 = *E.N.* 1140^{b} 4–6. 16–19: cf. *E.N.* 1140^{b} 22. 17: cf. *E.N.* 1103^{a} 8, 9. 20–23 = *E.N.* 1140^{b} 31–1141^{a} 8. 23–29 = *E.N.* 1141^{a} 9–^{b} 8.

[1] Reading αὐτή ἐστιν (coni. Spengel).

of science. So that it is evident that philosophy is compounded of intellect and science, so that it will deal with the same things with which intellect and science do.

Supposition is that whereby we are left in doubt about all things as to whether they are in a particular way or not.

Are wisdom and philosophy the same thing? Surely not! For philosophy has to do with things that can be demonstrated and are eternally the same, but wisdom has not to do with these, but with things that undergo change. I mean, for instance, straight or crooked or convex and the like are always what they are, but things expedient do not follow this analogy, so as never to change into anything else; they do change, and a given thing is expedient now, but not to-morrow, to this man but not to that, and is
1197b expedient in this way, but not in that way. Now wisdom has to do with things expedient, but philosophy not. Therefore philosophy and wisdom are not the same.

Is philosophy a virtue or not? It can become plain to us that it is a virtue by merely looking at wisdom. For if wisdom is, as we maintain, the virtue of one of the two rational parts, and wisdom is inferior to philosophy (for its objects are inferior; for philosophy has to do with the eternal and the divine, as we maintain, but wisdom with what is expedient for man), if, then, the inferior thing is a virtue, it is reasonable that the better should be a virtue, so that it is evident that philosophy is a virtue.

What is intelligence, and with what is it concerned? The sphere of intelligence is the same as that of wisdom, having to do with matters of action. For the intelligent man is doubtless so called from his capacity for deliberation, and in that he judges and sees a thing rightly. But his judgement is about small things and on small occasions. Intelligence, then, and the intelligent man are a part of wisdom and the wise man, and cannot be found apart from these; for you cannot separate the intelligent from the wise man.

The case would seem to be the same with cleverness.

32–b 3 = *E.N.* 1141a 22–28. 11–17 = *E.N.* 1142b 34–1143a 18.
18–26 = *E.N.* 1144a 23–37.

For cleverness and the clever man are not wisdom and the wise man; the wise man, however, is clever, wherefore also cleverness co-operates in a way with wisdom. But the bad man also is called clever; for instance, Mentor was thought to be clever, but he was not wise. For it is the part of the wise man and of wisdom to aim at the best things, and always to purpose and do these, but it is the part of cleverness and the clever man to consider by what means each object of action may be effected, and to provide these. Such, then, would seem to be the surroundings and sphere of the clever man.

It may raise a question and cause surprise that, when speaking of ethics and dealing with a department of statecraft, we are speaking about philosophy. Perhaps the reason is, firstly, that the inquiry about it will not appear foreign to our subject, if it is a virtue, as we maintain. Again, it is perhaps the part of the philosopher to glance also at subjects adjacent to his main interest. And it is necessary, when we are speaking about the contents of soul, to speak about them all; now philosophy is also in soul; so that we are not going beyond our proper subject in speaking about it.[1]

But as cleverness is to wisdom, so it would seem to be in the case of all the virtues. What I mean is that there are virtues which spring up even by nature in different persons, a sort of impulses in the individual, apart from reason, to courageous and just conduct and the like behaviour in accordance with virtue; and there are also 1198a
virtues due to habit and purpose. But the virtues that are accompanied with reason, when they supervene, are completely praiseworthy.

Now this natural virtue which is unaccompanied by reason, so long as it remains apart from reason, is of little account, and falls short of being praised, but when added to reason and purpose, it makes perfect virtue. Wherefore also the natural impulse to virtue co-operates with reason

36–1198a 9 = *E. N.* 1144b 1–17.

[1] The text is here unsound. Susemihl says of ψυχῆς, which appears in his text, that it is *aut lacunosum aut corruptum*.

and is not apart from reason. Nor, on the other hand, are reason and purpose quite perfected as regards being virtue without the natural impulse.

Wherefore Socrates was not speaking correctly when he said that virtue was reason, thinking that it was no use doing brave and just acts, unless one did them from knowledge and rational purpose. This was why he said that virtue was reason. Herein he was not right, but the men of the present day say better; for they say that virtue is doing what is good in accordance with right reason. Even they, indeed, are not right. For one might do what is just without any purpose at all or knowledge of the good, but from an irrational impulse, and yet do this rightly and in accordance with right reason (I mean he may have acted in the way that right reason would command); but all the same, this sort of conduct does not merit praise. But it is better to say, according to our definition, that it is the accompaniment by reason of the impulse to good. For that is virtue and that is praiseworthy.

The question might be raised whether wisdom is a virtue or not. It will be evident, however, from the following consideration that it is a virtue. For if justice and courage and the rest of the virtues, because they lead to the doing of right, are also praiseworthy, it is evident that wisdom will also be among the things that are praiseworthy and that rank as virtues. For wisdom also has an impulse towards those acts which courage has an impulse to do. For, speaking generally, courage acts as wisdom ordains, so that if it is itself praiseworthy for doing what wisdom ordains, wisdom will be in a perfect degree both praiseworthy and virtue.

But whether wisdom is practical or not one might see from this, namely, by looking at the sciences, for instance at housebuilding. For there is, as we say, in housebuilding one person who is called an architect, and another, who is subordinate to him, a housebuilder; and he is capable of making a house. But the architect also, inasmuch as he made the house, is capable of making a house. And the

10–21 = *E.N.* 1144b 18–30.

case is the same in all the other productive arts, in which there is a master-craftsman and his subordinate. The 1198b
master-craftsman therefore also will be capable of making something, and that the same thing which his subordinate is capable of making. If, then, the analogy holds in the case of the virtues, as is likely and reasonable, wisdom also will be practical. For all the virtues are practical, and wisdom is a kind of master-craftsman of them. For as it shall ordain, so the virtues and the virtuous act. Since then the virtues are practical, wisdom also will be practical.

But does this hold sway over all things in the soul, as is held and also questioned? Surely not! For it would not seem to do so over what is superior to itself; for instance, it does not hold sway over philosophy. But, it is said, this has charge of all, and is supreme in issuing commands. But perhaps it holds the same position as the steward in the household. For he is supreme over all and manages everything. But it does not follow that he holds sway over all; instead of that he is procuring leisure for the master, in order that he may not be hindered by necessary cares and so shut out from doing something that is noble and befitting. So and in like manner with him wisdom is, as it were, a kind of steward of philosophy, and is procuring leisure for it and for the doing of its work, by subduing the passions and keeping them in order.

1198b 9–20 = *E. N.* 1143b 33–36, 1145a 6–11.

BOOK II

AFTER this we must inquire into equity. What is it? 1
And what is its field and sphere? The equitable man with his equity is he who is inclined to take less than his legal rights. There are matters in which it is impossible for the lawgiver to enter into exact details in defining, and where he has to content himself with a general statement. When, then, a man gives way in these matters, and chooses those things which the lawgiver would have wished indeed to determine in detail,[1] but was not able to, such a man is equitable. It is not the way with him to take less than what is just absolutely; for he does not fall short of what is naturally and really just, but only of what is legally just in matters which the law left undetermined for want of power.

Considerateness[2] and the considerate man have to do 2
with the same things as equity, with points of justice that have been omitted by the lawgiver owing to the inexactness of his definitions. The considerate man criticizes the omissions of the lawgiver, and knows that, though things have been omitted by the lawgiver, they are nevertheless
1199a just. Such is the considerate man. Now considerateness is not found apart from equity. To the considerate man it belongs to judge, and to the equitable man to act in accordance with the judgement.

Good counsel is concerned with the same things as 3
wisdom (dealing with matters of action which concern

24–33 = *E. N.* 1137a 31–1138a 3. 34–1199a 3 = *E. N.* 1143a 19–24. 4–13 = *E. N.* 1142a 32–b 33.

[1] τῷ καθ' ἕκαστα. The τῷ is not required before καθ' ἕκαστα. But there was a growing tendency in Hellenistic Greek to prefix the article to such phrases.

[2] The Greek is εὐγνωμοσύνη, corresponding to the γνώμη of *E. N.* vi. 1143a 19. Εὐγνωμοσύνη is among the concomitants of virtue in *De Virtutibus et Vitiis*, 1251b 34. It does not appear in Eudemus.

choice and avoidance), and it is not found apart from wisdom. For wisdom leads to the doing of these things, while good counsel is a state or disposition, or whatever you are pleased to call it, which leads to the attainment of the best and most expedient in matters of action. Hence things that turn out right spontaneously do not seem to form the subject of good counsel. For where there is no reason which is on the look-out for what is best, you would not in that case say that a man to whom something turned out as it should be was well counselled, but lucky. For things that go right without the judgement of reason are due to good luck.

Is it the part of the just man to put himself on a level with everybody in his intercourse (I mean in the way of becoming all things to all men)? Surely not! For this would seem to be the part of a flatterer and obsequious person. But to suit his intercourse to the worth of each, this would seem to be the part of the man who is absolutely just and virtuous.

Here is also a difficulty that might be raised. If doing injustice is hurting somebody voluntarily and with full knowledge of the person and the manner and the end, and harm and injustice are in and concerned with good things, it follows that the doer of injustice and the unjust man will know what kind of things are good and what bad. But to know about these things is a peculiar property of the wise man and of wisdom. The absurdity then follows that wisdom, which is the greatest good, is attendant upon the unjust man. Surely it will not be thought that wisdom is attendant upon the unjust man. For the unjust man does not discern and is not able to judge between what is good in itself and what is good for him, but makes a mistake. But this is the province of wisdom, to be able to take a right view of these things (just as in matters of medicine we all know what is absolutely wholesome and what is productive of health, that hellebore and an aperient and surgery and cautery are wholesome and productive of health, and yet we do not possess the science of medicine), for without it we no longer know what is

good in particular cases, just as the doctor knows for whom a given thing is good and when and in what disposition; for herein the science of medicine displays itself. Now we may know things that are absolutely wholesome, and yet not have the science of medicine
1199b attendant upon us; and the same is the case with the unjust man. That in an absolute sense autocracy and government and power are good, he knows; but whether they are good for him or not, or when, or in what condition, that is what he does not also know. But this is just the business of wisdom, so that wisdom does not attend upon the unjust man. For the goods which he chooses and for which he commits injustice are what are absolutely good, not what are good for him. For wealth and office are good in themselves, but for him perhaps they are not good; for by obtaining wealth and office he will do much evil to himself and his friends, for he will not be able to make a right use of office.

Here also is a point which presents a difficulty and suggests inquiry. Can injustice be done to a bad man or not? For if injustice consists in hurt, and hurt in the deprivation of goods, it would seem not to hurt him. For the goods which he supposes to be good for him are not really so. For office and wealth will hurt the bad man who is not able to make a right use of them. If then they will hurt him by their presence, he who deprives him of these would not seem to be doing him an injustice. This kind of argument indeed will appear a paradox to the many. For all think that they are able to use office and power and wealth, but they are not right in this supposition. This is made plain by the lawgiver. For the lawgiver does not allow all to hold office, but there is a standard of age and means which must be possessed by him who is to hold office, implying that it is not possible for every one to do so. If then some one were to make it a grievance that he does not hold office or that he is not allowed to steer the ship, the answer would be, 'Well, you have nothing in your soul of a kind which will enable you to hold office or steer the ship.' In the case of the body we see that those cannot be in good health who apply to themselves things that are absolutely good, but if a man is to have his bad body in health, he must first apply to it water and a low diet. And when a man has his soul in a vicious state, in order that he may not work any ill must we not withhold him from wealth and office and power and things of that sort generally, the more so as soul is easier to move and more ready to change than body? For as the man whose body was bad was fit to be dieted in that way, so the man whose soul is bad is fit to live thus, without having any things of this sort.

This also presents a difficulty. For instance, when it is not possible at the same time to do brave and just acts, which is one to do? Now in the case of the natural virtues we said that there existed only the impulse to right without **1200^a** reason; but he who has choice has it in reason and the rational part. So that as soon as choice is present, perfect virtue will be there, which we said[1] was accompanied by wisdom, but not without the natural impulse to right. Nor will one virtue run counter to another, for its nature is to obey the dictates of reason, so that it inclines to that to which reason leads. For it is this which chooses the better. For the other virtues do not come into existence without wisdom, nor is wisdom perfect without the other virtues, but they co-operate in a way with one another, attending upon wisdom.

Nor less will the following present itself as a difficulty. Is it in the case of the virtues as it is in the case of the other goods, whether external or bodily? For these when they run to excess make men worse; for instance, when wealth becomes great it makes men supercilious and disagreeable. And so also with the other goods—office, honour, beauty, stature. Is it, then, thus in the case of virtue also, so that, if one comes to have justice or courage to excess, he will be worse? Surely not![2] But, it will be said, from virtue comes honour, and when honour be-

[1] 1197^b 36–1198^a 21.

[2] Instead of supplying another οὔ, we want to get rid of the φησίν, which may have crept in from below. ἢ οὔ is carried out below by ἢ τοῦτο οὐκ ἀληθές;

comes great, it makes men worse, so that it is evident that virtue when progressing to a great extent will make men worse. For virtue is the cause of honour, so that virtue also, if it becomes great, will make men worse. Surely this cannot be true! For virtue, though it may have many other functions, as it has, has this among the most special, to be able to make a right use of these and the like goods when they are there. If therefore the good man on there coming to him high honour or high office shall not make a right use of these, it shows that he is not a good man. Therefore neither honour nor office will make the good man worse, so that neither will virtue. But generally, since it was laid down by us at the start[1] that the virtues are mean states, it follows that the more any state is a virtue, the more it is a mean; so that not only will virtue as it becomes great not make a man worse, but it will make him better. For the mean in question was found[2] to be the mean between excess and defect in the passions. So much then for these matters.

After this we must make a new start and speak about 4
self-control and its opposite. But as the virtue and the vice are themselves of a strange nature, so the discussion which will ensue about them must necessarily be strange
1200b also. For this virtue is not like the rest. For in the rest reason and passion have an impulse towards the same objects and are not opposed to one another, but in the case of this reason and passion are opposed to one another. There are three things in the soul in respect of which we are called bad—vice, incontinence, brutality. About virtue and vice, then, their nature and their sphere, we have spoken above;[3] but now we must speak about incontinence and brutality.

Brutality is a kind of excessive vice. For when we see 5
some one utterly degraded, we say that he is not even a man but a brute, implying that there is a vice of brutality.

1200a 36–b 8 = *E.N.* 1145a 15–17. b 9–19 = *E.N.* 1145a 18–33.

[1] 1185b 13–32, 1186a 9–35, cf. 1186a 36–1187a 4. [2] 1186a 9–35.
[3] 1185a 14–1200a 34.

Now the virtue opposed to this is without a name, but this sort of thing is above man, a kind of heroic and divine virtue. But this virtue is without a name, because virtue does not belong to God. For God is superior to virtue and it is not in the way of virtue that his goodness lies. For, if it were, virtue would be better than God. For this reason the virtue which is opposed to the vice of brutality is without a name. But the usual antithesis to this kind of vice is divine and superhuman virtue. For as the vice of brutality transcends man, so also does the virtue opposed to it.

6 But with regard to incontinence and self-control we must first state the difficulties and the arguments which run counter to appearances, in order that, having viewed the matter together from the point of view of the difficulties and counter-arguments, and having examined these, we may see the truth about them so far as possible; for it will be more easy to see the truth in that way.

Now Socrates of old[1] used to annul and deny incontinence altogether, saying that no one would choose evil who knew it to be such. But the incontinent seems, while knowing things to be bad, to choose them all the same, letting himself be led by passion. Owing to such considerations he did not think that there was incontinence. But there he was wrong. For it is absurd that conviction of the truth of this argument should lead to the annulment of a fairly established fact. For men do display lack of self-control, and do things which they themselves know to be bad.

Since, then, there is such a thing as lack of self-control, does the incontinent possess some knowledge whereby he views and examines his bad acts? But, again, this would

20–24 = *E.N.* 1145^{b} 21–31. 25–32 = *E.N.* 1145^{b} 21–31.

[1] ὁ πρεσβύτης seems to be an instance of the well-known confusion of thought between living long and living long ago, which leads Horace (*Sat.* II. i. 34) to call Lucilius *senex*—

quo fit ut omnis
votiva pateat veluti descripta tabella
vita senis.

As a matter of fact, Lucilius died prematurely.

For Σωκράτης ὁ πρεσβύτης or γέρων cf. *E.E.* 1216^{b} 3, 1235^{a} 37.

not seem so. For it would be strange that the strongest and surest thing in us should be vanquished by anything. For knowledge is of all things in us the most permanent and the most constraining. So that this argument again runs counter to there being knowledge.[1]

Is it then not knowledge, but opinion? But if the incontinent man only has opinion, he will not be blame-
1201a worthy. For if he does something bad with respect to which he has no exact knowledge but only an opinion, one would make allowances for his siding with pleasure and doing what is bad, if he does not know for certain that it is bad, but only has an opinion; and those for whom we make allowances we do not blame. So that the incontinent, if he only has opinion, will not be to blame. But he is to blame. Such arguments then land us in difficulties. For one denied knowledge on the ground of absurd consequences, and the other again denied opinion on the ground that there were absurd consequences from that also.

Here is also a difficulty that might be raised. It is held that the temperate man is also self-controlled. Will this involve the temperate man's having vehement appetites? If then he is to be self-controlled, it will be necessary for him to have vehement appetites (for you would not speak of a man as self-controlled who masters moderate appetites); but if he is to have vehement appetites, in that case he will not be temperate (for the temperate is he who does not display appetite or feeling at all).

The following considerations again present a difficulty. For it results from the statements that the man who lacks self-control is sometimes praiseworthy and the man who possesses it blameworthy. For let it be supposed, it may be said, that some one has gone wrong in his reasoning, and let it appear to him as the result of his reasoning that what is right is wrong, but let appetite lead him to the right; then reason indeed will forbid his doing it, but being

38–1201a 9 = *E.N.* 1145b 31–1146a 9. 10–15 = *E.N.* 1145b 14, 15, 1146a 9–16. 16–35 = *E.N.* 1146a 16–21.

[1] Reading, without any marks of lacuna, ἐναντιοῦται τῷ μὴ εἶναι ἐπιστήμην.

led by appetite he does it (for such we found[1] was the incontinent man); he will therefore do what is right, supposing that appetite leads him thereto (but reason will try to hinder him; for let it be supposed that he is mistaken in his reasoning about right); it follows that he will be lacking in self-control, and yet be praiseworthy; for in so far as he does what is right, he is praiseworthy. The result then is a paradox.

Again, on the other hand, let his reason be mistaken, and let what is right not seem to him to be so, but let appetite lead him to the right. Now he is self-controlled who, though he has an appetite for a thing, yet does not act upon it owing to reason; therefore if his reason is wrong it will hinder him from doing what he has an appetite for;[2] therefore it hinders him from doing what is right (for to that we supposed that his appetite led him); but he who fails to do what is right, when it is his duty to do it, is blameworthy; therefore the man of self-control will sometimes be blameworthy. In this way then also the result is a paradox.

A difficulty might also be raised as to whether lack of self-control and the incontinent man display themselves in and about everything, for instance, property and honour and anger and glory (for people seem to be deficient in self-control with regard to all these things), or whether they do not, but lack of self-control has a certain definite sphere.

The above, then, are the points which present a difficulty; 1201b
but it is necessary to solve these difficulties. First, then, that which is connected with knowledge. For it appeared[3] to be an absurdity that one who possessed knowledge should cast it from him or fall away from it. But the same reasoning applies also to opinion; for it makes no difference whether it is opinion or knowledge. For if opinion is intensely firm and unalterable by persuasion,

36–39 = *E.N.* 1146b 2–5. b 1–9 = *E.N.* 1146b 6, 7, 24–31.

[1] 1188a 8 sq., 28 sqq., b 9 sqq., 1200b 27 sq.
[2] Such seems to be the required sense in a corrupt passage.
[3] 1200b 25–1201a 9.

it will not differ at all from knowledge, opinion carrying with it the belief that things are as people opine them to be; for instance, Heraclitus of Ephesus has this sort of opinion about his own dogmas.

But there is no paradox in the incontinent man's doing something bad, whether he has knowledge or opinion such as we describe. For there are two ways of knowing, one of which is the possessing knowledge (for we say that one knows when he possesses knowledge), the other is putting the knowledge into operation. He then who possesses the knowledge of right, but does not operate with it, is incontinent. When, then, he does not operate with this knowledge, it is nothing surprising that he should do what is bad, though he possesses the knowledge. For the case is the same as that of sleepers. For they, though they possess the knowledge, nevertheless in their sleep both do and suffer many disgusting things. For the knowledge is not operative in them. So it is in the case of the incontinent. For he seems like one asleep and does not operate with his knowledge. Thus, then, is the[1] difficulty solved. For the difficulty was whether the incontinent man at the moment of action expels his knowledge or falls away from it, both of which appear paradoxical.

But, again, the thing may be made manifest in this way, as we said in the *Analytics*[2] that the syllogism consists of two premisses, and that of these the first is universal, while the second is subsumed under it and is particular. For instance—

I know how to cure any one with a fever.
This man has a fever.
∴ I know how to cure this man.

Now there are things which I know with the knowledge of the universal, but not with that of the particular. Here then also mistake becomes possible to the man who pos-

9–24 = *E.N.* 1146^b 31–35. 24–1202^a 1 = *E.N.* 1146^b 35–1147^a 10.

---

[1] Reading δὴ ἡ (coni. Susemihl).
[2] Cf. *An. Pr.* i. 24, 25; but it is doubtful whether Aristotle's *Analytics* is actually referred to.

sesses the knowledge, for instance how to cure[1] any one with a fever; whether, however, a given person has a fever, I do not know. Similarly then in the case of the incontinent man who possesses the knowledge the same mistake will arise. For it is possible for the incontinent man to possess the knowledge of the universal, that such and such things are bad and hurtful, but yet not to know that these particular things are bad, so that while possessing knowledge in this way he will go wrong; for he has the universal knowledge, but not the particular. Neither, then, in this way is it at all a surprising result in the case of the incontinent man, that he who has the knowledge should do something bad. 1202a

For it is so in the case of persons who are drunk. For those who are drunk, when the intoxication has passed off, are themselves again. Reason was not expelled from them, nor was knowledge, but it was overcome by the intoxication, but when they have got rid of the intoxication, they are themselves again. So, then, it is with the incontinent. His passion gains the mastery and brings his reasoning to a standstill. But when the passion, like the intoxication, has been got rid of, he is himself again.

There was another argument[2] touching incontinence which presented a difficulty as seeming to show that the man who lacks self-control will sometimes be praiseworthy, and the man who possesses it blameworthy. But this is not the case. For the man who is deceived in his reason is neither continent nor incontinent, but only he who possesses right reason and thereby judges of right and wrong, and it is the man who disobeys this kind of reason who lacks self-control, while he who obeys it and is not led by his appetites is self-controlled. If a man does not think it disgraceful to strike his father and has a desire to strike him, but abstains from doing so, he is not a man of self-control. So that, since there is neither self-control nor its opposite in such cases, neither will lack of self-

2–7 = *E.N.* 1147a 10–18. 8–18 = *E.N.* 1151a 29–b 4.

[1] Omitting ἐπίσταμαι.

[2] 1201a 16–35.

control be praiseworthy nor self-control blameworthy in the way that was thought.

There are forms of incontinence which are morbid and others which are due to nature. For instance, such as these are morbid. There are some people who pluck their hairs and nibble them. If one masters this pleasure, then, he is not praiseworthy, nor blameworthy if he fails to do so, or not very much. As an instance of incontinence due to nature we may take the story of a son who was brought to trial in court for beating his father, and who defended himself by saying, 'Why, he did so to his own father', and, what 's more, who was acquitted, for the judges thought that his going wrong was due to nature. If, then, one were to master the impulse to beat his father, he is not praiseworthy. It is not, then, such forms of incontinence or continence as these of which we are now in search, but those for which we are called blameworthy or praiseworthy without qualification.

Of goods some are external, as wealth, office, honour, friends, glory; others necessary and concerned with the body, for instance, touch and taste [he, then, who is incontinent with respect to these, would appear to be incontinent without qualification[1]] and bodily pleasures. And the incontinence of which we are in search would seem to be concerned with just these. And the difficulty was[2] about the sphere of incontinence. As regards honour, then, a man is not incontinent without qualification; for he who is incontinent with regard to honour is praised in a way, as being ambitious. And generally when we call a man incontinent in the case of such things we do it with some addition, incontinent 'as regards honour or glory or
1202^{b} anger'. But when a man is incontinent in the strict sense we do not add the sphere, it being assumed in his case, and being manifest without the addition, what the sphere is.

19–29 = *E. N.* 1148^{b} 15–30, 1149^{b} 8–11. 30–^{b} 3 = *E. N.* 1148^{a} 22–^{b} 14.

[1] Rassow and Susemihl wish to put these words after 'and bodily pleasures'.

[2] 1201^{a} 35–39.

For he who is incontinent in the strict sense has to do with the pleasures and pains of the body.

It is evident also from the following consideration that incontinence has to do with these things. For since the incontinent man is blameworthy, the subject-matter of his incontinence ought also to be blameworthy. Now honour and glory and office and riches, and the other things with respect to which people are called incontinent, are not blameworthy, whereas bodily pleasures are blameworthy. Therefore, reasonably enough, the man who is concerned with[1] these more than he ought is called incontinent in the complete sense.

Among the so-called 'incontinences' with respect to other things that which is concerned with anger is the most blameworthy. But which is more blameworthy, this or incontinence with regard to pleasures? Now incontinence with regard to anger resembles servants who are eager to minister to one's needs. For they, when the master says 'Give me', are carried away by their eagerness, and before they hear what they ought to give, give something, and give the wrong thing. For often, when they ought to give a book, they give a pen. Something like this is the case with the man who cannot control his anger. For passion, as soon as it hears the first mention of injury, starts up to take vengeance, without waiting to hear whether it ought or ought not, or not so vehemently. This sort of impulse, then, to anger, which appears to be incontinence of anger, is not greatly to be blamed, but the impulse to pleasure is blameworthy. For this latter differs from the former owing to the injunction of reason to abstain, which it nevertheless acts against; for which reason it is more blameworthy than incontinence due to anger. For incontinence due to anger is a pain (for no one feels anger without being pained), but that which is due to appetite is attended with pleasure, for which reason it is more blameworthy. For incontinence due to pleasure seems to involve wantonness.

1202b 10–28 = *E. N.* 1149a 24–b 26.

---

[1] In 1202b 9 ἅν is evidently a misprint for ὧν.

Are self-control and endurance the same thing? Surely not! For self-control has to do with pleasures and the man of self-control is he who masters pleasures, but endurance has to do with pains. For the man of endurance is he who endures and undergoes pains. Again, lack of self-control and softness are not the same thing. For the soft person with his softness is he who does not undergo pains—not all of them, but such as any one else would undergo, if he had to; whereas the man who lacks self-control is he who is not able to endure pleasures, but succumbs to them and lets himself be led by them.

Again, there is another character who is called 'intem-
1203a perate'. Is the intemperate, then, the same with the incontinent? Surely not! For the intemperate is the kind of man who thinks that what he does is best and most expedient for himself, and who has no reason opposing the things which appear pleasant to himself, whereas the incontinent does possess reason which opposes his going in pursuit of those things to which his appetite leads.

But which is the more curable, the intemperate or the incontinent? On first sight, indeed, it might seem that it is not the incontinent. The intemperate, it may be urged, is more easy to cure; for if reason could be engendered in him, to teach him that things are bad, he will leave off doing them; but the incontinent man has reason, and yet acts as he does, so that such a person would seem to be incurable. But on the other hand which is in the worse condition, he who has no good at all, ⟨or he who has some good⟩ joined with these evils? Plainly the former, the more so inasmuch as it is the more valuable part that is in a bad condition. The incontinent man, then, does possess a good in his reason being right, while the intemperate does not. Again, reason is the principle in each. Now in the incontinent the principle, which is the most valuable thing, is in a good condition, but in the intemperate in

29–33 = *E.N.* 1150a 33–36. 33–38 = *E.N.* 1150a 14. 39: cf. *E.N.* 1150a 19–21. 1203a 6–20 = *E.N.* 1146a 31–b 2, 1150a 19–22, 1150b 29–1151a 28.

a bad; so that the intemperate will be worse than the incontinent. Again, like the vice of brutality of which we spoke, you cannot see it in a beast, but only in a human being (for brutality is a name for excessive vice). Why so? Just because a beast has in it no bad principle. Now the principle is reason. For which would do more evil, a lion, or Dionysius or Phalaris or Clearchus, or some of those monsters of wickedness? Plainly the latter. For their having in them a principle which is at the same time a bad principle contributes greatly to their powers of mischief, but in the beast there is no principle at all. In the intemperate, then, there is a bad principle. For inasmuch as he does bad acts and reason assents to these, and it seems to him that he ought to do these things, there is in him a principle which is not a sound one. Wherefore the incontinent would seem to be better than the intemperate.

There are two species of incontinence, one in the way of precipitancy and want of forethought, a kind that comes on suddenly (for instance, when we see a beautiful woman, we are at once affected in some way, and from the affection there ensues an impulse to do something which perhaps we ought not), the other a sort of weakness, but attended with reason which warns against action. Now the former would not seem to be very blameworthy. For this kind occurs even in the good, in those who are of warm temperament and of a rich natural endowment; but the other in 1203b
the cold and atrabilious, and such are blameworthy. Again, one may avoid being affected by fortifying oneself beforehand with the thought, 'There will come a pretty woman, so one must repress oneself.' So that, if he has fortified himself beforehand with a thought of this kind, he whose incontinence is due to the suddenness of the impression will not be affected at all, nor do anything wrong. But he who knows indeed from reason that he ought not, but gives in to pleasure and succumbs to it, is more blameworthy. The good man would never become incontinent in that way, and fortification by reason would be no cure for it. For this is the guide within the man, and yet he

30–b 11 = *E. N.* 1150b 19–28.

does not obey it, but gives in to pleasure, and succumbs with a contemptible sort of weakness.

Whether the temperate man is self-controlled was raised as a difficulty above,[1] but now let us speak of it. Yes, the temperate man is also self-controlled. For the man of self-control is not merely he who, when he has appetites in him, represses these owing to reason, but also he who is of such a kind that, though he has not appetites in him, he would repress them, if they did arise. But it is he who has not bad desires and who has his reason right with respect to these things who is temperate, while the man of self-control is he who has bad desires and who has his reason right with regard to these things; so that self-control will go along with temperance, and the temperate ⟨will be self-controlled, but not the self-controlled temperate⟩. For the temperate is he who does not feel passion, while the self-controlled man is he who does feel passion, or is capable of feeling it, but subdues it. But neither of these is actually the case with the temperate. Wherefore the self-controlled is not temperate.

But is the intemperate incontinent or the incontinent intemperate? Or does neither follow on the other? For the incontinent is he whose reason fights with his passions, but the intemperate is not of this sort, but he who in doing base deeds has the consent of his reason. Neither then is the intemperate like the incontinent nor the incontinent like the intemperate. Further, the intemperate is worse than the incontinent. For what comes by nature is harder to cure than what results from habit (for the reason why habit is held to be so strong is that it turns things into nature). The intemperate, then, is in himself the kind of man who is bad by nature, owing to which, and as a result of which, the reason in him is bad. But not so the incontinent. It is not true of him that his reason is not good because he is himself such (for he must needs have been bad, if he
1204^a were of himself by nature such as the bad). The inconti-

12–23 = *E.N.* 1151^b 32–1152^a 3. 24–1204^a 4 = *E.N.* 1152^a 4–6.

[1] 1201^a 9–16.

nent, then, seems to be bad by habit, but the intemperate by nature. Therefore the intemperate is the harder to cure. For one habit is dislodged by another, but nothing will dislodge nature.

But seeing that the incontinent is the kind of man who knows and is not deceived in his reason, while the wise man also is of the same kind, who views everything by right reason, is it possible for the wise man to be incontinent? Surely not! For though one might raise the foregoing difficulties, yet if we keep consistent with our former statements, the wise man will not be incontinent. For we said that the wise man was not merely he in whom right reason exists, but he who also does what appears in accordance with right reason to be best. Now if the wise man does what is best, the wise man will not be incontinent; but an incontinent man may be clever. For we distinguished above [1] between the clever and the wise as being different. For though their spheres are the same, yet the one does what he ought and the other does not. It is possible, then, for the clever man to be incontinent (for he does not succeed in doing what he ought), but it is not possible for the wise man to be incontinent.

7 After this we must speak about pleasure, since our discussion is on the subject of happiness, and all think that happiness is pleasure and living pleasantly, or not without pleasure. Even those who feel disgust at pleasure, and do not think that pleasure ought to be reckoned among goods, at least add the absence of pain; now to live without pain borders on pleasure. Therefore we must speak about pleasure, not merely because other people think that we ought, but because it is actually indispensable for us to do so. For since our discussion is about happiness, and we have defined [2] and declare happiness to be an exercise of virtue in a perfect life, and virtue has to do with pleasure and pain, it is indispensable to speak about pleasure, since happiness is not apart from pleasure.

5–18 = *E.N.* 1152a 6–15. 19–22: cf. *E.N.* 1098b 25.
22–31 = *E.N.* 1152b 3–7.

[1] 1197b 18–28, cf. 36 sq.

[2] 1184b 22–1185a 13.

First, then, let us mention the reasons which some people give for thinking that one ought not to regard pleasure as part of good. First, they say that pleasure is a becoming, and that a becoming is something incomplete, but that the good never occupies the place of the incomplete. Secondly, that there are some bad pleasures, whereas the good is never to be found in badness. Again, that it is found in all, both in the bad man and in the good, and in beasts
1204b wild and tame; but the good is unmixed with the bad and not promiscuous. And that pleasure is not the best thing, whereas the good is the best thing. And that it is an impediment to right action, and what tends to impede right cannot be good.

First, then, we must address ourselves to the first argument,[1] that about becoming, and must endeavour to dispose of this on the ground of its not being true. For, to begin with, not every pleasure is a becoming. For the pleasure which results from thought is not a becoming, nor that which comes from hearing and ⟨seeing and⟩ smelling. For it is not the effect of want, as in the other cases; for instance, those of eating and drinking. For these are the result of defect and excess, owing to the fulfilment of a want or the relief of an excess; which is why they are held to be a becoming. Now defect and excess are pain. There is therefore pain wherever there is a becoming of pleasure. But in the case of seeing and hearing and smelling there is no previous pain. For no one in taking pleasure in seeing or smelling was affected with pain beforehand. Similarly in the case of thought. One may speculate on something with pleasure without having felt any pain beforehand. So that there may be a pleasure which is not a becoming. If then pleasure, as their argument maintained, is not a good for this reason, namely, that it is a becoming, but there is some pleasure which is not a becoming, this pleasure may be good.

33–35 = *E.N.* 1152b 12–14. 35–b 2 = *E.N.* 1152b 19–22. 3 = *E.N.* 1152b 16, 17. 4–20 = *E.N.* 1152b 33–1153a 7.

[1] a 32–35.

But generally no pleasure is a becoming. For even the vulgar pleasures of eating and drinking are not becomings, but there is a mistake on the part of those who say that these pleasures are becomings. For they think that pleasure is a becoming because it ensues on the application of the remedy; but it is not. For there being a part of the soul with which we feel pleasure, this part of the soul acts and moves simultaneously with the application of the things which we need, and its movement and action are pleasure. Owing, then, to that part of the soul acting simultaneously with the application, or owing to its activity, they think that pleasure is a becoming, from the application being visible, but the part of the soul invisible. It is like thinking that man is body, because this is perceptible by sense, while the soul is not: but the[1] soul also exists. So it is also in this case; for there is a part of the soul with which we feel pleasure, which acts along with the application. Therefore no pleasure is a becoming.

And it is, they say, a conscious restoration to a normal state. ⟨This, however, cannot be accepted either.⟩ For there is pleasure without such restoration to a normal state. For restoration means the filling up of what by nature is wanting, but it is possible, as we maintain,[2] to **1205a**
feel pleasure without any want. For the want is pain, and we say that there is pleasure without pain and prior to pain. So that pleasure will not be a restoration in respect of a want. For in such pleasures there is no want. So that if the reason for thinking that pleasure is not a good was because it is a becoming, and it is found that no pleasure is a becoming, pleasure may be a good.

But next it is maintained[3] that some pleasures are not good. One can get a comprehensive view of this point as follows. Since we maintain that good is mentioned in all the categories (in that of substance and relation and

21–1205a 6 = *E.N.* 1153a 7–17. 7–15 = *E.E.* 1217b 25–1218a 1.

[1] Retaining ἢ (MSS.).

[2] 1204b 6–20.

[3] A reference to this view may have originally existed at 1204a 35 or b 1.

quantity and time and generally in all), this much is plain at once. Every activity of good is attended with a certain pleasure, so that, since good is in all the categories, pleasure also will be good; so that since the goods and pleasure are in these, and the pleasure that comes from the goods is pleasure, every pleasure will be good.[1]

At the same time it is manifest from this that pleasures differ in kind. For the categories are different in which pleasure is. For it is not as in the sciences, for instance grammar or any other science whatever. For if Lampros possesses the science of grammar, he as a grammarian will be disposed by this knowledge of grammar in the same way as any one else who possesses the science; there will not be two different sciences of grammar, that in Lampros and that in Ileus. But in the case of pleasure it is not so. For the pleasure which comes from drunkenness and that which comes from the commerce of the sexes do not dispose in the same way. Therefore pleasures would seem to differ in kind.

But another reason why pleasure was held by them[2] not to be good was because some pleasures are bad. But this sort of objection and this kind of judgement is not peculiar to pleasure, but applies also to nature and knowledge. For there is such a thing as a bad nature, for example that of worms and beetles and of ignoble creatures generally, but it does not follow that nature is a bad thing. In the same way there are bad branches of knowledge, for instance the mechanical; nevertheless it does not follow that knowledge is a bad thing, but both knowledge and nature are good in kind. For just as one must not form one's views of the quality of a statuary from his failures and bad workmanship, but from his successes, so one must not judge of the quality of knowledge or nature or of anything else from the bad, but from the good.

26, 27: cf. *E.N.* 1152b 20–22, 1153a 17–20, 1153b 7–9.

---

[1] It is difficult to understand how this conclusion is reached, and its truth is expressly denied in 1205b 2.

[2] 1204a 35 sq.

In the same way pleasure is good in kind, though there are bad pleasures—of that we ourselves are as well aware as any one. For since the natures of creatures differ in the way of bad and good, for instance that of man is good, but that of a wolf or some other beast bad, and in like manner there is one nature of a horse, another of a man, an ass, or a dog, and since pleasure is a restoration of each to its own nature from that which runs counter to it, it follows that this will be appropriate, that the bad nature should have the bad pleasure. For the thing is not the same for a horse and a man, any more than for any of the rest. But since their natures are different, their pleasures also are different. For pleasure, as we saw,[1] is a restoration, and the restoration, they maintain, restores to nature, so that the restoration of the bad nature is bad, and that of the good, good.

But those who assert that pleasure is not a good thing are in much the same case as those who, not knowing nectar, think that the gods drink wine, and that there is nothing more delightful than this. But this is owing to their ignorance. In much the same case, I say, are all those who assert that all pleasures are becoming, and therefore not a good. For owing to their not knowing other than bodily pleasures, and seeing these to be becomings and not good, for this reason they think in general that pleasure is not a good.

Since, then, there are pleasures both of a nature undergoing restoration and also of one in its normal state, for instance of the former the satisfactions which follow upon want, but of a nature in its normal state the pleasures of sight, hearing, and so on, the activities of the nature in its normal state will be better—'activities' I say, for the pleasures of both kinds are activities. It is evident, then, that the pleasures of sight, hearing, and thought will be best, since the bodily result from a satisfaction.

Again, this was also said[2] by way of showing that it

1205^b 29, 30: cf. *E.N.* 1153^a 28.

---

[1] 1204^b 36 sqq., 1205^b 6 sq.

[2] 1204^a 36–^{b} 1.

is not a good, that what exists in all and is common to all is not good. Such an objection might seem to be appropriate in the case of a man who covets honour and is actuated by that feeling. For the man who is covetous of honour is one who wishes to be sole possessor of something and by some such means to surpass all others; so he thinks that, if pleasure is to be a good, it too must be something of this sort. Surely this is not so, but, on the contrary, it would seem to be a good for this reason, that all things aim at it. For it is the nature of all things to aim at the good, so that, if all things aim at pleasure, pleasure must be good in kind.

1206a Again, it was denied[1] that pleasure is a good on the ground that it is an impediment. But their asserting it to be an impediment seems to arise from a wrong view of the matter. For the pleasure that comes from the performance of the action is not an impediment; if, however, it be a different pleasure, it is an impediment; for instance, the pleasure of intoxication is an impediment to action; but on this principle one kind of knowledge will be a hindrance to another, for one cannot exercise both at once. But why is knowledge not good, if it produces the pleasure that comes from knowledge? And will that pleasure be an impediment? Surely not; but it will intensify the action. For the pleasure is an incentive to increased action, if it comes from the action itself. For suppose the good man to be doing his acts of virtue, and to be doing them pleasantly; will he not much more exert himself in the action? And if he acts with pleasure, he will be virtuous, but if he does the right with pain, he is not virtuous. For pain attends upon what is due to compulsion, so that if one is pained at doing right, he is acting under compulsion; and he who acts under compulsion is not virtuous.

But indeed it is not possible to perform virtuous acts without pain or pleasure. The middle state does not

33–35 = *E.N.* 1153b 25–28. 1206a 1–25: cf. *E.N.* 1153a 20–23.

[1] 1204b 2 sq.

exist. Why so? Because virtue implies feeling, and feeling pain or pleasure, and there is nothing intermediate. It is evident, then, that virtue is either attended with pain or with pleasure. Now if one does the right with pain he is not good. So that virtue will not be attended with pain. Therefore with pleasure. Not only, then, is pleasure not an impediment, but it is actually an incentive to action, and generally virtue cannot be without the pleasure that comes from it.

There was another argument,[1] to the effect that there is no science which produces pleasure. But this is not true either. For cooks and garland-makers and perfumers are engaged in the production of pleasure. But indeed the other sciences do not have pleasure as end, but the end is with pleasure and not without it;[2] there is, therefore, a science productive of pleasure.

Again, there was another argument,[3] that it is not the best thing. But in that way and by the like reasoning you will annul the particular virtues. For courage is not the best thing. Is it, therefore, not a good? Surely this is absurd! And the same with the rest. Neither, then, is pleasure not a good simply because it is not the best thing.

To pass on, a difficulty of the following kind might be raised in the case of the virtues. I mean, since the reason sometimes masters the passions (for we say so in the case of the man of self-control), and the passions again conversely master the reason (as happens in the case of the incontinent), since, then, the irrational part of the soul, being **1206b**
vicious, masters the reason, which is well-disposed (for the incontinent man is of this kind), the reason in like manner, being in a bad condition, will master the passions, which are well-disposed and have their proper virtue, and if this should be the case, the result will be a bad use of virtue (for the reason being in a bad condition and using virtue will use it badly); now such a result would appear paradoxical.

[1] This argument is suspected to have dropped out at 1204b 1. It is to be found in *E.N.* vii. 1152b 18, and the answer to it in 1153a 23–27.

[2] Susemihl would place these words after 'production of pleasure' in l. 30.

[3] 1204b 1.

This difficulty it is easy to answer and resolve from what has been said by us before[1] about virtue. For we assert that then, and only then, is there virtue, when reason being in a good condition is commensurate with the passions, these possessing their proper virtue, and the passions with the reason; for in such a condition they will accord with one another, so that reason should always ordain what is best, and the passions being well disposed find it easy to carry out what reason ordains. If, then, the reason be in a bad condition, and the passions not, there will not be virtue owing to the failure of reason (for virtue consists in both). So that it is not possible to make a bad use of virtue.

Speaking generally, it is not the case, as the rest of the world think, that reason is the principle and guide to virtue, but rather the feelings. For there must first be produced in us (as indeed is the case) an irrational impulse to the right, and then later on reason must put the question to the vote and decide it. One may see this from the case of children and those who live without reason. For in these, apart from reason, there spring up, first, impulses of the feelings towards right, and reason supervening later and giving its vote the same way is the cause of right action. But if they have received from reason the principle that leads to right, the feelings do not necessarily follow and consent thereto, but often oppose it. Wherefore a right disposition of the feelings seems to be the principle that leads to virtue rather than the reason.

8

Since our discussion is about happiness, it will be connected with the preceding to speak about good fortune For the majority think that the happy must be the fortunate life, or not apart from good fortune, and perhaps they are right in thinking so. For it is not possible to be happy without external goods, over which fortune is supreme. Therefore we must speak about good fortune, saying gene-

1206b 30–1207b 18 = 1246b 37–1248b 7.

[1] 1202a 8–18, cf. 1201a 16–35 and 1197b 36–1198a 9.

rally who the fortunate man is, and what are his surroundings and his sphere.

First, then, one may raise difficulties by having recourse to the following considerations. One would not say of fortune that it is nature. For what nature is the cause of, that she produces for the most part or without exception,[1] but this is never the case with fortune—her effects are dis- 1207a
orderly and as it may chance; this is why we speak of 'chance' in the case of such things.

Neither would one identify it with any mind or right reason. For here more than ever is there order and uniformity, but not chance. Wherefore, where there is most of mind and reason, there is least chance, and where there is most chance, there is there least mind.

Can it be, then, that good fortune is a sort of care of the gods? Surely it will not be thought to be this! For we suppose that, if God is the disposer of such things, he assigns both good and evil in accordance with desert, whereas chance and the things of chance do really occur as it may chance. But if we assign such a dispensation to God, we shall be making him a bad judge or else unjust. And this is not befitting to God.

And yet outside of these there is no other position which one can assign to fortune, so that it is plain that it must be one of these. Now mind and reason and knowledge seem to be a thing utterly foreign to it. And yet neither would the care and providence of God seem to be good fortune, owing to its being found also in the bad, though it is not likely that God would have a care of the bad.

Nature, then, only is left as being most connected with good fortune. And good fortune and fortune generally displays itself in things that are not in our own power, and of which we are not masters nor able to bring them about. For which reason no one calls the just man, in so far as he is just, fortunate, nor yet the brave man, nor any other virtuous character. For these things are in our power to have or not to have. But it is just in such things as follow that we shall speak more appropriately of good fortune. For we

[1] Transferring ἀεί (l. 38) to after ᾖ (l. 39) (Susemihl).

do call the well-born fortunate, and generally the man who possesses such kinds of goods, whereof he is not himself the arbiter.

But all the same even there good fortune would not seem to be used in its strict sense. But there are more meanings than one of the term 'fortunate'. For we call a man fortunate to whom it has befallen to achieve some good beyond his own calculation, and him who has made a gain when he ought reasonably to have incurred a loss. Good fortune, then, consists in some good accruing beyond expectation, and in escaping some evil that might reasonably have been expected. But good fortune would seem to consist to a greater extent and more properly in the obtaining of good. For the obtaining of good would seem to be in itself a piece of good fortune, while the escaping evil is a piece of good fortune indirectly.

Good fortune, then, is nature without reason. For the fortunate man is he who apart from reason has an impulse to good things and obtains these, and this comes from nature. For there is in the soul by nature something of this sort whereby we move, not under the guidance of reason, towards things for which we are well fitted. And
1207b if one were to ask a man in this state, 'Why does it please you to do so?'—he would say, 'I don't know, except that it does please me,' being in the same condition as those who are inspired by religious frenzy; for they also have an impulse to do something apart from reason.

We cannot call good fortune by a proper name of its own, but we often say that it is a cause, though cause is not a suitable name for it. For a cause and its effect are different, and what is called a cause contains no reference to an impulse which attains good, in the way either of avoiding evil or on the other hand of obtaining good, when not thinking to obtain it. Good fortune, then, in this sense is different from the former, and this seems to result from the way in which things fall out, and to be good fortune indirectly. So that, if this also is to be called good fortune, at all events the other sort has a more intimate connexion with happiness, namely, that wherein the principle of impulse towards the attainment of goods is in the man himself.

Since, then, happiness cannot exist apart from external goods, and these result from good fortune, as we said just now,[1] it follows that it will work along with happiness. So much then about good fortune.

9 But since we have spoken about each of the virtues in detail, it remains to sum up the particulars under one general statement. There is a phrase, then, which is not badly used of the perfectly good man, namely, 'nobility and goodness.' For 'he is noble and good', they say, when a man is perfectly virtuous. For it is in the case of virtue that they use the expression 'noble and good'; for instance, they say that the just man is noble and good, the brave man, the temperate, and generally in the case of the virtues. Since, then, we make a dual division, and say that some things are noble and others good, and that some goods are absolutely good and others not so, calling 'noble' such things as the virtues and the actions which spring from them, and 'good', office, wealth, glory, honour, and the like, the noble and good man is he to whom the things that are absolutely good are good, and the things that are absolutely noble are noble. For such a man is noble and good. But he to whom things absolutely good are not good is not noble and good, any more than he would be thought to be in health to whom the things that are absolutely healthy are not healthy. For if the accession of wealth and office were to hurt anybody, they would not be choiceworthy, but he will choose to have for himself such things as will not hurt him. But
he who is of such a nature as to shrink from having anything **1208a**
good would not seem to be noble and good. But he for whom the possession of all good things is good and who is not spoilt by them, as, for instance, by wealth and power, such a man is noble and good.

10 But about acting rightly in accordance with the virtues

19–1208a 4 = *E.E.* 1248b 8–1249a 16. 5–30: cf. *E.N.* 1138b 18–24: *E.E.* 1249b 3–9.

[1] 1206b 33 sqq.

something indeed has been said,[1] but not enough. For we said that it was acting in accordance with right reason. But possibly one might be ignorant as to this very point, and might ask, 'What is acting in accordance with right reason? And where is right reason?' To act, then, in accordance with right reason is when the irrational part of the soul does not prevent the rational from displaying its own activity. For then only will the action be in accordance with right reason. For seeing that in the soul we have a something worse and a something better, and the worse is always for the sake of the better, as in the case of body and soul the body is for the sake of the soul, and then only shall we say that we have our body in a good state, when its state is such as not to hinder, but actually to help and take part in inciting towards the soul accomplishing its own work (for the worse is for the sake of the better, to aid the better in its work); when, then, the passions do not hinder the mind from performing its own work, then you will have what is done in accordance with right reason.

Yes, but perhaps some one may say, 'In what state must the passions be so as not to act as a hindrance, and when are they in this state? For I do not know.' This sort of thing is not easy to put into words, any more than the doctor finds it so. But when he has given orders that barley-gruel shall be administered to a patient in a fever, and you say to him, 'But how am I to know when he has a fever?'—he replies, 'When you see him pale.' But how am I to know when he is pale?' There the doctor loses patience with you, 'Well, if you can't perceive that much yourself, it's no good talking to you any more.'[2] The same thing applies in like manner to all such subjects. And the case is the same with regard to recognizing the passions. For one must contribute something oneself towards the perception.

But perhaps one might raise the following sort of question

[1] 1198^{a} 10–21, cf. 1196^{b} 4–10.

[2] The text here is corrupt and defective, but the above seems to represent the required meaning.

also, 'If I really know these things, shall I then be happy?' For they think they must be; whereas it is not so. For none of the other sciences transmits to the learner the use and exercise, but only the faculty. So in this case also the knowing of these things does not transmit the use (for happiness is an activity, as we maintain[1]), but the faculty, nor does happiness consist in the knowledge of what produces it, but comes from the use of these means. Now the use and exercise of these it is not the business of this treatise to impart, any more than any other science imparts 1208^b
the use of anything, but only the faculty.

11 In addition to all that has gone before, it is necessary to speak about friendship, saying what it is, and what are its circumstances and sphere. For since we see that it is co-extensive with life and presents itself on every occasion, and that it is a good, we must embrace it also in our view of happiness.

First, then, perhaps it will be as well to go through the difficulties and questions that are raised about it. Does friendship exist among the like, as is thought and said? For 'Jackdaw sits by jackdaw', as the proverb has it, and

'Unto the like God ever brings the like'.[2]

There is a story also of a dog that used always to sleep upon the same tile, and how Empedocles, on being asked, 'Why does the dog sleep on the same tile?' said, 'Because the dog has something that is like the tile', implying that it was owing to the likeness that the dog resorted to it.

But again, on the other hand, some people think that friendship occurs rather among opposites. Take the saying—

'Earth loves the shower, what time the plain is dry'.[3]

1208^b 3–6 = *E.N.* 1153^a 3–15: *E.E.* 1234^b 18–22. 7–10 = *E.N.* 1155^a 32–35: *E.E.* 1235^a 4–9. 11–14 = *E.N.* 1155^b 7: *E.E.* 1235^a 10–12. 15–20 = *E.N.* 1155^a 35–^{b}6: *E.E.* 1235^a 13–18.

---

[1] Cf. 1184^b 31 sqq., 1204^a 27 sq.

[2] Hom. *Od.* xvii. 218.

[3] Athenaeus xii. 600^a gives the context of this line of Euripides—

ἐρᾷ μὲν ὄμβρου γαῖ᾽, ὅταν ξηρὸν πέδον
ἄκαρπον αὐχμῷ νοτίδος ἐνδεῶς ἔχῃ·
ἐρᾷ δ᾽ ὁ σεμνὸς οὐρανὸς πληρούμενος
ὄμβρου πεσεῖν ἐς γαῖαν Ἀφροδίτης ὕπο.

But it is not known from what play it comes.

It is the opposite, they say, that loves to be friends with the opposite; for among the like there is no room for friendship. For the like, they say, has no need of the like, and more to the same effect.

Again, is it hard or easy to become a friend? Flatterers, at all events, who quickly gain a footing of close attendance, are not friends, though they appear to be.

Further, such difficulties as the following are raised. Will the good man be a friend to the bad? Or will he not? For friendship implies fidelity and steadfastness, and the bad man is not at all of this character. And will one bad man be a friend to another? Or will this not be the case either?

First, then, we must determine what kind of friendship we are in search of. For there is, people think, a friendship towards God and towards things without life, but here they are wrong. For friendship, we maintain, exists only where there can be a return of affection, but friendship towards God does not admit of love being returned, nor at all of loving. For it would be strange if one were to say that he loved Zeus. Neither is it possible to have affection returned by lifeless objects, though there is a love for such things, for instance wine or something else of that sort. Therefore it is not love towards God of which we are in search, nor love towards things without life, but love towards things with life, that is, where there can be a return of affection.

If, then, one were to inquire next what is the lovable, it is none other than the good. Now there is a difference between the lovable and what is to be loved, as between the desirable and what is to be desired. For that is desirable which is absolutely good, but that is to be desired
1209a by each which is good for him; so also that which is absolutely good is lovable, but that is to be loved which is good for oneself, so that the lovable is also to be loved, but that which is to be loved is not necessarily lovable.[1]

20–22 = *E.E.* 1235b 5–9. 22–25 = *E.N.* 1155b 11, 12: *E.E.* 1235a 31–33. 26–35: cf. *E.N.* 1155b 28–31, 1158b 35.

[1] Here the translation follows Bekker's text, which seems to convey the right meaning.

Here, then, we see the source of the difficulty as to whether the good man is a friend to the bad man or not. For what is good for oneself is in a way attached to the good, and so is that which is to be loved to the lovable, and it depends as a consequence upon the good that it should be pleasant and that it should be useful. Now the friendship of the virtuous lies in their loving one another; and they love one another in so far as they are lovable; and they are lovable in so far as they are good. 'The good man, then,' it will be replied, 'will not be a friend to the bad.' Nay, but he will. For since the good had as its consequence the useful and the pleasant, in so far as, though bad, he is agreeable, so far he is a friend; again, on the other hand, being useful, then so far as he is useful, so far is he a friend. But this sort of friendship will not depend upon lovableness. For the good, we saw,[1] was lovable, but the bad man is not lovable. Rather such a friendship will depend on a man's being one who is to be loved. For springing from the perfect friendship which exists among the good there are also these forms of friendship, that which refers to the pleasant and that which refers to the useful. He, then, whose love is based on the pleasant does not love with the love which is based on the good, nor does he whose friendship is based upon the useful. And these forms of friendship, that of the good, the pleasant, and the useful, are not indeed the same, nor yet absolutely different from one another, but hang in a way from the same head. Just so we call a knife surgical, a man surgical, and knowledge surgical. These are not called so in the same way, but the knife is called surgical from being useful in surgery, and the man from his being able to produce health, and the knowledge from its being cause and principle. Similarly, the forms of friendship are not all called so in the same way, the friendship of the virtuous which is based on the good, the friendship depending on pleasure, and that depending on utility. Nor yet is it

1209a 7: cf. *E.N.* 1156a 7–14.

[1] 1 sq.

a mere case of equivocation, but, while they are not actually the same, they have still in a way the same sphere and the same origin. If, therefore, some one were to say, 'He whose love is prompted by pleasure is not a friend to so-and-so; for his friendship is not based on the good,' such an one is having recourse to the friendship of the virtuous, which is a compound of all these, of the good and the pleasant and the useful, so that it is true that he is not a friend in respect of that friendship, but only in respect of the friendship depending on the pleasant or the useful.

Will the good man then be a friend to the good, or will he not? For the like, it is urged, has no need of the like. An argument of this sort is on the look-out for the friend-
1209b ship based on utility; for if they are friends in so far as the one has need of the other, they are in the friendship which is based on utility. But the friendship which is based on utility has been distinguished from that which is based on virtue or on pleasure. It is likely, then, that the virtuous should be much more friends; for they have all the qualifications for friendship, the good and the pleasant and the useful. But the good may also be a friend to the bad; for it may be that he is a friend in so far as he is agreeable. And the bad also to the bad; for it may be that they are friends in so far as they have the same interest. For we see this as a matter of fact, that, when persons have the same interest, they are friends owing to that interest, so that there will be nothing to prevent the bad also having to some extent the same interest.

Now friendship among the serious, which is founded on virtue and the good, is naturally the surest, the most abiding, and the finest form. For virtue, to which the friendship is due, is unchangeable, so that it is natural that this form of friendship should be unchangeable, whereas interest is never the same. Wherefore the friendship which rests on interest is never secure, but changes along with the interest; and the same with the friendship which rests on pleasure. The friendship, then, of the best men is that which arises from virtue, but that of the common run of

37–b 10: cf. *E.E.* 1238a 30–b 14.   11–17: cf. *E.N.* 1156b 7–12.

men depends upon utility, while that which rests on pleasure is found among vulgar and commonplace persons.

When people find their friends bad, the result is complaint and expressions of surprise; but it is nothing extraordinary. For when friendship has taken its start from pleasure, and this is why they are friends, or from interest, so soon as these fail the friendship does not continue. Very often the friendship does remain, but a man treats his friend badly, owing to which there are complaints; but neither is this anything out of the way, For your friendship with this man was not from the first founded on virtue, so that it is not extraordinary that he should do nothing of what virtue requires. The complaints, then, are unreasonable. Having formed their friendship with a view to pleasure, they think they ought to have the kind which is due to virtue; but that is not possible. For the friendship of pleasure and interest does not depend on virtue. Having entered then into a partnership in pleasure, they expect virtue, but there they are wrong. For virtue does not follow upon pleasure and utility, but both these follow upon virtue. For it would be strange not to suppose that the serious are the most agreeable to one another. For even the bad, as Euripides says, are pleasant to one another. 'The bad man is fused into one with the bad.'[1] For virtue does not follow upon pleasure, whereas pleasure does follow upon virtue.

But is it necessary that there should be pleasure in the friendship of the serious? Or is it not? It would be strange indeed to say that it is not. For if you deprive 1210a
them of the quality of being agreeable to one another, they will procure other friends, who are agreeable, to live with, for in view of that there is nothing more important than being agreeable. It would be curious then not to think that the virtuous ought above all others to live in common

[1] Quoted in *E. E.* vii. 2, § 41, in the form κακὸς κακῷ . . . συντέτηκεν ἡδονῇ. Dindorf (*Eur. Frag.* 310) gives these three lines as a fragment from the Bellerophontes—

'Ανὴρ δὲ χρηστὸς χρηστὸν οὐ μισεῖ ποτέ,
κακῷ κακός τε συντέτηκεν ἡδοναῖς,
φιλεῖ δὲ θοὐμόφυλον ἀνθρώπους ἄγειν.

one with another; and this cannot be without the element of pleasure. It will be necessary, then, as it seems, for them above all to be agreeable.

But since friendships have been divided into three species, and in the case of these the question was raised[1] whether friendship takes place in equality or in inequality,[2] the answer is that it may depend on either. For that which implies likeness is the friendship of the serious, and perfect friendship; but that which implies unlikeness is the friendship of utility. For the poor man is a friend to the rich owing to his own lack of what the wealthy man has in abundance, and the bad man to the good for the same reason. For owing to his lack of virtue he is for this reason a friend to him from whom he thinks he will get it. Among the unequal then there arises friendship based on utility. So that Euripides says,

'Earth loves the shower, what time the plain is dry,'[3]

intimating that the friendship of utility has place between these as opposites. For if you like to set down fire and water as the extreme opposites, these are useful to one another. For fire, they say, if it has not moisture, perishes, as this provides it with a kind of nutriment, but that to such an extent as it can get the better of; for if you make the moisture too great, it will obtain the mastery, and will cause the fire to go out, but if you supply it in moderation, it will be of service to it. It is evident, then, that friendship based on utility occurs among things the most opposite.

All the forms of friendship, both those in equality and those in inequality, are reducible to the three in our division. But in all the forms of friendship there is a difference that arises between the partners when they are not on a level in love or in benefaction or in service, or whatever else of the kind it may be. For when one exerts himself energetically, and the other is in defect, there is complaint and

[1] 1208b 8–20.

[2] Used here, as the context shows, for ὁμοιότης and ἀνομοιότης. There is no reference here to the distinction between friendships ἐν ἰσότητι and καθ' ὑπεροχήν of *E.N.* 1162a 35. Cf. *E.E.* 1239a 4.

[3] See 1208b 16.

blame on the score of the defect. Not but that the defect on the part of the one is plain to see in the case of such persons as have the same end in view in their friendship; for instance, if both are friends to one another on the ground of utility or of pleasure or of virtue. If, then, you do me more good than I do you, I do not even dispute that you ought to be loved more by me; but in a friendship where we are not friends with the same object, there is more room for differences. For the defect on one side or the other is not manifest. For instance, if one is a friend for pleasure and the other for interest, that is where the dispute will arise. For he who is superior in utility does not think the pleasure a fair exchange for the utility, and he who is more agreeable does not think that he receives in the utility an adequate return for the pleasure which he bestows. Where- 1210b
fore differences are more likely to arise in such kinds of friendship.

When men are friends on an unequal footing, those who are superior in wealth or anything of that sort do not think that they themselves ought to love, but think that they ought to be loved by their inferiors. But it is better to love than to be loved. For to love is a pleasurable activity and a good, whereas from being loved there results no activity to the object of the love. Again, it is better to know than to be known; for to be known and to be loved attaches even to things without life, but to know and to love only to things with life. Again, to be inclined to benefit is better than not; now he who loves is inclined to benefit, just in so far as he loves, but this is not the case with him who is loved, in so far as he is loved.

But owing to ambition men wish rather to be loved than to love, because of there being a certain superiority in being loved. For he who is loved has always a superiority in agreeableness or means or virtue, and the ambitious man reaches out after superiority. And those who are in a position of superiority do not think that they themselves ought to love, since they make a return to those who love them, in those things in which they are superior. And

1210b 14–22: cf. *E.N.* 1159a 12–17: *E.E.* 1239a 21–27.

again the others are inferior to them, for which reason the superiors do not think they themselves ought to love but to be loved. But he who is deficient in wealth or pleasures or virtue admires him who has a superiority in these things, and loves him owing to his getting these things or thinking that he will get them.

Now such friendships arise from sympathy, that is, from wishing good to some one. But the friendship which takes place in these cases has not all the required attributes. For often we wish good to one person and like to live with another. But ought we to say that these things are friendships or that they are characteristics of the perfect friendship which is founded on virtue? For in that friendship all these things are contained; for there is none other with whom we should more wish to live (for pleasantness and usefulness and virtue are attributes of the good man), and it is to him that we should most wish good, and to live and to live well we should wish to none other than he.

Whether a man can have friendship for and towards himself may be omitted for the present, but we shall speak of it later.[1] But all the things that we wish for a friend we wish for ourselves. For we wish to live along with ourselves (though that is perhaps unavoidable), and to live well, and to live, and the wishing of the good applies to none so much. Further, we are most sympathetic with ourselves; for if we meet with a defeat or fall into any kind of misfortune, we are at once grieved. So looking at the matter in this way it would seem that there is friend-
1211a ship towards oneself. In speaking then of such things as sympathy and living well and so on we are referring either to friendship towards ourselves or to the perfect friendship. For all these things are found in both. For the living together and the wish for a thing's being and for its well-being and all the rest are found in these.

Further, it may perhaps be thought that wherever justice is possible, there friendship may exist too. Wherefore

32, 33 = *E.N.* 1166a 33, 34. 34–1211a 5 = *E.N.* 1166a 1–33.
6–15 = *E.N.* 1159b 25–32 = *E.E.* 1241b 11–17.

[1] Cf. 1211a 16 sqq.

there are as many species of friendship as there are of just dealing. Now there can be justice between a foreigner and a citizen, between a slave and his master, between one citizen and another, between son and father, between wife and husband, and generally every form of association has its separate form of friendship. But the firmest of friendships would seem to be that with a foreigner; for they have no common aim about which to dispute, as is the case with fellow-citizens; for when these dispute with one another for the priority, they do not remain friends.

It will be in place now to speak about this, whether there is friendship towards oneself or not. Since then we see, as we said just a little above,[1] that the act of loving is recognized from the particulars, and it is to ourselves that we should most wish the particulars (the good, and being, and well-being; and we are most sympathetic with ourselves, and we most wish to live along with ourselves); therefore, if friendship is known from the particulars, and we should wish the particulars to belong to ourselves, it is plain that there is friendship towards ourselves, just as we maintained that there is injustice towards oneself.[2] Though, indeed, as it takes one person to inflict and another to receive an injury, while each individual is the same person, it appeared[3] for that reason that there was no injustice towards oneself. It is possible, however, as we said[4] on examining into the parts of the soul, when these, as they are more than one, are not in agreement, that then there should be injustice towards oneself. In the same way then there would seem to be friendship towards oneself. For the friend being, according to the proverb—when we wish to describe a very great friend, we say 'my soul and his are one'; since then the parts of the soul are more than one, then only will the soul be one, when the reason and the passions are in accord with one another (for so it will be one): so that when it has become one there will be

16–^{b}3 = *E.N.* 1168^{b} 1–10.

[1] 1211^{a} 1–5.
[2] 1196^{a} 28.
[3] 1196^{a} 6–25.
[4] 1196^{a} 25–30.

friendship towards oneself. And this friendship towards oneself will exist in the virtuous man; for in him alone the parts of the soul are in proper relation to one another owing to their not being at variance, since the bad man is never a friend to himself, for he is always at strife with himself. At all events the incontinent man, when he has
1211b done something to which pleasure prompts, not long afterwards repents and reviles himself. It is the same with the bad man in other vices. For he is always fighting with and opposing himself.

There is also a friendship in equality; for instance, that of comrades is on an equality in respect of number and capacity of good (for neither of them deserves more than the other to have a greater share of goods either in number or capacity or size, but what is equal; for comrades are supposed to be a kind of equals). But that between father and son is on an inequality, and that between ruler and subject, between worse and better, between wife and husband, and generally in all cases where there is one who occupies the position of worse or better in friendship. This friendship in inequality, indeed, is proportional. For in giving of good no one would ever give an equal share to the better and the worse, but always a greater to the one who was superior. And this is the proportionally equal. For the worse with a less good is in a kind of way equal to the better with a greater.

Among all the above-mentioned forms of friendship love 12
is in a way strongest in that which is based on kindred, and more particularly in the relation of father to son. Now why is it that the father loves the son more than the son the father? Is it, as some say rightly enough as regards the many, because the father has been a kind of benefactor to the son, and the son owes him a return for the benefit? Now this cause would seem to hold good in the friendship which is based on utility. But as we see it to be in the sciences, so it is here also. What I mean is that in some the end and the activity are the same, and there is not any

18–39 = *E.N.* 1167^{b} 17–1168^{a} 27 = *E.E.* 1241^{a} 35–^{b}9.

other end beyond the activity; for instance, to the flute-player the activity and end are the same (for to play the flute is both his end and his activity); but not to the art of housebuilding (for it has a different end beyond the activity); now friendship is a sort of activity, and there is not any other end beyond the act of loving, but just this. Now the father is always in a way more active owing to the son being a kind of production of his own. And this we see to be so in the other cases also. For all feel a sort of kindness towards what they have themselves produced. The father, then, feels a sort of kindness towards the son as being his own production, led on by memory and by hope. This is why the father loves the son more than the son the father.

There are other things which are called and are thought to be forms of friendship, about which we must inquire **1212[a]** whether they are friendship. For instance, goodwill is thought to be friendship. Now, speaking absolutely, goodwill would seem not to be friendship (for towards many persons and on many occasions we entertain a feeling of goodwill either from seeing or hearing some good about them. Does it follow then that we are friends? Surely not! For if some one felt goodwill towards Darius, when he was alive among the Persians, as some one may have done, it did not follow that he had a friendship towards Darius); but goodwill would seem to be sometimes the beginning of friendship, and goodwill may become friendship if, where one has the power to do good, there be added the wish to do it for the sake of the person towards whom the goodwill is felt. But goodwill implies moral quality and is relative to it. For no one is said to have a goodwill towards wine or towards anything else without life that is good or pleasant, but if any one be of a good character, goodwill is felt towards him. And goodwill is not separate from friendship, but acts in the same sphere. This is why it is thought to be friendship.

Unanimity borders close on friendship, if the kind of

40–1212[a] 13 = *E.N.* 1155[b] 32–1156[a] 5, 1166[b] 30–1167[a] 21: cf. *E.E.* 1241[a] 1–14. 14–26 = *E.N.* 1167[a] 22–32 = *E.E.* 1241[a] 15–33.

unanimity that you take be that which is strictly so called. For if one entertains the same notions as Empedocles and has the same views about the elements as he, is he unanimous with Empedocles? Surely not! Since the same thing would have to hold in any like case. For to begin with, the sphere of unanimity is not matters of thought but matters of action, and herein it is not in so far as they think the same, but in so far as in addition to thinking the same they have a purpose to do the same about what they think. For if both think to rule, but each of them thinks that he is to be ruler, are they therefore unanimous? Surely not. But if I wish to be ruler myself, and he wishes me to be so, then it is that we are unanimous. Unanimity, then, is found in matters of action coupled with the wish for the same thing. It is therefore the establishment of the same ruler in matters of action that is the sphere of unanimity in the strict sense.

Since there is, as we maintain,[1] such a thing as friendship 13
towards oneself, will the good man be a lover of self or not? Now the lover of self is he who does everything for his own sake in matters of advantage. The bad man is a lover of self (for he does everything for his own sake), but not the good man. For the reason why he is a good man is because he does so and so for the sake of another; wherefore he is not actuated by self-love. But it is true that all feel an impulse towards things that are good, and think that they themselves ought to have these in the highest degree. This is most apparent in the case of wealth and rule. Now the good man will resign these to another, not on the ground that it does not become him in the highest degree to have them, but if he sees that another will be able to make more use of these than he; but the rest of the world will not do this owing to ignorance
1212b (for they do not think they might make a bad use of such goods) or else owing to the ambition of ruling. But the good man will not be affected in either of these ways.

28-b23 = *E.N.* 1167a28–1169b2.

[1] Cf. 1211a16–b3.

Wherefore he is not a lover of self as regards such goods at least; but, if at all, in respect of the noble. For this is the only thing in which he will not resign his share, but in respect of things useful and pleasant he will. In the choice, then, of things in accordance with the noble he will display love of self, but in the choice which we describe as being prompted by the useful and the pleasant it is not he who will do so, but the bad man.

14 Will the good man love himself most of all or not? In a way he will love himself most and in a way not. For since we say[1] that the good man will resign goods in the way of utility to his friend, he will be loving his friend more than himself. Yes: but his resignation of such goods implies that he is compassing the noble for himself in resigning these to his friend. In a way, therefore, he is loving his friend more than himself, and in a way he is loving himself most. In respect of the useful he is loving his friend, but in respect of the noble and good he is loving himself most; for he is compassing these for himself as being noblest. He is therefore a lover of good, not a lover of self. For, if he does love himself, it is only because he is good. But the bad man is a lover of self. For he has nothing in the way of nobility for which he should love himself, but apart from these grounds he will love himself *qua* self. Wherefore it is he who will be called a lover of self in the strict sense.

15 It will come next to speak about self-sufficingness and the self-sufficing man. Will the self-sufficing man require friendship too? Or will he not, but will he be sufficient to himself as regards that also? For even the poets have such sayings as these—

What need of friends, when Heaven bestows the good?[2]

Whence also the difficulty arises, whether he who has all the goods and is self-sufficing will need a friend too? Or

1212^b 24–33 = *E. N.* 1169^b 3–13 = *E. E.* 1244^b 1–7.

---

[1] ^{a} 36 sq.

[2] Eur. *Orest.* 667. Quoted also in *E. N.* 1169^b 7, 8.

is it then that he will need him most? For to whom will he do good? Or with whom will he live? For surely he will not live alone. If, then, he will need these things, and these are not possible without friendship, the self-sufficing man will need friendship too. Now the analogy that is generally derived from God in discussions is not right there, nor will it be useful here. For if God is self-sufficing and has need of none, it does not follow that we shall need no one. For we hear this kind of thing said about God. Seeing that God, so it is said, possesses all goods and is self-sufficing, what will he do? We can hardly suppose that he will sleep. It follows, we are told, that he will
1213a contemplate something; for this is the noblest and the most appropriate employment. What, then, will he contemplate? For if he is to contemplate anything else, it must be something better than himself that he will contemplate. But this is absurd, that there should be anything better than God. Therefore he will contemplate himself. But this also is absurd. For if a human being surveys himself, we censure him as stupid. It will be absurd therefore, it is said, for God to contemplate himself. As to what God is to contemplate, then, we may let that pass. But the self-sufficingness about which we are conducting our inquiry is not that of God but of man, the question being whether the self-sufficing man will require friendship or not. If, then, when one looked upon a friend one could see the nature and attributes of the friend, . . . such as to be a second self, at least if you make a very great friend, as the saying has it, 'Here is another Heracles, a dear other self.' Since then it is both a most difficult thing, as some of the sages have said, to attain a knowledge of oneself, and also a most pleasant (for to know oneself is pleasant)—now we are not able to see what we are from ourselves (and that we cannot do so is plain from the way in which we blame others without being aware that we do the same things ourselves; and this is the effect of favour or passion, and there are many of us who are blinded by these things so that we judge not aright); as then when we wish to see our own face, we do

so by looking into the mirror, in the same way when we wish to know ourselves we can obtain that knowledge by looking at our friend. For the friend is, as we assert,[1] a second self. If, then, it is pleasant to know oneself, and it is not possible to know this without having some one else for a friend, the self-sufficing man will require friendship in order to know himself.

Again, if it is a fine thing, as it is, to do good when one has the goods of fortune, to whom will he do good? And with whom will he live? For surely he will not spend his time alone; for to live with some one is pleasant and necessary. If, then, these things are fine and pleasant and necessary, and these things cannot be without friendship, 1213b
the self-sufficing man will need friendship too.

16 Should one acquire many friends or few? They ought neither to be absolutely many nor yet few. For if they are many, it is difficult to apportion one's love to each. For in all other things also the weakness of our nature incapacitates us from reaching far. For we do not see far with our eyes, but if you set the object unduly far off, the sight fails owing to the weakness of nature; and the case is the same with hearing and with all other things alike. Failing, then, to show love through incapacity one would, not unjustly, incur accusations, and would not be a friend, as one would be loving only in name; but this is not what friendship means. Again, if they are many, one can never be quit of grief. For if they are many, it is always likely that something unfortunate will occur to one at least of them, and when these things take place grief is unavoidable. Nor yet, on the other hand, should one have few, only one or two, but a number commensurate with one's circumstances and one's own impulse to love.

17 After this we must inquire how one ought to treat a friend. This inquiry does not present itself in every friendship, but in that in which friends are most liable to

1213b 3-16 = *E. N.* 1170b 20–1171a 20 = *E. E.* 1245b 20-25.

[1] Cf. 11–13.

bring complaints against one another. They do not do this so much in the other cases; for instance, in the friendship between father and son there is no complaint such as the claim that we hear made in some forms of friendship, 'As I to you, so you to me,' failing which there is in those cases grave complaint. But between unequal friends equality is not expected, and the relation between father and son is on a footing of inequality, as is also that between wife and husband, or between servant and master, and generally between the worse and the better. They will therefore not have complaints of this sort. But it is between equal friends and in a friendship of that sort that a complaint of this kind arises. So we must inquire how we ought to treat a friend in the friendship between friends who are on a footing of equality.

* * * * * *

INDEX

1181–1199 = 81–99
1200 = 0
1201–1213 = 1–13

INDEX

INDEX

INDEX

INDEX

INDEX

PROPER NAMES

ETHICA EUDEMIA

DE VIRTUTIBUS ET VITIIS

BY

J. SOLOMON, M.A.

BALLIOL COLLEGE

OXFORD UNIVERSITY PRESS

AR. ETH. E.

PREFACE

WITH the permission of Messrs. Teubner I have followed in this translation the text of Susemihl (Leipzig 1884), who here as elsewhere has brought much light by obvious corrections and judicious punctuation. Where readings other than his are adopted they are mentioned with the names of their authors.

In the foot-notes are cited corresponding passages from the *Nicomachean Ethics* and *Magna Moralia*. Here the work of Susemihl has been of the greatest assistance.

The *Eudemian Ethics* and the *De Virtutibus et Vitiis* have not received much attention from scholars. Mr. Ross's suggestions have been of the greatest use to me; Fritzsche's commentary I have sometimes referred to with advantage, and also to some notes printed by Prof. Henry Jackson and kindly sent me by him some years ago. Prof. Jackson is also the author of an article in the *Journal of Philology*, xxxii, which has shed a flood of light on the corrupt passage, Bk. VII, chs. 13, 14. Of course the principal help to the understanding of the two treatises is the *Nicomachean Ethics*, their resemblances to and differences from which work are of great interest.

J. SOLOMON.

CONTENTS

EUDEMIAN ETHICS

BOOK I

BOOK II

CHAPTER I.

CHAPTER 6.

§ 1. Every animal and plant is an origin in its power of begetting. 1222^b 15–18.

2. But man alone originates actions. 1222^b 18–20.

3. First causes of movement are the true causes. 1222^b 20–23.

4–7. In necessary matter there are, strictly speaking, none such. 1222^b 23–41.

8. If there are any things contingent, their causes must be contingent. 1222^b 41—1223^a 4.

9. This is the case with the acts which are in a man's own power. 1223^a 4–9.

10. Now virtue and vice are concerned with these acts. 1223^a 9–15.

∴ Virtue and vice are voluntary. 1223^a 15–20.

CHAPTER 7.

§§ 1, 2. What is the voluntary?

It would seem to depend on one of three things—

(1) impulse,

(2) purpose,

(3) thought. 1223^a 21–28.

3. Impulse may be divided into—

(1) wish,

(2) passion,

(3) appetite.

4, 5. Proof that everything in accordance with appetite is voluntary.

(1) What runs counter to appetite is painful.

The painful is compulsory.

The compulsory is involuntary.

∴ What runs counter to appetite is involuntary.

∴ Giving way to appetite is voluntary. 1223^a 29–36.

6. (2) Giving way to appetite is incontinence.

Incontinence is vice.

Vice is wrongdoing.

Wrongdoing is voluntary.

∴ Giving way to appetite is voluntary. 1223^a 36–^{b} 3.

7. Proof of the contrary.

(1) Giving way to appetite is incontinence.

Incontinence is doing what one thinks to be bad.

Doing what one thinks to be bad is against one's wish.

What is against one's wish is involuntary.

∴ Giving way to appetite is involuntary. 1223^b 3–10.

8. (2) Acting contrary to appetite is continence.

Continence is a virtue.

Virtue is right-doing.

Right-doing is voluntary.

BOOK VII

FRIENDSHIP.

§ 33. There is always a pleasure in the recognition of the familiar. 1237ª 23–27.

34. Hence like loves like, and nothing is so pleasant to man as man.

If this is true of the imperfect types, it will be so of the perfect.

∴ Good men find pleasure in each other.

∴ Friendship is the mutual choice of the good and pleasant for their own sakes. 1237ª 27–33.

35. Or rather friendship itself is the state from which such choice proceeds. But the actuality is love and lies in him who loves.

∴ The joy is in loving, not in being loved. 1237ª 33–37.

36. The latter may be the case even with things devoid of life. 1237ª 37–40.

37. The pleasure of friendship consists in loving the friend for what he is in himself. 1237ª 40–ᵇ 5.

38. But some unpleasant accident may make one prefer to do so at a distance. 1237ᵇ 5–7.

39. True friendship is alone stable. 1237ᵇ 8–12.

40. Stability requires trust, and trust experience, and experience time. 1237ᵇ 12–17.

40, 41. The wish for friendship may be sudden, but not friendship itself. 1237ᵇ 17–23.

42. A proof is that calumny may affect the minds of those who have not made trial of one another. 1237ᵇ 23–26.

43. True friendship cannot exist between the bad; for they are distrustful. 1237ᵇ 27–30.

44. And they prefer their material interests to a friend. 1237ᵇ 30–34.

45. Since true friendship requires experience, it cannot exist among many. 1237ᵇ 34–36.

46. Old friends must not be exchanged for new, unless we know the new to be better. 1237ᵇ 36—1238ª 3.

47. However good in himself a man may be, if he is to be your friend he must be good to you. 1238ª 3–8.

48. To have many friends interferes with the active exercise of friendship. 1238ª 8–10.

49. Everything, then, serves to show that true friendship is essentially stable. 1238ª 11–15.

50, 51. Adversity is a better test of it than prosperity. 1238ª 15–20.

51, 52. The truly pleasant is that which pleases in the long run. 1238ª 21–29.

53. The primary form of friendship, then, depends on virtue, but not the others. 1238ª 30–34.

Aristocracy or monarchy and the friendship between father and son on the latter. 1241^b 33–40.

CHAPTER 10.

§§ 1, 2. There are friendships of—
kinsmen,
comrades,
fellow-citizens.

That of kinsmen may be based on proportional or numerical equality.

That of fellow-citizens is chiefly for the sake of utility. 1241^b 40—1242^a 11.

3, 4. This form gives scope for justice in the fullest sense.

But justice finds no place in such a relation as that of art to instrument. 1242^a 11–18.

5. How to treat a friend is a question of justice. 1242^a 19–22.

5, 6. Man is not merely a social, but also a domestic animal. 1242^a 22–27.

6–9. The household contains in itself the types of all political relations—
master and slave,
husband and wife,
father and son,
brethren. 1242^a 27–^{b} 1.

10–12. In unequal friendships justice does not present itself in the same light to both parties. 1242^b 2–16.

12, 13. Equalisation is effected by the superior having the larger share of honour, the inferior of gain. 1242^b 16–21.

14, 15. Political friendship aims at utility, and is based on equality. 1242^b 22–31.

16, 17. The friendship of utility is of two kinds—
(1) legal,
(2) moral. 1242^b 31–37.

17. Complaints are most likely to arise in the latter. 1242^b 37—1243^a 2.

18. And generally in the friendship of utility rather than in that of virtue or pleasure. 1243^a 2–6.

19, 20. Though the legal form lends itself less to complaints than the moral. 1243^a 6–14.

21–23. Is a service to be estimated by its value in itself or to the receiver? 1243^a 14–31.

24–29. Political friendship looks at the thing, moral at the intention. 1243^a 31–^{b} 14.

30–32. Friendships in which different objects are aimed at are a fertile source of dispute. 1243^b 15–27.

33–35. Such cases must be settled by proportion. 1243^b 27–38.

CONTENTS

BOOK VIII

CONTENTS

ON VIRTUES AND VICES

CONTENTS

ETHICA EUDEMIA

BOOK I

1 THE man who stated his judgement in the god's precinct in Delos made an inscription on the propylaeum to the temple of Leto, in which he separated from one another the good, the beautiful, and the pleasant as not all properties of the same thing; he wrote, 'Most beautiful is what is most just, but best is health, and pleasantest the obtaining of what one desires.' But let us disagree with him; for happiness is at once the most beautiful and best of all things and also the pleasantest. **1214**^{a}

Now about each thing and kind there are many views that are disputed and need investigation; of these some concern knowledge only, some the acquisition of things and the performance of acts as well. About those which involve speculative philosophy only we must at a suitable opportunity say what is relevant to that study. But first we must consider in what the happy life consists and how it is to be acquired, whether all who receive the epithet 'happy' become so by nature (as we become tall, short, or of different complexions), or by teaching (happiness being a sort of science), or by some sort of discipline—for men acquire many qualities neither by nature nor by teaching but by habituation, bad qualities if they are habituated to the bad, good if to the good. Or do men become happy in none of these ways, but either—like those possessed by nymphs or deities—through a sort of divine influence, being as it were inspired, or through chance? For many declare happiness to be identical with good luck.

That men, then, possess happiness through all or some or one of these causes is evident; for practically all new creations

1214^{a} 1–8 = *E. N.* 1099^{a} 24–30. 14–25 = *E. N.* 1099^{b} 9–11.
24–25 = *E. N.* 1099^{b} 7 sq.

come under these principles—for all acts arising from intelligence may be included among acts that arise from knowledge. Now to be happy, to live blissfully and beautifully, must consist mainly in three things, which seem most desirable; for some say prudence[1] is the greatest good, some virtue, and some
1214b pleasure. Some also dispute about the magnitude of the contribution made by each of these elements to happiness, some declaring the contribution of one to be greater, some that of another,—these regarding prudence as a greater good than virtue, those the opposite, while others regard pleasure as a greater good than either: and some consider the happy life to be compounded of all or of two of these, while others hold it to consist in one of them alone.

First then about these things we must enjoin every one 2
that has the power to live according to his own choice to set up for himself some object for the beautiful life to aim at, (whether honour or reputation or wealth or culture), with reference to which he will then do all his acts, since not to have one's life organized in view of some end is a mark of much folly. Then above all we must first define to ourselves without hurry or carelessness in which of our belongings the happy life is lodged, and what are the indispensable conditions of its attainment—for health is not the same as the indispensable conditions of health; and so it is with many other things, e.g. the beautiful life and its indispensable conditions are not identical. Of such things some are not peculiar to health or even to life, but common—to speak broadly—to all dispositions and actions, e.g. without breathing or being awake or having the power of movement we could enjoy neither good nor evil; but some are indispensable conditions in a more special sense and peculiar to each kind of thing, and these it is specially important to observe; e.g. the eating of meat and walking after meals are more peculiarly the indispensable conditions of a good physical state than the more general conditions mentioned above. For herein is the cause of the disputes about happy living,

30–33 = *E. N.* 1098b 22–26.

[1] 'Prudence,' the traditional rendering of φρόνησις.

its nature and causes; for some take to be elements in happiness what are merely its indispensable conditions.

3 To examine then all the views held about happiness is superfluous, for children, sick people, and the insane all have views, but no sane person would dispute over them; for such persons need not argument but years in which they may change, or else medical or political correction—for medicine, no less than stripes, is a correction. Similarly we have not to consider the views of the multitude (for they 1215a
talk without consideration about almost everything, and most about happiness); for it is absurd to apply argument to those who need not argument but suffering. But since every study has its special problems, evidently there are such relating to the best life and best existence; the opinions then that put these difficulties it is well to examine, for a disputant's refutation of what is opposed to his argument is a demonstration of the argument itself.

Further, it is proper not to neglect these considerations, especially with a view to that at which all inquiry should be directed, viz. the causes that enable us to share in the good and beautiful life—if any one finds it invidious to call it the blessed life—and with a view to the hope we may have of attaining each good. For if the beautiful life consists in what is due to fortune or nature, it would be something that many cannot hope for, since its acquisition is not in their power, nor attainable by their care or activity; but if it depends on the individual and his personal acts being of a certain character, then the supreme good would be both more general and more divine, more general because more would be able to possess it, more divine because happiness would then be the prize offered to those who make themselves and their acts of a certain character.

4 Most of the doubts and difficulties raised will become clear, if we define well what we ought to think happiness to be, whether that it consists merely in having the soul of a certain character—as some of the sages and older writers

28–1215a 3 = *E. N.* 1095a 28–30. 12–19: cf. *E. N.* 1099b 13–20. 22–25: cf. *E. N.* 1098b 29–1099a 7.

thought—or whether the man must indeed be of a certain character, but it is even more necessary that his acts should be of a certain character.

Now if we make a division of the kinds of life, some do not even pretend to this sort of well-being, being only pursued for the sake of what is necessary, e. g. those concerned with vulgar arts, or with commercial or servile occupations—by vulgar I mean arts pursued only with a view to reputation, by servile those which are sedentary and wage-earning, by commercial those connected with buying in markets [1] and huckstering in shops. But there are also three goods directed to a happy employment of life, those which we have above [2] called the three greatest of human goods, virtue, prudence, and pleasure. We thus see that there are three lives which all those choose who have power, viz. the
1215b lives of 'the political man', the philosopher, the voluptuary; for of these the philosopher intends to occupy himself with prudence and contemplation of truth, the 'political man' with noble acts (i. e. those springing from virtue), the voluptuary with bodily pleasures. Therefore the latter calls a [3] different person happy, as was indeed said before.[4] Anaxagoras of Clazomenae being asked, 'Who was the happiest of men?' answered, 'None of those you suppose, but one who would appear a strange being to you,' because he saw that the questioner thought it impossible for one not great and beautiful or rich to deserve the epithet 'happy', while he himself perhaps thought that the man who lived painlessly and pure of injustice or else engaged in some divine contemplation was really, as far as a man may be, blessed.

About many other things it is difficult to judge well, but 5
most difficult about that on which judgement seems to all easiest and the knowledge of it in the power of any man—viz. what of all that is found in living is desirable, and what, if

26–1215b 14 = *E. N.* 1095b 14–1096a 10.

---

[1] ὠνὰς ἀγοραίας for ἀγοράς (Fr. and Pb).
[2] Cf. 1214a 30–3.
[3] Sus.'s ⟨ἕτερος⟩ not wanted.
[4] Cf. 1214a 30–b5.

attained, would satisfy our desire. For there are many consequences of life that make men fling away life, as disease, excessive pain, storms, so that it is clear that, if one were given the power of choice, not to be born at all would, as far at least as these reasons go, have been desirable. Further, the life we lead as children is not desirable,[1] for no one in his senses would consent to return again to this. Further, many incidents involving neither pleasure nor pain or involving pleasure but not of a noble kind are such that, as far as they are concerned, non-existence is preferable to life. And generally, if one were to bring together all that all men do and experience but not willingly because not for its own sake, and were to add to this an existence of infinite duration, one would none the more on account of these experiences choose existence rather than non-existence. But further, neither for the pleasure of eating alone or that of sex, if all the other pleasures were removed that knowing or seeing or any other sense provides men with, would a single man value existence, unless he were utterly servile, for it is clear that to the man making this choice there would be no difference between being born a brute and a man; at any rate the
ox in Egypt, which they reverence as Apis, in most of such 1216a
matters has more power than many monarchs. We may say the same of the pleasure of sleeping. For what is the difference between sleeping an unbroken sleep from one's first day to one's last, say for a thousand or any number of years, and living the life of a plant? Plants at any rate seem to possess this sort of existence, and similarly children; for children, too, continue having their nature from their first coming into being in their mother's womb, but sleep the entire time. It is clear then from these considerations that men, though they look, fail to see what is well-being, what is the good in life.

And so they tell us that Anaxagoras answered a man who was raising problems of this sort and asking why one should choose rather to be born than not—'for the sake of

34: cf. *E. N.* 1095b 19 sq.

[1] Omitting τίς and the note of interrogation.

viewing the heavens and the whole order of the universe'. He, then, thought the choice of life for the sake of some sort of knowledge to be precious; but those who felicitate Sardanapallus or Smindyrides the Sybarite or any other of those who live the voluptuary's life, these seem all to place happiness in the feeling of pleasure. But others would rather choose virtuous deeds than either any sort of wisdom or sensual pleasures; at any rate some choose these not only for the sake of reputation, but even when they are not going to win credit by them; but most 'political' men are not truly so called; they are not in truth 'political', for the 'political' man is one who chooses noble acts for their own sake, while most take up the 'political' life for the sake of money and greed.

From what has been said, then, it is clear that all connect happiness with one or other of three lives, the 'political', the philosophic, and the voluptuary's. Now among these the nature and quality and sources of the pleasure of the body and sensual enjoyment are clear, so that we have not to inquire what such pleasures are, but whether they tend to happiness or not and how they tend, and whether—supposing it right to attach to the noble life certain pleasures—it is right to attach these, or whether some other sort of participation in these is a necessity, but the pleasures through which men rightly think the happy man to live pleasantly and not merely painlessly are different.

But about these let us inquire later.[1] First let us consider about virtue and prudence, the nature of each, and whether they are parts of the good life either in themselves or through **1216^b** the actions that arise from them, since all—or at least all important thinkers—connect happiness with these.

Socrates, then, the elder,[2] thought the knowledge of virtue to be the end, and used to inquire what is justice, what bravery and each of the parts of virtue; and his conduct

15: cf. *E.N.* 1095^b 21 sq. 21–23: cf. *E.N.* 1095^b 22 sq. 28, 29: cf. *E.N.* 1095^b 14–1096^a 5. 3–25: cf. *M.M.* 1182^a 1–7, and 1183^b 8–18.

[1] No such discussion is to be found in the treatise, but cf. *E.N.* 1153^b 7–25.

[2] Distinguished from the younger Socrates, a pupil of Plato.

was reasonable, for he thought all the virtues to be kinds of knowledge, so that to know justice and to be just came simultaneously; for the moment that we have learned geometry or architecture we are architects and geometers. Therefore he inquired what virtue is, not how or from what it arises. This is correct with regard to theoretical knowledge, for there is no other part of astronomy or physics or geometry except knowing and contemplating the nature of the things which are the subjects of those sciences; though nothing prevents them from being in an incidental way useful to us for much that we cannot do without. But the end of the productive sciences is different from science and knowledge, e.g. health from medical science, law and order (or something of the sort) from political science. Now to know anything that is noble is itself noble; but regarding virtue, at least, not to know what it is, but to know out of what it arises is most precious. For we do not wish to know what bravery is but to be brave, nor what justice is but to be just, just as we wish to be in health rather than to know what being in health is, and to have our body in good condition rather than to know what good condition is.

6 About all these matters we must try to get conviction by argument, using perceived facts as evidence and illustration. It would be best that all men should clearly concur with what we are going to say, but if that is unattainable, then that all should in some way at least concur. And this if converted they will do, for every man has some contribution to make to the truth, and with this as a starting-point we must give some sort of proof about these matters. For by advancing from true but obscure judgements he will arrive at clear ones, exchanging ever the usual confused statement for more real knowledge. Now in every inquiry there is a difference between philosophic and unphilosophic argument; therefore we should not think even in political philosophy that the sort of consideration which not only makes the nature of the thing evident but also its cause is superfluous;

20–25 = *E. N.* 1103b 26–29 : cf. *M. M.* I. 1. 26 sq. = *E. N.* 1098b 8 sq. 35–1217a 17 : cf. *E. N.* 1094b 11–27, 1095a 30–b 13.

for such consideration is in every inquiry the truly philosophic method. But this needs much caution. For there
1217a are some who, through thinking it to be the mark of a philosopher to make no arbitrary statement but always to give a reason, often unawares give reasons foreign to the subject and idle—this they do sometimes from ignorance, sometimes because they are charlatans—by which reasons even men experienced and able to act are trapped by those who neither have nor are capable of having practical and constructive intelligence. And this happens to them from want of culture; for inability in regard to each matter to distinguish reasonings appropriate to the subject from those foreign to it is want of culture. And it is well to criticize separately the reason that gives the cause and the conclusion both because of what has just been said,[1] viz. that one should attend not merely to what is inferred by argument, but often attend more to perceived facts—whereas now when men are unable to see a flaw in the argument they are compelled to believe what has been said—and because often that which seems to have been shown by argument is true indeed, but not for the cause which the argument assigns; for one may prove truth by means of falsehood, as is clear from the Analytics.[2]

After these further preliminary remarks let us start on 7
our discourse from what we have called[3] the first confused judgements, and then[4] seek to discover a clear judgement about the nature of happiness. Now this is admitted to be the greatest and best of human goods—we say human, for there might perhaps be a happiness peculiar to some superior being, e.g. a god; for of the other animals, which are inferior in their nature to men, none have a right to the epithet 'happy'; for no horse, bird, or fish is happy, nor anything the name of which does not imply some share of a

21 sq. = *E.N.* 1095a 16–20. 22–24 = *E.N.* 1102a 13: cf. *M.M.* 1182b 2–5. 24–29 = *E.N.* 1099b 32–1100a 1.

---

[1] Cf. 1216b 26–35.
[2] Cf. *Anal. Pr.* ii. cc. 2–4; *An. Post.* i. 75a 3 and 88a 20.
[3] Cf. 1216b 32 sq.
[4] ἔπειτα for ἐπὶ τό.

divine element in its nature; but in virtue of some other sort of participation in good things some have a better existence, some a worse.

But we must see later that this is so.[1] At present we say that of goods some are within the range of human action, some not; and this we say because some things—and therefore also some good things—are incapable of change, yet these are perhaps as to their nature the best. Some things, again, are within the range of action, but only to beings superior to us. But since 'within the range of action' is an ambiguous phrase—for both that for the sake of which we act and the things we do for its sake have to do with practice and thus we put among things within the range of action both health and wealth and the acts done for the sake of these ends, i.e. wholesome conduct and money-bringing conduct—it is clear that we must regard happiness as the best of what is within the range of action for man.

8 We must then examine what is the best, and in how 1217b
many senses we use the word. The answer is principally contained in three views.[2] For men say that the good *per se* is the best of all things, the good *per se* being that whose property is to be the original good and the cause by its presence in other things of their being good; both of which attributes belong to the Idea of good (I mean by 'both' that of being the original good and also the cause of other things being good by its presence in them); for good is predicated of this Idea most truly (other things being good by participation in and likeness to this); and this is the original good, for the destruction of that which is participated in involves also the destruction of that which participates in the Idea, and is named from its participation in it.

33–35: cf. *E. N.* 1141a 34 sqq., 1178b 7 sqq. 39 sq.: cf. *E. N.* 1095a 13–20. 2–1218a 38 = *E. N.* 1096a 11–1097a 13: cf. *M. M.* 1182b 10–1183b 8, 1205a 8–11.

[1] No such discussion is to be found in the existing treatise.

[2] The three views seem to be those referred to in 1218b 7–11, that this good we are seeking is (1) the Idea of Good, (2) the common good, (3) the good as end.

But this is the relation of the first to the later, so that the Idea of good is the good *per se*; for this is also (they say) separable from what participates in it, like all other Ideas.

The discussion, however, of this view belongs necessarily to another inquiry and one for the most part more logical, for arguments that are at once destructive and general belong to no other science but logic. But if we must speak briefly about these matters, we say first that it is to speak abstractly and idly to assert that there is an Idea whether of good or of anything whatever—this has been considered in many ways both in our popular and in our philosophic discussions. Next, however much there are Ideas and in particular an Idea of good, they are perhaps useless with a view to a good life and to action. For the good has many senses, as numerous as those of being. For being, as we have divided it in other works, signifies now what a thing is, now quality, now quantity, now time, and again some of it consists in passivity, some in activity; and the good is found in each of these modes, in substance as mind and God, in quality as justice, in quantity as moderation, in time as opportunity, while as examples of it in change, we have that which teaches and that which is being taught. As then being is not one in all that we have just mentioned, so neither is good; nor is there one science either of being or of the good; not even things named good in the same category are the objects of a single science, e.g. opportunity or moderation; but one science studies one kind of opportunity or moderation, and another another: e.g. opportunity and moderation in regard to food are studied by medicine and gymnastics, in military matters by the art of strategy, and similarly with other sorts of action, so that it can hardly be the province of one science to study the good *per se*.

1218a Further, in things having a natural succession, an earlier and a later, there is no common element beyond, and, further, separable from, them, for then there would be something prior to the first; for the common and separable

16 sq. = *E. N.* 1096b 30–32. 23–25 = *E. N.* 1096b 32–1097a 13. 25–1218a 1 = *E. N.* 1096a 23–34 : cf. *M. M.* 1183a 7–23. 1–8 = *E. N.* 1096a 17–23.

element would be prior, because with its destruction the first would be destroyed as well; e.g. if the double is the first of the multiples, then the universal multiple cannot be separable, for it would be prior to the double, if the common element turns out to be the Idea, as it would be if one made the common element separable: for if justice is good, and so also is bravery, there is then, they say, a good *per se*, for which they add '*per se*' to the general definition; but what could this mean except that it is 'eternal' and 'separable'? But what is white for many days is no whiter than that which is white for a single day; † so not even the common good would be identical with 'the Idea', for it is the common property of all†.[1]

But we should show the nature of the good *per se* in the opposite way to that now used. For now from what is not agreed to possess the good they demonstrate the things admitted to be good, e.g. from numbers they demonstrate that justice and health are goods, for they are arrangements and numbers, and it is assumed that goodness is a property of numbers and units because unity is the good itself. But they ought, from what are admitted to be goods, e.g. health, strength, and temperance, to demonstrate that beauty is present even more in the changeless; for all these things in the sensible world are order and rest; but if so, then the changeless is still more beautiful, for it has these attributes still more. And it is a bold way to demonstrate that unity is the good *per se* to say that numbers have desire; for no one says distinctly how they desire, but the saying is altogether too unqualified. And how can one suppose that there is desire where there is no life? One should consider seriously about this and not assume without reasons what it is not easy to believe even with reasons. And to say that all existing things desire some one good is not true; for each seeks its own special good, the eye vision, the body health, and so on.

There are then these difficulties in the way of there being

8-15 = *E.N.* 1096^{a} 34-^{b} 5. 15-24: cf. *M.M.* 1183^{a} 24-28.

[1] Sus.'s additions are rejected.

a good *per se*; further, it would be useless to political philosophy, which, like all others, has its particular good, e. g. as gymnastic has good bodily condition.

[Further, there is the argument written in the discourse[1]—that the Idea itself of good is useful to no art or to all arts in the same way. Further, it is not practicable.] And similarly neither is good as a universal either the good *per*
1218^{b} *se* (for it might belong even to a small good) or practicable; for medicine does not consider how to procure an attribute that may be an attribute of *anything*, but how to procure health; and so each of the other arts. But 'good' is ambiguous, and there is in it a noble part,[2] and part is practicable but the rest not so. The sort of good that is practicable is an object aimed at, but not the good in things unchanging.

It is clear, then,[3] that neither the Idea of good nor the good as universal is the good *per se* that we are actually seeking; for the one is unchanging and not practical, and the other though changing is still not practical. But the object aimed at as end is best, and the cause of all that comes under it, and first of all goods. This then would be the good *per se*, the end of all human action. And this would be what comes under the master-art of all, which is politics, economics, and prudence;[4] for these mental habits differ from all others by their being of this nature; whether they differ from one another must be stated later.[5] And that the end is the cause of all that comes under it, the method of teaching shows; for the teacher first defines the end and thence shows of each of the other things that it is good; for the end aimed at is the cause. E. g. since to be

38–^{b} 6: cf. *E. N.* 1097^{a} 16 sqq., 1096^{b} 32–35. 10–14 = *E. N.* 1094^{a} 24–^{b} 10, 1097^{a} 16–24: cf. 1095^{a} 13–16, 1094^{a} 18–28.

---

[1] The discourse seems to be the discussion of the Idea of Good in 1217^{b} 16–1218^{a} 32; 1217^{b} 19–25 is especially referred to.

[2] i. e. τὸ ἐν τοῖς ἀκινήτοις ἀγαθόν, for which cf. 1217^{a} 30, 1218^{a} 22, ^{b} 7.

[3] Putting comma after ἕνεκα, l. 6, and inserting οὖν after φανερόν, l. 7 (Brandis).

[4] Cf. *Eth. Nic.* vi.

[5] No such discussion is to be found in the existing treatise, but cf. *E. N.* 1141^{b} 21–1142^{a} 11.

in health is so and so, so and so[1] must needs be what conduces to it; the wholesome is the efficient cause of health and yet[2] only of its actual existence; it is not the cause of health being good. Further, no one demonstrates that health is good (except he is a sophist and no doctor, but one who produces deceptive arguments from inappropriate considerations), any more than any other principle.

†We must now consider, making a fresh start, in how many senses the good as the end of man, the best in the field of action, is the best of all, since this is best.†

22–24: cf. *M. M.* 1182^b 22–27, 1183^a 35 sq.

---

[1] τοδί for τόδε (Spengel).

[2] καίτοι for καὶ τότε (W. D. R.).

BOOK II

AFTER this let us start from a new beginning and speak 1
about what follows from it. All goods are either outside or in the soul, and of these those in the soul are more desirable; this distinction we make even in our popular discussions. For prudence, virtue, and pleasure are in the soul, and some or all of these seem to all to be the end. But of the contents of the soul some are states or faculties, others activities and movements.

Let this then be assumed, and also that virtue is the best state or condition or faculty of all things that have a use and work. This is clear by induction; for in all cases we lay this down: e.g. a garment has an excellence, for it has a work and use, and the best state of the garment is its excellence. Similarly a vessel, house, or anything else has an excellence; therefore so also has the soul, for it has a work. And let us assume that the better state has the better work; and as the states are to one another, so let us assume the corresponding works to be to one another. And the work of anything is its end; it is clear, therefore, from this that the work is better than the state; for the end is best, as being end: for we assume the best, the final stage, to be the end for the sake of which all else exists. That the work, then, is better than the state or condition is plain.

But 'work' has two senses; for some things have a work beyond mere employment, as architecture has a house and not the act of building, medicine health and not the act of curing and restoring to health; while the work of other things is just their employment, e.g. of vision seeing and of mathematical science contemplation. Hence, necessarily,

32–36 = *E. N.* 1098b 12–15, *M. M.* 1184b 1–6. 35: cf. *E. N.* 1098b 31 sqq. 37: cf. *E. N.* 1106a 15 sqq. 5 sqq.: cf. *E. N.* 1097b 23 sqq. 13–17 = *E. N.* 1094a 3–6: cf. *M. M.* 1184b 9–17, 1197a 3–10.

in those whose work is their employment the employment is more valuable than the state.

Having made these distinctions, we say that the work of a thing is also the work of its excellence, only not in the same sense, e.g. a shoe is the work both of the art of cobbling and of the action of cobbling. If, then, the art of cobbling and the good cobbler have an excellence, their work is a good shoe: and similarly with everything else.

Further, let the work of the soul be to produce living, this[1] consisting in employment and being awake—for slumber is a sort of inactivity and rest. Therefore, since the work must be one and the same both for the soul and for its excellence, the work of the excellence of the soul would be a good life. This, then, is the complete good, which (as we saw)[2] was happiness. And it is clear from our assumptions (for these were[3] that happiness was the best of things, and ends and the best goods were in the soul; and † it is itself either a state or an activity †),[4] since the activity is better than the state, and the best activity than the best state, and virtue is the best state, that the activity of the virtue of the soul is the best thing. But happiness, we saw,[5] was the best of things; therefore happiness is the activity of a good soul. But since happiness was[6] something complete, and living is either complete or incomplete and so also virtue—one virtue being a whole, the other a part—and the activity of what is incomplete is itself incomplete, therefore happiness would be the activity of a complete life in accordance with complete virtue.

And that we have rightly stated its genus and definition
common opinions prove. For to do well and to live well is 1219b
held to be identical with being happy, but each of these—

18–23 = *E.N.* 1098a 7 sqq.: cf. *M.M.* 1184b 17–21. 23–35 = *E.N.* 1098a 5–17: cf. *M.M.* 1184b 22–1185a 9–13. 23–25 = *E.N.* 1095b 30–33, 1102b 7 sq. 25–27 = *E.N.* 1098a 5 sq., 1098b 29–1099a 3. 35–b 6 = *E.N.* 1098a 17–20, 1100a 1–5: cf. *M.M.* 1185a 1–6.

---

[1] τοῦτο for τοῦ (Cook Wilson).
[2] 1218b 7–12.
[3] Cf. 1218b 7–12, 32–6; 1217a 21 sq.; cf. 39 sq.
[4] Corrupt: or something omitted (Sus.).
[5] 1217a 21 sq., 39 sq.
[6] Cf. 1218b 7–12.

living and doing—is an employment, an activity; for the practical life is one of using or employing, e.g. the smith produces a bridle, the good horseman uses it.

We find confirmation also in the common opinion that we cannot ascribe happiness † to an existence of a single day,† or to a child, or to each of the ages of life; and therefore Solon's advice holds good, never to congratulate a man when living, but only when his life is ended. For nothing incomplete is happy, not being whole.

Further, praise is given to virtue because of its actions, but to actions something higher than praise, the encomium. And we crown the actual conquerors, not those who have the power to conquer but do not actually conquer. Further, our judging the character of a man by his acts is a confirmation. Further, why is happiness not praised? Surely because other things are praised owing to this, either by their having reference to it or by their being parts of it. Therefore felicitation, praise, and encomium differ; for encomium is discourse relative to the particular act, praise declares the general nature of the man, but felicitation is for the end. This clears up the difficulty sometimes raised—why for half their lives the good are no better than the bad, for all are alike when asleep; the cause is that sleep is an inactivity, not an activity of the soul. Therefore, even if there is some other part of the soul, e.g. the vegetative, its excellence is not a part of entire virtue, any more than the excellence of the body is; for in sleep the vegetative part is more active, while the perceptive and the appetitive are incomplete in sleep. But as far as they do to some extent partake of movement, even the visions of the good are better than those of the bad, except so far as they are caused by disease or bodily defect.

After this we must consider the soul. For virtue belongs to the soul and essentially so. But since we are looking

6–8 = *E. N.* 1100^a 10 sqq.: cf. *M. M.* 1185^a 6–9. 8, 9 = *E. N.* 1101^b 31–34: cf. *M. M.* 1183^b 20–35. 9 sq.: cf. *E. N.* 1099^a 3–5. 11–16 = *E. N.* 1101^b 21–34: cf. *M. M.* 1183^b 20–35. 16–25 = *E. N.* 1102^a 28–^{b} 12: cf. *M. M.* 1185^a 9–13. 26 sq. = *E. N.* 1102^a 13–22. 26–1220^a 12: cf. *M. M.* 1185^a 36–^{b} 12, *E. N.* 1102^a 23–1103^a 10. 27–31 = *E. N.* 1102^b 13–1103^a 3.

for human virtue, let it be assumed that the parts of the soul partaking of reason are two, but that they partake not in the same way, but the one by its natural tendency to command, the other by its natural tendency to obey and listen; if there is a part without reason in some other sense, let it be disregarded. It makes no difference whether the soul is divisible or indivisible, so long as it has different faculties, namely those mentioned above, just as in the curved we have unseparated the concave and the convex, or, again, the straight and the white, yet the straight is not white except incidentally and is not the same in essence.[1]

We also neglect any other part of the soul that there may be, e.g. the vegetative, for the above-mentioned parts are peculiar to the human soul; therefore the virtues of the nutritive part, that concerned with growth, are not those of man. For, if we speak of him *qua* man, he must have the power of reasoning, a governing principle,[2] moral action; but reason governs not reason, but desire and the passions; he must then have these parts. And just as general good **1220a**
condition of the body is compounded of the partial excellences, so also the excellence of the soul, *qua* end.

But of virtue or excellence there are two species, the moral and the intellectual. For we praise not only the just but also the intelligent and the wise. For we assumed[3] that what is praiseworthy is either the virtue or its act, and these are not activities, but have activities. But since the intellectual virtues involve reason, they belong to that rational part of the soul which governs the soul by its possession of reason, while the moral belong to the part which is irrational but by its nature obedient to the part possessing reason; for we do not describe the character of a man by saying that he is wise or clever, but by saying that he is gentle or bold.

After this we must first consider moral virtue, its nature,

32–36 = *E. N.* 1102a 28–32. 36–1220a 4 = *E. N.* 1102a 32–b 12. 5–12 = *E. N.* 1103a 3–10: cf. *M. M.* 1185b 5–12. 8–11: cf. *E. N.* 1102b 13 sq., 30 sq.

---

[1] οὐσίᾳ τὸ αὐτό (Bonitz). [2] Retaining καί.
[3] Cf. 1219b 8 sqq., 15 sq., 1218b 37 sqq.

its parts—for our inquiry has been forced back on this—and how it is produced. We must make our search as all do in other things—they search having something to start with; so here, by means of true but indistinct judgements, we must[1] try to attain to what is true and distinct. For we are now in the condition of one who describes health as the best condition of the body, or Coriscus as the darkest man in the market-place; for what either of these is we do not know, but yet for the attainment of knowledge of either[2] it is worth while to be in this condition. First, then, let it be laid down that the best state is produced by the best means, and that with regard to everything the best is done from the excellence of that thing (e.g. the exercises and food are best which produce a good condition of body, and from such a condition men best perform exercises). Further, that every condition is produced and destroyed by some sort of application of the same things, e.g. health from food, exercises, and weather.[3] This is clear from induction. Virtue too, then, is that sort of condition which is produced by the best movements in the soul, and from which are produced the soul's best works and feelings; and by the same things, if they happen in one way, it is produced, but if they happen in another, it is destroyed. The employment of virtue is relative to the same things by which it is increased and destroyed, and it puts us in the best attitude towards them. A proof that both virtue and vice are concerned with the pleasant and the painful is that punishment being cure and operating through opposites, as the cure does in everything else, acts through these.

That moral virtue, then, is concerned with the pleasant 2
and the painful is clear. But since the character, being as
1220b its name indicates something that grows by habit[4]—and
that which is under guidance other than innate[5] is trained to

26–34 = *E. N.* 1104a 11–b 3: cf. *M. M.* 1185b 13–32. *E. N.* 1105a 14–17. 34–39 = *E. N.* 1104b 4–1105a 13: cf. *M. M.* 1185b 33–37. 39–b 6 = *E. N.* 1103a 14–23: cf. *M. M.* 1185b 38–1186a 8.

[1] δεῖ (MSS.) for ἀεί (Sus.).
[2] *αὐτοῖν* for *αὐτῆς* (rc. Mb).
[3] Cf. *Hist. An.* 601a 23 sq. (Fr.).
[4] ἦθος from ἔθος.
[5] ἀγωγὴν (W.D.R.) *μὴ ἔμφυτον* (Fr.).

a habit by frequent movement of a particular kind—is the active principle present after this process, but in things inanimate we do not see this (for even if you throw a stone upwards ten thousand times, it will never go upward except by compulsion),—consider, then, character to be this, viz. a quality in accordance with governing reason belonging to the irrational part of the soul which is yet able to obey the reason. Now we have to state in respect of what part of the soul we have character of this or that kind.[1] It will be in respect of the faculties of passion, in virtue of which men are spoken of as subject to passion, and in respect of the habits, in virtue of which men are described, in reference to those passions, either as feeling them in some way or as not feeling them. After this comes the division made in previous discussions[2] into the passions, faculties, and habits. By passions I mean such as anger, fear, shame, sensual desire—in general, all that is usually followed of itself by sensuous pleasure or pain. Quality does not depend on these—they are merely experienced—but on the faculties. By faculty I mean that in virtue of which men who act from their passions are called after them, e.g. are called irascible, insensible, amorous, bashful, shameless. And habits are the causes through which these faculties belong to us either in a reasonable way or the opposite, e.g. bravery, temperance, cowardice, intemperance.

3 After these distinctions we must notice that in everything continuous and divisible there is excess, deficiency, and the mean, and these in relation to one another or in relation to us, e.g. in the gymnastic or medical arts, in those of building and navigation, and in any sort of action, alike scientific and non-scientific, skilled and unskilled. For motion is continuous, and action is motion. In all the mean in relation to us is the best; for this is as knowledge

7–20 = *E.N.* 1105^{b} 19–1106^{a} 12: cf. *M.M.* 1186^{a} 9–17. 21–35 = *E.N.* 1106^{a} 26–^{b} 35: cf. *M.M.* 1186^{a} 17–32.

---

[1] *ποι' ἄττα* (*ποῖ' ἄττα* MSS.) for *ποιότης τά*.

[2] *διειλεγμένοις* Rass. for *ἀπηλλαγμένοις*: perhaps the author refers to *E. N.* 1105^{b} 20.

and reason direct us. And this everywhere also makes the best habit. This is clear both by induction and by reasoning. For opposites destroy one another, and extremes are opposite both to one another and to the mean; for the mean is to either extreme the other extreme, e.g. the equal is greater to the less, but less to the greater. Therefore moral virtue must have to do with the mean and be a sort of mediety. We must then notice what sort of mediety virtue is and about what sort of means; let each be taken from the list by way of illustration, and studied:

irascibility	lack of feeling	gentleness
audacity	cowardice	bravery
1221a shamelessness	shyness	modesty
intemperance	insensibility	temperance
envy	(unnamed)	righteous indignation
gain	loss	the just
lavishness	meanness	liberality
boastfulness	self-depreciation	sincerity
habit of flattery	habit of dislike	friendliness
servility	stubbornness	dignity
luxuriousness	submission to evils	endurance
vanity	meanness of spirit	greatness of spirit
extravagance	pettiness	magnificence
cunning	simplicity	prudence

These and similar are the passions that occur in the soul; they receive their names, some from being excesses, some from being defects. For the irascible is one who is angry more than he ought to be, and more quickly, and with more people than he ought; the unfeeling is deficient in regard to persons, occasions, and manner. The man who fears neither what, nor when, nor as he ought is confident; the man who fears what he ought not, and on the wrong occasions, and in the wrong manner is cowardly. So 'intemperate' is the name for one prone to sensual desire and exceeding in all possible ways, while he who is deficient and does not feel desire even so far as is good for him and

36–1221b 9 = *E.N.* 1107a 26–1108b 10. 13–b 17: cf. *M.M.* 1186a 17–32.

in accordance with nature, but is as much without feeling as a stone, is insensible. The man who makes profit from any source is greedy of gain; the man who makes it from none, or perhaps few,[1] is a 'waster'. The braggart is one who pretends to more than he possesses, the self-depreciator is one who pretends to less. The man who is more ready than is proper to join in praise is a flatterer; the man who is less ready is prone to dislike. To act in everything so as to give another pleasure is servility, but to give pleasure seldom and reluctantly is stubbornness. Further, one who can endure no pain, even if it is good for him, is luxurious; one who can endure all pain alike has no name literally applicable to him, but by metaphor is called hard, patient, or ready of submission. The vain man is he who thinks himself worthy of more than he is, while the poor-spirited thinks himself worthy of less. Further, the lavish is he who exceeds, the mean is he who is deficient, in every sort of expenditure. Similar are the stingy and the purse-proud; the latter exceeds what is fitting, the former falls short of it. The rogue aims at gain in any way and from any source; the simple not even from the right source. A man is envious in feeling pain at the sight of prosperity more often than he ought, for even those who deserve prosperity cause when prosperous pain to the envious; the opposite character has not so definite a name: he is one who shows 1221b
excess in not grieving even at the prosperity of the undeserving, but accepts all, as gluttons accept all food, while his opposite is impatient through envy.

It is superfluous to add to the definition that the particular relations to each thing should not be accidental; for no art, theoretical or productive, uses such additions to its definitions in speech or action; the addition is merely directed against logical quibbles against the arts. Take the above, then, as simple definitions, which will be made more accurate when we speak of the opposite habits.

But of these states themselves there are species with

10–15 = *E. N.* 1126a 8–31.

[1] ⟨εἴ γε⟩ before ὀλιγαχόθεν (Bussemaker).

names differing according as the excess is in time, in degree, or in the object provoking the state: e.g. one is quick-tempered through feeling anger quicker than one ought, irascible and passionate through feeling it more, acrid through one's tendency to retain one's anger, violent and abusive through the punishments one inflicts from anger. Epicures, gluttons, drunkards are so named from having a tendency contrary to reason to indulgence in one or the other kind of nutriment.[1]

Nor must we forget that some of the faults mentioned cannot be taken to depend on the manner of action, if manner means excess of passion: e.g. the adulterer is not so called from his excessive intercourse with married women; 'excess' is inapplicable here, but the act is simply in itself wicked; the passion and its character are expressed in the same word. Similarly with outrage. Hence men dispute the liability of their actions to be called by these names; they say that they had intercourse but did not commit adultery (for they acted ignorantly or by compulsion), or that they gave a blow but committed no outrage; and so they defend themselves against all other similar charges.

Having got so far, we must next say that, since there 4
are two parts of the soul, the virtues are divided correspondingly, those of the rational part being the intellectual, whose function is truth, whether about a thing's nature or genesis, while the others belong to the part irrational but appetitive—for not any and every part of the soul, supposing it to be divisible, is appetitive. Necessarily, then, the character must be bad or good by its pursuit or avoidance of certain pleasures and pains. This is clear from our classification[2] of the passions, powers, and states; for the powers and states are powers and states of the passions, and the passions are distinguished by pain and pleasure. So that for these reasons and also because of our previous

15–17: cf. *E.N.* 1118b 16–21. 18–26 = *E.N.* 1107a 8–27: cf. *M.M.* 1186a 36–b 3. 27–1222a 2: cf. *M.M.* 1186a 32–35. 32–1222a 5 = *E.N.* 1104b 3–1105a 13.

[1] i.e. food or drink.

[2] Cf. 1220b 7–20.

propositions[1] it follows that all moral virtue has to do with pleasures and pains. For by whatever things a soul tends to become better or worse, it is with regard to and in relation to these things that it finds pleasure. But we say men are bad through pleasures and pains, either by the pursuit 1222a
and avoidance of improper pleasures or pains or by their pursuit in an improper way. Therefore all readily define the virtues as insensibility or immobility as regards pleasures and pains, and vices as constituted by the opposites of these.

5 But since we have assumed[2] that virtue is that sort of habit from which men have a tendency to do the best actions, and through which they are in the best disposition towards what is best; and best is what is in accordance with right reason, and this is the mean between excess and defect relative to us; it would follow that moral virtue is a mean relative to each individual himself, and is concerned with certain means in pleasures and pains, in the pleasant and the painful. The mean will sometimes be in pleasures (for there too is excess and defect), sometimes in pains, sometimes in both. For he who is excessive in his feeling of delight exceeds in the pleasant, but he who exceeds in his feeling of pain, in the painful—and this either absolutely or with reference to some standard, e. g. when he differs from the majority of men; but the good man feels as he ought. But since there is a habit in consequence of which its possessor will in some cases admit the excess, in others the defect of the same thing, it follows that as these acts are opposed to one another and to the mean, so the habits will also be opposed to one another and to virtue.

It happens, however, that sometimes all these oppositions will be clearer, sometimes those on the side of excess, sometimes those on the side of defect. And the reason of the difference is that †the unlikeness or likeness to the mean is not always of the same kind†, but in one case one might change quicker from the excess to the middle habit, some-

2–5 = *E. N.* 1104b 24–28. 6–8 = *E. N.* 1104b 27 sq. 17–1222b 14 = *E. N.* 1108b 11–1109a 19: cf. *M. M.* 1186b 4–32.

---

[1] Cf. 1220a 26–37, b34, 35.

[2] Cf. 1218b 37 sqq.

times from the defect, and the person further distant seems more opposed; e. g. in regard to the body excess in exercise is healthier than defect, and nearer to the mean, but in food defect is healthier than excess. And so of those states of will which tend to training now some, now others, will show a greater tendency to health in case of the two acts of choice[1]—now those good at work, now those good at abstemiousness[2]; and he who is opposed to the moderate and the reasonable will be the man who avoids exercise, not both; and in the case of food the self-indulgent man, not the man who starves himself. And the reason is that from the start our nature does not diverge in the same way from the mean as regards all things; we are less inclined to exercise, and more inclined to indulgence. So it is too with regard to the soul. We regard, then, as the habit opposed to the mean, that towards which both our faults and men in general are more inclined—the other extreme, as though not existent, escapes our notice, being unperceived because of its rarity. Thus we oppose anger to gentleness, and the irascible to
1222b the gentle. Yet there is also excess in the direction of gentleness and readiness to be reconciled, and the repression of anger when one is struck. But the men prone to this are few, and all incline more to the opposite extreme; there is none of the spirit of reconciliation[3] in anger.

And since we have reached a list of the habits in regard to the several passions, with their excesses and defects, and the opposite habits in virtue of which men are as right reason directs them to be—(what right reason is, and with an eye to what standard we are to fix the mean, must be considered later[4])—it is clear that all the moral virtues and vices have to do with excesses and defects of pleasures and pains, and that pleasures and pains arise from the above-mentioned habits and passions. But the best habit is that which is the mean in respect of each class of things. It is clear then that all, or at least some, of the virtues will be connected with means.

[1] i. e. choice of amount of exercise, of amount of food.

[2] Keep *οἱ* and adjs. in masc., not fem. as Bz., Sus.

[3] καταλλακτικόν (Fr.).

[4] 1249a 21–b 23: cf. *E. N.* 1138b 15–34.

6 Let us, then, take another starting-point for the succeeding inquiry. Every substance is by nature a sort of principle; therefore each can produce many similar to itself, as man man, animals[1] in general animals, and plants plants. But in addition to this *man* alone of animals is also the source of certain actions; for no other animal would be said to act. Such principles, which are primary sources of movements, are called principles in the strict sense, and most properly such as have necessary results; God is doubtless a principle of this kind. The strict sense of 'principle' is not to be found among principles without movement, e. g. those of mathematics, though by analogy we use the name there also. For there, too, if the principle should change, practically all that is proved from it would alter; but its consequences do not change themselves, one being destroyed by another, except by destroying the assumption and, by its refutation, proving the truth.[2] But man is the source of a kind of movement, for action is movement. But since, as elsewhere, the source or principle is the cause of all that exists or arises through it, we must take the same view as in demonstrations. For if, supposing the triangle to have its angles equal to two right angles, the quadrilateral must have them equal to four right angles, it is clear that the property of the triangle is the cause of this last. And if the triangle should change, then so must the quadrilateral, having six right angles if the triangle has three, and eight if it has four: but if the former does not change but remains as it was before, so must the quadrilateral.

The necessity of what we are endeavouring to show is clear from the Analytics[3]; at present we can neither affirm nor deny anything with precision except just this.

Supposing there were no further cause for the triangle's

15–1123a 20 = *E. N.* 1113b 3–1115a 13: cf. *M. M.* 1187a 5–b 30. 15–20 = *E. N.* 1113b 16–18. 20: cf. *E. N.* 1099b 32–1100a 1, 1111a 25 sq.

[1] Omit ὂν (Sus.).

[2] e. g. if ἀρχή A led to B and C, of which C was absurd, then C by refuting A would refute the other consequence B.

[3] Cf. *Anal. Post.* i. 4.

having the above property, then the triangle would be a sort of principle or cause of all that comes later. So that if anything existent may have the opposite to its actual
1223^a qualities, so of necessity may its principles. For what results from the necessary is necessary; but the results of the contingent might be the opposite of what they are; what depends on men themselves forms a great portion of contingent matters, and men themselves are the sources of such contingent results. So that it is clear that all the acts of which man is the principle and controller may either happen or not happen, and that their happening or not happening—those at least of whose existence or non-existence he has the control—depends on him. But of what it depends on him to do or not to do, he is himself the cause; and what he is the cause of depends on him. And since virtue and vice and the acts that spring from them are respectively praised or blamed—for we do not praise or blame for what is due to necessity, or chance, or nature, but only for what we ourselves are causes of; for what another is the cause of, for that he bears the blame or praise—it is clear that virtue and vice have to do with matters where the man himself is the cause and source of his acts. We must then ascertain of what actions he is himself the source and cause. Now, we all admit that of acts that are voluntary and done from the deliberate choice of each man he is the cause, but of involuntary acts he is not himself the cause; and all that he does from deliberate choice he clearly does voluntarily. It is clear then that virtue and vice have to do with voluntary acts.

We must then ascertain what is the voluntary and the 7
involuntary, and what is deliberate choice, since by these virtue and vice are defined. First we must consider the voluntary and involuntary. Of three things it would seem to be one, agreement with either desire, or choice, or thought—that is, the voluntary would agree, the involuntary

4–9 = *E. N.* 1113^b 13–21. 9–13 = *E. N.* 1109^b 30–34. 21–^{b} 17 = *E. N.* 1109^b 30–1111^b 3. 21–^{b} 36: cf. *M. M.* 1187^b 31–1188^a 37.

would be contrary to one of these. But again, desire is divided into three sorts, wish, anger, and sensual appetite. We have, then, to distinguish these, and first to consider the case of agreement with sensual appetite.

Now all that is in agreement with sensual appetite would seem to be voluntary; for all the involuntary seems to be forced, and what is forced is painful, and so is all that men do and suffer from compulsion—as Evenus says,[1] 'all to which we are compelled is unpleasant.' So that if an act is painful it is forced on us, and if forced it is painful. But all that is contrary to sensual appetite is painful—for such appetite is for the pleasant—and therefore forced and involuntary; what then agrees with sensual appetite is voluntary; for these two are opposites. Further, all wickedness makes one more unjust, and incontinence seems to be wickedness, the incontinent being the sort of man that acts in accordance with his appetite and contrary to his reason, and shows his incontinence when he acts in accordance with his appetite; but to act unjustly is **1223b**
voluntary, so that the incontinent will act unjustly by acting according to his appetite; he will then act voluntarily, and what is done according to appetite is voluntary. †Indeed, it would be absurd that those who become incontinent should be more just.†[2]

From these considerations, then, the act done from appetite would seem voluntary, but from the following the opposite: what a man does voluntarily he wishes, and what he wishes to do he does voluntarily. But no one wishes what he thinks to be bad; but surely the man who acts incontinently does not do what he wishes, for to act incontinently is to act through appetite contrary to what the man thinks best; whence it results that the same man acts at the same time both voluntarily and involuntarily; but this is impossible. Further, the continent will do a just act, †and more so than incontinence†; for continence is a virtue, and virtue makes men more just. Now one acts continently whenever he acts against his appetite in accord-

[1] Fr. 8 Hiller.
[2] This should perhaps be transferred to a 36 or b 12 (Spengel).

ance with his reason. So that if to act justly is voluntary as to act unjustly is—for both these seem to be voluntary, and if the one is, so must the other be—but action contrary to appetite is involuntary, then the same man will at the same time do the same thing voluntarily and involuntarily.

The same argument may be applied to anger; for there is thought to be a continence and incontinence of anger just as there is of appetite; and what is contrary to our anger is painful, and the repression is forced, so that if the forced is involuntary, all acts done out of anger would be voluntary. Heraclitus, too, seems to be regarding the strength of anger when he says that the restraint of it is painful—'It is hard,' he says, 'to fight with anger; for it gives its life for what it desires.' But if it is impossible for a man voluntarily and involuntarily to do the same thing[1] at the same time, and in regard to[2] the same part of the act, then what is done from wish is more voluntary than that which is done from appetite or anger; and a proof of this is that we do many things voluntarily without anger or desire.

It remains then to consider whether to act from wish and to act voluntarily are identical. But this too seems impossible. For we assumed and all admit that wickedness makes men more unjust, and incontinence seems a kind of wickedness. But the opposite will result from the hypothesis above; for no one wishes what he thinks bad, but does it when he becomes[3] incontinent. If, then, to commit injustice is voluntary, and the voluntary is what agrees with wish, then when a man becomes incontinent he will be no longer committing injustice, but will be more just than before he became incontinent. But this is impossible.[4] That the voluntary then is not action in accordance with desire, nor the involuntary action in opposition to it, is clear.

But again, that action in accordance with, or in opposition 8
to, choice is not the true description of the voluntary and

18 sqq. = *E. N.* 1111a 24 sq.: cf. *M. M.* 1188a 23 sq. 22–24 = *E. N.* 1105a 7 sq. 37–1225a 1: cf. *M. M.* 1188a 38–b 14.

[1] Reading τὸ αὐτό (Pb Bekker).
[2] ἅμα καὶ κατά (Bz.).
[3] Reading γένηται, l. 33.
[4] Cf. 1223b 2.

involuntary is clear from the following considerations: it has been shown[1] that the act in agreement with wish was not involuntary, but rather that all that one wishes is 1224a voluntary, though it has also been shown[2] that one may do voluntarily what one does not wish. But we do many things from wish suddenly, but no one deliberately chooses an act suddenly.

But if, as we saw,[3] the voluntary must be one of these three—action according either to desire, choice, or thought, and it is not two of these, the remaining alternative is that the voluntary consists in action with some kind of thought. Advancing a little further, let us close our delimitation of the voluntary and the involuntary. To act on compulsion or not on compulsion seems connected with these terms; for we say that the enforced is involuntary, and all the involuntary is enforced: so that first we must consider the action done on compulsion, its nature and its relation to the voluntary and the involuntary. Now the enforced and the necessary, force and necessity, seem opposed to the voluntary and to persuasion in the case of acts done. Generally, we speak of enforced action and necessity even in the case of inanimate things; for we say that a stone moves upwards and fire downwards on compulsion and by force; but when they move according to their natural internal tendency, we do not call the act one due to force; nor do we call it voluntary either; there is no name for this antithesis; but when they move contrary to this tendency, then we say they move by force. So, too, among things living and among animals we often see things suffering and acting from force, when something from without moves them contrary to their own internal tendency. Now in the inanimate the moving principle is simple, but in the animated there is more than one principle; for desire and reason do not always agree. And so with the other animals the action on compulsion is simple (just as in the inanimate), for they have not desire and reason opposing one another, but live by desire; but man has both, that is

[1] Cf. 1223b 2 sq. and 24-27.

[2] Omit μόνον (J. S.): cf. 1223b 30-36 and 7-9.

[3] Cf. 1223a 23-26.

at a certain age, to which we attribute also the power of action; for we do not use this term of the child, nor of the brute, but only of the man who has come to act from reason.

So the compulsory act seems always painful, and no one acts from force and yet with pleasure. Hence there arises much dispute about the continent and incontinent, for each of them acts with two tendencies mutually opposed, so that (as the expression goes) the continent forcibly drags himself from the pleasant appetites (for he feels pain in dragging himself away against the resistance of desire), while the incontinent forcibly drags himself contrary to his reason. But still the latter seems less to be in pain; for appetite is for the pleasant, and this he follows with delight; so that the incontinent rather acts voluntarily and not from force, because he acts without pain. But persuasion is opposed
1224b to force and necessity, and the continent goes[1] towards what he is persuaded of, and so proceeds not from force but voluntarily. But appetite leads without persuading, being devoid of reason. We have, then, shown[2] that these alone seem to act from force and involuntarily, and why they seem to, viz. from a certain likeness to the enforced action, in virtue of which we attribute enforced action also to the inanimate. Yet if we add[3] the addition made in our definition, there also the statement becomes untrue. For it is only when something *external* moves a thing, or brings it to rest against its own internal tendency, that we say this happens by force; otherwise we do not say that it happens by force. But in the continent and the incontinent it is the present *internal* tendency that leads them, for they have both tendencies. So that neither acts on compulsion nor by force, but, as far at least as the above goes, voluntarily. For the external moving principle, that hinders or moves in opposition to the internal tendency, is what we call necessity, e.g. when we strike some one with the hand of one whose wish and appetite alike resist; but when the principle is from within, there is no force. Further, there

[1] ἄγεται should perhaps be read. [2] Cf. a 22 sq.
[3] Reading προσθείη (Spengel).

is both pleasure and pain in both; for the continent feels pain now in acting against his appetite, but has the pleasure of hope, i. e. that he will be presently benefited, or even the pleasure of being actually at present benefited because he is in health; while the incontinent is pleased at getting through his incontinency what he desires, but has a pain of expectation, thinking that he is doing ill. So that to say that both act from compulsion is not without reason, the one sometimes acting involuntarily owing to his desire, the other owing to his reason; these two, being separated, are thrust out by one another. Whence men apply the language to the soul as a whole, because we see something like the above in the case of[1] the elements of the soul. Now of the parts of the soul this may be said; but the soul as a whole, whether in the continent or the incontinent, acts voluntarily, and neither acts on compulsion, but one of the elements in them does, since by nature we have both. For reason is in them by nature, because if growth is permitted and not maimed, it will be there; and appetite, because it accompanies and is present in us from birth. But these are practically the two marks by which we define the natural—it is either that which is found with us as soon as we are born, or that which comes to us if growth is allowed to proceed regularly, e.g. grey hair, old age, and so on. So that either acts, in a way,[2] contrary to nature, and yet, broadly speaking, according to nature, but not the same nature. The puzzles then about the continent and incontinent are these—do both, or one of them, act on compulsion, so that they act involuntarily or else at the same time both on compulsion and voluntarily; that is, if the compulsory is involuntary, both voluntarily and involuntarily? And it 1225a
is tolerably clear from the above how these puzzles are to be met.

In another way, too, men are said to act by force and compulsion without any disagreement between reason and desire in them, viz. when they do what they consider both painful

2–36 = *E.N.* 1110a 4 sq.: cf. *M.M.* 1188b 14–24.

---

[1] ⟨ἐπὶ⟩ before τῶν (J. S.).
[2] ⟨πως⟩ (suggested by Sus.) after πράττει.

and bad, but they are threatened with stripes, imprisonment, or death, if they do not do it. Such acts they say they did on compulsion. Or shall we deny this, and say that all do the act itself voluntarily? for they had the power to abstain from doing it, and to submit to the suffering. Again perhaps one might say that some such acts were voluntary and some not. For whatever of the acts that a man does without wishing them he has the power to do or abstain from doing,[1] these he always does voluntarily and not by force; but those in which he has not this power, he does by force in a sense (but not absolutely), because he does not choose the very thing he does, but the purpose for which it is done, since there is a difference, too, in this. For if a man were to murder another that he might not catch him at blind man's buff he would be laughed at if he were to say that he acted by force, and on compulsion; there ought to be some greater and more painful evil that he would suffer if he did not commit the murder. For then he will act on compulsion, and either[2] by force, or at least not by nature, when he does something evil for the sake of good, or release from a greater evil; then he will at least act involuntarily, for such acts are not subject to his control. Hence, many regard love, anger in some cases, and natural conditions, as involuntary, as being too strong for nature; we feel indulgence for them as things capable of overpowering nature. A man would more seem to act from force and involuntarily, if he acted to escape violent than if to escape gentle pain, and generally if to escape pain than if to get pleasure. For that which depends on him—and all turns on this—is what his nature is able to bear; what it is not, what is not under the control of his natural desire or reason, that does not depend on him. Therefore those who are inspired and prophesy, though their act is one of thought, we still say have it not in their own power either to say what they said, or to do what they did. And so of acts done through appetite. So that some thoughts and passions do not depend on us, nor the acts following such thoughts

[1] μὴ πρᾶξαι ἢ πρᾶξαι instead of μὴ ὑπάρξαι ἢ ὑπάρξαι (Speng.).
[2] ἤ for μή (Bz.)

and reasonings, but, as Philolaus said, some arguments are too strong for us.

So that if the voluntary and involuntary had to be considered[1] in reference to the presence of force as well as from other points of view, let this be our final distinction. †Nothing obscures the idea of the voluntary so much as the use of the expression that men act from force and yet voluntarily†.

9 Since we have finished this subject, and we have found 1225b
the voluntary not to be defined either by desire or by choice, it remains to define it as that which depends on thought. The voluntary, then, seems opposed to the involuntary, and to act with knowledge of the person acted on, instrument and tendency—for sometimes one knows the object, e. g. as father, but not that the tendency of the act is to kill, not to save, as in the case of Pelias's daughters; or knows the object to be a drink but takes it to be a philtre or wine when it was really hemlock—seems opposed to action in ignorance of the person, instrument, or thing, if, that is, the action is essentially the effect of ignorance. All that is done owing to ignorance, whether of person, instrument, or thing, is involuntary; the opposite therefore is voluntary. All, then, that a man does—it being in his power to abstain from doing it—not in ignorance and owing to himself must needs be voluntary; voluntariness is this. But all that he does in ignorance and owing to his ignorance, he does involuntarily. But since science or knowledge is of two sorts, one the possession, the other the use of knowledge, the man who has, but does not use knowledge may in a sense be justly called ignorant, but in another sense not justly, e. g. if he had not used his knowledge owing to carelessness. Similarly, one might be blamed for not having the knowledge, if it were something easy or necessary and he does not have it because of carelessness or pleasure or pain. This, then, we must add to our definition.

36–b 16 = *E. N.* 1110b 18–1111a 21: cf. *M. M.* 1188b 25–38.

[1] Cf. 1224a 9–11.

Such, then, is the completion of our distinction of the voluntary and the involuntary.

Let us next speak about choice, first raising various diffi- 10
culties about it. For one might doubt to what genus it belongs and in which to place it, and whether the voluntary and the chosen are or are not the same. Now some insist that choice is either opinion or desire, and the inquirer might well think that it was one or the other, for both are found accompanying it. Now that it is not desire is plain; for then it would be either wish, appetite, or anger, for none desires without having experienced one of these feelings. But anger and appetite belong also to the brutes while choice does not; further, even those who are capable of both the former often choose without either anger or appetite; and when they are under the influence of those passions they do not choose but remain unmoved by them. Further, anger and appetite always involve pain, but we often choose without pain. But neither are wish and choice the same; for we often wish for what we know is impossible, e.g. to rule all mankind or to be immortal, but no one chooses such things unless ignorant of the impossibility, nor even what is possible, generally, if he does not think it in his power to do or to abstain from doing it. So that this is clear, that the object of choice must be one of the things in our own power. Similarly, choice is not an opinion nor,
1226^{a} generally, what one thinks; for the object of choice was [1] something in one's power and many things may be thought that are not, e.g. that the diagonal is commensurable; and further, choice is not either true or false. Nor yet is choice identical with our opinion about matters of practice which are in our own power, as when we think that we ought to do or not to do something. This argument applies to wish as well as to opinion; for no one chooses an end, but the means to an end, e.g. no one chooses to be in health, but to walk or to sit for the purpose of keeping well; no one chooses to be happy but to make money or run risks for the purpose of

17–1227^{a} 17 = *E.N.* 1111^{b} 4–1113^{a} 12: cf. *M.M.* 1189^{a} 1–^{b} 25.

[1] Cf. 1223^{a} 16–19.

being happy. And in general, in choosing we show both what we choose and for what we choose it, the latter being that for which we choose something else, the former that which we choose for something else. But it is the end that we specially *wish for*, and we *think* we ought to be healthy and happy. So that it is clear through this that choice is different both from opinion and from wish; for wish and opinion are specially of the end, but choice is not.

It is clear, then, that choice is not wish, or opinion, or judgement simply. But in what does it differ from these? How is it related to the voluntary? The answer to these questions will also make it clear what choice is. Of possible things, then, there are some such that we can deliberate about them, while about others we cannot. For some things are possible, but the production of them is not in our power, some being due to nature, others to other causes; and about these none would attempt to deliberate except in ignorance. But about others, not only existence and non-existence is possible, but also human deliberation; these are things the doing or not doing of which is in our own power. Therefore, we do not deliberate about the affairs of the Indians nor how the circle may be squared; for the first are not in *our* power, the second is wholly beyond the power of action; but we do not even deliberate about all things that may be done and that are in our power (by which it is clear that choice is not opinion simply), though the matters of choice and action belong to the class of things in our own power. One might then raise the problem—why do doctors deliberate about matters within their science, but not grammarians? The reason is that error may occur in two ways (either in reasoning or in perception when we are engaged in the very act), and in medicine one may go wrong in both ways, but in grammar one can do so only in respect of the perception and action, and if they inquired about this there would be no end to their inquiries. Since then choice is[1] neither opinion nor wish singly nor 1226b
yet both (for no one chooses suddenly, though he thinks he ought to act, and wishes, suddenly), it must be com-

[1] Omitting ἐστι προαίρεσίς (P[b]).

pounded of both, for both are found in a man choosing. But we must ask—how compounded out of these? The very name is some indication. For choice is not simply taking but taking one thing before another; and this is impossible without consideration and deliberation; therefore choice arises out of deliberate opinion.

Now about the end no one deliberates (this being fixed for all), but about that which tends to it—whether this or that tends to it, and—supposing this or that resolved on—how it is to be brought about. All consider this till they have brought the commencement of the production to a point in their own power. If then, no one deliberately chooses without some preparation, without some consideration whether it is better or worse to do so and so, and if one considers all that are in one's power of the means to the end which are capable of existing or not existing, it is clear that choice is a considered desire for something in one's own power; for we all consider what we choose, but we do not choose all that we consider. I call it considered when consideration is the source and cause of the desire, and the man desires because of the consideration. Therefore in the other animals choice does not exist, nor in man at every age or in every condition; for there is not consideration or judgement of the ground of an act; but it is quite possible that many animals have an opinion whether a thing is to be done or not; only thinking with consideration is impossible to them. For the considering part of the soul is that which observes a cause of some sort; and the object of an action is one of the causes; for we call cause that owing to which a thing comes about; but the purpose of a thing's existence or production is what we specially call its cause, e.g. of walking, the fetching of things, if this is the purpose for which one walks. Therefore, those who have no aim fixed have no inclination to deliberate. So that since, if a man of himself and not through ignorance does or abstains from that which is in his power to do or abstain from, he acts or abstains voluntarily, but we do many such things without deliberation or premeditation, it follows that all that has been deliberately chosen is voluntary, but not all the volun-

tary is deliberately chosen, and that all that is according to choice is voluntary, but not all that is voluntary is according to choice. And at the same time it is clear from this that those legislators define well who enact that some states of feeling are to be considered voluntary, some involuntary, and some premeditated; for if they are not thoroughly accurate, at least they approximate to the truth. But about this we will speak in our investigation of justice;[1] 1227a
meanwhile, it is clear that deliberate choice is not simply wish or simply opinion, but opinion and desire together when following as a conclusion from deliberation.

But since in deliberating one always deliberates for the sake of some end, and he who deliberates has always an aim by reference to which he judges what is expedient, no one deliberates about the end; this is the starting-point and assumption, like the assumptions in theoretical science (we have spoken about this shortly in the beginning of this work and minutely in the Analytics[2]). Every one's inquiry, whether made with or without art, is about what tends to the end, e.g. whether they shall go to war or not, when this is what they are deliberating about. But the cause or object will come first, e.g. wealth, pleasure, or anything else of the sort that happens to be our object. For the man deliberating deliberates if he has considered, from the point of view of the end, what[3] conduces to bringing the end within his own action, or what he at present can do towards the object. But the object or end is always something good by nature, and men deliberate about its partial constituents, e.g. the doctor whether he is to give a drug, or the general where he is to pitch his camp. To them the absolutely best end is good. But contrary to nature and by perversion[4] not the good but the apparent good is the end. And the reason is that some things cannot be used for anything but what their nature determines, e.g. sight; for one can see nothing

18–b 4 = *E.N.* 1113a 13–b 2. 18–b 11: cf. *M.M.* 1189b 25–1190a 7.

---

[1] Not in the existing treatise, but cf. *E.N.* 1135a 16–1136a 9.

[2] Cf. 1214b 6 sqq. and *An. Post.* i. 2.

[3] Omitting ἤ.

[4] διὰ στροφήν (Jackson).

but what is visible, nor hear anything but what is audible. But science enables us to do what does not belong to that science; for the same science is not similarly related to health and disease, but naturally to the former, contrary to nature to the latter. And similarly wish is of the good naturally, but of the bad contrary to nature, and by nature one wishes the good, but contrary to nature and through perversion[1] the bad as well.

But further, the corruption and perversion of a thing does not tend to anything at random but to the contrary or the intermediate between it and the contrary. For out of this province one cannot go, since error leads not to anything at random but to the contrary of truth where there is a contrary, and to that contrary which is according to the appropriate science contrary. Therefore, the error and the resulting choice must deviate from the mean towards the opposite—and the opposite of the mean is excess or defect. And the cause is pleasantness or painfulness; for we are so constituted that the pleasant appears good to the soul and the more pleasant better, while the painful appears bad and
1227b the more painful worse. So that from this also it is clear that virtue and vice have to do with pleasures and pains; for they have to do with objects of choice, and choice has to do with the good and bad or what seems such, and pleasure and pain naturally seem such.

It follows then, since moral virtue is itself a mean and wholly concerned with pleasures and pains, and vice lies in excess or defect and is concerned with the same matters as virtue, that moral virtue is a habit tending to choose the mean in relation to us in things pleasant and painful, in regard to which, according as one is pleased or pained, men are said to have a definite sort of character; for one is not said to have a special sort of character merely for liking what is sweet or what is bitter.

These distinctions having been made, let us say whether II
virtue makes the choice correct and the end right so that a man chooses for the right end, or whether (as some say) it makes

12–1228a 2: cf. *M. M.* 1190a 8–33.

[1] διὰ στροφήν (Jackson).

the reason so. But what does this is continence, for this preserves the reason. But virtue and continence differ. We must speak later about them,[1] since those who think that virtue makes the reason right, do so for this cause—namely, that [2] continence is of this nature and continence is one of the things we praise. Now that we have discussed preliminary questions let us state our view.[3] It is possible for the aim to be right, but for a man to go wrong in the means to that aim; and again the aim may be mistaken, while the means leading to it are right; or both may be mistaken. Does then virtue make the aim, or the means to that aim? We say the aim, because this is not attained by inference or reasoning. Let us assume this as starting-point. For the doctor does not ask whether one ought to be in health or not, but whether one ought to walk or not; nor does the trainer ask whether one ought to be in good condition or not, but whether one should wrestle or not. And similarly no art asks questions about the end; for as in theoretical sciences the assumptions are our starting-points, so in the productive the end is starting-point and assumed. E.g. we reason that since this body is to be made healthy, therefore so and so must be found in it if health is to be had—just as in geometry we argue, if the angles of the triangle are equal to two right angles, then so and so must be the case. The end aimed at is, then, the starting-point of our thought, the end of our thought the starting-point of action. If, then, of all correctness either reason or virtue is the cause, if reason is not the cause, then the end (but not the means) must owe its rightness to virtue. But the end is the object of the action; for all choice is of some thing and for the sake of some object. The object, then, is the mean, and virtue is the cause of this by choosing it.[4] Still choice is not of this but of the things done for the sake of this. To hit on these things—I mean what ought to be done for the sake of the object—belongs to another faculty; but of the rightness of

[1] Not in the existing treatise, but cf. *E.N.* 1150^{b} 29–1151^{a} 28, 1144^{a} 35.
[2] Read colon for full stop after *αἴτιον* and omit *γάρ*.
[3] Reading *λέγωμεν* (C^{r}).
[4] Omitting *οὗ ἕνεκα*.

the end of the choice the cause is virtue. And therefore it is from a man's choice that we judge his character—that is from the object for the sake of which he acts, not from the act itself. Similarly, vice makes the choice to be for the sake of the opposite object. If, then, a man, having it in his power to do the honourable and abstain from the base, does the opposite, it is clear that this man is not good. Hence, it follows that both vice and virtue are voluntary; for there is no necessity to do what is wicked. Therefore vice is blamable and virtue praiseworthy. For the involuntary if base or bad is not blamable, if good is not praiseworthy, but only the voluntary. Further, we praise and blame all men with regard to their choice rather than their acts (though activity is more desirable than virtue), because men may do bad acts under compulsion, but no one chooses them under compulsion. Further, it is only because it is not easy to see the nature of a man's choice that we are forced to judge of his character by his acts. The activity then is more desirable, but the choice more praiseworthy. And this both follows from our assumptions and is in agreement with observation.

2–19: cf. *M.M.* 1190a 34–b 6.

BOOK III

1 THAT there are mean states, then, in the virtues, and that these are states of deliberate purpose, and that the opposite states are vices and what these are, has been stated in its universal form. But let us take them individually and speak of them in order; and first let us speak of bravery. All are practically agreed that the brave man is concerned with fears and that bravery is one of the virtues. We distinguished also in the table[1] confidence and fear as contraries; in a sense they are, indeed, opposed to one another. Clearly, then, those named after these habits will be similarly opposed to one another, e.g. the coward, for he is so called from fearing more than he ought and being less confident than he ought, and the confident man, who is so called for fearing less than he ought and being more confident than he ought. (Hence they have names cognate to those of the qualities, e.g. 'confident' is cognate to 'confidence'.) So that since bravery is the best habit in regard to fear and confidence, and one should be neither like the confident (who are defective in one way, excessive in another) nor like the cowards (of whom the same may be said, only not about the same objects, but inversely, for they are defective in confidence and excessive in fear), it is clear that **1228^b**
the middle habit between confidence and cowardice is bravery, for this is the best.

The brave man seems to be in general fearless, the coward prone to fear; the latter fears many things and few, great things and small, and intensely and quickly, while his opposite fears either not at all or slightly and reluctantly

23–26 = *E. N.* 1114^b 26–29, 1115^a 4 sq. 26–1230^a 36 = *E. N.* 1115^a 5–1117^b 22: cf. *M. M.* 1190^b 9–1191^a 36. 31–35 = *E. N.* 1115^b 28–1116^a 2.

[1] Cf. 1221^a 17–19.

and seldom, and great things only. The brave endures even what is very formidable, the coward not even what is slightly formidable. What, then, does the brave man endure? First, is it the things that appear formidable to himself or to another? If the latter, his bravery would be no considerable matter. But if it is the things formidable to himself, then he must find many things formidable—formidable things[1] being things that cause fear to those who find them formidable, great fear if very formidable, slight fear if slightly formidable. Then it follows that the brave man feels much and serious fear; but on the contrary bravery seemed to make a man fearless, fearlessness consisting in fearing few things if any, and in fearing slightly and with reluctance. But perhaps we use 'formidable'—like 'pleasant' and 'good'—in two senses. Some things are pleasant or good absolutely, others to a particular person pleasant or good—but absolutely bad and not pleasant, e.g. what is useful to the wicked or pleasant to children as such; and similarly the formidable is either absolutely such or such to a particular person. What, then, a coward as such fears is not formidable to any one or but slightly so; but what is formidable to the majority of men or to human nature, that we call absolutely formidable. But the brave man shows himself fearless towards these and endures such things, they being to him formidable in one sense but in another not—formidable to him *qua* man, but not formidable to him except slightly so, or not at all, *qua* brave. These things, however, are terrible, for they are so to the majority of men. This is the reason, by the way, why the habit of the brave man is praised; his condition is analogous to that of the strong or healthy. For these are what they are, not because, in the case of the one, no toil, in the case of the other, no extreme,[2] crushes them, but because they are either unaffected absolutely or affected only to a slight extent by the things that affect the many

18–38 = *E. N.* 1115^b 7–15.

---

[1] Reading πολλά with some MSS. and Sus., omitting μεγάλα καί, and (after φοβερά) inserting τὰ δὲ φοβερά (Bz.).

[2] e.g. of temperature.

or the majority. The sick, then, and the weak and the cowardly are affected by the common affections, as well as by others, only more quickly and to a greater extent than the many, and further, by the things that affect the many they are wholly unaffected or but slightly affected.[1]

But it is still questioned whether anything is terrible to the brave man, whether he would not be incapable of fear. May we not allow him to be capable of it in the way above mentioned? For bravery consists in following reason, and **1229^{a}** reason bids one choose the noble. Therefore the man who endures the terrible from any other cause than this is either out of his wits or confident; but the man who does so for the sake of the noble is alone fearless and brave. The coward, then, fears even what he ought not, the confident is confident even when he ought not to be; the brave man both fears and is confident when he ought to be, and is in this sense a mean, for he is confident or fears as reason bids him. But reason does not bid a man to endure what is very painful or destructive unless it is noble; now the confident is confident about such things even if reason does not bid him be so, while the coward is not confident even if it does; the brave man alone is confident about them only if reason bids him.

There are five kinds of courage, so named from a certain analogy between them; for they all endure the same things but not for the same reasons. One is a civic courage, due to the sense of shame; another is military, due to experience and knowledge, not (as Socrates said[2]) of what is fearful, but of the resources they have to meet what is fearful. The third kind is due to inexperience and ignorance;[3] it is that which makes children and madmen face objects moving towards them and take hold of snakes. Another kind is due to hope, which makes those who have often been fortunate, or those who are drunk, face dangers—for wine makes them sanguine. Another

4: cf. *E.N.* 1115^{a} 29–31, 33. ^{b} 5, 12 sq., 21. 1116^{a} 15, ^{b} 2 sq.
12–31 = *E.N.* 1116^{a} 16–1117^{a} 27.

[1] This sentence is probably spurious, being a repetition of ll. 33–35.
[2] Cf. Plat. *Protag.* 360 D: omit ὅτι (Sylburg).
[3] Cf. 1229^{b} 26.

kind is due to irrational feeling, e.g. love or anger; for a man in love is rather confident than timid, and faces many dangers, like him who slew the tyrant in Metapontium or the man of whom stories are told in Crete. Similar is the action of anger or passion, for passion is beside itself. Hence wild boars are thought to be brave though they are not really so, for they behave as such when beside themselves, but at other times are variable, like confident men. But still the bravery of passion is above all natural (passion is invincible, and therefore children are excellent fighters); civic courage is the effect of law. But in truth none of these forms is courage, though all are useful for encouragement in danger.

So far we have spoken of the terrible generally; now it is best to distinguish further. In general, then, whatever is productive of fear is called fearful, and this is all that causes destructive pain. For those who expect some other pain may perhaps have another pain and another emotion but not fear, e.g. if a man foresees that he will suffer the pain of envy or of jealousy or of shame. But fear only occurs in connexion with the expectation of pains whose nature is to

1229b be destructive to life. Therefore men who are very effeminate as to some things are brave, and some who are hard and enduring are cowards. Indeed, it is thought practically the special mark of bravery to take up a certain attitude towards death and the pain of it. For if a man were so constituted as to be patient as reason requires towards heat and cold and similar not dangerous pains, but weak and timid about death, not for any other feeling, but just because it means destruction, while another was soft in regard to these but unaffected in regard to death, the former would seem cowardly, the latter brave; for we speak of danger also only in regard to such objects of fear as bring near to us that which will cause such destruction; when this seems close, then we speak of danger.

The objects of fear, then, in regard to which we call a man brave are, as we have said, those which appear capable of causing destructive pain, but only when they appear near

2-12: cf. *E.N.* 1115a 17-27.

and not far off, and are of such magnitude, real or apparent, as is not out of proportion to man, for some things must appear terrible to and must upset any man. For just as things hot and cold and certain other powers are too strong for us and the conditions of the human body, so it may be with regard to the emotions of the soul.

The cowardly, then, and the confident are misled by their habits; for to the coward what is not terrible seems terrible, and what is slightly terrible greatly so, while in the opposite way, to the confident the terrible seems safe and the very terrible but slightly so; but the brave man thinks things what they truly are. Therefore, if a man faces the terrible through ignorance (e.g. if a man faces in the transport of madness the attack of a thunderbolt), he is not brave, nor yet if, knowing the magnitude of the danger, he faces it through passion—as the Celts take up their arms to go to meet the waves; in general, all the bravery of barbarians involves passion. But some face danger also for other pleasures—for passion is not without a certain pleasure, involving as it does the hope of vengeance. But still, whether a man faces death for this or some other pleasure or to flee from greater evils, he would not justly be called brave. For if dying were pleasant, the profligate would have often died because of his incontinence, just as now—since what causes death is pleasant though not death itself—many knowingly incur death through their incontinence, but none of them would be thought brave even if they do it with perfect readiness to die. Nor is a man brave if he seeks death to avoid trouble, as many do; to use Agathon's words: 'Bad men too weak for toil are in love with death.' And so the poets narrate that Chiron, because of the pain of his wound, prayed for death and release from his immortality. Similarly, all who face dangers owing to experience are not really brave; this is what, perhaps, most soldiers do. For the truth is the exact opposite of what Socrates thought; he held that bravery was knowledge. But those who know how to ascend masts are confident not because

28–30 = *E. N.* 1115^b 26–29. 30–1230^a 4 = *E. N.* 1116^a 10–15, 1117^a 5–9. 4–16 = *E. N.* 1116^b 3–19: cf. 1115^b 1–4.

they know what is terrible, but because they know how to help themselves in dangers. Nor is all that makes men fight more boldly courage; for then, as Theognis puts it,[1] strength and wealth would be bravery—'every man' (he says) 'daunted by poverty'. Obviously some, though cowards, face dangers because of their experience, because they do not think them dangers, as they know how to help themselves; and a proof of this is that, when they think they can get no help and the danger is close at hand, they no longer face it. But it is where shame, among all such causes,[2] makes a man face danger that the man would most seem to be brave, as Homer says Hector faced the danger from Achilles—'and shame seized Hector';[3] and, again, 'Polydamas will be the first to taunt me'.[4] Such bravery is civic. But the true bravery is neither this nor any of the others, but like them, as is also the bravery of brutes which from passion run to meet the blow. For a man ought to hold his ground though frightened, not because he will incur disrepute, nor through anger, nor because he does not expect to be killed or has powers by which to protect himself; for in that case he will not even think that there is anything to be feared. But since all virtue implies deliberate choice—we have said before[5] what this means and that it makes a man choose everything for the sake of some end, and that the end is the noble—it is clear that bravery, because it is a virtue, will make a man face the fearful for some end, so that he does it neither through ignorance—for his virtue rather makes him judge correctly—nor for pleasure, but because the act is noble; since, if it be not noble but frantic, he does not face the danger, for that would be disgraceful. In regard, then, to what things bravery is a mean state, between what, and why, and the meaning of the fearful, we have now spoken tolerably adequately for our present purpose.

16–21 = *E. N.* 1116a 17–29. 21 sq. = *E. N.* 1116b 13–1117a 1.

---

[1] Cf. Theognis 177.
[2] Keep the MS. reading αἰτίων.
[3] These words do not exist in Homer as we know him.
[4] Iliad xxii. 100.
[5] Cf. 1227b 21–1228a 7.

2 After this we must try to draw certain distinctions regarding profligacy and temperance. 'Profligate' has many senses.[1] It is, in a sense, the unchastened and uncured, as the undivided is the not divided, and with the 1230b
same two classes, i. e. the one capable, the other incapable of division; for undivided means both what is incapable of division, and what is capable but not actually divided; and so with 'profligate'. For it is both that which by its nature refuses chastening, and that which is of a nature to accept but has not yet received chastening for the faults in regard to which the temperate man acts rightly—e. g. children. For we give them the same name as the profligate, but because of this latter kind of profligacy.[2] And, further, it is in different senses that we give the name to those hard to cure and to those whom it is quite impossible to cure through chastening. Profligacy, then, having many senses, it is clear that it has to do with certain pleasures and pains, and that the forms differ from one another and from other states by the kind of attitude towards these; we have already stated how, in the use of the word 'profligacy', we apply it to various states by analogy.[3] As to those who from insensibility are unmoved by these same pleasures, some call them insensible, while others describe them as such by other names; but this state is not very familiar or common because all rather err in the opposite direction, and it is congenital to all to be overcome by and to be sensible to such pleasures. It is the state chiefly of such as the boors introduced on the stage by comic writers, who keep aloof from even moderate and necessary pleasures.

But since temperance has to do with pleasures, it must also have to do with certain appetites; we must, then,

36–1231b 4 = *E.N.* 1117b 23–1119b 20: cf. *M.M.* 1191a 35–b 22. 38–b 20 = *E.N.* 1119a 34–b 18. 21–1231a 25 = *E.N.* 1117b 27–1118b 7.

---

[1] The two Greek words ἀκόλαστος and κεκολασμένος are cognate; we might get cognate words if for 'profligate' we might substitute the more special word 'unchaste', cognate to 'chastened'.

[2] i. e. ἀκόλαστος often means no more than 'naughty'.

[3] This seems to refer to words which must have been lost at 1221a 20.

ascertain which. For the temperate man does not exhibit his temperance in regard to all appetites and all pleasures, but about the objects, as it seems, of two senses, taste and touch, or rather really about those of touch alone. For his temperance is shown not in regard to visual pleasure in the beautiful (so long as it is unaccompanied by sexual appetite) or visual pain at the ugly; nor, again, in regard to the pleasure or pain of the ear at harmony or discord; nor, again, in regard to olfactory pleasure or pain at pleasant or disagreeable odours. Nor is a man called profligate for feeling or want of feeling in regard to such matters. For instance, if one sees a beautiful statue, or horse, or human being, or hears singing, without any accompanying wish for eating, drinking, or sexual indulgence, but only with the wish to see the beautiful and to hear the singers, he would not be thought profligate any more than those who were charmed by the Sirens. Temperance and profligacy have to do with those two senses whose objects are alone felt by and give pleasure and pain to brutes as well; and these are the senses of taste and touch, the brutes seeming insensible to
1231a the pleasures of practically all the other senses alike, e.g. harmony or beauty; for they obviously have no feeling worth mentioning at the mere sight of the beautiful or the hearing of the harmonious, except, perhaps, in some marvellous instances. And with regard to pleasant and disagreeable odours it is the same, though all their senses are sharper than ours. They do, indeed, feel pleasure at certain odours; but these gladden them accidentally and not of their own nature, being those that give us pleasure owing to expectation and memory, e.g. the pleasure from the scent of food or drinks; for these we enjoy because of a different pleasure, that of eating or drinking; the odours enjoyed for their own nature are such as those of flowers; (therefore Stratonicus neatly remarked that these smell beautifully, food, &c., pleasantly). Indeed, the brutes are not excited over every pleasure connected with taste, e.g. not over those which are felt in the tip of the tongue, but only over those that are felt in the gullet, the sensation being one of touch rather than of taste. Therefore gluttons pray not for

a long tongue but for the gullet of a crane, as did Philoxenus, the son of Eryxis. Therefore, broadly, we should regard profligacy as concerned with objects of touch. Similarly it is with such pleasures that the profligate man is concerned. For drunkenness, gluttony, lecherousness, gormandizing, and all such things are concerned with the above-mentioned senses; and these are the parts into which we divide profligacy. But in regard to the pleasures of sight, hearing, and smell, no one is called profligate if he is in excess, but we blame without considering disgraceful such faults, and all in regard to which we do not speak of men as continent; the incontinent are neither profligate nor temperate.

The man, then, so constituted as to be deficient in the pleasures in which all must in general partake and rejoice is insensible (or whatever else we ought to call him); the man in excess is profligate. For all naturally take delight in these objects and conceive appetites for them, and neither are nor are called profligate; for they neither exceed by rejoicing more than is right when they get them, nor by feeling greater pain than they ought when they miss them; nor are they insensible, for they are not deficient in the feeling of joy or pain, but rather in excess.

But since there is excess and defect in regard to these things, there is clearly also a mean, and this state is the best and opposed to both of the others; so that if the best state about the objects with which the profligate is concerned is temperance, temperance would be the mean state in regard to the above-mentioned sensible pleasures, the mean between profligacy and insensibility, the excess being 1231b
profligacy, and the defect either nameless or expressed by the names we have suggested. More accurate distinctions about the class of pleasures will be drawn in what is said later[1] about continence and incontinence.

3 In the same way we must ascertain what is gentleness and irascibility. For we see that the gentle is concerned

26–b 4 = *E.N.* 1118b 28–1119a 20. 5–26 = *E.N.* 1125b 26–1126b 9: cf. *M.M.* 1191b 23–38.

[1] Not to be found in the existing treatise.

with the pain that arises from anger, being characterized by a certain attitude towards this. We have given in our list[1] as opposed to the passionate, irascible, and savage—all such being names for the same state—the slavish and the senseless. For these are practically the names we apply to those who are not moved to anger even when they ought, but take insults easily and are humble towards contempt—for slowness to anger is opposed to quickness, violence to quietness, long persistence in that feeling of pain which we call anger to short. And since there is here, as we have said[2] there is elsewhere, excess and defect—for the irascible is one that feels anger more quickly, to a greater degree, and for a longer time, and when he ought not, and at what he ought not, and frequently, while the slavish is the opposite—it is clear that there is a mean to this inequality. Since, then, both the above-mentioned habits are wrong, it is clear that the mean state between them is good; for he is neither too soon nor too late, and does not feel anger when he ought not, nor feel no anger when he ought. So that since in regard to these emotions the best condition is gentleness, gentleness would be a mean state, and the gentle a mean between the irascible and the slavish.

Also magnanimity, magnificence, and liberality are mean 4
states—liberality being shown in the acquisition or expenditure of wealth. For the man who is more pleased than he ought to be with every acquisition and more pained than he ought to be at every expenditure is illiberal; he who feels less of both than he ought is lavish; he who feels both as he ought is liberal. (By 'as he ought', both in this and in the other cases, I mean 'as right reason directs'.) But since the two former show their nature respectively by excess and defect—and where there are extremes, there is also a mean and that is best, a single best for each kind of action—liberality must be the mean between lavishness and meanness in regard to the acquisition and expenditure

27–1232^{a} 18 = *E.N.* 1119^{b} 19–1122^{a} 18: cf. *M.M.* 1191^{b} 39–1192^{a} 20.

[1] Cf. 1221^{b} 12–15.

[2] Cf. 1220^{b} 21 sqq.

of wealth. I take wealth and the art of wealth in two senses; the art in one sense being the proper use of one's 1232a property (say of a shoe or a coat), in the other an accidental mode of using it—not the use of a shoe for a weight, but, say, the selling of it or letting it out for money; for here too the shoe is used. Now the lover of money is a man eager for actual money, which is a sign of possession taking the place of the accidental use of other possessions. But the illiberal man may even be lavish in the accidental pursuit of wealth, for it is in the natural pursuit of it that he aims at increase.[1] The lavish runs short of necessaries; but the liberal man gives his superfluities. There are also species of these genera which exceed or fall short as regards parts of the subject-matter of liberality, e.g. the sparing, the skinflint, the grasper at disgraceful gain, are all illiberal; the sparing is characterized by his refusal to spend, the grasper at disgraceful gain by his readiness to accept anything, the skinflint by his strong feeling over small amounts, while the man who has the sort of injustice that involves meanness is a false reckoner and cheat. And similarly one class of spendthrift is a waster by his disorderly expenditure, the other a fool who cannot bear the pain of calculation.

5 As to magnanimity we must define its specific nature from the qualities that we ascribe to the magnanimous. For just as with other things,[2] in virtue of their nearness and likeness up to a certain point, their divergence beyond that point escapes notice, so it is with magnanimity. Therefore, sometimes men really opposite lay claim to the same character, e.g. the lavish to that of the liberal, the self-willed to that of the dignified, the confident to that of the brave. For they are concerned with the same things, and are up to a certain point contiguous; thus the brave man and the confident are alike ready to face danger—but the former in one way, the latter in another; and these ways differ greatly.

19–1233a 30 = *E.N.* 1123a 34–1125a 34: cf. *M.M.* 1192a 21–36.

---

[1] This seems to mean that he might be lavish of money, if it brought him an increase of commodities.

[2] Omit ἃ (MSS.).

Now, we assert that the magnanimous man, as is indicated by the name we apply to him, is characterized by a certain greatness of soul and faculty; and so he seems like the dignified and the magnificent man, since[1] magnanimity seems to accompany *all* the virtues. †For[2] to distinguish correctly great goods from small is laudable. Now, those goods are thought great which are pursued by the man of the best habit in regard to what seem to be pleasures;[3] and magnanimity is the best habit. But every special virtue correctly distinguishes the greater from the less among its objects, as the wise man and virtue would direct, so that all the virtues seem to go with this one of magnanimity, or this with all the virtues.†

Further, it seems characteristic of the magnanimous man
1232^b to be disdainful; each virtue makes one disdainful of what is esteemed great contrary to reason (e.g. bravery disdains dangers of this kind—for it considers it disgraceful to hold them great;[4] and numbers are not always fearful: so the temperate disdains many great pleasures, and the liberal wealth). But this characteristic seems to belong to the magnanimous man because he cares about few things only, and those great, and not because some one else thinks them so. The magnanimous man would consider rather what one good man thinks than many ordinary men, as Antiphon after his condemnation said to Agathon when he praised his defence of himself. Contempt seems particularly the special characteristic of the magnanimous man; and, again, as regards honour, life, and wealth—about which mankind seems to care—he values none of them except honour. He would be pained if denied honour, and if ruled by one undeserving. He delights most of all when he obtains honour.

In this way he would seem to contradict himself; for to

28–30: cf. *E.N.* 1128^a 34 sq. 30: cf. *E.N.* 1125^a 12 sq. 37 sq.: cf. *E.N.* 1123^b 26 sq. 38 sq.: cf. *E.N.* 1124^b 5 sq., 29 10: cf. *E.N.* 1124^b 6–9. 12–14 sq.: cf. *E.N.* 1123^b 17–24, 34: 1124^a 12 sq.

[1] ὅτι for ὅτε (Sus.).

[2] 32–8 are unintelligible: the idea seems to be that magnanimity is implied in all the virtues, cf. 38 and 1232^b 25.

[3] δοκοῦντ' for τοιαῦτ' (Fr.).

[4] γὰρ ⟨ἡγεῖσθαι⟩, cf. 1233^a 30.

be[1] concerned above all with honour, and yet to disdain the multitude and[2] reputation, are inconsistent. So we must first distinguish. For honour, great or small, is of two kinds; for it may be given by a crowd of ordinary men or by those worthy of consideration; and, again, there is a difference according to the ground on which honour is given. For it is made great not merely by the number of those who give the honour or by their quality, but also by its being precious;[3] but in reality, power and all other goods are precious and worthy of pursuit only if they are truly great, so that there is no virtue without greatness; therefore every virtue, as we have said,[4] makes man magnanimous in regard to the object with which that virtue is concerned.[5] But still there is a single virtue, magnanimity, alongside of the other virtues, and he who has this must be called in a special sense magnanimous. But since some goods are precious and some not,[6] according to the distinction above[7] made, and of such goods some are in truth great and some small, and of these some men are worthy and think themselves so, among these we must look for the magnanimous man. There must be four different kinds of men. For a man may be worthy of great goods and think himself worthy of them, and again there may be small goods and a man worthy of them and thinking himself worthy; and we may have the opposites in regard to either kind of goods; for there may be a man worthy of small who thinks himself worthy of great and esteemed goods; and, again, one worthy of great but thinking himself worthy only of small. He then who is worthy of the small but thinks himself worthy of the great is blameable; for it is silly and not noble that he should obtain out of proportion to his worth: the man also is blameable who being worthy of great goods, because he possesses the gifts that make a man worthy, does not think himself worthy to share in them. There remains then the 1233a opposite of these two—the man who is worthy of great

[1] τὸ γάρ (best MSS.).
[2] Retaining καί of the MSS.
[3] ⟨τιμία⟩ for τιμίαν (J. S.).
[4] Cf. a39 sqq.
[5] i. e. every virtue is a species of magnanimity.
[6] Add οὔ after τὰ δ' (J. S.).
[7] l. 10 sqq.

goods and thinks himself worthy of them, such being his disposition; he is the mean between the other two and is praiseworthy. Since, then, in respect of the choice and use of honour and the other esteemed goods, the best-condition is magnanimity, and we define the magnanimous man [1] as being this, and not as being concerned with things useful; and since this mean is the most praiseworthy state, it is clear that magnanimity is a mean. But of the opposites, as shown in our list,[2] the quality consisting in thinking oneself worthy of great goods when not worthy is vanity—for we give the name of vain to those who think themselves worthy of great things though they are not; but the quality of not thinking oneself worthy of great things though one is, we call mean-spiritedness—for it is held to be the mark of the mean-spirited not to think himself worthy of any thing great though he possesses that for which he would justly be deemed worthy of it; hence, it follows that magnanimity is a mean between vanity and mean-spiritedness. The fourth of the sorts of men we have distinguished is neither wholly blameable nor yet magnanimous, not having to do with anything that possesses greatness, for he is neither worthy nor thinks himself worthy of great goods; therefore, he is not opposite to the magnanimous man; yet to be worthy and think oneself worthy of small goods might seem opposite to being worthy and thinking oneself worthy of great ones. But such a man is not opposite to the magnanimous man, for he is not to be blamed [3] (his habit being what reason directs); he is, in fact, similar in nature to the magnanimous man; for both think themselves worthy of what they really are worthy of. He might become magnanimous, for of whatever he is worthy of he will think himself worthy. But the mean-spirited man who, possessed of great and honourable qualities, does not think himself worthy of great good—what would he do if he deserved only small? Either [4] he would think himself worthy of

9-30 = *E.N.* 1125a 16–34, 1122b 30 sq.

[1] τὸν μεγαλόψυχον (MSS.).
[2] Cf. 1221a 10, 31 sq.
[3] Omitting μή (Bekker).
[4] ἢ for εἰ (most MSS. and Bekk.).

great goods and thus be vain, or else of still smaller than he has. Therefore, no one would call a man mean-spirited because, being an alien in a city, he does not claim to govern but submits, but only one who does not, being well born and thinking power a great thing.

6 The magnificent man is not concerned with any and every action or choice, but with expenditure—unless we use the name metaphorically; without expense there cannot be magnificence. It is the fitting in ornament, but ornament is not to be got out of ordinary expenditure, but consists in surpassing the merely necessary. The man, then, who tends to choose in great expenditure the fitting magnitude, and desires this sort of mean, and with a view to this sort of pleasure is magnificent; the man whose inclination is to something larger than necessary but out of harmony, has no name, though he is near to those called by some tasteless and showy: e. g. if a rich man, spending money on the 1233b
marriage of a favourite, thinks it sufficient to make such arrangements as one makes to entertain those who drink to the Good Genius,[1] he is shabby; while one who receives guests of this sort in the way suited to a marriage feast resembles the showy man, if he does it neither for the sake of reputation nor to gain power; but he who entertains suitably and as reason directs, is magnificent; for what looks well is the suitable; nothing unsuitable is fitting. And what one does should be fitting. † For in what is fitting is involved suitability both to the object † (e. g. one thing is fitting for a servant's, another for a favourite's wedding) and to the entertainer both in extent and kind, e. g. one thought [2] that the mission conducted by Themistocles to the Olympian games was not fitting to him because of his previous low station, but would have been to Cimon. But the man who is indifferent to questions of suitability is in none of the above classes.

Similarly with liberality; for a man may be neither liberal nor illiberal.

31–b 15 = *E.N.* 1122a 18–1123a 33 : cf. *M.M.* 1192a 21–36.

[1] A regular Greek toast.

[2] prps. ᾤοντο (Speng.).

In general of the other blameable or praiseworthy qualities 7
of character some are excesses, others defects, others means,
but of feelings, e.g. the envious man and the man who
rejoices over another's misfortunes. For, to consider the
habits to which they owe their names, envy is pain felt at
deserved good fortune, while the feeling of the man who
rejoices at misfortunes has itself no name,[1] but such a man
shows his nature by[2] rejoicing over undeserved ill fortune.
Between them is the man inclined to righteous indignation,
the name given by the ancients to pain felt at either good
or bad fortune if undeserved, or to joy felt at them if deserved.
Hence they make righteous indignation (*νέμεσις*) a god.
Shame is a mean between shamelessness and shyness; for
the man who thinks of no one's opinion is shameless, he who
thinks of every one's alike is shy, he who thinks only of that
of apparently good men is modest. Friendliness is a mean
between animosity and flattery; for the man who readily
accommodates himself in all respects to another's desires is
a flatterer; the man who opposes every desire is prone to
enmity; the man who neither accommodates himself to nor
resists every one's pleasure, but only accommodates himself to
what seems to be best, is friendly. Dignity is a mean between
self-will and too great obligingness; for the contemptuous
man who lives with no consideration for another is self-willed;
the man who adapts his whole life to another and is sub-
missive to everybody is too obliging; but he who acts thus
in certain cases but not in others, and only to those worthy,
is dignified. The sincere and simple, or, as he is called,
'downright' man, is a mean between the dissembler and the
charlatan. For the man who knowingly and falsely depre-
1234a ciates himself is a dissembler; the man who exalts himself
is a charlatan; the man who represents himself as he is, is
sincere, and in the Homeric phrase 'intelligent'; in general

18–26: cf. *M.M.* 1192b 18–29 (*E.N.* 1108b 1–7). 26–29 = *E.N.* 1128b 10–35: cf. *M.M.* 1193a 1–10. 29–34 = *E.N.* 1126b 10–1127a 12: cf. *M.M.* 1193a 20–28. 34–38: cf. *M.M.* 1192a 30–38. 38–1234a 3 = *E.N.* 1127a 13–b32: cf. *M.M.* 1193a 28–35.

[1] ἐστίν for ἐπὶ τό (Speng.).
[2] ἐστι for ἐπί (Casaubon); τῷ for τό (some MSS., Bekker).

the one loves truth, the other a lie. Wittiness also is a mean, the witty being a mean between the boorish or stiff and the buffoon. For just as the squeamish differs from the omnivorous in that the one takes little or nothing and that with reluctance, while the other accepts everything readily, so is the boor related to the vulgar buffoon; the one accepts nothing comic without difficulty, the other takes all easily and with pleasure. Neither attitude is right; one ought to accept some things and not others, as reason directs—and the man who does this is witty. The proof is the usual one; wittiness of this kind, supposing we do not use the word in some transferred sense, is the best habit, and the mean is praiseworthy, and the extremes blameable. But wit being of two kinds—one being delight in the comic, even when directed against one's self, if it be really comic, like a jeer, the other being the faculty of producing such things—the two sorts differ from one another but both are means. For the man that can [1] produce what a good judge will be pleased at, even if the joke is against himself, will be midway between the vulgar and the frigid man; this definition is better than that which merely requires the thing said to be not painful to the person jeered at, no matter what sort of man he is; one ought rather to please the man who is in the mean, for he is a good judge.

All these mean states are praiseworthy without being virtues; nor are their opposites vices—for they do not involve deliberate choice. All of them occur in the classifications of affections, for each is an affection. But since they are natural, they tend to the natural virtues; for, as will be said later,[2] each virtue is found both naturally and also otherwise, viz. as including thought. Envy then tends to injustice (for the acts arising from it affect another), righteous indignation to justice, shame to temperance—whence some even put temperance into this genus. The sincere and the false are respectively sensible and foolish.

4–23 = *E. N.* 1127^b 33–1128^b 3: cf. *M. M.* 1193^a 11–19.

[1] ὁ δυνάμενος (Sylb.).
[2] Not in the existing treatise, but cf. *E. N.* vi. 1144^b 1–17.

But the mean is more opposed to the extremes than these to one another, because the mean is found with neither, but
1234b the extremes often with one another, and sometimes the same people are at once cowardly and confident, or lavish in some ways, illiberal in others, and in general are lacking in uniformity in a bad sense—for if they lack uniformity in a good sense, men of the mean type are produced; since, in a way, both extremes are present in the mean.

The opposition between the mean and the extremes does not seem to be alike in both cases; sometimes the opposition is that of the excessive extreme, sometimes that of the defective, and the causes are the two first given [1]—rarity, e.g. of those insensible to pleasures, and the fact that the error to which we are most prone seems the more opposed to the mean. There is a third reason, namely, that the more like seems less opposite, e.g. confidence to bravery,[2] lavishness to liberality.

We have, then, spoken sufficiently about the other praiseworthy virtues; we must now speak of justice.

[1] Cf. 1222a 22–b4.
[2] prps. read τὸ θάρσος πρὸς τὴν ἀνδρείαν (Bz.).

BOOKS IV, V, VI = *ETH. N.* BKS. V, VI, VII.

BOOK VII

1 FRIENDSHIP, what it is and of what nature, who is a friend, and whether friendship has one or many senses (and if many, how many), and, further, how we should treat a friend, and what is justice in friendship—all this must be examined not less than any of the things that are noble and desirable in character. For it is thought to be the special business of the political art to produce friendship, and men say that virtue is useful for this, for those who are unjustly treated by one another cannot be friends to one another. Further, all say that justice and injustice are specially exhibited towards friends; the same man seems both good and a friend, and friendship seems a sort of moral habit; and if one wishes to act without injustice, it is enough[1] to make friends, for genuine friends do not act unjustly. But neither will men act unjustly if they are just; therefore justice and friendship are either the same or not far different.

Further, men believe a friend to be among the greatest of goods, and friendlessness and solitude to be most terrible, because all life and voluntary association is with friends; **1235^a**
for we spend our days with our family, kinsmen, or comrades, children, parents, or wife. The private justice practised to friends depends on ourselves alone, while justice towards all others is determined by the laws, and does not depend on us.

Many questions are raised about friendship. There is the view of those who include the external world and give the term an extended meaning; for some think that like is

18–22 = *E.N.* 1155^a 3: cf. *M.M.* 1208^b 3 sq. 22–1235^a 3 = *E.N.* 1155^a 3–31: cf. *M.M.* 1208^b 4–6. 4–29 = *E.N.* 1155^a 32–^{b} 9: cf. *M.M.* 1208^b 7–20.

[1] ἅλις for ἀλλ' εἰς (Jackson).

friend to like, whence the saying 'how God ever draws like to like';[1] or the saying 'crow to crow'; or 'thief knows thief, and wolf wolf'. The physicists even systematize the whole of nature on the principle that like goes to like—whence Empedocles said that the dog sat on the tile because it was most like it. Some, then, describe a friend thus, but others say that opposites are friends; for they say the loved and desired is in every case a friend, but the dry does not desire the dry but the moist—whence the sayings, 'Earth loves the rain',[2] and 'in all things change is pleasant'; but change is change to an opposite. And like hates like, for 'potter is jealous of potter',[3] and animals nourished from the same source are enemies. Such, then, is the discrepancy between these views; for some think the like a friend, and the opposite an enemy—'the less is ever the enemy of the more, and begins a day of hate'[4]; and, further, the places of contraries are separated, but friendship seems to bring together. But others think opposites are friends, and Heraclitus blames the poet who wrote 'may strife perish from among gods and men'[5]; for (says he) there could not be harmony without the low and the high note, nor living things without male and female, two opposites. There are, then, these two views about friendship; and when so far separated from one another both are too broad.[6] There are other views that come nearer to and are more suitable to observed facts. Some think that bad men cannot be friends but only the good; while others think it strange that mothers should not love their own children. (Even among the brutes we find such friendship; at least they choose to die for their children.) Some, again, think that we only regard the useful as a friend, their proof being that all pursue the useful, but the useless, even in themselves, they throw away (as old Socrates said,[7]
1235^{b} citing the case of our spittle, hairs, and nails), and that we cast off useless parts, and in the end at death our very

29–1235^{b} 12 = *E.N.* 1155^{b} 9–16: cf. *M.M.* 1208^{b} 22–25.

[1] *Od.* xvii. 218.
[2] Eur. fr. 898 Nauck.
[3] Hes. *Works and Days*, 25.
[4] Eurip. *Phoen.* 540.
[5] *Iliad* xviii. 107.
[6] Sus.'s καί unnecessary.
[7] Cf. Xen. *Mem.* i. 2. 54.

body, the corpse being useless; but those who have a use for it keep it, as in Egypt. Now all these things [i. e. likeness, contrariety, utility] seem opposed to one another; for the like is useless to the like, and contrariety is furthest removed from likeness, and the contrary is most useless to its contrary, for contraries destroy one another. Further, some think it easy to acquire a friend, others a very rare thing to recognize one, and impossible without misfortune; for all wish to seem friends to the prosperous. But others would have us distrust even those who remain with us in misfortune, alleging that they are deceiving us and making pretence, that by giving their company to us when we are in misfortune they may obtain our friendship when we are again prosperous.

2 We must, then, find a method that will best explain the views held on these topics, and also put an end to difficulties and contradictions. And this will happen if the contrary views are seen to be held with some show of reason; such a view will be most in harmony with the facts of observation; and both the contradictory statements will in the end stand, if what is said is true in one sense but untrue in another.

Another puzzle is whether the good or the pleasant is the object of love. For if we love what we *desire*—and love is of this kind, for 'none is a lover but one who ever loves'[1]—and if desire is for the pleasant, in this way the object of love would be the pleasant; but if it is what we *wish for*, then it is the good—the good and the pleasant being different.

About all these and the other cognate questions we must attempt to gain clear distinctions, starting from the following principle. The desired and the wished for is either the good or the apparent good. Now this is why the pleasant is desired, for it is an apparent good; for some think it such, and to some it appears such, though they do not

13–1236^a 15: cf. *M. M.* 1208^b 26–1209^a 3. 13–1236^a 6 = *E. N.* 1155^b 17–27.

[1] Eurip. *Troad.* 1051.

think so. For appearance and opinion do not reside in the same part of the soul. It is clear, then, that we love both the good and the pleasant.

This being settled, we must make another assumption. Of the good some is absolutely good, some good to a particular man, though not absolutely; and the same things are at once absolutely good and absolutely pleasant. For we say that what is advantageous to a body in health is absolutely good for a body, but not what is good for a sick body, such as drugs and the knife. Similarly, things absolutely pleasant to a body are those pleasant to a healthy and unaffected body, e. g. seeing in light, not in darkness, though the opposite is the case to one with ophthalmia. And the pleasanter wine is not that which is pleasant to one whose tongue has been spoilt by inebriety (for such men[1] add vinegar to it), but that which is pleasant to sensation
1236a unspoiled. So with the soul; what is pleasant not to children or brutes, but to the adult, is really pleasant; at least, when we remember both we choose the latter. And as the child or brute is to the adult man, so are the bad and foolish to the good and sensible. To these, that which suits their habit is pleasant, and that is the good and noble.

Since, then, 'good' has many meanings—for one thing we call good because its nature is such, and another because it is profitable and useful—and further, the pleasant is in part absolutely pleasant and absolutely good, and in part pleasant to a particular individual and apparent good; just as in the case of inanimate things we may choose and love a thing for either of these reasons, so in the case of a man loving one because of his character or because of virtue, another because he is profitable and useful, another because he is pleasant, and for pleasure. And[2] a man becomes a friend when he is loved and returns that love, and this is recognized by the two men in question.

There must, then, be three kinds of love, not all being so

7–15 = *E. N.* 1155b 27–1156a 5. 16–32 = *E. N.* 1156a 6–14: cf. *M. M.* 1209a 3–36.

[1] Read οὗτοι for οὔτ' (Sus.). [2] Read δέ for δή (Jackson).

named for one thing or as species of one genus, nor yet having the same name quite by mere accident. For all the senses of love are related to one which is the primary, just as is the case with the word 'medical', and[1] just as we speak of a medical soul, body, instrument, or act, but properly the name belongs to that primarily so called. The primary is that of which the definition is implied in the definition of all;[2] e.g. a medical instrument is one that a medical man would use, but the definition of the instrument is not implied in that of 'medical man'. Everywhere, then, we seek for the primary. But because the[3] universal is primary, they also take the primary[4] to be universal, and this is an error. And so they are not able to do justice to all the observed facts about friendship; for since one definition will not suit all, they think there are no other[5] friendships; but the others are friendships, only not similarly so. But they, finding the primary friendship will not suit, assuming it would be universal if really primary, deny that the other friendships even are friendships; whereas there are many species of friendship; this was part of what we have already said,[6] since we have distinguished the three senses of friendship—one due to virtue, another to usefulness, a third to pleasantness.

Of these the friendship based on usefulness is of course[7] that of the majority; men love one another because of their usefulness and to the extent of this; so we have the proverb 'Glaucus, a helper is a friend so long as[8] he fights', and 'the Athenians no longer know the Megarians'. But the friendship based on pleasure is that of the young, for they are sensitive to pleasure; therefore also their friendship easily changes; for with a change in their characters as they 1236b
grow up there is also a change in their pleasures. But the friendship based on virtue is that of the best men.

It is clear from this that the primary friendship, that of

33–1237b 7 = *E.N.* 1156a 14–1157a 16: cf. *M.M.* 1209b 11–19.
33–1236b 17 = *E.N.* 1156a 14–b 6.

---

[1] Omit stop after *ἰατρικόν* (Jackson) and omit *γάρ* (19).
[2] *πᾶσιν* for *ἡμῖν* (Bz., Jackson).
[3] *διὰ δὲ τὸ ⟨τὸ⟩ καθόλου εἶναι πρῶτον.*
[4] *⟨τὸ⟩ πρῶτον* (Speng.).
[5] Omit *τάς* (MSS.).
[6] Cf. ll. 7–17.
[7] *ἐστι νὴ Δία* (Jackson).
[8] *τόσσον φίλος* (Fr.), *ἔστε* (J. S.).

good men, is a mutual returning of love and purpose. For what is loved is dear to him who loves it, but a man loving another man is himself dear[1] also to the man loved. This friendship, then, is peculiar to man, for he alone perceives another's purpose. But the other friendships are found also among the brutes where utility is in some degree present, both between tame animals and men, and between animals themselves, as in the case mentioned by Herodotus[2] of the friendship between the sandpiper and the crocodile, and the coming together and parting of birds that soothsayers speak of. The bad may be friends to one another on the ground both of usefulness and of pleasure; but some deny them to be friends, because there is not the primary friendship between them; for a bad man will injure a bad man, and those who are injured by one another do not love one another; but in fact they love, only not with the primary friendship. Nothing prevents their loving with the other kinds; for owing to pleasure they put up with each other's injury, so long as they are[3] incontinent. But those whose love is based on pleasure do not seem to be friends, when we look carefully, because their friendship is not of the primary kind, being unstable, while that is stable; it is, however, as has been said,[4] a friendship, only not the primary kind but derived from it. To speak, then, of friendship in the primary sense only is to do violence to facts, and makes one assert paradoxes; but it is impossible for all friendships to come under one definition. The only alternative left is that in a sense there is only one friendship, the primary; but in a sense all kinds are friendship, not as possessing a common name accidentally without being specially related to one another, nor yet as falling under one species, but rather as in relation to one and the same thing.

†But since the same thing is at the same time absolutely good and absolutely pleasant (if nothing interferes), and the genuine friend is absolutely the friend in the primary sense, and such is the man desirable for himself (and he must be

17–1237b 7 = *E.N.* 1156b 7–17, 33–1157a 12.

---

[1] *αὐτὸς ὁ φιλῶν* for *ἀντιφιλῶν* (W.D.R.).

[2] Cf. Hdt. ii. 68.

[3] *ἕως ἄν* (Jackson).

[4] a 7–b 1.

such; for the man to whom[1] one wishes good to happen for himself, one must also desire to exist), the genuine friend is also absolutely pleasant; hence any sort of friend is thought pleasant†; but here one ought rather to distinguish further, for[2] the subject needs reflection. Is what is good for one's self or what is good absolutely dear? and is actual loving attended with pleasure, so that the loved object is pleasant, or not? For the two must be harmonized. For what is not absolutely good, but perhaps[3] bad, is something to avoid, and what is not good for one's self is nothing to one; but what is sought is that the absolutely good should be good in the further sense of being good to the individual. For the absolutely good is absolutely desirable, but for each 1237a individual his own; and these must agree. Virtue brings about this agreement, and the political art exists to make them agree for those to whom as yet they do not. And one who is a human being[4] is ready and on the road for this (for by nature that which is absolutely good is good to him), and man rather than woman, and the gifted rather than the ungifted; but the road is through pleasure; the noble must be pleasant. But when these two disagree a man cannot yet be perfectly good, for incontinence may arise; for it is in the disagreement of the good with the pleasant in the passions that incontinence occurs.

So that since the primary friendship is grounded on virtue, friends of this sort will be themselves absolutely good, and this not because they are useful, but in another way. For good to the individual and the absolutely good are two, and as with the profitable so with habits. For the absolutely profitable differs from what is profitable to certain people, as[5] taking exercise does from taking drugs. So that the habit called human virtue is of two kinds, for we will assume man to be one of the things excellent by nature; therefore[6] the virtue of the naturally excellent is an absolute good, but the virtue of that which is not thus

[1] For ὡς read ᾧ (Spengel).
[2] ἔχει γὰρ ἐπίστασιν, πότερον τό γε (Erasmus).
[3] ἄν πως for ἁπλῶς (Jackson).
[4] ⟨ὁ⟩ ἄνθρωπος (Jackson).
[5] τοισδί, ὃν τρόπον for τὸ καλὸν τοιοῦτον (Jackson).
[6] ἄρα for γάρ (Sus.).

good only to it. Similarly, then, with the pleasant. For here one must pause and examine whether friendship can exist without pleasure, how such a friendship differs from other friendship, and on which of the two—goodness or pleasure—the loving depends, whether one loves a man because he is good even if not pleasant, and in any case not for his pleasantness. Now, loving having two senses,[1] does actual love seem to involve pleasure because activity is good? It is clear that just as in science what we have recently contemplated and learnt is most perceptible † because of its pleasantness †, so also is the recognition of the familiar, and the same account applies to both. Naturally, at least, the absolutely good is absolutely pleasant, and pleasant to those to whom it is good. From which it at once follows that like takes pleasure in like, and that nothing is so pleasant to man as man; and if this is so even before they are perfect, it is clear it must be so when they are perfected; and the good man is perfect. But if active loving is a mutual choice with pleasure in each other's acquaintanceship, it is clear that in general the primary friendship is a reciprocal choice of the absolutely good and pleasant because it is good and pleasant; and friendship itself[2] is the habit from which such choice springs. For its function is an activity, and this is not external, but in the one who feels love, but the function of every faculty is external; for it is in something different or in one's self *qua* different. Therefore to love is to feel pleasure, but not to be loved; † for to be loved is the activity of what is lovable, but to love is the activity of friendship also †; and the one is found only in the animate, the other also in the inanimate, for even inanimate things are loved. But since active loving is to treat the loved[3] *qua*
1237b loved, and the friend is loved by the friend *qua* friend and not *qua* musician or doctor, the pleasure coming from him merely as being himself is the pleasure of friendship; for he loves the object as himself and not for being something else.[4] So that if he does not rejoice in him for being good the primary friendship does not exist, nor should any of his

[1] Potential and actual love.
[2] αὐτὴ ἡ φιλία (St. G. Stock).
[3] τῷ φιλουμένῳ (Fritzsche).
[4] ἄλλο (Jackson).

incidental qualities hinder more than his goodness gives pleasure. For if[1] a man has an unpleasant odour he is left. For he must be content with goodwill without actual association.[2] This then is primary friendship, and all admit it to be friendship. It is through it that the other friendships seem friendships to some, but are doubted to be such by others. For friendship seems something stable, and this alone is stable. For a formed decision is stable, and where we do not act quickly or easily, we get the decision right. There is no stable friendship without confidence, but confidence needs time. One must then make trial, as Theognis says,[3] 'You cannot know the mind of man or woman till you have tried them as you might cattle.' Nor is a friend made except through time; they do indeed wish to be friends, and such a state easily passes muster as friendship. For when men are eager to be friends, by performing every friendly service to one another they think they not merely wish to be, but are friends. But it happens with friendship as with other things; as man is not in health merely because he wishes to be so, neither are men at once friends as soon as they wish to be friends. The proof is that men in this condition, without having made trial of one another, are easily made enemies; wherever each has allowed the other to test him, they are not easily made enemies; but where they have not, they will be persuaded whenever those who try to break up the friendship produce evidence. It is clear at the same time that this friendship does not exist between the bad, for the bad man feels distrust and is malignant to all, measuring others by himself. Therefore the good are more easily deceived unless experience has taught them distrust. But the bad prefer natural goods to a friend and none of them loves a man so much as things; therefore they are not friends. The proverbial 'community among friends' is not found among them; the friend is made a part of things, not things regarded as part of the friend. The primary friendship then is not found between

8–1238a 29 = *E. N.* 1156b 17–32.

---

[1] εἰ (Bekk.). [2] *ἀγαπητὸν γὰρ τὸ εὐνοεῖν* (W. D. R.) *συζῆν δὲ μή* (J. S.).
[3] Theog. 125.

many, for it is hard to test many men, for one would have to live with each. Nor should one choose a friend like a garment. Yet in all things it seems the mark of a sensible man to choose the better of two alternatives; and if one has used the worse garment for a long time and not the better, the better is to be chosen, but not in place of an old friend one of whom you do not know whether he is better.
1238a For a friend is not to be had without trial nor in a single day, but there is need of time and so 'the bushel of salt' has become proverbial. He must also be not merely good absolutely but good for you, if the[1] friend is to be a friend to you. For a man is good absolutely by being good, but a friend by being good for another, and absolutely good and friend when these two attributes are combined † so that what is absolutely good is good for the other, or else not absolutely good,[2] but good to another in the sense of useful.† But the need of active loving also prevents one from being at the same time a friend to many; for one cannot be active towards many at the same time.

From these facts then it is clear that it is correctly said that friendship is a stable thing, just as happiness is a thing sufficient in itself. It has been rightly said, 'for nature is stable but not wealth',[3] but it is still better to say 'virtue' than 'nature'; and Time is said to show the friend,[4] and bad fortune rather than good fortune. For then it is clear that the goods of friends are common (for these alone instead of things naturally good and evil—which are the matters with which good and bad fortune are concerned—choose a man rather than the existence of some of those things and the non-existence of others). But misfortune shows those who are not really friends, but friends only for some accidental utility. But time reveals both sorts; for even the useful man does not show his usefulness quickly, as the pleasant man does his pleasantness; yet the absolutely pleasant is not quick to show himself either. For men are like wines

[1] *εἰ ὁ* for *εἰ δή* (Bu.).

[2] *τοῦτο τῷ* for *τὸ τούτου* (Jackson), *ᾖ* for *εἰ* (Π²), *σπουδαῖος* for *σπουδαίῳ* (Fritzsche).

[3] Eur. *Elect.* 941.

[4] *ὅ τε* for *ὅτι* before *χρόνος*, *φίλον* for *φιλούμενον* (Jackson).

and meats; the pleasantness of them shows itself quickly, but if it continues longer it is unpleasant and not sweet, and so it is with men. For the absolutely pleasant[1] must be determined as such by the end it realizes and the time for which it continues pleasant. Even the vulgar would admit this, judging not[2] merely according to results but in the way in which, speaking of a drink, they call it sweeter. For this is unpleasant not[3] for the result but from not being continuous, though it deceives us at the start.

The first friendship then—by reason of which the others get the name—is that based on virtue and due to the pleasure of virtue, as has been said before;[4] the other kinds occur also in children, brutes, and bad men, whence the sayings, 'like is pleased with like' and 'bad adheres to bad from pleasure'.[5] And[6] the bad may be pleasant to one another, not *qua* bad or *qua* neither good nor bad, but (say) as both being musicians, or the one fond of music and the other a musician, and inasmuch as all have some good in them, and in this way they harmonize with one another. Further, they might be useful and profitable to one another, not absolutely but in relation to their purpose, in virtue of[7] 1238b
some neutral characteristic. Also a bad man may be a friend to a good,[8] the bad being of use to the good in relation to the good man's existing purpose, the good to the incontinent in relation to his existing purpose, and to the bad in relation to his natural purpose. And he will wish for his friend what is good, the absolutely good absolutely, and conditionally what is good for the friend, so far as poverty or illness is of advantage to him—and these for the sake of absolute goods; taking a medicine is an instance, for that no one wishes, but wishes only for some particular purpose. Further, a good man and a bad man may be friends in the way in which those not good might be friends to one another. A man might be pleasant, not as bad but as partaking in some common property, e.g. as being

[1] Omitting *καί* with the MSS.

[2] *οὐκ* (MSS.) for *ὅτι*.

[3] ⟨*οὐ*⟩ before *διά* (Jackson).

[4] Cf. 1236^b 2–1237^b 8.

[5] Eur. fr. 298 Nauck.

[6] *ἐνδέχεται δέ* (MSS.).

[7] *προαίρεσιν ᾗ* (W. D. R.).

[8] *τῷ ἐπιεικεῖ φαῦλον* (Bekker).

musical, or again, so far as there is something good in all (for which reason some might be glad to associate even with the good), or in so far as they suit each individual; for all have something of the good.

These then are three kinds of friendship; and in all 3
of them the word friendship implies a kind of equality. For even those who are friends through virtue are mutually friends by a sort of equality of virtue.

But another variety is the friendship of superiority to inferiority, e.g. as the virtue of a god is superior to that of a man (for this is another kind of friendship)—and in general that of ruler to subject; just as justice in this case is different, for here it is a proportional equality, not numerical equality. Into this class falls the relation of father to son and of benefactor to beneficiary; and there are varieties of these again, e.g. there is a difference between the relation of father to son, and of husband to wife, the latter being that of ruler to subject, the former that of benefactor to beneficiary. In these varieties there is not at all, or at least not in equal degree, the return of love for love. For it would be ridiculous to accuse God because the love one receives in return from him is not equal to the love given him, or for the subject[1] to make the same complaint against his ruler. For the part of a ruler is to receive not to give love, or at least to give love in a different way. And the pleasure is different, and[2] that of the man who needs nothing over his own possessions or child, and that of him who lacks over what comes to him, are not the same. Similarly also with those who are friends through use or pleasure, some are on an equal footing with each other, in others there is the relation of superiority and inferiority. Therefore those who think themselves to be on the former footing find fault if the other is not equally useful to and a benefactor of them; and similarly with regard to pleasure. This is obvious in the case of lover and beloved; for this is

15–1240a 4: cf. *M. M.* 1210a 6–22. 15–39 ≑ *E. N.* 1158b 1–19.

[1] ὁ ἀρχόμενος for καὶ ἀρχομένῳ (Bz.).
[2] καὶ ⟨ἡ⟩ ἡδονὴ διαφέρει, οὐδ᾽ ἐν (Jackson).

frequently a cause of strife between them. The lover does not perceive that the passion in each has not[1] the same reason; therefore Aenicus has said 'a beloved, not a lover, would say such things'.[2] But they think that there is the same reason for the passion of each.

4 There being, then, as has been said,[3] three kinds of 1239a
friendship—based on virtue, utility, and pleasantness—these again are subdivided each into two, one kind based on equality, the other on superiority. Both are friendships, but only those between whom there is equality are friends; it would be absurd for a man to be the friend of a child, yet certainly he loves and is loved by him. Sometimes the superior ought to be loved, but if he loves, he is reproached for loving one undeserving; for measurement is made by the worth of the friends and a sort of [i. e. proportional] equality. Some then, owing to inferiority in age, do not deserve to receive an equal love, and others because of virtue or birth or some other such superiority possessed by the other person. The superior ought to[4] claim either not to return the love or not to return it in the same measure, whether in the friendship of utility, pleasure, or virtue. Where the superiority is small, disputes naturally arise; for the small is in some cases of no account, e. g. in weighing wood, though not in weighing gold. But men judge wrongly what is small; for their own good by its nearness seems great, that of another by its distance small. But when the difference is excessive, then not even those affected seek to make out that their love should be returned or equally returned, e. g. as if a man were to claim this from God. It is clear then that men are friends when on an equality with each other, but we may have return of love without their being friends. And it is clear why men seek the friendship of superiority rather than that of equality; for in the

1–b 6 = *E. N.* 1158b 20–1159a 33. 17–19 = *E. N.* 1158b 33–1159a 5: cf. *M. M.* 1208b 29–31. 21–b 6 = *E. N.* 1159a 13–b 1: cf. *M. M.* 1210b 6–32.

[1] ἐστὶ τῆς προθυμίας (Fritzsche).
[2] διὸ εἴρηκεν Αἴνικος· ἐρώμενος τοιαῦτ' ἄν, οὐκ ἐρῶν λέγοι (Jackson).
[3] Cf. 1236a 7–1238b 15.
[4] δεῖ for ἀεί (Cook Wilson).

former they obtain both love and superiority. Therefore with some the flatterer is more valued than the friend, for he procures the appearance of both love and superiority for the object of his flattery. The ambitious are especially of this kind; for to be an object of admiration involves superiority. By nature some grow up loving, and others ambitious; the former is one who delights rather in loving than in being loved, the other is rather fond of honour. He, then, who delights in being loved and admired really loves superiority; the other, the loving, is fond of the pleasure of loving.[1] This by his mere activity of loving he must[2] have; for to be loved is an accident; one may be loved without knowing it, but not love. Loving, rather than being loved, depends on lovingness; being loved rather depends on the nature of the object of love. And here is a proof. The friend or lover would choose, if both were not possible, rather to know than to be known, as we see women do when allowing others to adopt their children,[3] e. g. Antiphon's Andromache. For wishing to be known seems to be felt on one's own account and in order to get, not to do, some good; but wishing to know is felt in order
1239b that one may do and love. Therefore we praise those who persist in their love towards the dead; for they know but are not known. That, then, there are several sorts of friendship, that they are three in number, and what are the differences between being loved and having love returned, and between friends on an equality and friends in a relation of superiority and inferiority, has now been stated.

But since 'friendly' is also used more universally, as was 5
indeed said at the beginning,[4] by those who take in extraneous considerations—some saying that the like is friendly, and some the contrary,—we must speak also of the relation of these friendships to those previously

6–1240a 7 = *E. N.* 1159b 10–24.

---

1 τῆς . . . ἡδονῆς (MSS.).
2 ἀνάγκῃ ἐνεργοῦντι for ἀνάγκη ἐνεργοῦντα (J. S.).
3 ὑποβολαῖς (Vict.); cf. Plat. *Rep.* 538 A and *Eth. Nic.* 1159a 28.
4 Cf. 1235a 4 sqq.

mentioned. The like is brought both under the pleasant and under the good, for the good is simple, but the bad various in form; and the good man is ever like himself and does not change in character; but the bad and the foolish are quite different in the evening from what they were in the morning. Therefore unless the bad come to some agreement, they are not friends to one another but are parted; but unstable friendship is not friendship. So thus the like is friendly, because the good is like; but it may also be friendly because of pleasure; for those like one another have the same pleasures, and everything too is by nature pleasant to itself. Therefore the voices, habits, and company of those of the same species are pleasantest to each side, even in the animals other than man; and in this way it is possible for even the bad to love one another: 'pleasure glues the bad to the bad.'[1]

But opposites are friendly through usefulness; for the like is useless to itself; therefore master needs slave, and slave master; man and wife need one another, and the opposite is pleasant and desired *qua* useful, not as included in the end but as a means towards it. For when a thing has obtained what it desires, it has reached its end and no longer desires the opposite, e. g. heat does not desire cold, nor dryness moisture. Yet in a sense the love of the contrary is love of the good; for the opposites desire one another because of the mean; they desire one another like tallies[2] because thus out of the two arises a single mean. Further, the love is accidentally of the opposite, but *per se* of the mean, for opposites desire not one another but the mean. For if over-chilled they return to the mean by being warmed, and if over-warmed by being chilled. And so with everything else. Otherwise they are ever desiring, never in the mean states; but that which is in the mean delights without desire in what is naturally pleasant, while the others delight in all that puts them out of their natural condition. This kind of relation then is found also among inanimate things; but love occurs when the relation is found among the living. Therefore some delight in what 1240a

[1] Cf. 1238a 34.

[2] Cf. Plat. *Symp.* 191 D.

is unlike themselves, the rigid in the witty, the energetic in the lazy; for they reduce each other to the mean state. Accidentally, then, as has been said,[1] opposites are friendly, because of the good.

The number then of kinds of friendship, and the different senses in which we speak of 'friends' and of persons as 'loving' and 'loved', both where this constitutes friendship and where it does not, have now been stated.

The question whether[2] a man is a friend to himself 6
or not requires much inquiry. For some think that every man is above all a friend to himself; and they use this friendship as a canon by which to test his friendship to all other friends. If we look to argument and to the properties usually thought characteristic of friends, then the two kinds of friendship are in some of these respects opposed to one another, but in others alike. For this friendship—that to oneself—is, in a way, friendship by analogy, not absolutely. For loving and being loved requires two separate individuals. Therefore a man is a friend to himself rather in the sense in which we have described[3] the incontinent and continent as willing or unwilling, namely in the sense that the parts of his soul are in a certain relation to each other; and all problems of this sort have a similar explanation, e. g. whether a man can be a friend or enemy to himself, and whether a man can wrong himself. For all these relations require two separate individuals; so far then as the soul is two, these relations can in a sense belong to it; so far as these two are not separate, the relations cannot belong to it.

By a man's attitude to himself the other modes of friendship, under which we are accustomed to consider friendship in this discourse, are[4] determined.[5] For a man seems to us a friend, who wishes the good or what he thinks to be such to some one, not on his own account but for the sake of that

8–b39 = *E.N.* 1166a 1–b29: cf. *M.M.* 1210b 33–1211a 5.

1 Cf. 1239b 32 sq.
2 δὲ τοῦ αὐτόν (τοῦ omitted accidentally by Susemihl).
3 Cf. 1223a 36–b17.
4 εἰσίν for ὡς (Speng., Jackson).
5 φίλον εἶναι ὡρισμένοι (Jackson).

other; or, in another way, if he wishes for another man existence—even if he is not bestowing goods, still less[1] existence—on that other's account and not on his own, he would seem most of all to be a friend to him.[2] And in yet another manner he would be a friend to him whom he wishes to live with merely for the sake of his company and for no other reason; thus fathers wish the existence of their sons, but prefer to live with others. Now[3] these various ways of friendship are discordant with one another. For some think they are not loved, unless the other wishes them this or that good,[4] some unless their existence or their society is desired. Further, to sorrow with the sorrowing, for no other reason than their sorrow, we shall regard as love (e. g. slaves towards their masters feel grief because their masters when in trouble are cruel to them, not for the sake of the masters themselves)—as mothers feel towards their children, and birds that share one another's pains. For the friend wants, if possible,[5] not merely to feel pain along with his friend, but to feel the same pain, e. g. to feel thirsty when he is thirsty, if that were possible, and if not,[6] then to feel a pain as like as possible. The same words are applicable to joy, which, if felt for no other reason than that the other feels joy, is a sign of friendship. Further, 1240b
we say about friendship such things as that friendship is equality, and true friends a single soul. All such phrases point back to the single individual; for a man wishes good to himself[7] in this fashion; for no one benefits himself for some further reason or speaks well of himself for a certain consideration, because his action is that of an individual;[8] for he who shows that he loves wishes not to love but to be thought to love.[9] And wishing the existence above all of the friend, living with him, sharing his joy and his

1–3 = *E. N.* 1168b 6–8.

[1] ⟨μήτοι⟩ for μὴ τῷ (Jackson).
[2] φίλος εἶναι for φιλεῖν (Jackson).
[3] δέ for δή (Spengel).
[4] τοδὶ αὐτοῖς for τὸ ἑαυτοῖς (Jackson).
[5] τε for γε (MSS.).
[6] εἴ τε μή (Jackson).
[7] αὑτῷ (Jackson).
[8] χάριν τοσοῦδε λέγει, ὅτι (Jackson).
[9] δοκεῖν γὰρ φιλεῖν βούλεται (Jackson).

grief, unity of soul with the friend, the impossibility of even living without one another, and the dying together are characteristic of a single individual. (For such is the condition of the individual and he is perhaps company to himself.) All these characters then[1] we find in the relation of the good man to himself. In the bad man, e. g. the incontinent, there is variance, and for this reason it seems possible for a man to be at enmity with himself; but so far as he is single and indivisible, he is an object of desire to himself.[2] Such is the good man, the man whose friendship is based on virtue, for the wicked man is not one but many, in the same day other than himself and fickle. So that a man's friendship for himself is at bottom friendship towards the good; for because a man is in a sense like himself,[3] single, and good for himself, so far he is a friend and object of desire to himself. And this is natural to man; but the bad man is unnatural. The good man never finds fault with himself at the moment of his act, like the incontinent, nor the later with the earlier man, like the penitent, nor the earlier with the later, like the liar. Generally, if it is necessary to distinguish as the sophists do, he is related to himself as 'Coriscus' to 'good Coriscus'.[4] †For it is clear that some identical portion of them is good†; for when they blame themselves, they kill themselves. But every one seems good to himself. But the man that is good absolutely, seeks to be a friend to himself, as has been said,[5] since he has within him two parts which by nature desire to be friends and which it is impossible to tear apart. Therefore in the case of man each is thought to be the friend of himself; but not so with the other animals; e. g. the horse is himself to himself . . .[6] therefore not a friend. Nor are children, till they have attained the power of deliberate choice; for already then the mind is at variance with the appetite. One's friendship to oneself resembles the friendship arising from kinship; for neither bond can be dissolved by one's own power; but, even if

[1] δή for δέ (Jackson).
[2] αὑτῷ for αὑτοῦ (MSS.).
[3] ὅμοιος (Bekker).
[4] Cf. *Soph. El.* c. 17.
[5] Cf. a13–21.
[6] A lacuna in the text.

they quarrel, the kinsmen remain kinsmen; and so the man remains one so long as he lives.

The various senses then of loving, and how all friendships reduce to the primary kind, is clear from what has been said.

7 It is appropriate to the inquiry to study agreement of 1241a
feeling and kindly feeling; for some identify these, and others think they cannot exist apart. Now kindly feeling is not altogether different from friendship, nor yet the same; for when we distinguish friendship according to its three sorts, kindly feeling is found neither in the friendship of usefulness nor in that of pleasure. For if one wishes well to the other because that is useful to one, one would be so wishing not for the object's sake, but for his own; but goodwill seems like . . .[1] to be not for the sake of[2] him who feels the goodwill, but for the sake of him towards whom it is felt. But[3] if goodwill existed in the friendship towards the pleasant, then men would feel goodwill towards things inanimate. So that it is clear that goodwill is concerned with the friendship that depends on character; but goodwill shows itself in merely wishing, friendship in also doing what one wishes. For goodwill is the beginning of friendship; every friend has goodwill, but not all who have goodwill are friends. He who has goodwill only is like a man at the beginning, and therefore it is the beginning of friendship, not friendship itself.

For friends seem to agree in feeling, and those who agree in feeling seem to be friends. Friendly agreement is not about all things, but only about things that may be done by those in agreement and what relates to their common life. Nor[4] is it agreement merely in thought or merely in desire, for it is possible to know one thing and desire the opposite,[5] as in the incontinent the motives disagree, nor if a man agrees with another in deliberate choice, does he

1–14 = *E.N.* 1166b 30–1167a 21: cf. *M.M.* 1211b 40–1212a 12.
15–33 = *E.N.* 1167a 22–b 16: cf. *M.M.* 1212a 13–27.

---

[1] A lacuna here, possibly 'virtuous friendship' (Sus.).
[2] ἕνεκα for εὔνοια (Jackson).
[3] δέ for δή (Π[2] Bekker).
[4] οὐδέ for οὔτε (coni. Susemihl).
[5] νοεῖν καὶ for τὸ κινοῦν.

necessarily agree in desire.[1] Agreement is only found in the case of good men; at least, bad men when they choose and desire the same things[2] harm one another. Agreement, like friendship, does not appear to have a single meaning; but still in its primary and natural form it is morally good; and so the bad cannot agree; the agreement of the bad, when they choose and desire the same things, is something different. And the two parties must so desire the same thing that it is possible for both to get what they desire;[3] for if they desire that which cannot belong to both, they will quarrel; but those in agreement will not quarrel. There is agreement when the two parties make the same choice as to who is to rule, who to be ruled, meaning by 'the same', not that each one should choose himself, but that both should choose the same person. Agreement is the friendship of fellow citizens. So much then about agreement and goodwill.

It is disputed why benefactors are more fond of the **8**
benefited than the benefited of their benefactors. The opposite seems to be just. One might suppose it happens from consideration of utility and what is profitable to oneself; for the benefactor has a debt due to him, while the benefited has to repay a debt. This, however, is not all; the reason is partly the general natural principle—activity
1241ᵇ is more desirable. There is the same relation between the effect and the activity, the benefited being as it were an effect or creation of the benefactor. Hence in animals their strong feeling for their children, both in begetting them and in preserving them afterwards. And so fathers love their children—and still more mothers—more than they are loved by them. And these again love their own children more than their parents, because nothing is so good as activity; in fact, mothers love more than fathers because they think the children to be more their own creation; for

34–^{b}11 = *E.N.* 1167^{b} 17–1168^{a} 27: cf. *M.M.* 1211^{b} 18–39.

---

[1] οὐδ' εἰ . . . ὁμονοεῖ (rc. Pᵇ).

[2] ταὐτά (Bekker).

[3] e.g. Charles V and Francis I did not 'agree'—as the former said—because both desired Milan.

the amount of work is measured by the difficulty, and the mother suffers more in birth. So much then for friendship towards oneself and among more than one.

9 But both justice seems to be a sort of equality and friendship also involves equality, if the saying is not wrong that 'love is equality'.[1] Now constitutions are all of them a particular form of justice; for a constitution is a partnership, and every partnership rests on justice, so that whatever be the number of species of friendship, there are the same of justice and partnership; these all border on one another, and the species of one have differences akin to those of the other. But since there is the same relation between soul and body, artisan and tool, and master and slave, between each of these pairs there is no partnership; for they are not two, but the first term in each is one, and the second a part of this one, but not itself one.[2] Nor is the good to be divided between the two, but that of both belongs to the one for the sake of which the pair exists. For the body is the soul's congenital tool, while the slave is as it were a part and detachable tool of the master, the tool being a sort of inanimate slave.

The other partnerships are a part of the civic partnership, e. g. those of the phratries and priestly colleges[3] or pecuniary partnerships.[4] All constitutions are found together in the household, both the true and the corrupt forms, for the same thing is true in constitutions[5] as of harmonies. The government of the children by the father is royal, the relation of husband and wife aristocratic, the relation of brothers that of a commonwealth; the corruption of these three are tyranny, oligarchy, and democracy. The forms of justice then are also so many in number.

But since equality is either numerical or proportional, there will be various species of justice, friendship, and

11–1242^b 1 = *E. N.* 1159^b 25–1162^a 33.

---

[1] Keeping ἤ.

[2] οὐ δ' ἕν for οὐδέν (Jackson).

[3] ὀργέων (L. and S. s.v. ὀργεών s. fin.) or ὀργεώνων (Dietsche).

[4] Omit ἔτι πολιτεῖαι as dittography (Fr.).

[5] Omit τῶν (Spengel). For the sense cf. *Pol.* 1342^a 24.

partnership ; on numerical equality rests the commonwealth,[1] and the friendship of comrades—both being measured by the same standard, on proportional the aristocratic (which is best),[2] and the royal. For the same thing is not just for the superior and the inferior; what is proportional is just. Such is the friendship between father and child; and the same sort of thing may be seen in partnerships.

1242a We speak of friendships of kinsmen, comrades, partners, 10
the so-called 'civic friendship'. That of kinsmen has more than one species, that of brothers, that of father and sons. There is the friendship based on proportion, as that of the father to his children, and that based on mere number, e. g. that of brothers, for this latter resembles the friendship of comrades; for here too age gives certain privileges. Civic friendship has been established mainly in accordance with utility; for men seem to have come together because each is not sufficient for himself, though they would have come together anyhow for the sake of living in company. Only the civic friendship and its parallel corruption are not merely friendships, but the partnership is that of friends;[3] other friendships rest on the relation of superiority. The justice belonging to the friendship of those useful to one another is pre-eminently justice, for it is civic or political justice. The concurrence of the saw and the art that uses it is of another sort; for it is not for some end common to both—it is like instrument and soul—but for the sake of the user. It is true that the tool itself[4] receives attention, and it is just that it should receive it, for its function, that is; for it exists for the sake of its function. And the essence of a gimlet is twofold, but more properly it is its activity, namely boring. In this class come the body and a slave, as has been said before.[5]

To inquire, then, how to behave to a friend is to look for a particular kind of justice, for generally all justice is in

[1] Dispensing with Susemihl's addition of δημοκρατική.
[2] ἡ ἀρίστη (W. D. R.).
[3] Cf. 1239a 4, 5.
[4] αὐτὸ τό for τοῦτο (Bz.).
[5] Cf. 1241b 17–24.

relation to a friend. For justice involves a number of individuals who are partners, and the friend is a partner either in family or in one's scheme of life. For man is not merely a political but also a household-maintaining animal, and his unions are not, like those of the other animals, confined to certain times, and formed with any chance partner, whether male or female; but in a special sense man is not a lonely being,[1] but has a tendency to partnership with those to whom he is by nature akin. There would, then, be partnership and a kind of justice, even if there were no State; and the household is a kind of friendship; the relation, indeed, of master and servant is that of an art and its tools, a soul and its body; and these are not friendships, nor forms of justice, but something similar to justice; just as health is not justice, but something similar. But the friendship of man and wife is a friendship based on utility, a partnership; that of father and son is the same as that of God to man, of the benefactor to the benefited, and in general of the natural ruler to the natural subject. That of brothers to one another is eminently that of comrades, inasmuch as it involves equality[2]—'for I was not declared a bastard brother to him; but the same Zeus, my king, was called the father of both of us.'[3] For this is the language of men that seek equality. Therefore in the household first we 1242b
have the sources and springs of friendship, of political organization, and of justice.

But since there are three sorts of friendship, based on virtue, utility, and pleasantness respectively, and two varieties of each of these—for each of them may imply either superiority or equality—and the justice involved in these is clear from the debates that have been held on it, in a friendship between superior and inferior the claim for proportion takes different forms, the superior's claim being one for inverse proportion, i. e. as he is to the inferior, so should what he receives from the inferior be to what the inferior

2–21 = *E. N.* 1162a 34–b4, 1163a 24–b27.

[1] *ἀλλ' ἰδίᾳ οὐ μοναυλικόν* for the gibberish *ἀλλ' αἱ διὰ δύμον αὐλικόν* (Speng.).

[2] *ᾗ κατ' ἰσότητα* (Jackson).

[3] Soph. Fr. 684 Nauck.

receives from him, he being in the position of ruler to subject; if he cannot get that, he demands at least numerical equality. For so it is in the other associations, the two members enjoying an equality sometimes of number, sometimes of ratio. For if they contributed numerically equal sums of money, they divide an equal amount, and by an equal number; if not equal sums, then they divide proportionally. But the inferior inverts this proportion and joins crosswise.[1] But in this way the superior would seem to come off the worse, and friendship and partnership to be a gratuitous burden. Equality must then be restored and proportion created by some other means; and this means is honour, which by nature belongs to a ruler or god in relation to a subject. The profit and the honour must be equated.

But civic friendship is that resting on equality; it is based on utility; and just as cities are friends to one another, so in the like way are citizens. 'The Athenians no longer know the Megarians';[2] nor do citizens one another, when they are no longer useful to one another, and the friendship is merely a temporary one for a particular exchange of goods.[3] There is here, too, the relation of ruler and subject which is neither the natural relation, nor that involved in kingship, but each is ruler and ruled in turn; nor is it either's purpose to act with the free beneficence of a god,[4] but that he may share equally in the good and in the burdensome service. Civic friendship, then, claims to be one based on equality. But of the friendship of utility there are two kinds, the strictly legal and the moral. Civic friendship looks to equality and to the object as sellers and buyers do; hence the proverb 'a fixed wage for a friend'. When, then, friendship proceeds by contract, it is of the civic and strictly legal kind;[5] but when each of the two parties

21–1243^{b} 14 = *E. N.* 1162^{b} 16–1163^{a} 23.

---

[1] i. e. he claims that *A*'s receipt shall not be to *B*'s as *A*'s contribution to *B*'s, but as *B*'s contribution to *A*'s.

[2] *Fr. eleg.* adesp. 6 Bergk.

[3] Cf. *E. N.* 1162^{b} 26.

[4] ποιῇ ὡς ὁ θεός (ὡς omitted by mistake in Susemihl).

[5] Reading καθ' ὁμολογίαν ᾖ, πολιτικὴ αὕτη φιλία καὶ νομική (Fr. and apparently the Vetus Versio).

leaves the return for his services to be fixed by the other, we have the moral friendship, that of comrades. Therefore recrimination is very frequent in this sort of friendship; and the reason is that it is unnatural; for friendships based on utility and based on virtue are different; but these wish to have both together, associating together really for the sake of utility, but representing their friendship as moral, like that of good men; pretending to trust one another they 1243a
make out their friendship to be not merely legal. For in general there are more recriminations in the useful friendship than in either of the other two (for virtue is not given to recrimination, and pleasant friends having got what they wanted, and given what they had, are done with it; but useful friends do not dissolve their association at once, if their relations are not merely legal but those of comrades); still the legal form of useful friendship is free from recrimination. The legal association is dissolved by a money-payment (for it measures equality in money), but the moral is dissolved by voluntary consent. Therefore in some countries the law forbids lawsuits for voluntary transactions between those who associate thus as friends, and rightly; for good men do not go to law[1] with one another; and such as these have dealings with one another as good men themselves, and dealing with men who can be trusted.[2] In this kind of friendship it is uncertain how either will recriminate on the other, seeing that they trust each other, not in a limited legal way but on the basis of their characters.

It is a further problem on which of two grounds we are to determine what is just, whether by looking to the amount of the service rendered, or to what was its character for the recipient; for, to borrow the language of Theognis,[3] the service may be 'Small to thee, O goddess, but great to me'. Or the opposite may happen, as in the saying, 'this is sport to you but death to me.' Hence, as we have said,[4] come recriminations. For the benefactor claims a return on the

[1] δίκῃ for δίκαιον (J. S.). [2] πιστοῖς (Jackson). [3] Theog. 14.
[4] Reading ὥσπερ εἴρηται (coni. Fritzsche), or possibly εἴρηται alone may bear this sense. The reference is to 1242b 37.

ground of having done a great service, because he has done it at the request of the other, or with some other plea of the great value of the benefit to the other's interest, saying nothing about what it was to himself; while the recipient insists on its value to the benefactor, not on its value to himself. †Sometimes the receiver inverts the position,† insisting how little the benefit has turned out to him, while the doer insists on its great magnitude[1] to *him*, e.g. if at considerable risk one has benefited another to the extent of a drachma, the one insists on the greatness of the risk, the other on the smallness of the money, just as in the repayment of money—for there the dispute is on this point—the one claims the value of it when it was lent, the other concedes only the value of it now when it is returned, unless they have made an explicit provision in the contract. Civic friendship, then, looks to the agreement and the thing, moral friendship to the purpose; here then we have more truly justice, and a friendly justice. The reason of the quarrel is that moral friendship is more noble, but useful friendship more necessary; men come,[2] then, proposing to be moral friends, i.e. friends through virtue; but when some private interest stands in the way,[3] they show clearly they were not so. For the multitude aim at the noble only when they
1243b have plenty of everything else; and at noble friendship similarly. So that it is clear what distinctions should be drawn in these matters. If the two are moral friends, we must look to see if the purpose of each is equal; and then nothing more should be claimed by either from the other. But if their friendship is of the useful or civic kind, we must consider what would have been profitable lines for an agreement. And if one declares that they are friends on one basis, but the other on the other, it is not honourable, if one ought to *do* something in return, merely to use fine language; and so too, in the other case,[4] but since they have not

[1] Omit *μέγα* as a gloss (J. S.). [2] *ἔρχονται* (P[b] Bekker).
[3] *ἀντικρούσῃ* for *ἄντικρυς ᾖ* (Jackson).
[4] i.e. if it really was a business agreement, it is not honourable for one party to get off by saying it was a 'moral' friendship; and if it really was a 'moral' friendship, it is not honourable for one party to claim a return as if it had been a business agreement.

declared their friendship a moral friendship, some one[1] must be made judge, so that neither cheats the other by a false pretence; and so each must put up with his luck. But that moral friendship is based on purpose is clear, since even if after receiving great benefits one does not repay them through inability, but repays only to the extent of his ability, he acts honourably; and God is satisfied at getting sacrifices as good as our power allows. But a seller of goods will not be satisfied if the buyer says he cannot pay more; nor will a lender of money.

Recriminations are common in dissimilar friendships, where[2] action and reaction are not in the same straight line; and it is not easy to see what is just. For it is hard to measure by just this one unit different directions; we find this in the relation of lovers, for there the one pursues the other as the one pleasant person,[3] in order to live with him, while the latter seeks the other at times for his utility. When the love is over, one changes as the other changes. Then they calculate the *quid pro quo*;[4] thus Python and Pammenes quarrelled; and so in general do teacher[5] and pupil (for knowledge and money have no common measure), and so Herodicus the doctor quarrelled with a patient who paid him only a small fee; such too was the case of the king and the lyre-player; the former regarded his associate as pleasant, the latter his as useful; and so the king, when he had to pay, chose to regard himself as an associate of the pleasant kind, and said that just as the player had given him pleasure by singing, so he had given the player pleasure by his promise. But it is clear here too how one should decide; the measurement must be by one measure, only here not by a number[6] but by a ratio; we must measure by proportion, just as one measures in the associations of citizens. For how is a cobbler to have dealings with a farmer

15–38 = *E. N.* 1163^b 28–1164^b 21: cf. *M. M.* 1210^a 24–^{b}6.

---

[1] Reading *τινά* (Bekker). [2] *ταῖς* for *τοῖς* (Bz.).
[3] Keeping *τόν* with the MSS.
[4] *τί ἀντὶ τίνος* for the MSS. reading *παντί τινος* (Jackson).
[5] Reading *καὶ ὅλως διδάσκαλος* (MSS.).
[6] *οὐκ ἀριθμῷ* for *οὐχ ὅρῳ* (Jackson).

unless one equates the work of the two by proportion? so to all whose exchanges are not of the same for the same, proportion is the measure, e.g. if the one complains that he has given wisdom, and the other that he has given money, we must measure first the ratio of wisdom to wealth,[1] and then what has been given for each. For if the one gives half of the lesser, and the other does not give even a small fraction of the greater object, it is clear that the latter does injustice. Here, too, there may be a dispute at the start, if one party pretends they have come together for use, and the other denies this and alleges that they have met from some other kind of friendship.

1244a As regards the good man who is loved for his virtue, we must consider whether we ought to render useful services and help to him, or to one who makes a return and has power. This is the same problem as whether we ought rather to benefit a friend or a virtuous man. For if a man is both virtuous and a friend,[2] there is perhaps no great difficulty, if one does not exaggerate the one quality and minimize the other, making him very much of a friend, but not much of a good man. But in other cases many problems arise, e.g. if the one has been [3] but will no longer remain so, and the other will be but is not yet what he is going to be, or the one was but is not, and the other is but has not been and will not be. But the other [4] is a harder question. For perhaps Euripides is right in saying, 'A word is your just pay for a word,[5] but a deed for him who has given deeds.'[6] And one must not do everything for one's father, but there are some things also one should do for one's mother, though a father is the better of the two. For, indeed, even to Zeus we do not sacrifice all things, nor does he have all honours but only some. Perhaps, then, there are things which should be rendered to the useful friend and others to the good one; e.g. because a man gives you II

1–36 = *E.N.* 1164b 22–1165a 35.

[1] τί σοφία πρὸς τὸν πλοῦτον (J. S.).
[2] Reading ἂν μὲν γὰρ φίλος (MSS.).
[3] Perhaps understand φίλος.
[4] Cf. l. a 2.
[5] Reading λόγον . . . λόγου (Bekk.).
[6] Fr. 882 Nauck.

food and what is necessary, you need not give him your society; nor, therefore, need you give the man to whom you grant your society that which not he but the useful friend[1] gives. †Those who doing this give all to the object of their love, when they ought not, are worthless.†

And the various definitions of friendship that we give in our discourse all belong to friendship in some sense, but not to the same friendship. To the useful friend applies the fact that one wishes what is good for him, and to a benefactor, and in fact to any[2] kind of friend—for this definition does not distinguish the class of friendship; to another we should wish existence, of another we should wish the society, to the friend on the basis of pleasure sympathy in joy and grief is the proper gift. All these definitions are appropriate to some friendship, but none to a single unique thing, friendship. Hence there are many definitions, and each appears to belong to a single unique thing, viz. friendship, though really it does not, e.g. the purpose to maintain the friend's existence. For the superior friend and benefactor wishes the existence of that which he has made, and to him who has given one existence one ought to give it in return, but not necessarily one's society; that gift is for the pleasant friend.

Some friends wrong one another; they love rather the things than the possessor of them; and so they love the persons much as they choose wine because it is pleasant, or wealth because it is useful; for wealth is more useful than its owner. Therefore the owner is indignant,[3] as if the other had preferred his wealth to him as to something inferior. But the other side complain in turn; for they now look to find in him a good man, when before they looked for one pleasant or useful.

12 We must also consider about independence and friendship, 1244^b
and the relations they have to one another. For one might doubt whether, if a man be in all respects independent, he

1–1245^b 19 = *E.N.* 1169^b 3–1170^b 19: cf. *M.M.* 1212^b 24–1213^b 2, *E.N.* 1171^a 21–^{b}28.

[1] ⟨ὁ⟩ χρήσιμος (coni. Susemihl).

[2] ὁποίῳ δὴ for ὁποῖος δέ (Jackson).

[3] διὸ δὴ ἀγανακτεῖ (rc. P^b).

will have a friend, if one seeks a friend from want and the good man[1] is perfectly independent.[2] If the possessor of virtue is happy, why should he need a friend? For the independent man neither needs useful people nor people to cheer him, nor society; his own society is enough for him. This is most plain in the case of a god; for it is clear that, needing nothing, he will not need a friend, nor have one, supposing that he does not need one.[3] So that the happiest man will least need a friend, and only as far as it is impossible for him to be independent. Therefore the man who lives the best life must have fewest friends, and they must always be becoming fewer, and he must show no eagerness for men to become his friends, but despise not merely the useful but even men desirable for society. But surely this makes it all the clearer that the friend is not for use or help, but that the friend through virtue[4] is the only friend. For when we need nothing, then we all seek others to share our enjoyment, those whom we may benefit rather than those who will benefit us. And we judge better when independent than when in want, and most of all we then seek friends worthy to be lived with. But as to this problem, we must see if we have not been partially right, and partially missed the truth owing to our illustration.[5] It will be clear if we ascertain what is life in its active sense and as end. Clearly, it is perception and knowledge, and therefore life in society is perception and knowledge in common. And mere perception and mere knowledge[6] is most desirable to every one, and hence the desire of living is congenital in all; for living must be regarded as a kind of knowledge. If then we were to cut off and abstract mere knowledge and its opposite—this passes unnoticed in the argument as we have given it, but in fact need not remain unnoticed—there would be no difference between this and another's knowing instead

[1] *ἀγαθός* (W.D.R.).

[2] Reading a comma after *φίλος*, l. 3, and a full-stop after *αὐταρκέστατος*.

[3] *εἴ γε μηθὲν δέοιτό του* (Jackson).

[4] *ἀλλ' ὁ δι' ἀρετήν* (Aldine, Bekker).

[5] Of the case of man from that of God: cf. 1245b 13 sqq.

[6] *αὐτὸ τό* for MS. *τὸ αὐτό bis* (J.S.).

of oneself; and this is like another's living instead of oneself.[1] But[2] naturally the perception and knowledge of oneself is more desirable. For we must take two things into consideration, that life is desirable and also the good, and thence that it is desirable that such a nature should belong to oneself[3] as belongs to them. If, then, of such a pair of corresponding 1245a
series[4] there is always one series of the desirable, and the known and the perceived are in general constituted by their participation in the nature of the determined,[5] .... so that to wish to perceive one's self is to wish oneself to be of a certain definite character,—since, then, we are not in ourselves possessed of each of such characters, but only by participation in these qualities in perceiving and knowing—for the perceiver becomes perceived in that way and in that respect in which he first perceives, and according to the way in which and the object which he perceives; and the knower becomes known in the same way—therefore it is for this reason that one always desires to live, because one always desires to know; and this is because he himself wishes to be the object known. The choice to live with others might seem, from a certain point of view, silly—(first, in the case of things common also to the other animals, e. g. eating together, drinking together; for what is the difference between doing these things in the neighbourhood of others or apart from them, if you take away speech? But even to share in speech of a casual kind does not make the case different. Further, for friends who are self-dependent neither teaching nor learning is possible; for if one learns, he is not as he should be: and if he teaches, his friend is not; and likeness is friendship)—but surely it is obviously so, and all of us find greater pleasure in sharing good things with friends as far as these come to[6] each—I mean the greatest good one can share; but to some it falls to share in bodily delights, to others in artistic contemplation, to others in philosophy. And the friend must be present

[1] τῷ for τοῦ.
[2] δέ (MSS.) for δή.
[3] αὑτοῖς for αὐτὸ τοῖς (Bz.).
[4] As that of the Pythagoreans, One, Good &c. X Many, Bad &c.
[5] τὸ ὡρισμένον belonging to the 'desirable' series of the συστοιχία or pair of series.
[6] ἑκάστῳ for ἕκαστον (W.D.R.).

too; whence the proverb, 'distant friends are a burden', so that men must not be at a distance from one another when there is friendship between them. Hence sensuous love seems like friendship; for the lover aims at the society of his beloved, but not as ideally he ought, but in a merely sensuous way.

The argument, then, says what we have before mentioned, raising difficulties; but the facts are as we saw later, so that it is clear that the objector is in a way misleading us. We must see the truth from this: a friend wants to be, in the words of the proverb, 'another Heracles', 'a second self': but he is severed from his friend, and it is hard to find in two people the characteristics of a single individual. But though a friend is by nature what is[1] most akin to his friend, one man is like another in body, and another like him in soul, and one like him in one part of the body or soul, and another like him in another. But none the less[2] does a friend wish to be as it were a separate self. Therefore to perceive a friend must be in a way to perceive one's self and to know one's self.[3] So that even the vulgar forms of pleasure and life in the society of a friend are naturally pleasant (for perception of the friend always takes place at the same time), but still more the communion in the diviner pleasures. And the reason is, that it is always pleasanter
1245b to see one's self enjoying the superior good. And this is sometimes a passion, sometimes an action, sometimes something else. But if it is pleasant for a man himself to live well and also his friend, and in their common life to engage in mutually helpful activity, their partnership surely would be above all in things included in the end. Therefore men should contemplate in common and feast in common, only not on the pleasures of food or on necessary pleasures; such society does not[4] seem to be true society, but sensuous enjoyment. But the end which each can attain is that in which he desires the society of another; if that is not possible, men desire to benefit and be benefited by friends in preference to others. That society then is right, that all

[1] ὅ (MSS.) for τό.
[2] γε for τε (Sylburg).
[3] Omitting τὸν φίλον γνωρίζειν τό.
[4] ⟨ὁμιλίαι γὰρ οὐχ⟩ (Sus.).

wish it above all things, and that the happiest and best man tends especially to do so, is clear. But that the contrary appeared as the conclusion of the argument was also reasonable, since the argument said what was true. For it is in respect of the comparison of the two cases [1] that the solution is found,[2] the case compared being in itself truly enough stated. For because God is not such as to need a friend, the argument claims [3] the same of the man who resembles God. But by this reasoning the virtuous man will not even think; for the perfection of God is not in this, but in being superior to thinking of aught beside himself. The reason is, that with us welfare involves a something beyond us, but the deity is his own well-being.

As to our seeking and praying for many friends, while we say that the man who has many friends has no friend, both are correct. For if it is possible to live with and share the perceptions of many at the same time, it is most desirable that these should be as numerous as possible; but since this is most difficult, the activity of joint perception must exist among fewer. So that it is not only hard to get many friends—for probation is necessary—but also to use them when you have got them.

Sometimes we wish the object of our love to be happy away from us, sometimes to share the same fortune as ourselves; the wish to be together is characteristic of friendship. For if the two can both be together and be happy, all choose this; but if they cannot be both, then we choose as [4] the mother of Heracles might have chosen, e. g. that her son should be a god rather than in her company but a serf to Eurystheus. One might say something like the jesting remark [5] of the Laconian,[6] when some one bade him in a storm to summon the Dioscuri.

15–19: cf. *M. M.* 1212b 37–1213b 4. 20–1246a 25: cf. *M. M.* 1213b 3–17, 1245b 20–5 = *E. N.* 1170b 20–1171a 20. 26–1246a 25 = *E. N.* 1171a 21–b28.

---

[1] Cf. 1244b 7. [2] Omitting οὐκ. [3] ἀξιοῖ (Bz.).

[4] μὴ ἐνδεχομένου δὲ ἅμα, ὥσπερ (Jackson).

[5] ὅ for ὅν (Jackson).

[6] He doubtless said that being in trouble himself he did not wish to involve the Dioscuri in it.

It appears to be the mark of one who loves to keep the object of his love from sharing in hardships, but of the beloved to wish to share them; the conduct of both is reasonable. For nothing ought to be so painful to a friend as his friend should be pleasant to him,[1] but it is thought that he ought not to choose what is for his own interest. Therefore men keep their friends from participation in their calamities; their own suffering is enough, that they may
1246a not show themselves studying their own interest, and choosing joy at the cost of a friend's pain, or relief by not bearing their troubles alone. But since both well-being and participation are desirable, it is clear that participation with a smaller good is more desirable than to enjoy a greater good in solitude. But since the weight to be attached to participation is not ascertained, men differ, and some think that participation in all things at once is the mark of friendship, e.g. they say that it is better to dine together than separately, though having the same food: others wish them to share prosperity,[2] since (they say) if[3] one takes extreme cases, great adversity in company is on a par[4] with great prosperity enjoyed alone. We have something similar in the case of ill-fortune. For sometimes we wish our friends to be absent and we wish to give them no pain, when they are not going to be of any use to us; at another time we find it pleasantest for them to be present. But this contradiction is quite reasonable. For this happens in consequence of what we have mentioned above,[5] and because we often simply avoid the sight of a friend in pain or in bad condition, as we should the sight of ourselves so placed; yet to see a friend is as pleasant as anything can be (because of the above-mentioned[6] cause), and, indeed,[7] to see him ill is pleasant if you are ill yourself. So that whichever of these two is the pleasanter decides us whether to wish the friend present or not. This also happens, for the same reason, in the case of the worse sort of men; for they are most

[1] *ὡς ἡδὺ τὸν φίλον* (MSS.).
[2] *οἱ δ' ἅμα* (Spengel) *μὲν τοῦ εὖ βούλονται* (Jackson).
[3] *ἐπειδὴ εἰ* (Jackson).
[4] *ὁμολόγους εἶναι ἅμα* (Jackson).
[5] Cf. 1245b 26–1246a 1.
[6] Cf. 1245a 26–b9.
[7] *μήν* for *μή*.

anxious that their friends should not fare well nor even exist if they themselves have to fare badly.[1] Therefore some kill the objects of their love with themselves. For they think that if the objects of their love are to survive they perceive their own trouble more acutely, just as one who remembered that once he had been happy would feel it more than if he thought himself to be always unhappy.

13 Here one might raise a question. One can use each thing both for its natural purpose and otherwise, and either *per se* or again[2] *per accidens*, as, for instance, one might use the eye, as eye,[3] for seeing, and also for falsely seeing by squinting, so that one thing appears as two. Both these uses are due to the eye being an eye, but it was possible to use the eye in another way—*per accidens*,[4] e. g. if one could sell or eat it. Knowledge may be used similarly[5]; it is possible to use it really or to do what is wrong, e. g. when a man voluntarily writes incorrectly, to make knowledge into ignorance for the time, as dancing-girls sometimes exchange the uses of the hand and the foot,[6] and use the foot as a hand and the hand as a foot. If, then, all the virtues are kinds of knowledge, one might use justice also as injustice, and so one would be unjust and do unjust actions from justice, as ignorant things may be done from knowledge. But if this is impossible, it is clear that the 1246b
virtues are not species of knowledge. And even if ignorance cannot proceed from knowledge, but only error and the doing of the same things as[7] proceed from ignorance, it must be remembered that from justice one will not act as from injustice. But since Prudence[8] is knowledge and something true, it may behave like knowledge;[9] one might act imprudently though possessed of prudence, and commit the errors of the imprudent. But if the use of each thing[10]

[1] *ἂν ἀνάγκη αὑτοῖς κακῶς* (W. D. R.).
[2] *ᾗ αὐτὸ ἢ αὖ* (Jackson).
[3] *οἷον ᾗ ὀφθαλμός* (Jackson).
[4] *ὅτι μὲν ὀφθαλμός ἐστιν, ᾗν δ' ὀφθαλμῷ, ἄλλῃ δέ, κατὰ συμβεβηκός* (Jackson).
[5] *ἐπιστήμῃ* (Spengel).
[6] *μεταστρέψασαι τὴν χεῖρα καὶ ⟨τὸν πόδα⟩* (Jackson).
[7] Omitting *ἅ*.
[8] 'Prudence' as usual = moral wisdom.
[9] *κἀκείνη* (MSS.).
[10] *ἡ ἑκάστου χρεία* (MSS.).

as such were single,[1] then in so acting men would still be acting prudently. Over other kinds of knowledge, then, there is something superior that diverts them; but how can there be any knowledge that diverts the highest knowledge of all? There is no longer any knowledge or intuitive reason to do this. But neither can virtue do it, for prudence *uses* that; for the virtue of the ruling part uses that of the subject. Who is there then whose prudence is thus diverted? Perhaps the position is like that of incontinence, which is said to be a vice of the irrational part of the soul. The incontinent man is in a sense[2] intemperate; he has reason, but supposing appetite to be strong it will twist him and he will draw the opposite conclusion. Or is it an obvious consequence[3] that, similarly, if there is virtue in the irrational part, but folly[4] in the rational, they are transformed in yet another way.[5] Thus it will be possible to use justice unjustly[6] and badly, and prudence foolishly—and therefore the opposite uses will also be possible. For it is absurd that vice occurring sometimes in the irrational part should twist the virtue in the rational part and make the man ignorant, but that virtue in the irrational part,[7] when folly[8] is present[9] in the rational, should not divert the latter and make the man judge prudently and as is right, and again, prudence in the rational part should not make the intemperance in the irrational part act temperately. This seems the very essence of continence. And therefore we shall also get prudent action arising out of ignorance. But all these consequences are absurd, especially that of acting prudently out of ignorance, for we certainly do not see this[10] in any other case, e. g. intemperance perverts[11] one's medical or grammatical knowledge. But at any rate we may say that not[12] ignorance, if opposite, (for[13] it has no superiority), but virtue, is rather related in this way to vice in general. For whatever the unjust[14] can do, the just can do;

[1] It was shown in a28–30 that it is not.
[2] πως (Jackson).
[3] ἦ ἔστι δῆλον (Jackson).
[4] ἄνοια (MSS.).
[5] ἑτέρᾳ (Jackson).
[6] τ' οὐ for τό (Jackson).
[7] ⟨ἡ⟩ ἐν τῷ ἀλόγῳ (Jackson).
[8] ἀνοίας (MSS.).
[9] ⟨ἐν τῷ λογιστικῷ⟩ (Susemihl).
[10] οὐδαμῶς (MSS.).
[11] Omit οὐ.
[12] οὐ for ὁ (Jackson).
[13] διό in Susemihl is a misprint for διά.
[14] καὶ γὰρ ἃ ὁ ἄδικος πάντα ὁ δίκαιος δύναται (Jackson).

and in general powerlessness is covered by power. And so it is clear that prudence and virtue go together, and that those complex states are states of one in whom prudence and virtue are not combined,[1] and the Socratic saying that nothing is stronger than prudence is right. But when Socrates said this of knowledge he was wrong. For prudence is virtue and not scientific knowledge, but another kind of cognition.

14 But since not only prudence and virtue produce well-doing, but we say also that the fortunate 'do well', thus assuming that good fortune produces well-doing and the 1247a
same results as knowledge,[2] we must inquire whether it is or is not by nature that one man is fortunate, another not, and what is the truth about these things. For that there are fortunate men we see, who though silly are often successful in matters controlled by fortune, some also[3] in matters involving art but into which chance largely enters, e.g. strategy and navigation. Does their success, then, arise from some acquired mental condition, or do they effect fortunate results not because of their own acquired qualities at all (at present men take the latter view, regarding them as having some special natural endowment); does nature, rather, make men with different qualities so that they differ from birth; as some are blue-eyed and some black-eyed because they have some particular part[4] of a particular nature, so are some lucky and others unlucky? For that they do not succeed through prudence is clear, for prudence is not irrational but can give a reason why it acts as it does; but they could not say why they succeed; that would be art. Further, it is clear that they succeed though imprudent,[5] and not merely imprudent about other things —that would not be strange at all, e.g. Hippocrates was a geometer, but in other respects was thought foolish and imprudent, and once on a voyage was robbed of much money by the customs-collectors at Byzantium, owing to his silliness, as we are told—but imprudent in the very

[1] ἀγαθοί, ἐκεῖναι δ' ἄλλου ἕξεις (Jackson).
[2] τῇ ἐπιστήμῃ for τῆς ἐπιστήμης (Speng.)
[3] οἱ δὲ καί (Bekker).
[4] τῷ τοδὶ τοιονδὶ ἔχειν (J. S.).
[5] ὅτι δέ, φανερόν, ὄντες ἄφρονες (Jackson).

business in which they are lucky. For in navigation not the cleverest are the most fortunate, but it is as in throwing dice, where one throws nothing, another throws something; so a man is lucky according as nature determines.[1] Or is it because he is loved, as the phrase is, by a god, success being something coming from without, as a worse-built vessel often sails better, not owing to itself but because it has a good pilot? But, if so, the[2] fortunate man has a good pilot, namely, the divinity. But it is absurd that a god or divinity should love such a man and not the best and most prudent. If, then, success must be due either to nature or intelligence[3] or some sort of protection, and the latter two causes are out of the question, then the fortunate must be so by nature. But, on the other hand, Nature is the cause of the absolutely uniform or of the usual, Fortune the opposite. If, then, it is thought that unexpected success is due to chance, but that, if it *is* through chance that one is fortunate, the cause of his fortune is not the sort of cause that produces always or usually the same result[4]—further, if a person succeeds or fails because he is a certain sort of man, just as a man sees badly because he is blue-eyed, then it follows that not fortune but nature is the cause; the man then is not fortunate but rather naturally gifted. So we must say that the people we call fortunate are not so through
1247b fortune; therefore they are not fortunate, for those goods only are in the disposal of fortune of which good fortune is the cause.

But if this is so, shall we say that fortune does not exist at all, or that it exists but is not a cause? No, it must both exist and be a cause. It will, then, also cause good or evil to certain people. But whether it is to be wholly removed, and we *ought* to say that nothing happens by chance, but *do* say that chance is a cause simply because, though there is some other cause, we do not see it (and therefore, in defining chance, some make it a cause incalculable to human reasoning, taking it to be a genuine reality)—this would be

[1] Omitting πολύ (MSS.) and reading καθὰ ἦν φύσει (Jackson).
[2] οὕτως ὁ (Sus.).
[3] νῷ (Jackson).
[4] Colon after πολύ (W. D. R.).

matter for another inquiry. But since we see people who are fortunate once only, why should they not be fortunate a second time for the same reason,[1] and a third time? For the same antecedent is cause of the same consequent.[2] Then this cannot be a matter of chance. But when the same event follows from indefinite[3] and undetermined antecedents, it will be for a particular man[4] good or evil, but there will not be the science that comes by experience[5] of it, since otherwise some lucky people[6] would have learned it, or even—as Socrates said[7]—all the sciences would have been kinds of good luck. What, then, prevents such things happening to a man often in succession, not because he has a certain character,[8] but as, say, dice might continually throw a lucky number? But again, are there not in the soul impulses, some from reason and others from irrational desire, the latter being the earlier? For if the impulse arising from appetite for the pleasant is natural, the desire also would by nature[9] march in each case[10] towards the good. If, then, some have a fortunate natural endowment—as musical[11] people, though they have not learned to sing, are fortunately endowed in this way—and move without reason in the direction[12] given them by their nature, and desire that which they ought at the time and in the manner they ought, such men are successful, even if they are foolish and irrational, just as the others will sing[13] well though not able to teach singing. And such men are fortunate, namely those who generally succeed without the aid of reason. Men, then, who are fortunate will be so by nature. Perhaps, however, 'good fortune' is a phrase with several senses. For some things are done from impulse and are due to deliberate choice, and others not, but the opposite; and if, in the former cases, they succeed where they seem to have reasoned badly, we say that they have been lucky; and again, in the

[1] *πάλιν ἂν διὰ τὸ* (MSS.) *αὐτὸ* (B[f]) *κατορθώσαιεν* (Jackson).
[2] *τοῦ γὰρ αἰτοῦ τὸ αὐτὸ αἴτιον* (B[f], Jackson).
[3] *ἀπ' ἀπείρων* (B[f], Jackson).
[4] *τῳ* for *τό* (Jackson).
[5] *ἡ δι'* (MSS.) *ἐμπειρίαν* (B[f]).
[6] *εὐτυχεῖς* (MSS.).
[7] *Euthyd.* 279 D.
[8] *ὅτι τοιοσδί* (Jackson).
[9] *καὶ ἡ ὄρεξις φύσει* (MSS.).
[10] *πάντοτε* (B[f], Jackson).
[11] *οἱ ᾠδικοί* (Sylburg). Cf. 1238[a] 36.
[12] *ᾗ ἡ φύσις* (Jackson).
[13] *ᾄσονται* (Sylburg).

latter cases, if they wished for a different good or less of the good than they got.[1] Men who are lucky in the former way,[2] then, may be fortunate by nature, for the impulse and the desire was for the right object[3] and succeeded, but the reasoning was silly; and people in this case, when it happens that their reasoning seems incorrect but desire is the cause of their reasoning, are saved by the rightness of their desire[4]; but on another occasion a man reasons again in this way owing to appetite and turns out unfortunate.

But in the other cases[5] how can the good luck be due to
1248a a natural goodness in desire and appetite? But surely the good fortune and chance spoken of here and in the other case[6] are the same, or else there is more than one sort of good fortune, and chance has two meanings.[7] But since we see some men lucky contrary to all knowledge and right reasonings, it is clear that the cause of luck must be something different from these. But is it luck or not by which a man desires[8] what and when he ought, though for him[9] human reasoning could not lead to this? For that is not altogether unreasonable, whereof[10] the desire is natural, though reason is misled by something. The man, then, is thought to have good luck, because luck is the cause of things contrary to reason, and this is contrary to reason (for it is contrary to science and the universal). But probably it does not spring from chance, but seems so for the above reason. So that this argument shows not that good luck[11] is due to nature, but that not all who seem to be lucky are successful owing to fortune, but rather owing to nature; nor does it show that there is no such thing as fortune, nor that fortune is not the cause of anything,[12] but only not of all that it seems to be the cause of. This, however, one might question: whether fortune is the cause of just this, viz. desiring what and when one ought. But will it not in

[1] ἐβούλοντο ἄλλο ἢ ἔλαττον ἢ ἔλαβον τἀγαθόν (Jackson).
[2] Cf. ll. 29, 30.
[3] οὗ δεῖ (MSS.).
[4] εἶναι τύχη, ἡ δ' αὐτοῦ αἰτία οὖσα, αὕτη ὀρθὴ οὖσα ἔσωσεν (Spengel).
[5] Cf. l. 30 τὰ δ' οὔ.
[6] κἀκείνη (MSS.).
[7] καὶ τύχη διττή to follow αἱ εὐτυχίαι (Speng.).
[8] ᾗ ἐπεθύμησεν (Fritzsche).
[9] ὅτε ἔδει ᾧ (Jackson).
[10] οὗ γε (Jackson).
[11] εὐτυχεῖται (Bf).
[12] ὅτι οὐδέν ἐστι τύχη, οὐδ' ὅτι οὐκ ἔστι τύχη αἰτία οὐθενός (Jackson).

this case be the cause of everything, even of thought and deliberation? For one does not deliberate after previous deliberation which itself presupposed deliberation, but there is some starting-point; nor does one think after thinking previously to thinking, and so *ad infinitum*. Thought, then, is not the starting-point of thinking nor deliberation of deliberation. What, then, can be the starting-point except chance? Thus everything would come from chance. Perhaps there is a starting-point with none other outside it, and this can act in this sort of way by being such as it is.[1] The object of our search is this—what is the commencement of movement in the soul? The answer is clear: as in the universe, so in the soul, God moves everything.[2] For in a sense the divine element in us moves everything. The starting-point of reasoning is not reasoning, but something greater. What, then, could be greater even than knowledge and intellect but God? Not virtue, for virtue is an instrument of the intellect. And for this reason, as I said a while ago,[3] those are called fortunate who, whatever they start on,[4] succeed in it without being good at reasoning. And deliberation is of no advantage to them, for they have in them a principle that is better than intellect and deliberation, while the others have not this but have intellect; they have inspiration, but they cannot deliberate. For, though lacking reason, they attain the attribute of the[5] prudent and wise—that their divination is speedy; and we must mark off as included in it all but the judgement that comes from reasoning; in some cases it is due to experience, in others to habituation in the[6] use of reflection: and both experience and habituation use God. This quality sees well the future and the present, and these[7] are the men in whom the reasoning-power is relaxed. Hence we have the melancholic men, the dreamers of what is true. For the moving prin- 1248b
ciple seems to become stronger when the reasoning-power is relaxed. So the blind remember better, their memory being

[1] *αὕτη δὲ διὰ τὸ τοιαύτη γε εἶναι τοιοῦτο* (Jackson).
[2] *δῆλον δή· ὥσπερ . . . καὶ πᾶν* (MSS.) *ἐκεῖ κινεῖ* (Jackson).
[3] *ὃ πάλαι ἔλεγον* (Jackson). Cf. 1247^b 26. [4] *οἳ ⟨οἳ⟩* (W. D. R.).
[5] *ἐπιτυγχάνουσι καὶ τοῦ τῶν* (Sylb.)
[6] *τοῦ* for *τε ἐν* (J. S.). [7] *οὗτοι* for *οὗτος* (J. S.).

freed from concern with the visible.[1] It is clear, then, that there are two kinds of good luck, the one divine—and so the lucky seem to succeed owing to God[2]; men of this sort seem to succeed in following their aim, the others to succeed contrary to their aim; both are irrational, but the one is persistent good luck, the other not.

About each virtue by itself we have already spoken; now since we have distinguished[3] their natures separately, we must describe clearly the excellence that arises out of the combination of them, what we have already[4] called nobility and goodness. That he who truly deserves this denomination must have the separate virtues is clear; it cannot be otherwise with other things either, for no one is healthy in his entire body and yet healthy in no part of it, but the most numerous and important parts, if not all, must be in the same condition as the whole. Now goodness and nobility-and-goodness differ not only in name but also in themselves. For all goods have ends which are to be chosen for their own sake. Of these, we call noble those which, existing all of them for their own sake, are praised. For these are those which are the source of praised acts and are themselves praised, such as justice itself and just acts; also temperate acts,[5] for temperance is praised, but health is not praised, for its effect is not; nor vigorous action, for vigour is not. These are good but not praised. Induction makes this clear about the rest, too. A good man, then, is one for whom the natural goods are good. For the goods men fight for and think the greatest—honour, wealth, bodily excellences, good fortune, and power—are naturally good, but may be to some hurtful because of their dispositions. For neither the imprudent nor the unjust nor the intemperate would get any good from the employment of them, any more than an invalid from the food of a healthy man, or one weak and maimed from the equipment of one in health and sound in all limbs. A man

[1] τοῦ πρὸς τοῖς ὁρατοῖς εἶναι τὸ μνημονεῦον (W. D. R.).
[2] Omitting ᾗ δὲ φύσει.
[3] Cf. 1228a 25–1234b 14.
[4] Not in the existing treatise.
[5] αἱ for οἱ.

is noble and good because those goods which are noble are possessed by him for themselves, and because he practises the noble and for its own sake, the noble being the virtues and the acts that proceed from virtue. There is also what we may call the 'civic' disposition, such as the Laconians have, and others like them might have; its nature would be something like this—there are some who think one should have virtue, but only for the sake of the natural goods, and so such men are good (for the natural goods are good[1] for them), 1249a
but they have not nobility and goodness. For it is not true of them that they acquire the noble for itself, that they purpose acts good and noble at once[2]—more than this, that what is not noble by nature but good by nature is noble to them; for objects are noble when a man's motives for acting and choosing them are noble. Wherefore[3] to the noble and good man the naturally good is noble—for what is just is noble, justice is proportion to merit, and the perfect man merits these things; or what is fitting is noble, and to the perfect man these things, wealth, high birth, and power, are fitting. So that to the perfect man things profitable are also noble; but to the many the profitable and the noble do not coincide, for things absolutely good are not good for them as they are for the good man; to the 'noble and good' man they are also noble, for he does many noble deeds by reason of them.[4] But the man who thinks he ought to have the virtues for the sake of external goods does deeds that are noble[5] only *per accidens*. 'Nobility and goodness', then, is complete virtue.

About pleasure, too, we have spoken,[6] what it is and in what sense good; we have said that the absolutely pleasant is also noble, and the absolutely good pleasant. But pleasure only arises in action; therefore the truly happy man will also live most pleasantly: that this should be so is no idle demand of man.

But since the doctor has a standard by reference to which

[1] ἀγαθὰ ἀγαθά (cf. 1248b 26).
[2] καλὰ κἀγαθά (W. D. R.).
[3] διό for διότι.
[4] δι' αὐτά (MSS.).
[5] Omitting τά, which is not in the MSS.
[6] Not in the existing treatise, but cf. *E. N.* 1152b 1–1154b 31.

he distinguishes the healthy[1] from the unhealthy body, and with reference to which each thing up to a certain point ought to be done and is wholesome,[2] while if less or more is done health is the result no longer, so in regard to actions and choice of what is naturally good but not praiseworthy,
1249b the good man should have a standard both of disposition and of choice, and similarly in regard to avoidance of excess[3] or deficiency of wealth and good fortune, the standard being —as above said[4]—'as reason directs'; this corresponds to saying in regard to diet that the standard should be medical science and its principles. But this, though true, is not clear. One must, then, here as elsewhere, live with reference to the ruling principle and with reference to the formed habit and[5] the activity of the ruling principle, as the slave must live with reference to that of the master, and each of us by the rule proper to him. But since man is by nature composed of a ruling and a subject part, each of us should live according to the governing element within himself—but this is ambiguous, for medical science governs in one sense, health in another, the former existing for the latter. And so it is with the theoretic faculty; for God is not an imperative ruler, but is the end with a view to which prudence issues its commands (the word 'end' is ambiguous, and has been distinguished elsewhere),[6] for God at least needs nothing. What choice, then, or possession of the natural goods—whether bodily goods, wealth, friends, or other things—will most produce the contemplation of God, that choice or possession is best; this is the noblest standard, but any that through deficiency or excess hinders one from the contemplation and service of God is bad; this man possesses in his soul, and this is the best standard for the soul—to perceive the irrational part of the soul, as such, as little as possible.

So much, then, for the standard[7] of perfection and the object of the absolute goods.

[1] τὸ ὑγιαῖνον (Pb) σῶμα (MSS.).
[2] καὶ ὑγιεινόν for καὶ εὖ ὑγιαῖνον (W. D. R.).
[3] καὶ περὶ φυγῆς χρημάτων (MSS.).
[4] Cf. 1222a 6–10, b7, 1231b 32 sq.
[5] καί for κατά (W. D. R.).
[6] Cf. *Met.* Λ. 72b 2, *Phys.* 194a36, *De An.* 415b2, 20. The two senses of τὸ οὗ ἕνεκα are (1) the person or thing for whose good a thing is done, (2) the end for which something is done. God is οὗ ἕνεκα in sense (2).
[7] τις in Susemihl is a misprint for τίς.

DE VIRTUTIBUS ET VITIIS

1 THE noble is the object of praise, the base of blame: at 1249a
the head of what is noble stand the virtues, at the head of what is base the vices; the virtues, then, are objects of praise, but so also are the causes of the virtues and their accompaniments and results, including the acts they give rise to: the opposites are objects of blame.

If in agreement with Plato we take the soul to have three parts, then prudence is the virtue of the rational, 1249b
gentleness and bravery of the passionate, temperance and continence of the appetitive; and of the soul as a whole, justice, liberality, and magnanimity. Folly is the vice of the rational, irascibility and cowardice of the passionate, intemperance and incontinence of the appetitive; and of 1250a
the soul as a whole, injustice, illiberality, and small-mindedness.

2 Prudence is a virtue of the rational part capable of procuring all that tends to happiness. Gentleness is a virtue of the passionate part, through which men become difficult to stir to anger. Bravery is a virtue of the passionate part, through which men are difficult to scare by apprehension of death. Temperance is a virtue of the appetitive part, by which men cease to desire bad sensual pleasures. Continence is a virtue of the appetitive part, by which men check by thinking the appetite that rushes to bad pleasures. Justice is a virtue of the soul that distributes to each according to his desert. Liberality is a virtue of the soul ready to spend on noble objects. Magnanimity is a virtue of the soul, by which men are able to bear good and bad fortune, honour and dishonour.

3 Folly is a vice of the rational part, causing evil living.

Irascibility is a vice of the passionate part, through which men are easily stirred to anger. Cowardice is a vice of the passionate part, through which men are scared by apprehensions, especially such as relate to death. Intemperance is a vice of the appetitive part, by which men become desirous of bad sensual pleasures. Incontinence is a vice of the appetitive part, through which one chooses bad pleasures, though thinking opposes this. Injustice is a vice of the soul, through which men become covetous of more than they deserve. Illiberality is a vice of the soul, through which men aim at gain from every source. Little-mindedness is a vice of the soul, which makes men unable to bear alike good and bad fortune, alike honour and dishonour.

To prudence belongs right decision, right judgement as to 4
what is good and bad and all in life that is to be chosen and avoided, noble use of all the goods that belong to us, correctness in social intercourse, the grasping of the right moment, the sagacious use of word and deed, the possession of experience of all that is useful. Memory, experience, tact, good judgement, sagacity—each of these either arises from prudence or accompanies it. Or possibly some of them are, as it were, subsidiary causes of prudence (such as experience and memory), while others are, as it were, parts of it, e.g. good judgement and sagacity.

To gentleness belongs the power to bear with moderation accusations and[1] slights, not to rush hastily to vengeance, not to be easily stirred to anger, to be without bitterness or contentiousness in one's character, to have in one's soul quietude and steadfastness.

To bravery belongs slowness to be scared by apprehensions of death, to be of good courage in dangers and bold
1250b in facing risks, and to choose a noble death rather than preservation in some base way, and to be the cause of victory. Also it belongs to bravery to labour, to endure, and to choose to play the man. And there accompanies it readiness to dare, high spirits, and confidence; and further, fondness for toil and endurance.

[1] Omit μετρίας as dittography (Bas.[2], Bekker).

To temperance belongs absence of admiration for the enjoyment of bodily pleasures, absence of desire for all base sensual enjoyment, fear of just ill-repute, an ordered course of life, alike in small things and in great. And temperance is accompanied by discipline, orderliness, shame, caution.

5 To continence belongs the power to restrain by reason the appetite when rushing to base enjoyment of pleasures, endurance, steadfastness under natural want and pain.

To justice belongs the capacity to distribute to each his deserts, to preserve ancestral customs and laws and also the written law, to be truthful in matters of importance, to observe one's agreements. First among acts of justice come those towards the gods, then those to deified spirits, then those towards one's country and parents, then those towards the departed: amongst these comes piety, which is either a part of justice or an accompaniment of it. Also justice is accompanied by purity, truth, trust, and hatred of wickedness.

To liberality it belongs to be profuse of money on praiseworthy objects, to be extravagant in spending on a proper purpose, to be helpful and kind in disputed matters, and not to take from improper sources. The liberal man is also clean in his dress and house, ready to provide himself with what is not strictly necessary but beautiful and enjoyable without profit, inclined to keep all animals that have anything peculiar or marvellous about them. Liberality is accompanied by a suppleness and ductility of disposition, by kindness, by pitifulness, by love for friends, for foreign intimates, for what is noble.

It belongs to magnanimity to bear nobly and bravely alike good and bad fortune, honour and dishonour; not to admire luxury or attention or power or victory in contests, but to have a sort of depth and greatness of soul. The magnanimous is one who neither values living highly nor is fond of life, but is in disposition simple and noble, one who can be injured and is not prompt to avenge himself. The accompaniments of magnanimity are simpleness, nobleness, and truth.

To folly it belongs to judge things badly, to decide 6
badly, to be bad in social intercourse, to use badly present
1251a goods, to think erroneously about what is good and noble as regards life. Folly is accompanied by ignorance, inexperience, incontinence, tactlessness, shortness of memory.

Of irascibility there are three species—promptness to anger, peevishness, sullenness. It is the mark of the angry man to be unable to bear small slights or defeats, to be ready to punish, prompt at revenge, easily moved to anger by any chance word or deed. The accompaniments of irascibility are a disposition easily excited, ready changes of feeling, attention to small matters, vexation at small things, and all these rapid and on slight occasion.

To cowardice it belongs to be easily moved by unimportant apprehensions, especially if relating to death or maiming of the body, and to suppose preservation in any manner to be better than a noble death. Its accompaniments are softness, unmanliness, despair, love of life. Beneath it, however, is a sort of caution of disposition and slowness to quarrel.

To intemperance it belongs to choose the enjoyments of hurtful and base pleasures, to suppose that those living in such pleasures are in the highest sense happy, to love laughter, jeering, wit, and levity in word and deed. Its accompaniments are disarrangement, shamelessness, disorder, luxury, ease, negligence, contempt, dissipation.

To incontinence it belongs to choose the enjoyment of pleasures though reason forbids, to partake of them none the less though believing it to be better not to partake of them, and while thinking one ought to do what is noble and profitable still to abstain from these for the sake of pleasures. The accompaniments of incontinence are effeminacy, negligence, and generally the same as those of intemperance.

Of injustice there are three species — impiety, greed, 7
outrage. Impiety is wrong-doing towards gods, deified spirits, the departed, one's parents, and one's country. Greed is wrong-doing in regard to agreements, claiming a share of the object in dispute beyond one's deserts. Out-

rage occurs when in providing pleasure for oneself one brings shame on others, whence Evenus says of it 'That which while gaining nothing still wrongs another'. It belongs to injustice to violate ancestral customs and laws, to disobey enactments and rulers, to lie, to commit perjury, to violate agreements and pledges. The accompaniments 1251b of injustice are quibbling, charlatanry, unamiability, pretence, malignity, unscrupulousness.

Of illiberality there are three species, pursuit of disgraceful gain, parsimony, stinginess: pursuit of disgraceful gain, in so far as such men seek gain from all sources and think more of the profit than of the shame; parsimony, in so far as they are unready to spend money on a suitable purpose; stinginess, in so far as, while spending, they spend in small sums and badly, and are more hurt than profited from not spending in season. It belongs to illiberality to value money above everything, and to think no reproach can ever attach to what yields a profit. The life of the illiberal is servile, suited to a slave, and sordid, remote from ambition and liberality. The accompaniments of illiberality are attention to small matters, sullenness, small-mindedness, self-humiliation, lack of measure, ignobility, misanthropy.

It belongs to small-mindedness to be able to bear neither honour nor dishonour, neither good nor ill fortune, but to grow braggart when honoured, to be elated at small prosperities, to be unable to bear even the smallest deprivation of honour, to regard any ill-success whatever as a great misfortune, to bewail oneself and to be impatient over everything. Further, the small-minded man is such as to call every slight an outrage and a dishonour, even such as are inflicted through ignorance or forgetfulness. The accompaniments of small-mindedness are attention to small things, grumbling, hopelessness, self-humiliation.

8 In general it belongs to virtue to make the condition of the soul good, using quiet and ordered motions and in agreement with itself throughout all its parts: whence the condition of a good soul seems a pattern of a good political constitution. It belongs also to virtue to do good

to the worthy, to love the good and to hate the bad; not to be prompt either to chastise or seek vengeance, but to be placable, kindly, and forgiving. Its accompaniments are worth, equity, indulgence, good hope, good memory, and further all such qualities as love of home, love of friends, love of comrades, love of one's foreign intimates, love of men, love of the noble: all these qualities are among the laudable. The marks of vice are the opposites, and its accompaniments the opposites; and all these marks and accompaniments of vice belong to the class of the blameable.

INDEX

EUDEMIAN ETHICS

1214^a 1—1249^b 25 = 14^a 1—49^b 25.

INDEX

INDEX

INDEX

INDEX

INDEX

PROPER NAMES

INDEX

VIRTUES AND VICES

1249a 26—1251b 39 = 49a 26—51b 39.

PROPER NAMES